Pitt Series in Policy and Institutional Studies

Pitt Series in Policy and Institutional Studies

Bert A. Rockman, Editor

Perceptions and Behavior in Soviet Foreign Policy

Perceptions and Behavior in Soviet Foreign Policy

•

RICHARD K. HERRMANN

UNIVERSITY OF PITTSBURGH PRESS

Series in Russian and East European Studies No. 7

Published by the University of Pittsburgh Press, Pittsburgh, Pa. 15260
Copyright © 1985, University of Pittsburgh Press
All rights reserved
Feffer and Simons, Inc., London
Manufactured in the United States of America

Library of Congress Cataloging in Publication Data

Herrmann, Richard K., 1952–
    Perceptions and behavior in Soviet foreign policy.

    (Pitt series in policy and institutional studies)
    Bibliography: p. 249.
    Includes index.
    1. Soviet Union—Foreign relations—1953–1975.
2. Soviet Union—Foreign relations—1975–
3. International relations. I. Title. II. Series.
DK274.H46 1985   327.47   85-1047
ISBN 0-8229-3814-6

To my mother and the memory of my father

Contents

Tables

Figures

List of Acronyms

ABM   Antiballistic missile

ADE   Armored division equivalent

APC   Armored personnel carrier

ASEAN Association of Southeast Asian Nations

BPA   Basic Principles Agreement (Moscow Summit, 1972)

CDU   Christian Democratic Union (West Germany)

CMEA   Council for Mutual Economic Assistance (Warsaw Pact)

CPSU   Communist party of the Soviet Union

CSU   Christian Social Union (West Germany)

DIA   Defense Intelligence Agency

DRV   Democratic Republic of Vietnam (North Vietnam)

FRG   Federal Republic of Germany (West Germany)

GDR   German Democratic Republic (East Germany)

ICBM   Intercontinental ballistic missile

IDF   Israeli Defense Forces

INF   Intermediate-range nuclear missile

JMC   Joint Military Commission (Vietnam War)

MIRV   Multiple independently targeted reentry vehicle

NLF   National Liberation Front (North Vietnam)

NSC   National Security Council

OPEC   Organization of Petroleum Exporting Countries

PCC   Political Consultative Committee

PCP	Portuguese Communist party
PDRY	South Yemen
PLO	Palestine Liberation Organization
PRC	People's Republic of China
PRG	Provisional Revolutionary Government (Vietnam)
RDF	Rapid Deployment Force
SALT	Strategic Arms Limitation Talks
SAM	Surface-to-air missile
SPD	Social Democratic party (West Germany)
UAR	United Arab Republic
WTO	Warsaw Treaty Organization

Acknowledgments

THIS BOOK has taken a number of years to write and many people have helped me along the way. I owe a great deal to Carl Beck. He encouraged me to pursue the study of the Soviet Union and East European societies and gave generously of his time, intellectual guidance, and professional support. I regret he did not live to see this project's conclusion. I also am grateful for the support of the Ford Foundation. Its fellowship in International Security–Arms Control and Soviet and East European Area Studies helped me considerably in doing much of the research for this book. Charles Hermann and the Mershon Center at Ohio State University also were generous with research support in the summer of 1983 and have provided me with many opportunities to discuss my ideas and engage in serious debates over many of the issues I have struggled with in this book.

A number of scholars have read all or parts of the original manuscript and have helped significantly in developing the conceptual framework and the case studies. Margaret Hermann and Ole Holsti read the theoretical chapters and provided useful advice. Robert Jervis and Bert Rockman read the entire manuscript and gave me a great many very helpful ideas on theory, substance, and presentation. Philip Stewart made his data on Politburo speeches available, for which I am grateful, and has always been willing to discuss the hard choices and difficult judgments inherent in any interpretation of Soviet policy.

I owe a special debt of gratitude to Richard Cottam. His ideas on the analysis of foreign policy motivation and perceptions have influenced my work greatly. He read the many early drafts of this work and gave me important criticisms and guidance on both the theoretical and substantive details of the study. His encouragement and advice helped me to see this book through to completion.

A number of people have helped in preparing the presentation of my ideas. Margaret Best has assisted me in running the computer programs on Politburo speeches. Jim Ludwig has also given generously of his programming skills. Karen Frank helped me shorten the original manuscript and tighten some of the language. Carol Robertson helped compile and type the bibliography. Jane Flanders at the University of Pittsburgh Press has been a tremendous help as copy editor and a pleasure to work with.

Finally, I would like to thank my wife Peg for her constant encouragement and help. She has typed the manuscript in its several different forms and has shared with me the trials and tribulations of writing a book.

I am grateful to all who helped me. Naturally on a subject as controversial as Soviet perceptions and motives many who contributed to my thinking did so by arguing with me about the evidence and my reasoning. Certainly no one should hold them responsible for the decisions and judgments I finally reached. I alone am responsible for the work's shortcomings.

Introduction

FOR WHAT reasons do nations act in international affairs? The problem of correctly discerning motivation underlying foreign policy has plagued many theories of international relations. Because diagnosing political causation is so essential to strategy, attribution of motives cannot be ignored or wisely left to mere assumption. One principal purpose of this work is to develop a more systematic approach to the analysis of foreign policy motivation.

A second purpose is to apply the developed framework to an analysis of Soviet foreign policy over the last two decades. My reasons for this are obvious, since the diagnosis of Soviet motives is central to American strategy and remains an issue of intense controversy. Because the interpretation of so many cases of Soviet international behavior (in Angola, Afghanistan, the Middle East) rests on assumptions concerning Soviet strategy, this study is designed specifically to examine dominant Soviet views of the United States and their impact on strategy.

I approach the Soviet case from the perspective of international relations, following a tradition in foreign policy analysis and political psychology that emphasizes the perceptions of national leaders. Patterns and insights discovered in research on perceptions and cognitions are used as a theoretical foundation for the conceptual scheme I develop here. I pay special attention to the concept of perception and to the problem of inferring the perceptions and motives of a nation's leaders on the basis of that nation's behavior in international politics. While theories drawn from political psychology are important to my framework, my purpose is not to test these theories, but rather to explore their utility in analyzing Soviet foreign policy.

To draw conclusions about the motives influencing a nation's leaders, theorists of international relations often use concepts like *perceptions, aims, expected utilities, initiators,* and *defenders.* Despite their popularity, these concepts are rarely measured and examined critically. Most often it is simply assumed that readers know what they mean. Because these judgments are so critical, I want to focus substantial attention upon them.

My analysis of Soviet foreign policy behavior will not be a detailed chronicle and the historian looking for a microscopic focus on a single case will not find it here. Instead I will discuss the various explanations of Soviet foreign policy behavior, focusing on the arguments and inferences that can be drawn from Soviet actions. I assume that the central questions regarding strategy revolve around what people think certain actions mean. The factual details of the USSR's behavior are usually less controversial than what these actions tell us about Soviet perceptions or aims.

Many psychologists are interested in how people interpret social and political events. These attribution theorists would suggest that Soviet foreign policy, like the international behavior of any state, can be explained by a combination of internal predispositions and external constraints. An international relations perspective may simplify the internal decisional process, while a comparative perspective might simplify the external international context. I will try to pay attention to the domestic scene in Moscow, but admit at the outset that my emphasis is on the USSR's behavior in its international context. The rationale for this is partly based on limitations of scope and space, but primarily reflects an assumption about the importance of understanding the global context as well as particular regional influences when interpreting Soviet behavior.

I argue that the meanings an observer attaches to Soviet foreign policy usually depend upon that observer's definitions of the situation and regional circumstances. An interpretation requires not only knowledge about a nation's actions but also an analysis of the specific arenas in which that nation carries out its foreign policy. My hope is to complement other studies that have concentrated upon debate in Moscow and have given less attention to the analysis of actual policy. Thus my focus here will be on an analysis of international behavior and strategy.

Some of the ideas for this book were generated by the debate over whether or not the United States should "play the China card." The notion of using Communist China, after a normalization of U.S.-Chinese relations, to contain the Soviet Union raised a number of fundamental questions among U.S. observers about Soviet perceptions and foreign policy. There were several propositions about the effect Sino-American rapprochement would have on Soviet behavior. One claimed that the strategic shift would lead to a heightened Soviet interest in detente and greater restraint in Vietnam. Other theorists worried that it would lead to tougher Soviet policies and, with hindsight, later pointed to the USSR's invasion of Afghanistan and Vietnam's occupation of Cambodia as proof of their position. In both cases the arguments hinged on judgments about Soviet perceptions. Would the American tie to China simply foreclose perceived opportunities for the USSR or exacerbate perceived threats?

Although it is impossible to determine which Soviet actions were caused by Sino-American rapprochement, the debate over this question will be evident throughout the book. It has affected both the scope and time span chosen for this study. Because the changing nature of Soviet-American-Chinese relations is so important in the international system, I will analyze Soviet behavior at three crucial moments in that relationship. The first opens in 1967 when American-Chinese relations were very hostile and Soviet-American reconciliation hardly begun. The second, beginning in 1972, represents a benchmark period in both Sino-American ties and Soviet-American detente. The third begins in 1979 as U.S.-PRC normalization was achieved and U.S.-Soviet relations were rapidly deteriorating.

Before entering this substantive analysis, I will begin by reconsidering several well-articulated perspectives. My intention in the initial chapter is not to summarize the American debate but rather to identify what general propositions deserve attention. An analysis of American views must be the starting point for a study of Soviet policy because it is from these competing perspectives that the most important questions and hypotheses are derived. The second chapter takes up the theoretical and methodological dilemmas entailed in studying the perceptions of other countries held by a nation's leaders. After reviewing other efforts to tackle these problems, I try to lay out a research strategy that builds on the successful aspects of previous studies. In this enterprise I will apply several theories about psychology and strategy that can be useful when analyzing Soviet images of the United States and U.S. foreign policy.

After the empirical study in chapters 3–5, the book concludes with a summation of the findings. In the last chapter I return to the basic questions raised in chapter 1 and try to relate my conclusions to three different perspectives on Soviet behavior.

Perceptions and Behavior in Soviet Foreign Policy

Chapter 1

American Perceptions of Soviet Foreign Policy: Three Theories

Decision-makers will usually benefit from making their beliefs and values more explicit. . . . It is often more fruitful to debate the merits of two opposed images or theories as a whole rather than to argue over the interpretation of each individual incident. . . . Particularly dangerous is the tendency to take the most important questions for granted. . . . This often involves taking too many things for granted and failing to scrutinize basic assumptions.

—Robert Jervis,
*Perception and Misperception
in International Politics*

HOW SHOULD the United States deal with the Soviet Union? The answers to this critical question emerge from different interpretations of Soviet foreign policy and the motives behind it. The crux of the strategic question is this: will Western pressure to contain the USSR lead to desired concessions and a Soviet foreign policy amenable to U.S. preferences, or will it lead to a retrenchment and consolidation of Soviet resolve to resist such pressure? Conversely, if the United States strives to allay Soviet fears and security concerns, will this make leaders in Moscow more accommodating and cooperative in their foreign policy, or will they exploit new opportunities for expansion? Glenn Snyder and Paul Diesing put the central question this way:

Whether to be firm and tough toward an adversary, in order to deter him, but at the risk of provoking his anger or fear and heightened conflict, or to conciliate him in the hope of reducing sources of conflict, but at the risk of strengthening him and causing him to miscalculate one's own resolve, is a perennial and central dilemma of international relations. A rational resolution of this dilemma depends most of all on an accurate assessment of the long run interests and intentions of the opponent. If his aims are limited, conciliation of his specific grievances may be cheaper than engaging in a power struggle with him. If they are possibly unlimited, the rational choice is to deter him with countervailing power and a resolve to use it.[1]

Interpreting why the Soviet Union behaves as it does is a difficult and controversial task. Some observers perceive Soviet actions as defensive, while others see the same events as proof of expansionist intentions. It is not surprising, therefore, that many scholars of international politics and Soviet-American relations alike have sought ways to circumvent analysis of motives. Hans Morgenthau, like other Realists, argues that guessing at motivational causes is so problematic that all observers can do is to treat power as a "currency" of politics.[2] Whatever the aims of a country's foreign policy, it needs power to achieve them; interests are defined in terms of power, and a desire for power is the immediate motive of foreign policy. In this scheme, a country's actions are driven by nothing more specific than an interest in power relative to other actors. The analyst may refrain from imputing any more precise motivations.

Realism has been criticized from many angles. It has been attacked as too simple, its concepts undefined, and its empirical claims doubtful.[3] Although these debates are important, the central issues for this study are first, how successful is Realism in side-stepping the basic problem of judging motives, and second, how useful is it in helping analysts deal with the Soviet Union? I have concluded that the effort to avoid the attribution of motives in foreign policy has been more illusory than real.

While introducing the notion of power as currency, Realism does not develop the more central concept of value. It fails to answer basic analytical questions analogous to asking why people spend their money, or what they are likely to spend it on; these remain beyond the reach of the Realist paradigm. Like a market analysis attentive to available money and not values, the general theory can offer only limited insight into which strategic actions are likely to affect an adversary's behavior and in what manner. This being the case, Realism often implicitly introduces motivational claims. Causes and motives are assumed or asserted rather than systematically considered. The most essential interpretive claim is not left out but simply left undefended.

Few will dispute the idea that the Soviet Union is interested in power. It is widely recognized that the USSR works to enhance certain dimensions of influence and seeks to establish its own competitive positions vis-à-vis the United States. However, focusing on the means undertaken to achieve these ends does not address the basic strategic problem. What constitutes an opportunity and why the USSR is predisposed to take opportunities remain unclear. Does it act because it perceives U.S. behavior as threatening, or to exploit perceived weaknesses? Because American strategy is often based on answers to this question, the problem remains fundamental. Hans Morgenthau understood this dilemma. In addition to his arguments about power, he introduced the ideas that nations act to preserve the status quo, to advance imperialist aims, and to gain prestige:

> The fundamental question that confronts the public officials responsible for the conduct of foreign policy as well as citizens trying to form an intelligent opinion on international issues . . . concerns the character of the foreign policy pursued by another nation and, in consequence, the kind of foreign policy that ought to be adopted with regard to it. Is the foreign policy of the other nation imperialist, or is it not? In other words, does it seek to overthrow the existing distribution of power or does it only contemplate adjustments within the general framework of the existing status quo? The answer to that question has determined the fate of nations, and the wrong answer has often meant deadly peril or actual destruction; for upon the correctness of that answer depends the success of the foreign policy derived from it.[4]

The analysis of Soviet foreign policy is a perennial issue in American politics. Arguments over the aims of Soviet policy and how the United States should respond to it have often taken on highly polemical tones. The heat of this debate has persuaded some scholars that it is preferable to avoid motivational issues altogether. The Harvard Nuclear Study Group has argued that focusing on motives is not only divisive but also an impediment to strategic decision making. The group suggests, for example: "Such debates obscure the central issue, which is the effect, not the motive, of Soviet actions. We can never 'know' exactly what motivates the Soviet leadership. What the West can know is that certain Soviet actions are not in its interests and the central issue is, then, how best to encourage Soviet restraint in such dangerous areas."[5]

Focusing on effects and not motives may help in evaluating the relationship between Soviet actions and U.S. interests, but does not provide an adequate basis for planning American responses. How can we construct strategies that might restrain the Soviets without a thoughtful analysis of what stimulates their actions? If Soviet leaders decide to act because they see an opportunity to exploit what appears to be an American or regional vulnerability, then demonstrating U.S. resolve to deter them might encourage restraint. On the other hand, if the leaders in the Kremlin decide to act because they perceive U.S. actions as posing an intense threat, and believe it to be more dangerous not to act than to act, then a tough U.S. response might not produce restraint, but instead spark an even more aggressive Soviet reaction.

In medicine, recognizing that a disease has undesirable or bad effects is not a great help in prescribing treatment. A similar logic holds in foreign policy analysis. The effects of Soviet behavior may be seen as a problem, but this does not provide much strategic guidance. The causes of that behavior must be sought before diagnosis can lead to a prescription. That the diagnosis will be inexact and uncertain does not make it unimportant.

The American analyst studying Soviet foreign policy is often subject to the pressures of several different roles. Because of the political implications of a strategic diagnosis, experts are often pulled into the debate over interpretation. They may be asked to evaluate as positive or negative the potential impact of Soviet behavior on U.S. interests. This task is somewhat analogous to determining if the physical developments that follow from a treatment are good or bad. By itself the process of defining interests and then evaluating the possible impact of Soviet behavior will not lead to a logical prescription for responding to it. When experts are asked to suggest strategy, they move into a slightly different role. Here they are required to analyze the causes of Soviet behavior along with the simpler statement of the problem. This role demands scholarly detachment and a comprehension of Soviet perceptions and aims. The objective is to formulate a strategy that might be effective in altering Soviet behavior.

Because policy toward the Soviet Union is so central in American political debates, it is difficult for analysts of Soviet policy to perform this diagnostic task with great detachment. Americans seem to be psychologically inclined to conclude that if Soviet behavior jeopardizes U.S. interests, then damaging U.S. interests was probably the aim of that behavior. Seldom does the public debate go beyond this immediate explanation to search for more complex underlying reasons why the USSR might have taken these actions. As a result, normative judgments can be so clear and intense that an independent diagnosis might be difficult to present publicly even if the analyst has struggled for detachment. This is especially true when analysts conclude that the Soviets' "hideous" and "outrageous" behavior that everyone condemns was driven by a deeply felt concern for their own security interests and prestige. In this case, the careful analyst's diagnosis should lead to a differentiated strategy sensitive to Soviet security concerns and designed to defuse Soviet paranoia and frustration. Yet this advice is likely to be badly out of step with a political climate that demands condemnation and firm punitive action. Unfortunately, if the analyst's diagnosis is proven correct, a punitive policy offers little hope of altering Soviet behavior in a positive direction.

Interpreting the motives behind another nation's foreign policy presents a paradox. Many scholars recognize the importance of such analysis in formulating strategy, and are convinced of the significance of the diagnostic problem.[6] At the same time, there are few systematic procedures for inferring aims and perceptions, and many are inclined to guess at motives or to write off the task as impossible. Although searching for motives is important, the process of inferring them from events is difficult to systematize. The same action, for example, can be stimulated by different motives, while a single motive can produce various actions. Moreover, in large countries such as the Soviet Union, so many interests are likely to motivate behavior that even a complex mixture of possible variables is certain to simplify the set of causal factors.

Despite the difficulties associated with inferring the causes of behavior, attributing motives is nevertheless pervasive in analyses of foreign policy. My rationale in this effort to study Soviet perceptions and aims rests on five basic premises. First, I view "science" as essentially a "problem-solving activity."[7] When addressing the problems of Soviet-American relations, and in particular possible general policies that the United States might follow, I find the task of attributing aims to Soviet behavior a primary endeavor, even though the difficulties inherent in the task preclude definitive conclusions. Yet I will address central questions, even if the answers are likely to be only tentative and relative.

Second, I begin with a claim that analyses of Soviet international behavior must seek and interpret causes if they are to help to solve problems. Events, acts, and patterns in behavior can be described without introducing motivational concepts. Facts, however, do not speak for themselves. They acquire meaning and significance only when the analyst begins to infer causes for them. Rigorous and scientific techniques of measuring data will not by themselves produce "acceptable answers" to the "interesting questions."[8] The process of inferring meaning needs to be as systematic and as well thought out as the techniques of measurement. The analytical logic is likely to be more important in shaping the results than the refinement of behavioral measures.

In less abstract terms, this second premise states that analysts do attribute aims to Soviet foreign policy when they make their data relevant to important strategic problems. The task is not impossible; it is done all the time. Calling the task impossible usually means that it is impossible to perform the task systematically or "scientifically" and that it can only be done through intuition and argument. I maintain that drawing inferences about Soviet aims is fundamentally an intellectual task. It relies on wisdom, to be sure. Techniques of measurement may make the data more reliable but will not necessarily improve interpretation. However, interpretation can be improved or at least clarified by systematic development and explicit presentation.

Third, because I approach my subject from a problem-solving perspective, I assume that there are likely to be a number of solutions to any given problem, each entailing different risks and costs. Efforts to diagnose and treat cancer have not led to painless and safe panaceas and it is unlikely that efforts to diagnose Soviet perceptions and aims will produce risk-free solutions either. What constitutes a solution is clearly a relative notion and one solution must be compared with others. This project will consider three alternative views of Soviet policy, not with the pretension that one can be identified as the true explanation but rather with the more modest hope that they can be compared with each other and their relative fit with the data evaluated. I hope that this enterprise will also provide a basis for estimating their expected utility that is sensitive to both their possible costs and risks.

Fourth, the two key concepts in this study are *motivation* and *perception*. Motivation refers to the compound of factors predisposing a country to move in a certain direction in foreign policy. Arguing persuasively against single-cause explanations, Richard Cottam introduces the idea that behavior is influenced by multiple causes and defines more specific motives for foreign policy like economic interests, messianic commitments to ideology, the pressure to protect or expand a frontier, vested interests in the bureaucracy or the military, and personal power of the leader.[9] The general thrust of a compound of motives can be described at a more aggregate level with terms like national defense and political expansion, paralleling Morgenthau's ideas. I will refer to these more general concepts as *aims*. *Perception* is defined as the construction of reality regarding the behavior of another nation or nations in which foreign policy decisions are made.

A nation's motives and perceptions are conceived of as concepts. They are introduced for descriptive purposes, not because they are conceived of as real "attributes" possessed by the USSR, as if the nation were a single being. In social psychology the concept of "trait" was traditionally reified and treated as a concrete entity; however, behavioral psychologists have redefined the idea as a concept designed simply to describe a pattern of behavior and have warned against the fallacy of reification.[10] I take this warning seriously. It is impossible to climb into the minds of Soviet leaders and it is equally obvious that the USSR as a national actor does not have "motives." To reify the concepts of motivation and perception will lead to a search for "real" motives or "real" perceptions that simply do not exist. This mistake may lead to the conclusion that these entities cannot be observed and in turn to the abandonment of systematic efforts to infer causes. No concepts can be "observed."[11] They are not real items that could be seen if only we had better access to Soviet decision makers. Concepts are strictly analytical and will be operationalized in chapter 2. They refer to elements in a simplified model of Soviet foreign policy that provide the dynamic in an "interpretative understanding."[12]

Fifth, and finally, I assume that an analysis that focuses exclusively on the internal predispositions of the USSR or exclusively on the international environment surrounding the USSR will be incomplete. In order to analyze the interaction of a country's predispositions with the stimuli and constraints in the international system, one must deal with both levels of analysis.[13] The effect of internal factors can be inferred only if the environmental conditions can be defined along with the actions they would predict. Behavior that the environment produces can only be deduced if one posits certain assumptions about internal predispositions. For example, to test whether or not the Soviet Union seizes opportunities for expansion, we must be able to define what environmental conditions actually constitute an opportunity for the USSR. On the other hand, we can gauge the effect of an environmental constraint like a foreign deterrent only by identifying a nation's predisposition to act.

Structural approaches concentrating on the USSR's position in the world are considered inadequate for the problem-solving task for three reasons. First, the distribution of power, as Realist theorists have argued, predicts outcomes, not actions. Many wars have been initiated by countries that ended up losing. As Wayne Ferris finds, it may be a change in relative military capability that predicts the outbreak of conflict better than the balance of power.[14] In the nuclear era, neither the United States nor the USSR is interested in an ultimate showdown or a test of who could win a conflict. The critical questions raised at the outset relate to Soviet actions and how to affect them. To address these issues, as both J. David Singer and Kenneth Waltz have argued, it can be useful to focus at both the national and the international levels of analysis.

Singer has pointed out that a scholar introduces considerable methodological complexities by focusing at the national rather than the international system level.[15] He raises two problems connected with inferring a nation's leaders' motives and perceptions. As stated in premise four, I hope to avoid reifying these concepts and plan instead to link them to empirical indicators in chapter 2. Waltz, who like Singer prefers the greater simplicity of the international system level, nevertheless recognizes the explanatory and strategic importance of the national level of analysis. Waltz argues, "Structually we can describe and understand the pressures states are subject to. We cannot predict how they will react to the pressures without knowledge of their internal predispositions."[16] Structural theories like Realism are general theories of international relations, not theories of specific foreign policies. To use the structural approach as a tool in strategic diagnosis of a particular case would both misunderstand its level of argument and reify its concepts. Hans Morgenthau dismissed the use of balance-of-power logic for explaining specific policies as "ideology"—a tag he equated to propaganda.[17]

Second, the concept of the balance of power as a factor in foreign policy decisions can predict outcomes only if the analyst assumes a country will exercise the objective potential it possesses. One can rarely make such an assumption in political affairs. Actual tests of strength are rare and ultimate tests of strength through all-out war are rarer still; in fact, they are absent in Soviet-American relations. Consequently, potential power alone is not likely to predict the results of policy decisions. Outcomes depend on decisions to act and to invest various amounts of resources in a given enterprise. Leverage, which is critical in bargaining, is not simply a function of a nation's potential power but is dependent on the nation's self-perceptions, its perceptions of the adversary, and varying degress of motivation between the two nations.[18]

Third, structural theories cannot avoid the problem of describing the environment. They tend to assume the accuracy of the analyst's perceptions of the situation. But how to estimate relative economic and military capability remains a subjective decision. Notions like "necessity" and "opportunity" do not relate to conditions that can be objectively identified. At the extremes, of course, one can point to illustrations such as the necessity of leaving a burning house, but in the real case of politics, situations are rarely so clear.[19] Concepts like "need," which in the biological-technical realm seem to have identifiable limits related to survival, in the political world are related to preferences.[20] Because of the different implications of attributing behavior to necessity rather than choice, it is not surprising that propagandists will attribute their country's "good" behavior to a predisposition to do the right thing and "bad" behavior to necessity. The bases of the necessity in certain preferred conditions are likely to be left unexplored.

Psychologists have found that it is not only propagandists who are biased in their evaluation of environmental determinants. They find the same inclinations among naive observers.[21] This does not preclude the study of environmental conditions such as the existence of an opportunity, but does suggest that we must try to comprehend not only the analyst's perception of the environmental conditions but also the subject's perception of the external system and the threats and opportunities it presents.

Although estimating Soviet perceptions and aims is difficult, it is done quite frequently. Claims about motives are usually the core ideas in competing theories about Soviet international behavior. In the United States, three dominant theories assume the following: (1) that the Soviet Union is motivated by a determination to spread communism and dominate the world, (2) that Moscow seeks to expand its influence by exploiting opportunities while protecting its security, and (3) that the USSR is primarily committed to self-defense. Each theory requires a brief review.

Three Perspectives on Soviet Motives

American images of the Soviet Union are aligned along a spectrum running between the "hard-line" and the "soft-line" approaches.[22] Such variation in interpretation is related to estimates of the relative importance to Soviet foreign policy of expansionist aims versus self-defense. Any number of views might be identified along this continuum; I will focus on only three typical examples. Quite naturally, this will make a complex debate seem artificially simple. My purpose is not to examine each argument in detail but rather to identify the propositions that lie at the center of the dispute.

These three viewpoints about Soviet motives are popular among the American elite. Ole Holsti and James Rosenau have found that among Americans who are highly attentive to foreign policy three distinct and mutually exclusive "belief systems" are common.[23] Integral to each is an image of the USSR. I have labeled them communist expansionism, realpolitik expansionism, and realpolitik self-defense.[24]

To provide a richer picture of these arguments, I have drawn on the work of authors whose descriptions of Soviet motives resemble the three distinct "beliefs" found by Holsti and Rosenau. My intention is not to critique any particular scholar's work but rather to develop the main lines of argument in each perspective. I have examined only part of these analysts' works, and then not as representative of their personal perspectives but rather as examples of the claims about the USSR that Holsti and Rosenau found to be typical. Each presentation by necessity simplifies a complicated viewpoint and focuses only on how it describes Soviet aims and motives. My intent is merely to capture the central architecture or key foundations of alternative interpretations with no pretense that these sketches reproduce all the complexity and subtleties of differing perspectives.

By focusing only on motivation I may exaggerate the differences among these perspectives. On a number of important points they are in agreement. All three, for example, recognize that the USSR is a powerful country that can threaten the interests of the United States. All agree that it has extended a repressive imperial control upon peoples and nations living near its frontiers and has employed its military might in brutal fashion in various parts of the world. Moreover, they all regard these military and imperial actions as "bad."

While the perspectives agree on the undesirability of various Soviet actions, they disagree profoundly over what causes the USSR to engage in these activities. Consequently, analysts differ sharply over what strategic prescriptions the United States ought to follow in response to them. They disagree on how to prevent potential threats from materializing and on how to remedy existing unacceptable situations.

The reviews that follow treat each perspective as an argument that leads to a prescription for dealing with the Soviet Union. I examine these arguments to see what possible propositions might be derived from them. Then I will test these propositions against a body of empirical evidence and use them to compare the relative accuracy and utility of the differing theories. At this point, however, the issue is not whether a view is the most accurate or useful description of Soviet behavior but whether it can be translated into a meaningful proposition. Can it be tested against empirical evidence? Is it even theoretically possible to disconfirm its accuracy?

I treat each motivational claim as a simple model. In evaluating a model, one must answer two important questions. First, is it internally logical and clearly stated? Second, is it relevant when describing Soviet foreign policy? To address the second question, one must have some way of comparing the model to empirical evidence. If the model does not generate expectations that can be compared to historical evidence, then its relevance cannot be evaluated and the model is thus questionable. The appearance of consequences predicted by a model, while enhancing its relative merit, of course does not prove its importance. Even though it may be logically impossible to prove the accuracy of a model, if it is going to be evaluated and compared to others, it must at least yield predictions that in theory could be falsified.

Theory 1: Communist Expansionism

In this view the Soviet Union is described as bent on achieving global hegemony and establishing worldwide communism.[25] Moscow's "imperial adventurism" and "quest for supremacy" are attributed not to unfortunate policy choices in the Kremlin but rather to the unavoidable product of its political system. This assessment claims that Soviet leaders rule over a totalitarian system and seek to impose on the world a universal ideology. It assumes that Soviet leaders need foreign expansion and victory over other political systems in order to preserve their domestic dominance. The mainspring of communist expansion is said to be the totalitarian system. At its core are the self-interested rulers who are described as using foreign conquests both to demonstrate the legitimacy of their vanguard role, and to distract the public's attention from their domestic failures.

Proponents of this assessment sometimes depict Soviet behavior as that of a "paper tiger." They see a constant probing for easy prey and a quick retreat in the face of solid resolution and resistance. The more sophisticated describe Soviet policy as guided by the "art of operation" and relate the USSR's instrumental behavior to a set of tactical rules of bargaining.[26] With only military power to rely on, and facing serious internal vulnerabilities, the Communist leadership, according to this view, seeks every opportunity to expand Soviet influence and to undermine American positions. Picturing the USSR as inherently weak, proponents of this theory argue that American power can be used to contain Soviet expansion. They suggest that if the United States denies the USSR foreign policy successes, the Communists will be compelled to turn inward, effecting changes in the system.

The central claims of the communist expansionism diagnosis are difficult to evaluate because they are nonfalsifiable. By arguing that the expansion-minded Communists are at the same time very unwilling to run risks, and instead seek easy victories, one can discount the lack of observable Soviet efforts toward expansion. In the same vein, by picturing the USSR as a "paper tiger," proponents of this theory can interpret evidence inconsistent with the expansionist proposition as evidence of Soviet restraint in the face of U.S. strength; the USSR was simply "compelled to behave." Testing the causal claims is made more difficult by the complementary disclaimer that much of Soviet behavior is designed to lull the West into a false sense of complacency and thus failure to act cannot be counted as disconfirming evidence.[27]

At times advocates of this perspective back up their claims with evidence drawn from the history of Russian expansion over the centuries and the backgrounds and personalities of members of the Soviet elite. The chronicle of Russian and Soviet history, which certainly includes a drive for expansion, does not prove that expansionism is at present the motive for Soviet behavior. The dangers of historical determinism are well known. The fact that Russian leaders a century ago aspired to have warm-water ports is no assurance that current leaders are so inclined. To assert without evidence drawn from the contemporary scene that expansionist aspirations transcend generations and motivate current leaders badly distorts the nation-state concept. It introduces a determinism that not only is without foundation but also violates the logic of empirical investigation.[28]

The claims about the Russian character or the legacy of the muzhik, or peasant, personality run the risk of stereotyping and provoke angry rejections by proud Russian nationalists.[29] From a social scientist's perspective, these general claims—even if they could be proven accurate, which seems highly dubious—cannot serve as evidence for describing particular members of the elite. Some of these arguments claim that an individual's background such as peasant birth predicts or even determines his or her contemporary political orientation. This claim is difficult to defend and minimizes the importance of education and training. Even if it were a useful general rule, it still would not substantiate the description of a particular individual. Specialists on the Soviet leadership have found it difficult to associate personal background with political attitudes.[30] Moreover, given the closed nature of the Soviet system, even the most diligent analysts have found it hard to determine the political attitudes of specific leaders.[31]

Theory 2: Realpolitik Expansionism

A second set of analysts argue that the USSR may optimally desire world domination, but that the Soviet Union is not actively driven by this aim; instead, it is simply opportunistic.[32] The advocates of this second view tend to minimize the importance of communist ideology in determining Soviet foreign policy, concluding instead that the USSR is a "great power" and as such will compete for influence and security as all major states do. At times some advocates of this diagnosis minimize the importance of intentions and suggest that power politics or Realism guides their examination. They make clear, however, that in their judgment the USSR is expansionist whereas the United States favors the status quo. While emphasizing the expansionist impulse as dominant, this perspective argues that the Soviet leadership is averse to taking risks. Rather than being adventurous, the USSR is better described as opportunistic. The advocates of this view claim that the Soviet leadership will take a "long view of history" and will await opportunities for expansion if they can predict low costs for exploiting them.

While suggesting that the USSR is thoroughly committed to revising the international status quo, proponents of this theory also describe the Soviet Union as a profoundly insecure and defensive state. They argue that it is striving to protect its empire and its security relations in Europe by trying to regulate the central, direct, bilateral aspects of the relationship with the United States. Simultaneously, it is said to be promoting political change and Soviet expansion in the Third World. According to this view, the Soviet Union is attempting to weaken U.S. strategic power in peripheral contests so as to allow Soviet exploitation of aspirations for social, political, and economic change in Third World countries. Moscow is said to take advantage of regional conflicts to expand its power. This diagnosis attributes Soviet actions in the Third World not only to revisionist aspirations but also to defensive concerns. It describes the Soviet Union as plagued by internal weaknesses and vulnerabilities such as ideological exhaustion, agricultural crises, energy shortages, demographic and labor dilemmas, ethnic conflicts, bureaucratic inefficiency, and the inability to shift comfortably to intensive economic development. Consequently, the diagnosis tends to attribute Soviet actions and perceived successes in Third World affairs to military intervention and a failure in U.S. policy. Soviet military ventures, it says, succeed primarily because the United States fails to use its strength either to raise adequate costs to deter Soviet action, or to teach the USSR that military intervention will not pay. In the long run, however, it sees Soviet success in the Third World as very limited, constrained not so much by U.S. counteraction as by the Soviet Union's own inability to facilitate economic development.

Proponents of theory 2 prescribe a strategy of containment that firmly denies Soviet expansion but simultaneously offers a second track of possible cooperation. Combining expansionist and defensive concerns, this dual-track strategy is not suggested as a means to produce change in Soviet system, since according to this theory externally compelled or influenced system change is beyond the capacity of the United States. Instead, they insist that the United States must prepare a long-term, probably permanent, policy of deterrence toward the USSR.

The realpolitik-expansionist theory depicts the USSR as opportunistic, exploiting opportunities for extending its influence that promise reasonable benefit and entail minimum risk or cost. This notion, like the "paper tiger" image of theory 1, is hard to evaluate because it does not lead to clear predictions about Soviet behavior. In most formulations it remains nonfalsifiable. It cannot be subjected to empirical tests without a working definition of "opportunity," and analysts promoting this diagnosis have not defined it adequately. They tend to argue that when the USSR acts, this is evidence of the Soviets taking advantage of an opportunity, and failure to act proves lack of opportunity. Such a tautological definition makes it impossible to test whether the USSR seizes opportunities when they appear, whether it exercises restraint, or whether it is likely to do one or the other in different times and places.

One major problem in ascertaining what constitutes an opportunity for the Soviets is related to the additional claim that leaders in Moscow are averse to taking risks. "Risk" is a subjective concept intricately tied to varying perceptions, and is thus hard to identify. The degree of fear of violence or retaliation said to be inherent in Soviet action will depend not only on one's analysis of Soviet behavior but also on judgments about the probable reaction of the United States or other nations. Analysts disagree on these questions and argue over the likelihood of reactions and escalation of conflict.[33] Since even Western analysts disagree among themselves as to whether the USSR may have taken a risk, no doubt Soviet analysts also have varying estimates of the risks involved in their contemplated behavior, and different ones from those of outsiders. One must either create an operational framework that can decipher the risk as it is perceived in Moscow, or combine the notion of taking a risk with the concept of seizing an opportunity and its related conditions.

The operational testing of what represents an opportunity for Soviet leaders is further complicated by the complementary notion that they are especially sensitive to what any action will cost them. This suggests that in cases where an expected payoff far exceeds expected costs (assuming these could be known), the Soviets may still not see an opportunity because of the significant expected costs entailed in taking action. Someone, for example, might recognize opportunities for Soviet action in the Persian Gulf, but would explain the USSR's inaction as the result of a decision by Soviet leaders to wait for another opportunity with still lower costs and greater hopes of success. The argument makes good sense, but creates difficulties for the analyst trying to infer a nation's aims. The claim is essentially teleological in that it explains current evidence with a speculation about future intentions.[34]

The argument that Soviet leaders are averse to taking risks and incurring costs makes it difficult to identify what they see as an opportunity. More important, it raises fundamental questions about measuring the aims of Soviet foreign policy. If the USSR is unwilling to risk significant resources to expand its territory, why should expansion be treated as a major motive of Soviet behavior? Economists interested in measuring what particular individuals perceive as valuable or useful in any given action have introduced the notion of sacrificial scales attached to choices.[35] The amount an actor is willing to risk and what he is willing to pay are presented as precisely the measures of what he values. Preferences that an actor reveals through behavior are then better indicators of values and aims than declared or assumed preferences. This logic seems equally appropriate in the analysis of Soviet foreign policy. If the USSR is seen to be unwilling to risk resources or to make significant sacrifices for expansion, then one cannot conclude that Soviet leaders are primarily motivated by a desire for expansion. Likewise, to argue that the Soviets will take unilateral action to their own advantage if an opportunity offers itself, but only if little or nothing is required of them, is to cast doubt on the importance of a desire for expansion as a cause of their behavior. The refinement of this diagnosis and its test will require that we not only define and measure "opportunity" but also locate the point at which the Soviets' willingness to take risks and to pay for expansion is so low that a given action is no longer an expansionist matter.

Without a clear and explicit definition of opportunity, it is also difficult to consider whether theory 2 takes nonoccurrences into account. Most Soviet restraint will be attributed to lack of opportunity, by definition. Without an independent definition of opportunity, it becomes impossible to test whether this theory ignores important cases when the Soviets failed to act in the face of opportunity. The perspective in general is likely to include symptomatic expectations quite similar to those of theory 1.

Theory 3: Realpolitik Defense

A third diagnosis of the Soviet Union's foreign policy is attentive to the issues raised in power politics but concludes that the USSR is better described as defensive.[36] The Soviet Union is presented as a profoundly conservative state primarily motivated by security concerns; its leaders seek to stabilize their international relations so as to allow for greater concentration on internal problems of development. The USSR's domination of Eastern Europe is not attributed to "any conscious desire to mistreat or oppress the peoples involved." This claim is in fact explicitly rejected. Instead, such "imperial" control of nations in its orbit, while not condoned, is attributed to security interests.

The proponents of theory 3 generally ascribe to Soviet leaders a geostrategic approach that identifies other nations as important elements in the superpower contest. Soviet involvement in the Third World is described as analogous to U.S. interference there. It is attributed to "cold war" bipolar perceptions of political contests. The USSR is also described as having less global political leverage than the United States and as disadvantaged in the alliance systems it can mobilize. In addition, it is said to face many serious domestic problems such as paralysis and backwardness in industrial and technological development, low labor productivity, strains caused by ethnic and nationalist loyalties among its member republics, a deficient agricultural system, and a multitude of inefficiencies related to the centralized bureaucratic system, public apathy, and a disaffected intellectual class. While proponents of theory 3 acknowledge these problems to be serious, they do not think that the system is in danger of imminent crisis. They conclude that the Soviet bureaucracy is "highly stable" and very unlikely to crack or capitulate to Western pressure.

Describing security as the primary motive driving Soviet behavior, advocates of theory 3 argue for a disengagement strategy that would reduce perceptions of mutual threat in both Moscow and Washington. The prescription is intended to reduce fears in Moscow rather than to manipulate these diagnosed Soviet anxieties as in a deterrence strategy. It is also designed to lend support to reformist elements in the Kremlin who, by prevailing over "conservatives" and "neo-Stalinists," may lead to modifications in the Soviet system.

Those who argue that Soviet leaders are primarily motivated by a concern for self-defense face the conceptual problem of identifying what actions constitute self-defense. The proponents of theory 3 recognize that an expanded notion of defense can be used to describe actions that could just as easily be called cases of expansion. As Robert Jervis has noted, "In extreme cases, states that seek security may believe that the best, if not the only, route to that goal is to attack and expand."[37] Clearly, a maximum conception of what is necessary for Soviet security could sanction an almost unlimited expansion of Soviet influence. Some actions like an unprovoked assault on France or a demand that West Germany must accept a Communist government, most Western analysts would agree, go beyond what could be considered actions taken in self-defense. These hypothetical cases, however, are not of great interest because they do not help to clarify less extreme behavior in specific regional settings. Moscow's minor moves that may be preliminary indicators of some change in foreign policy are far more interesting. In these situations the scene is more complicated, the actions more likely, and there is less consensus about whether to interpret a given action as motivated by security concerns. Although the task is one of definition, it nevertheless is essential and is too often neglected. Without a definition, the general claim cannot be empirically tested.

This definitional problem is complicated by the notion of what constitutes provocation. Behavior that is defined as "reactive" is treated as confirming the self-defense theory, while other actions that might disprove the proposition are attributed to perceived provocations. The problem for the analyst is to determine which actions should be treated as responses to provocations and at what point they can be attributed to motives other than a concern for self-defense.

Soviet support for Vietnam's invasion of Cambodia raised this fundamental problem. The act could be attributed to a defensive impulse vis-à-vis China and described in Realist terms as simply a shift in the balance of power. The shift in power represented by Chinese-Japanese and Sino-American rapprochement, the Realist could argue, led to an adjustment in Soviet influence in Southeast Asia represented by Vietnam's control of Cambodia. The act, however, called into question the limits of the self-defense explanation. The act after all forced a revision in Cambodia through military occupation and dismembered China's alliance in Southeast Asia. The fact that Pol Pot was a hideous leader or that the United States failed to raise equal objections to the ouster of Idi Amin by foreign intervention, arguments often made by the Soviets, does not change the facts of their behavior.

Recognizing that issues are often linked, as in the above example, is common in theories of American foreign policy.[38] When Americans think about containment, they often explain U.S. behavior in one region as a reaction to Soviet behavior. The American involvement in Vietnam is often seen as a defensive move responding to a broader threat of communist expansion. An American leader might reason that if the Soviets gain in one area, then the United States must counter this challenge, sometimes in a different area. Understanding containment as a strategy allows the leader to link a number of actions across different arenas into an interrelated set of policies. However, integrating the issues in the Soviet case above, while just as necessary, will be not only controversial but also hard to substantiate because of the closed nature of the Soviet system.

As a general rule, it seems that when tensions among great powers rise, so does the value their leaders place on allies and clients. When Britain and France were great competitors, British interests in Egypt fluctuated according to the intensity of the perceived threat from France.[39] The same pattern in Soviet-American relations is central to theory 3. To argue that security is a primary motive behind the USSR's policy toward Cambodia, one must show that Soviet leaders perceived threats from the United States or China and that these concerns were related to specific actions. Because of the closed nature of Soviet decision making, the argument will often depend on plausibility and conjecture.

The self-defense theory is generally based on evidence parallel to that used to bolster the other two arguments. For example, it is often based on a reading of Soviet history that emphasizes periodic invasions of Russia and domestic hardships rather than a desire for expansion; or it may cite statements coming from Moscow that stress security concerns. In cases that the realpolitik-expansionist argument defines as opportunistic and mischievous, the logic of theory 3 makes different assumptions about actions in different areas and contrary estimates of available Soviet options, drawing a picture of restraint and patience. The lack of definition and failure to clarify auxiliary assumptions, problems that plague the other two arguments, also trouble this one. One lesson from attribution theory that seems clear is that in order to test propositions about internal motivations, one must explicitly define the environmental situation in which actions take place.[40]

Theories About Motivation and Foreign Policy Analysis

Because the interpretation of Soviet policy is at the center of U.S. strategy, the above three theories about the causes of Soviet behavior are at the core of intense political debate. Those who borrow from the various theories and operate with fundamentally different assumptions about the aims of Soviet policy describe the strategic suggestions of the competing interpretations as incomprehensible or worse. Proponents of the first (expansionist) theory, for example, are inclined to see the strategy following from the self-defense view as appeasement. Those favoring theory 2 at times describe the advice of the first group as romantic and unrealistic while depicting the advocates of military disengagement as naive. On the other hand, advocates of theory 3 can conclude that proponents of the hard-line containment strategy of the first theory are insensitive to the dangers of military escalation and war. They also decide that adherents to the second theory are unwilling to pursue real compromises instead of looking for what is advantageous to the United States. Advocates of the third theory claim that the prescriptions for containment in theories 1 and 2 overextend U.S. power and the rightful exercise of its influence. They doubt that the USSR can be changed for the better with outside pressure and find advocates of the second theory overconfident about the United States' ability to control the international environment (especially in the Third World) outside the USSR. Proponents of the two expansionist interpretations describe advocates of the third theory as defeatists or isolationists.

Alexander George has recently argued that "crisis prevention may well be considered the orphan of strategic studies."[41] Despite the charged polemics and ideological convictions, however, all three perspectives offer strategies for pursuing peace and preventing crises. The wisdom of these prescriptions of course is heavily dependent on the accuracy of their assumptions about Soviet motives. Scholars interested in peace research and conflict resolution, consequently, have few more important tasks than evaluating competing theories about Soviet motives.

Basic research designed to test these interpretive theories is necessary. Philosophers of science have argued that the key contribution that social scientists can make is the understanding of causes. In the study of Soviet international behavior, it is often theories about aims that define competing paradigms.[42] How to test the usefulness of the different theories should be an aim of academic research. It is not enough to accept one interpretive paradigm a priori and then merely chronicle behavior in the light of that theory.

Inferring motivation is essential not only for research on comparative foreign policy, and Soviet behavior in particular, but also for the study of human conflict in general. Analytical models such as game theories should be assessed not for their "truth" but rather for their relevance as simplified representations.[43] In the more sophisticated models, this requires the identification of an actor's perceptions, motives, and subjective analysis of the utility of a given action.[44] Naturally, if these models are to be used to represent Soviet behavior, judgments on motives are necessary. As should be clear from the intense dispute among advocates of the three theories, judgments about motives will not be resolved by reference to area experts.[45] A similar dilemma remains in deterrence studies where the primary starting point is identifying an "initiator" and a "defender" rather than why the action was initiated. The value of a prescription for deterrence must be based on knowledge of motives.[46]

The social psychologist Fritz Heider has argued that an observer explains social and political actions as a function of the motives and capabilities attributed to the actor.[47] Attribution theory can help identify the basic differences among the three perspectives, but has no ready method for gauging the relative accuracy of the competing descriptions. Yet accuracy and usefulness are the criteria used to judge which paradigm to adopt. This is the most important decision a scholar studying Soviet foreign policy makes. Only by attributing a motive can one interpret a pattern of behavior and understand a chronicle of events or a set of data. For politicians, it serves as an absolutely necessary foundation for the logical formulation of strategy.[48]

It is disturbing that all three competing theories remain essentially nonfalsifiable and thus immune from empirical evaluation. Each remains too largely dependent on an assertion, ideological commitment, or "enlightened" assumption. Proceeding from one viewpoint or another, a scholar can muster illustrations to support any original claim. The enterprise in the political arena can resemble a lawyer's advocacy more than a searching inquiry.

Although an apparent political victory for one theory or another may define the limits of a debate, scholars must continue to recognize the central premises on which the entire strategic paradigm rests and insist that these be defended not by acts of faith or political power but by empirical evidence logically reviewed. If it is true that "shared images" define the limits of any debate about strategy within government bureaucracies, then independent scholars must continue to examine the basic theoretical assumptions.[49] The central diagnostic question should not be closed in order to protect the integrity of the strategy a government has chosen. In an era when the implementation of strategy often develops a bureaucratic momentum of its own, it is vital that independent analysts continue to test and question the basic political diagnosis that justifies it.

Describing the diagnostic function of theory, Alexander George presents the scholar's challenge in this way:

> Disagreements on what is the correct basic view of the opponent tend to become linked somewhat prematurely and rigidly with competing policy preferences. The ensuing struggle over policy choices then tends to squeeze out the possibility of a more systematic and objective analysis of the fundamental disagreement over the nature of the opponent. One of the most challenging tasks for those interested in the further development of policy-relevant theory, therefore, is to find ways of reexamining dominant images

and of adjudicating in a scholarly way disputes over the correct image of adversaries.[50]

The following study is driven by a recognition of the importance of the question of motives, yet I have few illusions about the prospects for "solving the problem" in any definitive sense. Any new effort to tackle the old problem can only be humbled by Robert Jervis's observation: "Although mountains of governmental memoranda and scholarly books have been written about the Soviet Union, I suspect that few people have been convinced by anyone else's arguments. Similarly, the past thirty-five years have seen all sorts of Soviet and American actions, but the basic debate has not been resolved."[51]

If Jervis is correct, there are many explanations for why analyses of Soviet behavior and aims have not been able to convince people who did not already agree with the conclusions. Psychological and political factors may be partially responsible, for surely if scholars do not approach the issues with an open mind and a commitment to detachment, the prospects for a productive dialogue are limited. The difficulty of the task, however, is also certainly to blame. Any analysis will depend on definitions of key concepts like what constitutes expansion or self-defense and on complex inferences from complicated data. Moreover, to test empirically these concepts and others, such as what represents an opportunity, we must have detailed pictures of situations, pictures that are themselves controversial and often necessarily include speculations about the credibility of deterrent threats and degrees of risk. These issues cannot be avoided and should be debated. They will not necessarily be resolved by more data and are usually not only more important than a particular fact about Soviet behavior, but are the real issue of controversy.

Debate that rests only on assumptions, however, will not be very productive if the central concepts remain undefined. The arguments will simply concern semantics and eschew the real questions. More critically, if the formulations of the central arguments remain nonfalsifiable and immune from empirical consideration, then the debate will be largely theoretical and increasingly divorced from Soviet foreign policy. Perhaps the interpretive debate can be advanced by making the definitional and logical issues explicit.

Although many scholars have analyzed Soviet foreign policy, relatively few studies have tried to test the rival theories regarding motivation. The following chapter looks briefly at several methods that have been used. It then develops a conceptual framework that integrates some of the strengths of previous efforts. This conceptual and theoretical approach is specifically designed to address the central dispute over Soviet aims. My hope is to provide a strategy for evaluating the competing theories that is based on empirical evidence.

Chapter 2

Inferring Perceptions in Foreign Policy Research: A Theoretical Approach

WHY DID the Soviet Union invade Afghanistan? Was it to secure its southern frontier? Was it to threaten Western access to the Persian Gulf? Perhaps it was simply to defend its credibility as a major power. We all may have our own theories, but each will include some estimate of what must have been Soviet perceptions of the situation and likely motives for the invasion. Usually the basic judgment about the aims guiding an action is related to a more immediate notion of what the actor perceived in the situation. Perceptions in turn can be inferred from two types of evidence: (1) what the actor says, and (2) what the actor does. This chapter will review how others have used these two types of evidence to estimate Soviet perceptions of international affairs. Rather than reporting the substantive findings, I will highlight the methodological lessons that can be drawn from previous research. The last two sections of the chapter will introduce a conceptual framework that will be applied throughout the rest of the book. This framework will provide a theoretical background and a systematic method for analyzing the images or metaphors found in statements about foreign policy and other nations, as well as strategic behavior.

Propositions About Soviet Perceptions and Motives

Various concepts about leaders' perceptions of world events are used to explain Soviet foreign policy decisions. Two perspectives on the Soviet Union's involvement in the horn of Africa, the southern Arabian peninsula, and Afghanistan illustrate this point. They can be thought of as propositions about Soviet leaders' perceptions and indirectly about Soviet foreign policy aims.

Proposition 1. One way to interpret Soviet intervention in Afghanistan and elsewhere is to emphasize regional opportunities and American inaction. In this view the United States' acceptance of "peaceful coexistence" and its losses in Southeast Asia are said to have sent a signal of

U.S. weakness to Moscow. The decline of U.S. nuclear superiority, coupled with a failure to use force successfully in Vietnam and Angola, are seen as eroding the United States' power to deter Soviet action. Soviet interventions in other nations are described as opportunistic seizing of the advantage in low-risk and low-cost situations.

This first hypothesis emphasizes the notion of *perceived opportunity*. It suggests that Soviet actions are a result of Soviet assessments "of the effect that Vietnam, Chile, and Watergate had come to have on the ability of the United States to function as an effective competitor in the developing world."[1] Regional crises are not seen as caused by the Soviet Union but rather as having presented irresistible opportunities for Soviet action. As Rajan Menon explains about Angola, Ethiopia, and Afghanistan, "Each resulted from complex indigenous factors. Moscow intervened because there seemed to be no compelling reason not to do so."[2] What might be labeled the "opportunities for gain" proposition is formulated concisely by Aryeh Yodfat. It has two parts:

(1) Use of opportunities. The Soviets frequently try to extend their influence and expand their presence by sending military and civilian advisers, supplying military equipment and providing economic aid. This occurs when it is the Soviet perception that the U.S.A. does not wish to risk a confrontation and would prefer to retreat. This trend is apparent in the Soviet interventions—directly or by proxy—in Afghanistan, Ethiopia, Angola and other places.

(2) Caution. The Soviets attempt to avoid direct intervention in local conflicts that might involve them in a confrontation with the U.S.A. This trend becomes evident when the U.S.S.R. concludes that the U.S.A. had the will and determination to oppose the Soviets, by force if necessary, and that such clashes might escalate into direct U.S.-Soviet conflict. This was the situation in Iran, South Yemen, Lebanon and other places.[3]

Proposition 2. Another interpretation argues that after 1975–1976 Soviet leaders were less optimistic about possibilities for taking advantage of world situations and more pessimistic about the threats of impending losses if their efforts should fail. In this view Soviet observers are said to have perceived substantial American "will" despite U.S. setbacks. It assumes that they perceived mounting regional opposition to threatened interference with heightened anxiety. Soviet interventions in other nations' affairs are attributed to concerns with security and regional influence. They are seen as driven less by perceptions of opportunity and more by *perceptions of threat*.

This second proposition assumes that the USSR seizes opportunities but argues that the specific cases of Soviet interference near the Persian Gulf were associated with efforts to preserve control in that area. They were not related directly to American weakness or regional vacuums of power. Dennis Ross summarizes the proposition:

The Soviets have demonstrated an ability to act decisively; but in each case the Soviets were impelled to act by the prospective costs of *not* acting and *not* by the expected gains of their action. What one might conclude from these cases of overt Soviet military intervention is that the Soviets are far more prepared to run risks over *defending* their gains—thereby pre-empting or averting potential "failures"—than they are over attempts to extend them.[4]

Mark Katz relates the argument to perceived risk and to the USSR's commitment to change:

What this means is that the Soviet Union has intervened not to fight for change in the status quo, but to protect what has already been established, despite the fact that a Marxist government may have only very recently come to power. The Soviets now look at American actions in local wars not to learn how to expand their sphere of influence in the Third World, but to prevent the loss of allies to forces that would be hostile to the U.S.S.R. if they came to power. This is yet another indication that the Soviets have come to conclude that indigenous forces in the Third World are not always friends, but may sometimes be enemies whom it is necessary to fight against if Soviet interests are to be protected.[5]

These propositions differ in their claims about Soviet perceptions of the United States. They agree that before taking action in the Middle East and Africa Soviet leaders concluded that the benefits outweighed the costs and that opportunities for intervention existed. This is undisputed. However, they disagree over the nature of the perceived opportunity. Did the leaders in the Kremlin see an opportunity to exploit political unrest in certain countries and see American will and potency as declining? Or did they perceive an opportunity to secure Soviet defenses in the face of a larger perceived threat from the United States and other regional adversaries? The basic motivational issue is translated into an argument about Soviet perceptions and how Soviet leaders define risk. The expansionist argument (proposition 1) is linked to the idea of perceived opportunity, while a self-defense interpretation assumes that they perceived a threat in the situation. Because of these connections, the study of perceptions may provide a logical and useful avenue for inferring Soviet aims.

The value of studying perceptions is currently in some dispute. Arthur Stein argues from the logic of game theory that an actor's perceptions really matter only in certain situations.[6] He suggests that perception affects the choice of strategy only when a decision is contingent on the actions of others. Although Stein restates the security dilemma and the well-known potential errors (seen by Morgenthau and others) of misreading an imperialist state as a defensive one or vice versa, nevertheless he argues that in some cases perceptions are not decisive. In many cases action is not contingent on another's behavior. Thus studying perceptions may not be worthwhile.[7] The logic is correct but the argument is unpersuasive in the Soviet case. The determinants of a dominant strategy may be rooted in a perceptual belief such as a conviction that an adversary acts in bad faith, and whether or not an action is contingent on another's behavior is itself a matter of debate, depending on one's perception of the situation.

Actions that may appear unrelated to the detached observer may be linked in the perceptions of decision makers. Stein suggests that a decision maker may simply take cues from another nation's immediately preceding behavior and preferences reflected in past choices. These cues and reflected lessons, however, can look very different to different observers.[8] Defining the political antecedent and what it stimulated is often difficult. Observers can link issues and arenas subjectively, making it difficult to predict which cues they are attentive to and what connections between them they may draw. It is striking how histories of American foreign policy can describe cues and choices so differently. John Gaddis suggests that a relaxation of American vigilance invited Soviet adventurism in the Third World.[9] Fred Halliday, on the other hand, argues that continuing American belligerence stimulated a reaction from the Soviets.[10]

Arthur Stein, doubting the importance of perceptual research, joins the argument: "The Soviet decision to invade Afghanistan was almost certainly not contingent on an assessment of the likely Western response but instead dictated by the nature of regional politics."[11] Stein's example of noncontingent behavior, however, illustrates precisely the importance of perceptions. In a survey of American leaders conducted by Ole Holsti and James Rosenau, only 30 percent of the respondents agreed that the Soviet move in Afghanistan was related to the protection of the USSR's southern border. Fifty-four percent felt the action was directly related to a decline in American influence, while 66 percent agreed with the proposition that the invasion was one step in a larger plan to control the Persian Gulf area. With 62 percent concluding that the episode proved the need for a U.S. base in the Middle East, it seems clear that for many the Soviet action was seen as contingent on the response of the United States.[12]

At this point, whether the Soviet act was contingent on other behavior or not is less significant than what the case reveals about the importance of perceptions. Defining the environment in which an act takes place is based on the analyst's perceptions and an understanding of how political leaders see the situation. Trying to predict how Soviet leaders might see the situation from an analyst's claims about external conditions seems particularly suspect. Despite the research obstacles, some empirical exploration of Soviet perceptions of the United States is required.

Soviet Perceptions of the United States: Lessons from Previous Research

Although many have recognized that international relations depend on how leaders perceive other countries, there are not many frameworks for actually studying such perceptions and misperceptions. A number of problems and likely errors have been identified.[13] Robert Jervis, Alexander George, and John Steinbruner provide useful insights into the forms that perceptions may take, but have not confronted adequately the methodological problems of inferring perceptions.[14] Archives may sometimes make the task easier, when available, but are not a panacea. What to make of verbal statements is still problematic. In contemporary conflicts and especially in the Soviet case, full documentation is obviously unavailable; diagnosis cannot be reduced to simply reading statements at face value. Instead, a theory and strategy for inferring perceptions will be necessary. The scheme developed here builds on the psychological patterns that have been discovered in studies of perception and misperception, and uses these insights as a theoretical basis for studying the contemporary images of other nations that Soviet leaders put forward.

In addition to conceptual and theoretical work on decision making in foreign policy, experts on the USSR have struggled to decipher Soviet views of the world.[15] In this effort they always confront two questions: which leaders or what organs should be studied, and how can perceptions be inferred?

At the height of the cold war, the decisional process in Moscow was described as monolithic and rigidly hierarchical. As the atmosphere changed, and U.S.-Soviet relations relaxed, the sense of threat dissipated and other, more complex models were advanced to describe the Soviet Union. First, more actors were presumed to be important; second, more values were presumed to be important to these actors. A monolithic picture posited one actor—the dictator—and one motivating value—personal power. A slightly more complex feudal model included several actors who were each interested in personal power.[16] A conflict model introduced several actors, each with several objectives, including power and policy preferences.[17] A bureaucratic model called for a focus on multiple institutional actors, each with role-determined interests.[18] Another view posited multiple actors, personal and institutional, each committed to a variety of values, including a desire for power, demands of a role, ideology, and policy preferences.[19]

Because scholars have seen the decisional process differently, their studies of Soviet perceptions have taken a number of forms.[20] Some focus on only one voice at the state level. Others examine multiple voices and try to identify differences across bureaucracies. Still others have broadened their focus to include voices that are not institutionally bound and sometimes are far from the centers of power. In each case, once the research is focused, another problem arises: how can perceptions be inferred from statements taken from censored media?

There are many potential pitfalls in trying to infer perceptions from what Soviet leaders say. Certainly a good deal of what is said is propaganda designed to justify Soviet behavior and mobilize domestic support. Western experts are familiar with the network of institutes in Moscow and Soviet writers, academic specialists, and journalists whose function is to study international affairs. Most assume that these Soviet representatives are also working to shape the understanding that foreigners have of Soviet viewpoints. In a relationship where military deterrence and diplomatic bargaining depend on perceptions of the adversary and on the adversary's perceptions of the USSR, it would be naive to take all that is said at face value.

Realizing that nobody can read all the Soviet writings on foreign affairs and that treating all statements as genuine would be naive, analysts tend to concentrate on a portion of the media and select certain statements as indicative of Soviet perceptions. This selection raises a host of methodological questions, most critical of which is how to distinguish between statements that reflect true perceptions and those that are propaganda.[21]

Someone who is convinced that Soviet leaders act because they perceive an opportunity can find quotations to support this claim. Someone else committed to a self-defense interpretation can readily find plenty of statements as ready ammunition. One's understanding of the media can unfortunately merely reflect one's prior beliefs about Soviet motives. If this is the case, the study of perceptions will be of limited value as a basis for inferring aims. Evidence will be selected according to prior assumptions. If one starts from a particular perspective, say for example the expansionist view, then one can simply discount statements that do not conform as propaganda or as appeals to a particular audience. In an adversarial relationship such as that between the United States and the USSR, one might suspect that such a bias would be reinforced by both governmental and public sentiment. American analysts would be likely to see as most prominent those statements that may indicate aggressive intent. Soviet analysts likewise would be inclined to seize on the confrontational parts of American speeches.

Social scientists committed to studying decision making have tried to find ways to use texts without falling into the traps of either naivete or methodological circularity. They have tried to reduce the bias in the selection of verbal data.[22] First, they suggest that it is important to differentiate among sources because there are differences between them. While a common line may exist, an analyst should not assume that sources are interchangeable. Second, the analyst must be on the alert for exceptions. A study must be reliable and provide some assurance that the quotations used as evidence are not taken out of context and are not rare exceptions to the dominant theme. Third, differences across voices may be important. A standard line may be obligatory, and therefore detailed exceptions or omissions may reveal policy disputes. Furthermore, if the censors ensure that all statements include certain obligatory formulations, then variation may be most evident in relative emphasis rather than absolute differences.

Although Soviet statements can be studied systematically and reliably, the problems of drawing inferences from them remain. If perceptions are thought of as concepts, it is not clear why they ought to be treated as equal to the text in the Soviet press.[23] Is it sensible to assume that perceptions of threat or opportunity and perceptions of another nation's military capability are likely to be directly stated in the Soviet media?[24] Awareness of political realities argues against taking the images presented in the press at face value, and logic argues against interpreting the press on the basis of prior assumptions about motives. Psychologists might argue that, even if they choose to speak with candor, leaders are unlikely to be aware of their own views. At the base of this problem is a reasonable skepticism: what appears in the Soviet media may not correspond to the actual international behavior of the USSR. Soviet leaders may be very generous with supportive propaganda, yet quite stingy with real material assistance. Conversely, they may speak often of disarmament while investing heavily in the development of weapons. In either case, we might do better to infer the prevailing perceptions of Soviet leaders from policy choices than from verbal posturing.

William Zimmerman and Glen Palmer have explored the relationship between words and deeds in Soviet foreign policy. They find that while the Soviet media rarely lie in a direct sense, verbal statements of intent are not always good predictors of policy behavior.[25] Certainly one explanation for this fact can be related to the predictable biases in political propaganda. With omissions, selective evidence, and ambiguous data, one can paint a picture of Soviet foreign policy that does not reveal likely behavior. Zimmerman and Palmer find, however, that the verbal imagery in the language of a key spokesperson, while not directly pointing to behavior, can be a very good predictor of policy.[26] In the area of military expenditures, for example, they find that the minister of finance's statements of intent do not predict the investment decisions he will make. On the other hand, they find that the minister's statements about the United States, as conveyed in the language of a speech or written document, is impressively good evidence for predicting increases in defense spending. This finding and the notion of using verbal images and metaphors as indirect indicators will figure prominently in the framework developed below.[27]

Comparing verbal behavior and policy choices as two sources of evidence for inferring how national leaders perceive the international situation raises an interesting problem in the Soviet case. The two types of evidence are at different levels of analysis. Verbal statements come from individual and institutional actors, while the policy outcome is the result of the decisional process. Only if one assumes that a particular political leader has total control, or that all domestic actors are the same, would one expect a strong correlation between the verbal behavior of a particular leader and the resultant behavior of the state. Because the Soviet system is closed, it is difficult to obtain information about the policy choices of specific leaders. The analyst is left with evidence at two levels: the verbal statements of leaders and the policy behavior of the state.

Because the verbal contributions to the decisional process and the policy results evident in Soviet behavior are at different levels of analysis, I introduce the notion of *prevailing view,* defined as the generally accepted construction of reality in which foreign policy decisions are made. This construction of reality may not be characteristic of any particular leader. Instead, it is thought of as a result of the overall decisional process that can be measured and observed in state behavior and specified verbal reports.

This study will analyze Soviet behavior at the state level rather than focusing on individual leaders. I am sensitive to the dangers of treating the state in an anthropomorphic fashion and introduce the concept of prevailing view strictly for analytic reasons. Because available data exists only at the two incommensurate levels, there is no way to avoid this simplification completely unless strategic behavior is not included as evidence. A premise of this study is that committed policy behavior is more significant than verbal statements and therefore the focus at the state level is imperative.

Inferring a prevailing view from Soviet behavior is no mean task. As in the study of verbal statements, the direct observation of behavior provides data but not meaning. The analyst must introduce a theory and set of decision rules to connect the USSR's actions to propositions about perceptions and motives guiding those actions. As should be clear from the first chapter, this has not been done very often. William Gamson and Andre Modigliani have pioneered an effort in this direction, however.[28] More recently, Davis Bobrow has attempted to infer the "grand design" best attributable to Soviet policy.[29]

Bobrow's study, like that of Gamson and Modigliani, has the advantage of analytical rigor and rests on behavioral evidence, but has not escaped criticism of its data base. For example, Bobrow's data do not include any indirect Soviet-American competition in third countries, a feature of the cold war that Alexander George and others have argued is important.[30] Gamson's and Modigliani's work, on the other hand, rests exclusively on the index of the *New York Times* and misses events that were not reported in that paper or became known in a later period.[31] Moreover, it requires the sequencing of events into action-reaction pairs that may impute aims at the time of coding. This is a problem that scholars working with data about events have not resolved.[32] Perhaps the most troublesome complaint leveled against these aggregate data bases is that in collecting them, scholars must make crucial decisions and value judgments in order to generate the data. Some readers would like to follow the derivation of the evidence in each case.[33] This is particularly obvious in the collection of data concerning military deployments and spending.[34] It is equally applicable with respect to major political events such as the Soviet occupation of Afghanistan.[35]

Dissatisfied with aggregate data bases, some leading scholars have returned to a greater reliance on case studies in which the controversial nature of the evidence can be more fully discussed.[36] Unfortunately, in many of these cases the analytical rigor designed to test central perceptual and motivational propositions is abandoned in favor of a statement of belief in one of the three major theories discussed in chapter 1.[37] Obviously, if analysts attempt to understand how national leaders perceive their situation by making certain assumptions about motives, then the inferred perceptions cannot be used in a strategy for testing the rival theories about motivation.[38] This dilemma is not a function of the case study approach. It can be avoided in a careful study that considers rival propositions, their expectations regarding foreign policy behavior, and the pattern of Soviet actions in a given region.[39]

Perhaps the major limitation in the case study approach is the difficulty of providing a strategic context beyond the specific region. Soviet actions in the Middle East and Angola, for example, may be part of a general strategic interaction with the United States, China, or both, and thus are properly understood as part of a larger pattern that would not be observable in a regional case study. A case study may find the Soviet Union determined to preserve its influence in the Middle East and reduce American presence there, but be unable to determine the reasons for this interest in influence without enlarging its focus to include the broader issues of Soviet-American and Soviet-Chinese relations.

It is always easier to pose the basic question regarding motives and point out dilemmas in various research strategies than it is to construct an approach that tries to address the central issues. The study that follows will be guided by a conceptual framework that attempts to build on the lessons of previous efforts. The two types of evidence that this study will employ are verbal images found in speeches and statements reported in the Soviet media and the USSR's international behavior.

Analyzing the Verbal Images in Soviet Foreign Policy Statements

Studying the images of foreign countries that leaders present to their publics through metaphorical or figurative language can be a valuable enterprise revealing these leaders' dominant perceptions of themselves, other nations, and the international situation.[40] Images, however, must be treated as indirect indicators of perceptions. The analysis of the content of a speech or document should be informed by a theory defining what various word-pictures and metaphors mean. Images are not the same as perceptions. Images are the conscious pictures, descriptions of foreign countries that a leader presents through language. Images are linguistic realities and can be identified. Perceptions, on the other hand, are concepts that underlie decision making and are not linguistically observable. They are inferred from images.

If perceptions are thought of as theoretical constructs, then the question is which of several possible patterns of perception is the most useful description of the views that dominate Soviet decision making at any given time? In the following section the components of several alternative perceptual models will be introduced. These are conceived of as building blocks that can be combined in different groupings and posited as possible simplified representations of the prevailing view among Soviet leaders. After identifying these concepts and perceptual patterns, I will address the more difficult question of how to determine the relevance or utility of any particular one. This second task is essentially a theoretical enterprise that attempts logically to connect each perceptual model with an observable pattern of images that occur in speeches and documents.

There are four basic concepts related to a political leader's perceptions of other nations that are fundamental to this research. Each can describe a part of the construction of reality in which foreign policy decisions are made. They are as follows:

1. If leaders believe that another nation poses a challenge to preferred political values, they perceive that nation as a *threat.*
2. If leaders observe a chance to foster preferred political values, either through direct exploitation or cooperative alliances, they perceive a situation as offering an *opportunity.*[41]
3. If leaders believe the culture of their own country to be superior, comparable, or inferior to that of another, they emphasize *cultural differences.*
4. If leaders believe the capabilities of their own country to be superior, comparable, or inferior to that of another, they emphasize *differences in capability.*

Using these foreign policy concepts, we can develop patterns to describe different perceptions of other nations. The concepts can be thought of as three sets of building blocks. In the first set are perceived threat and opportunity; in the second set, perceived cultural inferiority, parity, or superiority; and in the third set perceived advantage, parity, or disadvantage in power and capability. When one combines a block from each set, one can form patterns to describe ideal perceptions of a foreign country. The general procedure can lead to a number of patterns that

Table 1. Perceptions of Other Nations Indicated by Common Descriptive Metaphors Found in Foreign Policy Statements

Metaphor	Perception of Other Nation		
	Character of Foreign Policy Toward One's Own Nation	Capability Compared to One's Own	Cultural Level Compared to One's Own
Enemy	Threatening	Comparable	Comparable
Barbarian	Threatening	Greater	Inferior
Degenerate	Presenting an opportunity	Comparable but declining	Comparable but declining
Ally	Presenting a derived opportunity[1]	Comparable	Comparable
Dependent ally	Presenting a derived opportunity	Inferior	Comparable
Child	Presenting an opportunity	Inferior	Inferior
Satellite[2]	Threatening	Inferior	Comparable

1. A derived opportunity is one gained through cooperation, not exploitation or domination.
2. That is, a satellite of another nation that is seen as an enemy.

are theoretically and politically interesting. Some of the possible combinations are presented in table 1.

The three sets of concepts reflect assumptions about the dimensions or structure of each perception.[42] They are all defined in relational terms and are posited as the central components of a perception of a foreign country. The first dimension of threat and opportunity corresponds directly to the basic interpretive questions raised earlier in this chapter and in chapter 1. It is assumed to be necessary to capture the basic direction of the perceived relationship. The other two dimensions are introduced as important modifiers that interact with the central dimension to represent substantially different perceived relationships. The metaphors that are used to describe the observed country, and in turn to label the pattern of perceptions the metaphors reveal, illustrate the need for the modifying dimensions.

The three kinds of perceptions that are captured by the concepts introduced above are not independent. Following a gestalt tradition, I assume that they interact as if in a system and when combined into patterns act as models representing integrated wholes.[43] For both conceptual and methodological reasons I will not examine them independently. Rather, the patterns will be treated as models and linked to verbal and behavioral indicators. Three kinds of perceptual responses can be described thus:

1. *Defensive:* A defensive response is evoked by a perception of threat from a state seen as having similar capability and a comparable culture.
2. *Expansionist:* The expansionist response is evoked by a perception of directly available opportunity in a state seen as having similar capability and a comparable culture.
3. *Imperialist:* The imperialist response is evoked by a perception of opportunity in the interaction with a state that is seen as having much less capability and an inferior culture.

These perceptual patterns can be used as referents in describing Soviet perceptions but cannot be directly observed in the censored media. It would be naive to infer perceptions of threat or opportunity from the mere appearance of these words in political statements, censored articles, or interviews. A theory is required to operationalize these perceptual concepts.

Models are not true or false, but are either relevant or irrelevant. The question raised in the beginning of this chapter—why did the Soviet Union invade Afghanistan?—can be reformulated thus: which pattern, defensive or expansionist, best describes Soviet perceptions of the United States? Of course, the two models are not mutually exclusive and both may provide some description of the Soviet prevailing view. The question of relative utility, however, remains. One way to evaluate the relevance of a model is to deduce what one would expect the dominant Soviet leaders to do and say if the model were a useful representation of their perceptions. In other words, if the defensive pattern were a good representation, what would one expect to see in Soviet imagery? What different imagery would one expect if the expansionist pattern were a useful description? To answer these operational questions, we turn to the research done on misperceptions, which is very helpful.

In analyzing American beliefs about the USSR, Robert Jervis has found it useful to compare these images not to his claims about reality but to well-known patterns of misperceptions in international politics.[44] If the imagery parallels common perceptual simplifications, an analyst might doubt its accuracy and, more important, draw inferences about the likely causes of this misperception. Jervis and others studying perception have found common cognitive inclinations that lead to recognizable patterns of misinterpretation. The tendency to perceive more coherence and rationality in another nation's behavior than is merited and to assume that its decisional process is more centralized than is the case are two of many identified misperceptions.[45]

Underlying many of the empirically identified perceptual tendencies is a theory of cognitive consistency that derives from Fritz Heider's balance theory. Balance theory claims that an individual has an unconscious tendency to balance sentiment and conscious perceptions (for Heider unit relation). Heider's notion was a rather simple one. He suggested that in naive psychology subjects tend to develop conscious images of others that are balanced with their emotional sentiment toward the other.[46] He assumed that inconsistencies between the two, like hearing nice things about people you hate, produce dissonance and are generally minimized by cognitive processes.

It may be possible to use these psychological insights to link the patterns of perception just described with observable images. In other words, it may be possible to use the theory of cognitive consistency plus the identified patterns of simplification to predict how the combination of perceptions in one of the models will affect the linguistic imagery that is consciously produced. The method developed below builds on the studies of cognitive processes in decision making in an effort to make their insights useful in a strategic diagnosis of Soviet world views.

To deduce indicators for each perceptual pattern, I rely on balance theory. I assume that in the ideal case of extreme threat or an extremely inviting opportunity, political leaders would accept an image of reality that makes a decision easier. As in John Steinbruner's cognitive model, subjects will tend to construct a picture in which values are not in competition.[47] The simplification thus produced will make it possible to take decisive action without any complex tradeoffs, such as choosing between self-interest and morality. By treating concepts of perception as though they determine the verbal images that leaders of one nation use to describe another, we can link each ideal pattern with a stereotype. The perceptions prevailing in a nation can then be inferred from the stereotypes its leaders are inclined to draw upon in verbal statements. The idea might be illustrated by a medical analogy. Diseases have symptoms; by looking at the symptoms, one can identify a disease. In a similar way, perceptual concepts have corresponding stereotypes; by looking at the stereotypes leaders use, one can infer how one nation's leaders perceive other nations, the relation between other countries and themselves, and the world situation in general.

This method assumes that a subject will tend to simplify reality and that this simplification process will be guided by the perceptions of threat, opportunity, differences in capability and culture between nations. I recognize that perceptions may not be balanced, but am assuming that in the ideal case the theory applies.[48] I am constructing referents with which to gauge the degree of simplification in imagery and am not assuming that everyone's views will resemble the balanced stereotypes. In cognitive psychology what I am calling a stereotype might be thought of as a schema that happens to be balanced.[49] I postulate that such descriptive simplification regarding another country can be observed in three common areas of misperception: the description of the motivation underlying foreign policy behavior, the description of a nation's capability, and the description of its decisional process.

This method does not compare Soviet images to "reality" as the analyst sees it, but rather compares them to certain extreme stereotypes. The anchor point is labeled *complex* and simply designates an image that does not resemble a stereotype. The characteristics of the complex view have been defined by Richard Cottam:

> Motivation. Motivational complexity will be granted governments in this situation. There will be little tendency to ascribe a judgment of good or bad to the policy thrust associated with motivations. Defense is likely to be perceived as a significant aspect of motivation.

> Capability. Capability judgments will be made on the basis of empirical estimates of industrial and resource base, armed forces, equipment, training rather than on estimates of aggressive will and cunning from which power advantage derives.

> Style and Decisional Locus. A highly diversified decisional process will be seen, with decisions made incrementally rather than coldly rationally in accordance with a detailed and preordained plan.[50]

The stereotypical character of a subject's imagery can be represented comparatively in graphic form. See figure 1, which presents the extreme stereotypes. Two sets of stereotypes are presented, each with three poles: *enemy, ally,* and *degenerate; enemy, ally,* and *child.*

The Defensive Pattern and the "Enemy" Stereotype

The most commonly developed and best-known response to another nation is the defensive one; therefore, this pattern is considered first. If a great threat is perceived from another state thought to have both similar economic and military capability and a comparable culture, a nation's leaders will tend to characterize that state as an "enemy." The "enemy" stereotype allows leaders to respond to the perceived challenge with total conviction and absolute certainty of both the political imperative and moral correctness of their aims and means.[51] Characterizing the "enemy" as diabolically evil, a leader can suspend moral restrictions on his own nation's actions. He can then impose his nation's preferred values with coercive strategies and tactics of force that would normally appear reprehensible. The argument in its simplest form is that if people perceive a dire threat to their preferred values, they are inclined to hate the source of that threat. They are likely to see the source of threat in terms that allow them to forego moral restraints and use all the forces available to defeat the challenge and ensure their preferences. The perceived threat leads a subject to accept a picture that aligns conscious perceptions with subjective attitudes so as to facilitate decisive action. The stereotype is well known and can be summarized thus:[52]

Motivation: The "enemy" state's motivation is represented in an extremely simple fashion (usually by a monocausal explanation), emphasizing the aggressive drive for expansion and power of the leader and the nation-state. The state's motives are quickly judged to be evil and unjustified.

Capabilities and Power: The "enemy" state's power is seen as derived from the weakness of one's own state. If directly met with strong opposition, it will be exposed as a "paper tiger."

Decisional Process: The decision-making style of the "enemy" state is described as extremely rational and conspiratorial; its leaders are able to plot and execute complex, sinister plans. "Enemy" decision makers act as a unified monolith bonded together in common cause.[53]

Figure 1. Perceptual Maps for Summarizing the Analysis of Images

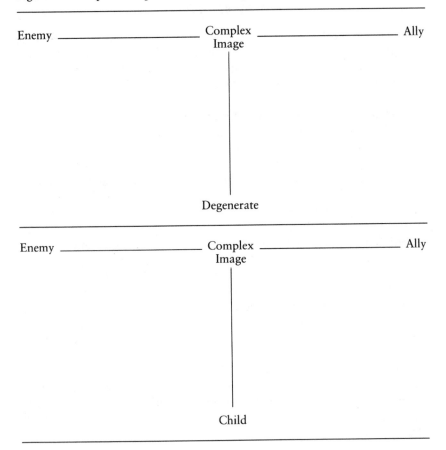

The Expansionist Pattern and the "Degenerate" Stereotype

The expansionist response is less commonly developed. While the effects of perceived threat and the "enemy" stereotype have received great attention in foreign policy studies, far less work has been devoted to perceptions of other nations as presenting an opportunity and the stereotypical imagery that these perceptions may produce. A most fascinating and politically important pattern to study is that stimulated by a perceived opportunity in another country seen to be comparable in capability and culture to one's own. One may wonder how a leader could perceive an opportunity to exploit another country if that country is also seen as possessing comparable instruments of power. Historically, however, we know Adolf Hitler not only saw opportunities vis-à-vis France and Britain but also persuaded large sections of the German population to agree with him. Because some scholars contend that the USSR today is an expansionist power similar to Nazi Germany, it is essential that the patterns of perceived opportunity and the stereotypical images that can be used as indicators (and early warning signs) be fully developed theoretically.

If a nation's leaders perceive a great opportunity to exploit another state that is also perceived to have both a power capability and a culture comparable to their own, they will tend to characterize that state and its people as "degenerate." Such a perception of opportunity may be related to a variety of factors, such as the state's economic interests, its national grandeur, or the political power of its leaders, but it may also involve a motive of self-defense. A self-defense motive can be relevant if a third state is involved that is seen as an enemy. In this case leaders might perceive an opportunity to use the target state as an asset against the third state. The desire to seize this opportunity might incline the latter to see the target state as "degenerate" and in need of foreign intervention.

The "degenerate" stereotype balances with the perception of opportunity so as to allow a nation to seize full advantage of a perceived opportunity. The stereotype frees the subject from inhibitions about violating principles, such as respect for another nation's independence and self-determination, and relaxes the moral constraints against using violence and coercion. By depicting another country as morally decadent, the stereotype allows political leaders to seize the opportunity and to define their interventions as necessary and beneficial for the "degenerate" nation. It helps to reestablish their own "moral integrity" by justifying the exploitation as a great mission to save the observed country from its own immorality. This rationalization results in the stereotype summarized below:

Motivation: The "degenerate" state is described as immoral, perverted, spiritually empty, and rotting from hedonistic self-indulgence. It is likely to be seen as passively accepting the loss of its past power and possessions.

Capabilities and Power: The "degenerate" state is less strong than it might be because of a paralyzing lack of will. Its potential power is discounted because of its unwillingness to actively defend itself or enter into confrontations.

Decisional Process: Decision making in the "degenerate" state is seen as corrupt and immoral, incompetent and indecisive, confused and perhaps even anarchic. The "degenerate" state lacks focused leadership, organization, and discipline.

The Imperialist Pattern and the "Child" Stereotype

Still another pattern developed from one nation's responses to another is the imperialist response. While the expansionist pattern and "degenerate" stereotype, just described, are valuable in detecting behavior that is associated with perceived opportunity, it is limited to cases where cultures are seen as comparable. This may be useful in analyzing Hitler's revisionist conquest of France and northern Europe, but does not apply to the type of imperialism that was manifest in the European colonization of Asia and Africa. In this colonial experience, opportunities to exploit other nations or peoples were perceived in regions where the culture and power capability were perceived as inferior to that of the exploiter. The stereotype was different.

If leaders perceive a great opportunity in another nation thought to have less capability and an inferior culture, they will tend to characterize the people of that nation as less mature than theirs, and as childlike. The "child" stereotype allows a nation to seize an opportunity with full vigor and without any moral inhibitions against violating other peoples' human dignity or their right to national self-determination. It depicts the observed people as too immature and backward to be treated as civilized human beings and justifies actions that deny them their freedom. The stereotype defines the observed people as not yet ready or willing to accept the responsibilities of independent political institutions. It reduces dissonance by allowing a nation to impose its will on another and to use that country while simultaneously congratulating itself for its "moral correctness" and even "charitable self-sacrifice." The stereotype interprets intervention and control as fulfilling a great moral mission, spreading civilization and modernization to the backward areas of the world.

One significant aspect of the "child" stereotype is that it justifies extreme coercion. Those in the observed nation who refuse to abide by the imposed wishes are classified as agitators under the influence of a third power—probably an enemy. This is an important feature because, as in other patterns, what a nation perceives as an opportunity may relate to a variety of motives such as the observed nation's economic interests, its grandeur, and the political power of its leaders. It also may involve a motive of defense. If an intense threat is perceived from a foreign country, a corresponding opportunity for containing the enemy may be perceived in a third state. The stereotype resulting from this pattern is summarized below:

Motivation: The elite of the "childlike" state is sharply divided between those willing to cooperate with the observer's country and those who are not. The cooperative elite are characterized as enlightened, responsible modernizers, benign and morally correct. Those unwilling to cooperate are described as irresponsible agitators and immoral radicals.

Capabilities and Power: The "childlike" state is less strong than it might be because of the incompetence of its leaders and the cultural inferiority of its people. Potential power is discounted because of the elite's inability to handle advanced technology or sophisticated administrative techniques without the constant tutelage of advisors.

Decisional Process: Decision making among the cooperative elite is pictured as relatively tolerant, incremental, and moderately diversified, but plagued with incompetence. That of the uncooperative elite is conspiratorial, xenophobic, and despotic. The cooperative element is seen as trying to modernize a traditional society by imposing unpopular changes that are justified and not repressive. The uncooperative element is seen as unified around a dictator and comprising a limited number of extremists who may be described as agents of a foreign power. The people are described as too immature politically to have any significant political opinions or to support any genuine nationalist movement.

The method for analyzing the metaphors and figurative language in foreign policy statements posits three conceptual patterns and examines each of these patterns through a stereotype. The rationale is based on assumptions of gestalt psychology and assumes the interdependence of various elements in cognitive structures. Deducing operational stereotypes for each perceptual pattern entails Heider's balance theory and is also based on empirical studies of cognitive process and misperception. Several case studies corroborate this approach. The association between an "enemy" image and perceived threat has been noted in several studies.[54] Richard Cottam has studied nineteenth-century British views of Egypt in order to examine the validity of the "child" stereotype and the imperialist pattern.[55] An examination of Adolf Hitler's views of France suggests that the expansionist model is often associated with the "degenerate" stereotype. In strictly analytical terms, the dimensions of each pattern determine the simplification process and the inclination to see other nations in terms of stereotypes. The approach is summarized in table 2.

The perceptions of a nation's leaders regarding other countries can be inferred from the imagery they use in speeches and written documents. Soviet statements will be examined in this study but their con-

Table 2. Stereotyped Descriptions of Other Nations That Are Symptomatic of Three Perceptual Responses to Their Foreign Policy Behavior

Response Pattern	Conceptual Dimensions Describing the Perception of the Other Nation	Stereotype That Operationalizes the Perceptual Concept[1]
Defensive	Threatening Possessing similar capability Comparable in culture	Enemy
Expansionist	Presenting an opportunity Possessing similar capability Comparable in culture	Degenerate
Imperialist	Presenting an opportunity Possessing less capability Inferior in culture	Child

1. These operational indicators are deduced using balance theory as a guide. They represent schemas that are perfectly balanced with the desire to respond to either threat or opportunity.

tent will not be taken as a literal reflection of the perceptions of Soviet leaders. Statements will be compared to the possible stereotypes of other nations they suggest—particularly the United States. This task will require comparing Soviet images of the United States with each of the three stereotypes: "enemy," "degenerate," and "child." The operational question will be how much the prevailing imagery in Soviet statements entails the "enemy" and "degenerate" stereotypes—the "child" stereotype is not applicable. The direction and degree of simplification found in the statements, rather than the literal text, will be used as the measure of perception.

The stereotypes are developed at a level of generality that corresponds to what others have called "shared images."[56] They are not spelled out at a level of tactical detail and phraseology at which some Kremlinologists operate. They are not designed to uncover fine distinctions in argument but rather are set up to tap general perceptions of the United States. This level is the most appropriate for tackling the interpretive questions raised at the outset. It has limitations. It will miss subtle differences in phrases or omissions that are significant in the "esoteric communications" in the Soviet media. It will tend to find more similarity in imagery than a more fine-tuned instrument would and thus omit interesting differences among Soviet voices. If my purpose were to study internal Soviet politics, these limits could be debilitating. They seem acceptable, however, given the focus on the prevailing view and the international behavior of the USSR.

My choice is to study the Soviet Union's foreign policy behavior over the past fifteen years. This task in itself is so important and so large that a focus on domestic politics is beyond my scope. At the level of state action and shared images, bureaucratic issues may be less important than at the level of policy implementation. In the Cuban missile crisis, for example, the essential U.S. decision was that the missiles must be taken out. The bureaucratic issues were less salient in this decision and became factors when the discussion turned to the tactical question of how to get the missiles out.[57] The inclination here is not to assume a unitary actor but to summarize the decisional process with the notion of prevailing view.

The idea of prevailing view is not introduced in order to ignore internal differences but rather is designed to capture perception at the state level. It is a conceptual picture of the result of the domestic process that complements actual state behavior. Because strategic actions will constitute the core of my evidence, it is the prevailing view that is most relevant. Thus I treat certain Soviet voices as if they articulated the composite image of the United States derived from speeches and published documents.

Statements of General Secretary Brezhnev, resolutions of the Central Committee of the CPSU, and editorials appearing in *Pravda* and *Izvestia* will be regarded as the authoritative sources for the prevailing view. Unfortunately, the image of the United States in these sources is not very detailed. To develop a richer picture of the prevailing imagery, I will use other articles in *Pravda* and *Izvestia* to flesh out this skeletal image.[58]

This fleshing out must be done carefully. It is important not to mix significantly different images. To avoid this, I use only articles that follow the main lines set by the Communist spokesmen. Furthermore, I include only those parts of additional articles that follow the prevailing image. This should not present unacceptable problems, given the focus on shared images. My aim is to capture what is common in Soviet pictures of the United States. This is easier than trying to decipher what is different. Articles that disagree on some programmatic issues may share a common general image. Where differences are noticeable, I will point them out.

Other studies of Soviet perceptions have found significant differences in the Soviet media.[59] At times analysts have been able to identify some leaders as more "hawkish" and others as having more confidence in detente. The focus on prevailing view may tend to blur these distinctions. To compensate for possible problems that such diversity may entail, in the conclusion I will consider competing images within the Politburo. The Politburo study will draw on a reliable data base that codes every speech or article written by each Politburo member during the 1970s. It will test the reliability of the imagery presented in the case studies and reveal the possible distortion involved in treating Secretary Brezhnev as a prevailing voice. It will also provide a systematic consideration of the differences in perception that are evident at the highest echelons of decision making.

To summarize: the purpose of studying verbal images is to determine what they reveal about Soviet perceptions of the United States. I make no effort to speculate on the psychological and personality factors that might explain why each individual holds these views. It is assumed from consistency theory that leaders may present a psychologically "balanced" picture or rationalization that justifies the state's behavior. By studying which stereotypical justifications are invoked, whether by the subjects themselves or by the prevailing censor, one can infer the Soviets' perceptions of threat and opportunity presented by the current world situation.

Statements offered by Communist spokesmen will not be dismissed simply because of the audience they are addressed to or because of my sense that the image is being advocated only for domestic political reasons. Verbal images should not be selectively sampled to fit an a priori assumption about Soviet perceptions. I compensate for the potential naivete entailed in this decision by giving greater priority to strategic actions. It is the international behavior of the USSR, not its publicly presented images of the United States, that should be the primary evidence for testing my propositions regarding Soviet perceptions and motives.

Analyzing Strategic Behavior

Studying the images that appear in speeches and published statements is not the same as studying Soviet foreign policy. Studying the strategic behavior of the USSR is a necessary task and a hard one, raising serious problems in data collection and coverage. There is no reliable way to evaluate the effects of missing data. Outsiders have no knowledge about what the universe of Soviet actions may have been. Some information is kept secret; much of what is made public is distorted for political or bureaucratic reasons, or both; and an undetermined portion is simply not available for collection by any source to which Westerners have access. Certainly these limits pose problems, but they do not preclude research. A great deal of evidence is available in event archives, news indexes, memoirs, and secondary sources. A more difficult problem than lack of information is determining what the known facts mean.

When actions can be identified, what they indicate about Soviet perceptions or motives remains controversial. For example, what does Soviet military assistance to a Third World "liberation" movement indicate? Is this encouraging turmoil or contributing to stability? Obviously, the answer to this question requires an assumption about the causes of turmoil and the prospects for peaceful resolution. Can arming parties opposed to American interests be simply defined as promoting violence, while U.S. military deliveries to counterelites is considered stabilizing?[60]

What Soviet actions would promote peace and on what terms? Does opposing U.S. terms indicate a lack of interest in peace, or rather a commitment to peace on other terms? Clear propositions defining what Soviet actions indicate have not been carefully developed. The nonfalsifiable nature of all three major competing perspectives testifies to this. We need to define and differentiate between Soviet actions that indicate perceived threat and patterns that indicate perceived opportunity.

It seems plausible that if the prevailing Soviet elite regard the United States as a threatening adversary, then Soviet international behavior will resemble a *containment* strategy. The logic of dealing with a country perceived as threatening with a strategy of containment is familiar to Americans. The strategy is designed to prevent a state from acquiring new allies or sources of political power. In the nuclear era it generally includes two major methods of raising unacceptable costs for the enemy: constructing political alliances and military deterrence. The containment strategy includes the development and support of political allies that present obstacles to the target state's acquisition of new partners and influence. This may be accomplished either directly, by encircling the target state, or indirectly, by confronting its regional allies. It also includes a commitment to military deterrence which in this era means the development and deployment of an arsenal of nuclear and conventional weapons capable of convincingly threatening the adversary.

A containment strategy can be pursued with different degrees of commitment that range from a selective pattern of alliances and maintaining nuclear detente to a pattern of broadly reinforced alliance coalitions and military modernization. Commitment to a containment effort can be thought of as the willingness to pay for its implementation. It is measured on the following scale: no support—propaganda support—economic assistance—sale of military equipment—donation of weapons and advisors—deployment of combat troops—nuclear threat invoking extended deterrence—total support.

To gauge the degree to which the USSR's actions regarding the United States resemble a containment pattern, I suggest the following criteria:

1. Commitment, measured in terms of sacrifice and risk, to protecting the government and territorial integrity of political allies, which in various regions of the world are in contest with allies supported by the United States;
2. Commitment, measured in terms of sacrifice and risk, to ensuring the continuation of existing political alliances;
3. Commitment to developing a nuclear deterrent based on weapons development and deployment instead of negotiations.

If Soviet policy is not motivated by self-defense motives, and is instead best attributed to expansionist aims, then one would not expect the containment pattern. One would expect Soviet behavior to resemble a strategy of *revisionism* regarding the political status quo that supersedes containment. Revisionism is not as widely used a concept as is containment, especially in the United States. I am using this word to describe a strategy that promotes change in an adversary's position and alters the political status quo. It is intended to operationalize the strategy one would expect if the Soviet Union were what Henry Kissinger called a "revolutionary power."[61] It corresponds historically to Adolf Hitler's efforts to "revise" the European order and the international system.[62] A revisionist strategy is characterized by demands that force the target state's acceptance of political change. Revisionism includes acts that both demand that the target state, or its ally, abandon a present position, relationship, or even its government, and enforces compliance. As with other strategies, revisionism can be pursued with different degrees of commitment. They may range from demands for political rollback that are backed by little more than propaganda to political demands enforced by military occupation. Political demands backed by subversion and intervention are somewhere in the middle.

This study will use the following criteria to gauge the degree to which the USSR's actions resemble a strategy of revisionism:

1. Commitment, as measured by sacrifice, risk, and power employed, to forcing the target state to retreat from a political position or political allegiance;
2. Commitment to forcing the United States or its allies to accept changes in either government, territory, or both;
3. Commitment to developing and deploying a military arsenal so superior to that of the United States that compliance with ultimatums is assured.

Containment and revisionism may be thought of as models of strategic behavior that correspond to the motives of self-defense and political expansion. By defining each and spelling out the general indicators of both, I hope to use these models to guide the analysis of Soviet policy. It is not practical to catalogue all Soviet actions, nor would doing so lead necessarily to any interpretive understanding. The two models introduced here will help define what information to search for, and if it is found what such information means about Soviet aims. The models will be put to the test in specific arenas of Soviet-American interaction like the Middle East. They will be used to define what Soviet actions in the area are consistent with a containment strategy and what indicate a revisionist attempt to force political change and expand Soviet domination.

In essence the strategic models will provide the decision rules that will be used to analyze Soviet foreign policy behavior. They are conceived of in a "hierarchy of inclusiveness."[63] A containment strategy is expected when security and national defense are of high priority and are seen as minimum commitments for a revisionist strategy. Revisionist behavior is defined as surpassing the kinds of actions that could easily be explained as befitting a containment pattern. It is assumed that a drive for political expansion includes a commitment to self-defense. The specific actions that separate one model from the other will be spelled out in each arena of interaction. Defining the expectations of both models may not "prove" the validity of the connection between them and the aims associated with them, but at least will spell out clearly the logic on which the interpretive judgments are based.[64] Moreover, it will force the analyst to search for and consider data that may support and disprove both propositions. As will be discussed below, evidence that fits the predictions of the revisionist model can be used to challenge the relevance of the containment model, but the absence of actions consistent with the revisionist model does not necessarily disprove its importance.

The study of Soviet behavior that follows is organized as a focused comparison.[65] Organization by arenas rather than simply cases seems most compatible with the global character of the strategic models. Several case studies are developed from each arena during a specific period. They are not selected at random but correspond to the arenas in which Soviet commitments were clearly greatest and in turn strategic questions evidently most salient. The period covered, 1967–1979, begins in the era prior to Sino-American rapprochement—1967 being a benchmark year—and ends with the culmination of U.S.-Chinese strategic cooperation. For 1967 the study will concentrate on Soviet behavior in the development of strategic nuclear weapons, and in Central Europe, the Middle East, and Southeast Asia. In 1972 a concentration on South Asia will be added. In 1979 Southwest Asia will be substituted for Southeast Asia.

In each arena the two general strategic models—containment and revisionism—will be translated into concrete expectations. The actual policy commitments demonstrated by Soviet actions will then be compared to the various predictions of each model. The resemblance between the USSR's behavior and the competing predictions will be judged in each arena for each period. By making separate evaluations, one can identify variations across arenas and changes over time. Furthermore, the focus on several areas will allow for more sensitivity to connections among issues and from one arena to another and make global generalizations possible. However, in some cases no judgment will be possible because the situation was so complex that it was impossible to decide whether Soviet actions were consistent with the containment or the revisionist model.

Translating the strategic models into specific policy expectations requires a good deal of situational analysis. At this level, there are several obstacles that argue against trying to quantify the data. First, the predictions in each arena are likely to be specific to one policy or another and to raise questions where the facts themselves are in dispute. Concerning strategic arms, for example, collecting the data is at times a controversial enterprise. In other arenas, like Southeast Asia, it is not always clear which events can be reasonably attributed to Soviet intervention and influence. It is inappropriate to disguise these issues or to present a false sense of precision by introducing a numerical relationship. Second, the notion of commitment requires the analysis of incommensurate variables. Rather than trying to code the evidence into an index, I will simply spell out information on aid, arms, or other foreign policy commitments such as pledges of support. Third, the situational context is so important for operationalizing the strategic models that to consider the most interesting questions, one must examine specific pieces of evidence in detail. After all, the definition of the situation will determine the predictions of each model and in turn the meaning that can be attributed to Soviet behavior. As Charles McClelland, a leader in the use of quantified events data, has argued: "The crucial factor is the situation and situational contexts are highly variable. It is possible that scaling events on a continuum of conflict tells us more about the judges than about the meaning of the events."[66]

Both strategic models lead to predictions about Soviet foreign policy behavior. If the predictions of the revisionist model resemble actual Soviet behavior, then the containment model is superseded and assumed to be less relevant than the revisionist one. If the containment predictions are fulfilled, but the USSR does not engage in the actions predicted by the revisionist model, then these "nonoccurrences" become significant and may argue against the revisionist description.[67] Defining what the revisionist model would predict, however, and how significant a nonoccurrence is requires a careful contextual argument. It is necessary to speculate on what the USSR could have done if it were determined to expand its influence and how risky alternative behavior might have been. The case study method would help to explain what actions would follow from a revisionist model and would provide for a contextual analysis of nonoccurrences.

If Soviet actions toward another country do not demonstrate an interest in forcing political change, this departure from the revisionist model can be attributed to two different sets of factors. On the one hand, it may indicate a lack of desire for expansion. On the other hand, it may be attributed to the strength of external constraints that prevent the USSR from pursuing a revisionist course. This second explanation suggests that the USSR is predisposed to expansion but cannot proceed in the present circumstances; it may be deterred by some combination of external forces. If we do not observe evidence of forced revisionism regarding a target state, this can be explained not by questioning expansionism as a motive but by invoking what might be called the *deterrence caveat*. This is basically a warning to reexamine the evidence to see that the estimate of Soviet capabilities that led to the initial prediction of revisionism does in fact correspond to the available means at their disposal. The Soviets' actions could have been blocked by a deterrent.

Before rejecting the revisionist model and concluding that the containment pattern is more appropriate, one must examine the deterrence caveat carefully. The credibility of external constraints must be discussed, as must the risks involved in possible Soviet action. There is a great danger of bias in this process. American analysts concerned about the USSR as a threat to their homeland are likely to attribute Soviet behavior to internal predispositions and Soviet inaction to environmental constraints.[68] They may be inclined to think that if the Soviets do not act as the revisionist expectation would predict, it is because they cannot. If this explanation is not scrutinized and empirical measures of Soviet capabilities are not carefully considered in each arena, the claim will remain nonfalsifiable. To fight against this bias, we may find it useful to study the tactics available to the USSR and to look critically at the credibility of American deterrents and those of other nations.

Examining the likelihood of possible U.S. counteraction and estimating the riskiness of possible Soviet acts obviously requires subjective evaluations. These judgments are difficult to make, yet are essential in determining the importance of nonoccurrences. Counteractions that the United States might have made in response to Soviet actions cannot be naively inferred from U.S. government statements alone. One purpose of such pronouncements is to enhance the psychological power of the U.S. deterrent. Leaders in Moscow are unlikely to predict U.S. behavior exclusively on the basis of government proclamations. Evaluations of the power of a deterrent must derive not only from government claims but also from the relative weight of Soviet capabilities and options in a given arena.

In most cases, Soviet capabilities in international affairs must be compared to two different types of options: first, the USSR could take a more active stance by courting other countries in the region, and second, it could intimidate regional parties through coercive means. To decide if the inaction is significant, one must consider both avenues. If the Soviets could have moved at a fairly low cost, then the nonoccurrence of an event that might have been predicted demonstrates relatively significant restraint on their part. The unwillingness to run risks or expend resources indicates that they place a low value on a policy of forced revisionism. Conversely, if the risks and costs of taking some kind of action were exorbitant, then nonaction is more difficult to decipher. It indicates an unwillingness to spend heavily for revisionism but does not rule out the possibility that if the costs were more moderate, the USSR might have moved. The estimate of the risk not taken will obviously be a critical judgment when one analyzes Soviet strategic behavior. However, whether the potential risks and cost of a given course of action actually deterred the leaders in Moscow in any given instance is impossible to say with certainty. As anyone familiar with

Figure 2. Flow Chart for the Analysis of Two Strategic Models: Revisionism and Containment

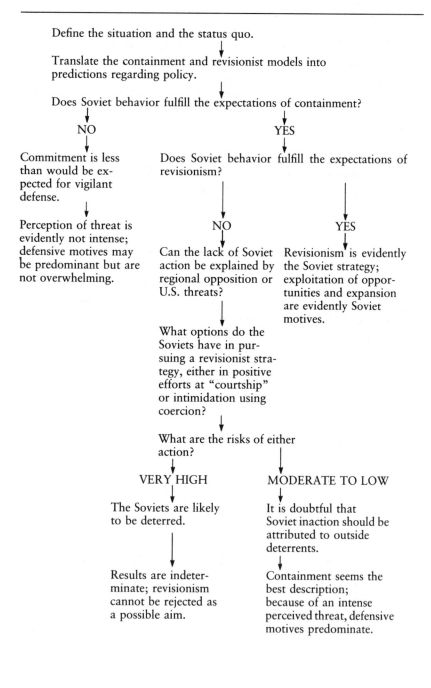

Define the situation and the status quo.

Translate the containment and revisionist models into predictions regarding policy.

Does Soviet behavior fulfill the expectations of containment?

NO

YES

Commitment is less than would be expected for vigilant defense.

Does Soviet behavior fulfill the expectations of revisionism?

Perception of threat is evidently not intense; defensive motives may be predominant but are not overwhelming.

NO

YES

Can the lack of Soviet action be explained by regional opposition or U.S. threats?

Revisionism is evidently the Soviet strategy; exploitation of opportunities and expansion are evidently Soviet motives.

What options do the Soviets have in pursuing a revisionist strategy, either in positive efforts at "courtship" or intimidation using coercion?

What are the risks of either action?

VERY HIGH

MODERATE TO LOW

The Soviets are likely to be deterred.

It is doubtful that Soviet inaction should be attributed to outside deterrents.

Results are indeterminate; revisionism cannot be rejected as a possible aim.

Containment seems the best description; because of an intense perceived threat, defensive motives predominate.

deterrence theory knows, it is nearly impossible to prove in any specific case that deterrence worked.[69] The best that can be offered is a careful and, it is hoped, judicious evaluation of the wisdom in attributing Soviet inaction to external deterrents rather than to a lack of desire.

In the following study I examine both verbal imagery in Soviet speeches and documents and foreign policy behavior and try to evaluate the resemblance between this evidence and what might be predicted regarding the Soviets' perceptions of the United States and chosen strategies in foreign relations. Using these theoretical frameworks, I apply explicit definitions and theories to the data. I do not pretend that this will prove which interpretation is "scientifically" correct. This is not my purpose. What I can do is organize the analysis and explain why certain inferences can be drawn and what judgments need to be and are being made. The frameworks help to evaluate in a scholarly manner the strengths and weaknesses of competing perspectives on Soviet foreign policy. They make explicit the assumptions, definitions, and judgments that are integral to the analysis and are necessary if the conclusions are to be replicated. By the same token, the frameworks identify how other data and arguments could alter the outcome.

This study is divided into three periods. Each opens with a brief introduction to contemporary Sino-American relations. This sets the environment at the international level. As mentioned in the preface, I am assuming that Sino-American-Soviet relations define an important part of the strategic context in which Soviet perceptions are formed. The research will then turn to verbal imagery from which conclusions can be drawn regarding the perceptions the images reveal. Following the examination of what Soviet spokesman said, the study turns to what the USSR did in the designated arenas. In each arena the analysis will apply the two strategic models: containment and revisionism. (See figure 2.) Each discussion will close with a summation of the findings and conclude with a judgment on the general aims of the USSR during that period.

Chapter 3

Soviet Perceptions and Foreign Policy, 1967

IN 1967 American-Chinese relations were visibly hostile. Leaders in both Washington and Peking warned of war and described one another in harsh adversarial terms. Secretary of State Dean Rusk, for example, described China as driven by a "fanatical and bellicose Marxist-Leninist-Maoist doctrine of world revolution" and as bent on Asian and world domination.[1] Comparing the ambitions of the Chinese leaders to those of Hitler, Secretary Rusk argued that they were neither "serious" nor "sober" and held a "view of the world and of life itself" that was "unreal." The United States remained committed to containing China with an alliance system "stretching from Korea and Japan right around to the subcontinent."[2] By the close of 1966 the containment effort included hundreds of thousands of troops in Vietnam with periodic clashes between U.S. and Chinese air forces along the Chinese–North Vietnamese frontiers.[3] Early in the year the U.S. State Department, responding to Chinese declarations, announced that the United States would attack the Chinese mainland should the PRC engage its troops in Vietnam.[4]

Chinese leaders were no kinder in their attitudes toward the United States. They pictured it as imperialistic and called it a demon motivated by the most base and illegitimate motives.[5] Labeling the United States a "paper tiger," the Maoists prepared for a "people's war" and confrontations that would "expose" the inherent weakness of the "imperialist aggressor." The Cultural Revolution (1966–1967) intensified the commitment to this strategy and prompted large-scale domestic mobilization. The PRC also courted allies in Africa and the Middle East on an anti-American, anti-imperialist platform, albeit with rather meager success. In January 1967 it suspended the periodic talks with the United States in Warsaw as apparent retaliation for American bombings in North Vietnam.

In 1950 a central element in China's anti-imperialist strategy was its alliance with the USSR. By 1967 this relationship had collapsed and Sino-Soviet relations were as hostile as Sino-American ones. Strident Chinese polemics depicted the USSR as a particularly vile and aggressive enemy bent on exploitation and domination. The long litany of crimes attributed to the Soviet Union included, among others, the imposition of unequal treaties and in effect the occupation of "disputed" territory, active "subversion" in Sinkiang, and support of "reactionary India."[6] Above all, the Maoist leadership directed special fire against the "obscene" Soviet "capitulation" to and "collusion" with American "imperialism."[7] While the Sino-Soviet conflict was certainly not exclusively a result of the USSR's advocacy of "peaceful coexistence" with the United States, many analysts consider the shift in Soviet ideology an important element in the split with China.

Sino-Soviet relations not only sounded hostile; they were visibly tense. In 1966 and 1967 the Chinese intensified military fortifications along the Soviet frontier and reinforced deployments in the Far East, Inner Mongolia, and Sinkiang. As part of the antirevisionist, anti-Soviet aspects of the Cultural Revolution, they initiated dramatic purges in Sinkiang, Tibet, and Inner Mongolia against what were labeled "counterrevolutionary nationalism" and forces of Soviet subversion.[8] In the diplomatic realm, China orchestrated attacks on the Soviet embassy in Peking and staged massive anti-Soviet demonstrations.[9] Beyond these domestic actions, China countered Soviet overtures to India by allying with Pakistan and refused to cooperate in Soviet efforts to aid North Vietnam.[10] It accused Moscow of endeavoring to encircle China with a "bulkhead" in Southeast Asia.

American officials saw the conflicts between China and the Soviet Union as real but were not inclined to cooperate with China against the USSR.[11] Quite the contrary: important voices in Washington suggested that the United States and the Soviet Union had "parallel" appreciation for restraint and responsible behavior that China had not yet acquired.[12] While the prevailing U.S. view of the USSR followed the "enemy" pattern, it was much less stereotypical than it had been a decade earlier. American leaders continued to describe the USSR as an expansionist state and remained committed to a containment strategy, but introduced important nuances in American policy.[13] Foremost among these was an interest in "peaceful coexistence" and dialogue with the Soviet Union. Many hoped to reduce the risk of a catastrophic nuclear exchange by stabilizing the deterrent relationship. The communications "hot line" was in place, as were preliminary restrictions on the testing and proliferation of nuclear weapons.

The Soviet Union remained the primary adversary in American foreign policy discussions, but was increasingly seen as a cautious power that recognized the suicidal nature of nuclear war. U.S. officials were less sanguine about the rationality of China's leaders. They expressed concerns that the revolutionary and radical zeal of the Maoists might propel China into a nuclear confrontation. The notion of using a "China card" against the USSR received little attention.

During the first period of this study, beginning in 1967, the "great strategic triangle" was characterized by a rather intense three-way hostility between the United States, China, and the Soviet Union. Many American leaders continued to insist that a communist collusion between Peking and Moscow existed and presented a combined threat to the United States. Chinese leaders insisted that "American imperialism" and "Soviet revisionism" or "social imperialism" had joined forces against Maoist China. As the following section will illustrate, Soviet leaders also felt that the other two powers were colluding against them. The Soviets charged that the PRC was increasingly serving American purposes, if not engaging in active conspiracy.

Soviet Images of the United States in 1967

Images of Sino-American Relations

Although American and Chinese leaders perceived Sino-American relations as hostile, Soviet spokesmen described emerging cooperation. Leaders in the Kremlin accused China, which was said to be ruled by Maoist fanatics, of "splitting" the socialists' stand against American activities and thus "objectively serving the interests of imperialism." Premier Kosygin claimed: "The unprecedented anti-Soviet campaign now under way in China, the attempts of the present Chinese leaders to split the socialist camp, and their schismatic actions in the international Communist movement are a service to imperialism."[14] The Maoist "splitting," according to Soviet spokesmen, invited American aggression and simply opened a vacuum for "imperialist" domination of Asia.[15] Although some journalists charged "direct complicity," most spokesmen only hinted at Sino-American collusion. They implied instead that the anti-Soviet character of Maoist policy was exciting American interest in using China for their own purposes. *Pravda*'s editorial explained: "Hatred for the Soviet Union has always been the common ground on which enemies of socialism have come together. It is no accident that interest in China has risen so much at present in the circles of imperialist reaction, where the prospects and possibilities of rapprochement with that country are being discussed with increasing persistence."[16]

Soviet spokesmen said that the Maoists had established "anti-Sovietism" as the "main direction" of Chinese foreign policy. Their image of China resembled a mixture of both the "enemy" and "child" stereotypes. Describing a sharp split between Maoists and healthy forces in China, they saw a dichotomized political elite, as is typical of the "child" stereotype. Moreover, they characterized the Maoists as fanatical in their commitment to a messianic ideology. Their thirst for power was said to be driving China backward into a medieval era.[17] On the other hand, as befits the "enemy" stereotype, Soviet spokesmen also described the Maoists as "great power chauvinists" and "nationalists" bent on expansion and domination in Asia.

Using a theme remarkably similar to American views of Soviet expansion, a *Pravda* editorial in 1967 argued that the Maoists were trying to use foreign policy expansion to compensate for domestic failure: "Doing everything possible to create the impression among the Chinese people that they are encircled on all sides by enemies, the Peking rulers are trying to rally them on the basis of nationalism and want to distract the working masses from the real problems facing the country and to justify the military-bureaucratic dictatorship of Mao Tse-tung and his stooges."[18] As is typical of the "enemy" stereotype, the image that *Pravda* presented highlighted the inherent weakness of the Maoist dictatorship: "The actions of Mao Tse-tung's grouping essentially are dictated not by their strength but by their weakness, the fear of their own party and their own people. The latest developments show that there are sufficient grounds for such fear on the part of the Chinese leaders."[19]

While much of the imagery that Soviet spokesmen offered resembled the "enemy" stereotype, it seemed to indicate that their conception of China was even closer to the "child" stereotype. Not only was the elite pictured as divided, but also the Maoists were contemptuously described as immature, uneducated, and primitive. Secretary Brezhnev dismissed them simply as "young students without political tempering, experience of life or understanding of Marxism-Leninism," and as "intoxicated with their impunity."[20] *Pravda* explained that, due to incompetent and inept leadership, China was in the midst of profound crisis and economic collapse.[21] The Soviet spokesmen described a tightly organized "military bureaucratic dictatorship" with a cadre of obedient stooges and storm troopers, but they concluded that the Maoists were incapable of sophisticated organization.[22] The inability to organize was attributed to the immaturity and lack of self-restraint among the fanatics that followed their idol, Mao.

The image, as would be expected, also described a "healthy" element in China deserving Soviet assistance. Spokesmen in Moscow claimed that China could not advance "along the path of social and economic progress" without the help of the "economically, politically and culturally more advanced" countries, such as the USSR.[23]

The mixed image of China presented by Soviet leaders seemed to indicate that the Maoists' anti-Soviet line was not perceived as an intense direct threat, but rather as a strategic opportunity that played into the hands of the United States. Actual Soviet behavior matched the ambiguity of the prevailing imagery and resembled, with low commitment to each, patterns of both containment and aggressive interference. The USSR, for example, increased its forces on the Chinese frontier, moved troops into Mongolia, and enhanced its ties with India, Vietnam, and North Korea.[24] All these actions seemed designed to encircle and contain China.

Simultaneously, the Soviets moved to intimidate China. The USSR increased its propaganda calling for the overthrow of the Maoist regime and funneled aid to potentially pro-Soviet factions within China. It also publicly reminded China that the USSR had once supported the idea of the creation of an independent East Turkestan Republic. The threat to exploit ethnic differences in China was only thinly disguised. While denying that they had plans to launch a preemptive nuclear first strike, the Soviets took care to make it clear to the Chinese that such a threat existed.[25]

Soviet behavior and the imagery used in foreign policy statements indicated that the threats and opportunities the dominant leaders in Moscow perceived in China were ambiguous and most likely partially derived from the analysis of American foreign policy. They seemed to define opportunities in terms of enhancing Soviet policy vis-à-vis the United States, while they saw threats following from the weakening of "anti-imperialist forces." The anti-Soviet policy of the Maoists was said to invite more active American aggression both because it weakened the unity of socialist forces and because it required the USSR to divert resources away from its competition with the United States, which remained clearly at the center of the prevailing Soviet world view.

Images of the United States

Motivation. Soviet spokesmen in 1967 described the United States as an expansionist power ultimately seeking world domination. Premier Kosygin claimed that it was precisely this American drive for imperial expansion that was the main cause of persisting international tensions.[26] The United States was not simply another imperialist state; it was "the chief force of aggression and reaction." In Secretary Brezhnev's words, for example, the United States "remains the embodiment of the worst reaction, bloody violence and aggression, and presents a serious threat to peace and security of all peoples, and we cannot nor do we have the right, to forget this."[27] In his picture, the United States was seen as captured by the messianic concept of the "American age," and as striving to establish superior strength with which to undermine Soviet alliances and achieve an American world empire.[28]

Soviet leaders often pointed to the United States' involvement in Vietnam as the most dramatic illustration of their charges. Vietnam was consistently cited as the "main obstacle" to detente in Soviet-American relations and as "the most serious threat to world peace today." American military actions in Vietnam were generally interpreted as proof of U.S. imperialism. *Pravda* explained that the American policy in Vietnam was trying "to force the Vietnamese people to submit to Washington's bidding, to transform South Vietnam into a permanent American military base and to intimidate the peoples of Asia, Africa, and Latin America who are waging a struggle for national liberation."[29] Tensions in the Near East, the Caribbean, Asia, and Greece were all attributed to one "common link," the "creator" of "all the hotbeds of danger, that being the United States."[30]

Soviet spokesmen also pointed to the Middle East as an example of the "imperialist," "aggressive," and "exploitative" character of American foreign policy. In June 1967, when the Arab-Israeli War broke out, Soviet leaders identified the United States as the primary culprit and argued that the Pentagon had "whipped up the Israeli general staff" and incited the regional expansionism of the Zionists.[31] A resolution adopted by the plenary session of the CPSU Central Committee on June 21, 1967, read as follows: "Israel's aggression is the result of a plot by the most reactionary forces of international imperialism, and foremost the U.S.A."[32] The United States, it said, wanted to take the Arabs' wealth and crush their independence. American interference in the Middle East was all described as part of a global strategy to control the world.

Depicting the United States as an aggressive, expansionist, and evil state bent on world empire, the prevailing image derived from the statements of Soviet leaders resembled the "enemy" stereotype in every major respect. Regarding motivation, the image lacked any similarity to the "degenerate" stereotype. It portrayed the United States as aggressively and violently active rather than passive. The United States was seen as attempting to expand its influence, not cut its losses.

Capabilities and Power: Soviet leaders in 1967 clearly described the United States as a superpower with enormous strength and resources, but they argued that it could not successfully pursue its imperial ambitions. The collective might of the socialist community could contain the expansionist aggression of the United States. As Secretary A. P. Kirilenko put it: "The might of the socialist commonwealth, and primarily the U.S.S.R., is preventing the imperialist forces from acting as they like."[33] The general argument claimed that only firm socialist resolve and unity could effectively "rebuff" American imperialism and preserve peace.

The shift in the balance of forces between the two world powers was an important element in the picture. Soviet spokesmen consistently argued that only the might of the USSR and socialist unity prevented further U.S. expansion.[34] They concluded that increases in Soviet military capability helped to ensure peace. The imagery of their statements indicated that the United States was "compelled" to conform to peaceful norms as the USSR enforced peaceful coexistence as a check on imperialism.

The picture of American aspirations being contained by Soviet resistance develops a theme parallel to the "paper tiger" aspect of the "enemy" stereotype. While the Communist spokesmen did not use the label "paper tiger" or claim that American power derived from Soviet weakness, their image of the United States included, in a more positive formulation, essentially the same idea. They described the United States as constantly probing for expansion and domination, but, when faced with Soviet power and socialist resistance, forced to retreat. Soviet power was seen as preventing further "imperial domination" and in turn strengthening peace; conversely, Soviet weakness would lead to American expansion. The United States, as in the "enemy" stereotype, would derive its power from the lack of opposition.

The United States was not pictured as weak, but rather as having "lost its strategic invulnerability." It was said to no longer possess either superior strength or sufficient capability to control political change in the Third World. I. Shatalov, like others, explained the shift in the balance of forces not by pointing to an American decline but rather to the mounting might of national liberation movements and socialism in the Third World:

> There have been radical changes in the world, and they have been caused not by the decreasing strength of the biggest imperialist state, but by the growing political, economic, and military might of he countries united in the Socialist system. The changes in the balance of forces between the Socialist and the imperialist systems have a considerable restraining influence on those who wish to unleash a world military conflict."[35]

While the balance of forces in world affairs was described as shifting to the benefit of "national liberation" and "socialism," the United States was still described as a very competitive, even "militaristic" society. The prevailing leaders in Moscow never described the United States as soft or weak of will, but, quite the contrary, as driven by a highly aggressive "ruling circle." It was not seen as decadent or unwilling to defend its interests, but as a country continuing to assert its imperial domination even when it no longer possessed the influence to do so successfully. Y. Melnikov described the theme perhaps most pointedly; his remarks illustrate how different the image was in 1967 from the "degenerate" stereotype:

> There is a steadily widening discrepancy between the doctrines of U.S. ruling circles and the actual relation of forces in the world, between the aspirations and the possibilities of American imperialism, between the general accepted standards of international law and the arbitrary acts of the White House, the Pentagon, and American diplomacy. Hence, the growing number of dangerous miscalculations and the increasingly adventurist policy of the Administration. Hence, its failures attributed in Washington to insufficient use of strength and, as a result, further gambles and escalation of unavailing violence."[36]

Decisional Process. Soviet spokesmen in 1967 attributed a number of conspiracies and diversionary tactics to the United States.[37] American foreign policy was characterized as crafty and fundamentally subversive, and was blamed for elaborate political conspiracies. President Johnson's "bridge-building" policy, for example, was described as simply a "cover for efforts to weaken cohesion among the countries of the

Socialist community and ultimately to divide them."[38] While this picture of U.S. decisional style resembled the "enemy" stereotype, Soviet spokesmen did not describe the locus of decision making in such stereotypical fashion.

American politics was seen as basically split between the "ruling circles," identified as financial, industrial, and military leaders, and the great mass of the people, who were described as having only limited control over the ruling elite. The "ruling circles" were not described as monolithic, as in an "enemy" stereotype, but as seriously divided on a number of issues. While the entire ruling elite was categorized as bourgeois, it was also dichotomized between "sober and raving voices."[39] The sober voices, depicted as "moderate, realistically thinking representatives," were contrasted to "belligerently minded figures," who were at times labeled "madmen." In this image, the "circles of extreme reaction" welcomed American military involvement abroad and international tension as vehicles for their own power and wealth. The realistic, moderate circles, on the other hand, were said to oppose U.S. aggression, most particularly in Vietnam, and to favor peaceful coexistence. The balance between the sober and raving voices was described as shifting, with increasing numbers of prominent figures advocating sober U.S. policy. Nevertheless, Soviet spokesmen concluded that the aggressive and imperialist elements were still predominant in 1967.

Differences within the U.S. ruling circles were acknowledged, although not consistently, with some Soviet journalists depicting real competition.[40] Authoritative voices, however, concluded that there was a general interest in economic expansion that united the ruling capitalist elite around a basically imperialist foreign policy. Decisions were not made by a single monolithic power, but were made from a rather narrow base representing general agreement on policy. While the image did not fit any stereotype perfectly, the degree of complexity was still very low and the outlines of the "enemy" pattern clear. Soviet observers did not present the U.S. decisional process as confused, lacking in organizational discipline, or indecisive. Their image of the United States in 1967 shared little with the "degenerate" stereotype.

The "enemy" imagery drawn from Soviet statements about U.S. relations with China suggests that in 1967 the prevailing view in Moscow conformed to the defensive model. However, this conclusion is drawn strictly from censored Soviet news media and propaganda. As I explained in chapter 2, one must carefully study the USSR's strategic actions vis-à-vis the United States during this period before attempting any serious judgments concerning Soviet perceptions. The next section will analyze and evaluate Soviet behavior in four arenas of competition in light of the various hypotheses about strategy. These arenas are: the development of strategic nuclear weapons, Central Europe, the Middle East, and Southeast Asia.

Soviet Foreign Policy Behavior in 1967

Strategic Nuclear Weapons

The development of strategic nuclear weapons has become an issue of immense importance in Soviet-American relations. One reason that the strategic balance between the two nations remains central to analyses of Soviet foreign policy is the belief that military capability determines the limits of any nation's actions; therefore, it is more important than intention. For analytical purposes, this belief treats the USSR's capability as an indicator of its intentions and suggests that trends in the deployment of weapons can be useful evidence when we consider the containment and revisionist hypotheses regarding Soviet foreign policy behavior.

A containment strategy would assume that peace is best guaranteed by maintaining one's own military strength. Consequently, if the Soviets pursued this strategy, one could predict that the USSR would deploy nuclear systems capable of deterring potential enemy challenges. Furthermore, one would expect that leaders in the Kremlin would be reluctant to substitute U.S.-Soviet agreements for unilateral Soviet power.

The deployment of weapons and the refusal to accept negotiated limits can reach a point, however, where such actions are consistent with a revisionist strategy. According to this second model, Soviet developments would move beyond an essential equivalence with the United States and toward a force capable of compelling American acquiescence. Calculating at what point weapon deployments actually demonstrate a nation's superiority over an adversary is one of the most controversial issues in national security analysis. Military forces must be compared to missions, which in the strategic nuclear era could include both intimidation and actual combat.

In 1967 the United States continued to enjoy advantages in the nuclear competition.[41] Soviet development, however, was escalating rapidly. Between 1966 and 1967 the USSR doubled its intercontinental ballistic missile (ICBM) force, even though continuing to lag behind American deployments.[42] Soviet leaders refused to discuss arms control, evidently seriously believing that an agreement would only codify their disadvantage. When President Johnson tried to raise these issues, Premier Kosygin quickly linked them to U.S. policy in third areas, the Middle East and Vietnam in particular.[43] Although the Soviets accepted marginal limitations on weapons in outer space and nuclear proliferation, these agreements seemed designed to stabilize the deterrent relationship and to limit further the American advantage in the arms race. As could be expected of a nation following a containment strategy, the Soviets were not willing to accept detente on the basis of American superiority and would not negotiate on strategic limits or regional conditions until they achieved more nearly equal strength.

Although the USSR did not possess a strategic advantage in the mid-1960s, it began a process of weapons development at that time that

Table 3. U.S. and Soviet Strategic Nuclear Forces, 1960–1982

	United States		Soviet Union	
	Launchers & Bombers	Warheads & Bombs	Launchers & Bombers	Warheads & Bombs
1960–1961				
ICBM	12	12	50	50
SLBM	48	48	48	48
Aircraft	540	2,160	190	380
Total	600	2,220	288	478
1967				
ICBM	1,054	1,054	475	475
SLBM	656	656	120	120
Aircraft	540	2,160	155	310
Total	2,250	3,870	750	905
1972				
ICBM	1,054	1,454	1,530	1,530
SLBM	656	2,832	560	560
Aircraft	457	1,828	140	280
Total	2,167	6,114	2,230	2,370
1977				
ICBM	1,054	2,154	1,477	2,061
SLBM	656	5,440	909	909
Aircraft	369	1,476	135	270
Total	2,079	9,070	2,521	3,240
1982				
ICBM	1,052	2,152	1,398	5,158
SLBM	544	4,656	950	2,570
Aircraft	332	2,708	156	313
Total	1,928	9,516	2,504	8,041

Sources: *The Military Balance, 1967* (London: IISS, 1967), pp. 5–9; ibid. (1972), pp. 4, 6–7, 65; ibid. (1977–78), pp. 5, 8, 77; Anthony H. Cordesman, "M-X and the Balance of Power: Reasserting America's Strength," *Armed Forces Journal*, Dec. 1982, pp. 22–51.

Key: ICBM = Intercontinental ballistic missiles
SLBM = Submarine-launched ballistic missiles

appeared to many Americans as a drive for superiority. Even though Soviet foreign policy behavior in 1967 failed to conform to the revisionist pattern, such an interpretation of their motives might be more convincing if one considers the process that began at this time and has continued into the 1980s.

There are many ways to compare Soviet and American weapons. All of them are limited; superiority in the nuclear era is hard to define. Table 3 and figure 3 chart the growth in U.S. and Soviet launchers and

Figure 3. U.S. and Soviet Nuclear Warheads, Bombs, and Launchers, 1961–1982

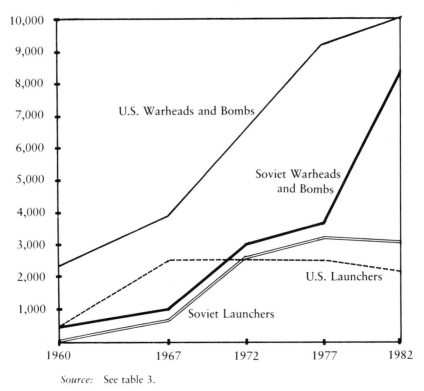

Source: See table 3.

warheads, but statistics provide very poor estimates of relative power. The systems are asymmetrical in many characteristics that are more important than numbers. For this initial period it is impossible to say whether or not the Soviets were striving for superiority. They were far behind on both quantitiative and qualitative measures. The complex issues associated with defining superiority and relative ability to carry out military missions must be deferred until our analysis of the 1979–1980 period, when the arsenals were more nearly equivalent.

The most difficult dilemma in trying to use military capability as an indicator of foreign policy intentions is that a drive for superiority can be consistent with a defensive as well as an expansionist motive. Americans traditionally—and some more currently—have argued that military superiority is the best guarantee of peace and that even a first-strike capability can be an integral part of a containment strategy. The problem only highlights the well-known limitations of trying to infer a nation's motivation from its capability. The competition for strategic advantage does not provide an adequate data base for testing motivational theories.

Political competition in regional arenas is an essential focus for analysis of Soviet foreign policy strategies not only because the regional disputes are "linked" to bilateral talks but also because they are the arenas in which differences between containment and revisionist strategies are most clearly evident. If Soviet leaders do perceive opportunities deriving from the competition for strategic superiority over the United States, then theoretically the effect of such perceptions should be visible in regional competition. Soviet behavior in three areas—Europe, the Middle East, and Southeast Asia—are studied here.

Central Europe

At the Karlovy Vary Conference of Communist and Workers' parties held in April 1967, Leonid Brezhnev, speaking for the Soviet delegation, explained that the conflict in Europe was inseparable from the worldwide struggle and represented the most critical arena of cold war confrontation.[44] While the general secretary presented the American challenge as global and called for worldwide resistance, he said that first and foremost American pressure in Central Europe had to be contained. Here he argued that the United States worked through West Germany. Brezhnev described the situation in this way:

> The aggressive forces of American and West German imperialism pose a threat to peace in Europe. What is the foundation for the increasingly close partnership of these forces? For American imperialism, collusion with F.R.G. ruling circles is the chief means—convenient for the U.S.A. and not too expensive—of maintaining its strategic military positions in Europe. It provides the U.S.A. with levers of pressure on the policies and economics of the Western European countries. As for the West German politicians by their reckoning the partnership with the U.S.A. will open up practical opportunities for them to carry out their revanchist schemes. . . . The military presence of the U.S.A. in Europe encourages West German imperialism.[45]

The Federal Republic of Germany (FRG) was not defined as a satellite of the United States. Rather, it was seen as an imperialist power in its own right driven by intense nationalism and revanchist aspirations: "It is a desire for aggression and territorial seizures. It is reliance on military force, which engenders the rapid growth of militarism. It is frenzied nationalism which inevitably creates international tension and a military threat."[46] Two academicians writing in *Pravda* explained: "An extensive program of foreign-policy expansion has been worked out in Bonn. The ideas of anti-communism, revanchism, and extremely bellicose chauvinism constitute the ideological foundation of the Federal Republic's foreign policy."[47]

The postwar division of Germany and reconstruction of Poland became political facts that, while not recognized as legitimate by the United States, constituted the status quo according to the Soviet Union. The USSR insisted that Germany either be unified and neutral, or divided into two equal states, one in each of the cold war blocs. The United States, on the other hand, insisted that Germany be united and free to join NATO, or divided, with the western state recognized as the only legitimate German government. After the situation reached several flash points in the heat of the cold war, the central dilemma still remained, with the Soviet Union insisting that the West recognize the German Democratic Republic (GDR), and Poland's western frontier.[48] Leaders in Washington and Bonn refused these Soviet demands. Change, nevertheless, was under way.

In December 1966 a Grand Coalition emerged in West Germany that married two different views of the USSR and two different traditions in national strategy. The leading party, the Christian Democratic Union (CDU), led by Kurt Kiesinger, emerged from a legacy that identified the USSR in stereotypical "enemy" terms and endorsed a "policy of strength" and a strategy of containment through NATO. Willy Brandt (the vice-chancellor and foreign minister) and the Social Democratic party (SPD), on the other hand, came from a different historical legacy. The SPD in the mid-1950s had opposed West Germany's entry into NATO.[49] Both parties by 1967 were committed to NATO but were also increasingly interested in Soviet proposals for peaceful coexistence in Central Europe. Brandt was anxious to promote a relaxation of tensions in Europe and began by renouncing West German ambitions for nuclear weapons and by acknowledging "respect," though not recognition, for Poland's frontier on the Oder-Neisse.

Soviet spokesmen were not impressed by the SPD's membership in the Grand Coalition and concluded that it reflected the Social Democrats' acceptance of the conservatives' platform. As would be expected because of the "enemy" stereotype, they also dismissed President Johnson's "bridge-building" initiative and the West German dialogue as a disguise for the traditional expansionist aspirations of West German imperialism.[50] In *Pravda* the FRG's change in "rhetoric" was described:

> The apologists for West German imperialism, enjoying the support of the Social Democratic leaders who have entered the Bonn government, are now engaged in a search for a "reformed nationalism" that could include the claim of West German imperialism to domination in Europe and at the same time retain some kind of "democratic" and "peaceful" cloak, which is necessary to mask the true goals of the West German ruling circles. This is the essence of the recent "change of concepts" in Bonn.[51]

At the Karlovy Vary conference, Brezhnev expressed similar skepticism: "Is it not clear that the new government is using this means merely to delude European public opinion, in order to escape isolation and thereby assure itself a firmer position for achieving its designs?"[52] On another occasion, Brezhnev described the "new policy" as a deceitful maneuver and reaffirmed an "enemy" image: "The entire practical content of F.R.G. policy is still the same, for the present, as it has been hitherto: a policy of revenge, a policy of militarism, a policy that denies the real situation in Europe and that infringes on the rights and territories of other states and peoples."[53]

The "enemy" stereotype that runs throughout the prevailing Soviet image of the United States and West Germany in 1967 indicates a dominant sense of threat. If this is the case, one might expect that the Soviets were following a policy of containment vis-à-vis the West. To test this strategic hypothesis, one must define the status quo. This, of course, depends on a somewhat arbitrary decision about time. I have decided to establish as the status quo the conditions existing in 1967— that is, the de facto existence of East Germany as a separate state, Poland's new boundaries, and the nonrecognition of these postwar developments by the West.[54] An ideal Soviet containment strategy would include policies protecting the two de facto developments and policies weakening West German resistance to recognizing them. In particular, these would include military deployments in the East, a stronger Warsaw Pact alliance, and efforts to limit the FRG's support in the West. On the other hand, a revisionist strategy would include, at a minimum, commitment to programs forcing Western recognition of the East German government or Poland's altered frontiers, and ideally it would mean commitment to actions forcing a retreat of the West or coercing change in Bonn.

Three sets of Soviet actions are relevant to the containment model: the commitment to protecting the status of East Germany and the borders of Poland, enforcing cohesion via the Warsaw Pact, isolating West Germany, and promoting West European recognition of the existing situation. All three merit a brief review.

The USSR's support for the recognition of the GDR as an equal sovereign state and to the acceptance of Poland's existing frontiers was unequivocal.[55] Soviet leaders pledged to use all of the USSR's might and even go to war should anyone challenge these commitments.[56] They backed up these pledges with twenty-six combat divisions, twenty of which were already in East Germany.[57]

The Soviet Union also mobilized and enforced solidarity in the Warsaw Pact. In January 1967 Romania responded favorably to the FRG's new overtures to the East. It established relations with West Germany even though the West Germans continued to deny East Germany's sovereignty or recognize Poland's altered frontiers. The USSR moved quickly to criticize this precedent and to reinforce cohesion among the alliance as would be expected in a containment strategy. Only days after Romania established relations, the Soviet Union convened a foreign ministers' meeting of the Warsaw Treaty Organization. The declared purpose was to formulate a common WTO policy and to stress a united commitment to the GDR and Poland.[58] Unity was also given highest priority at the Karlovy Vary Conference of Communist and Workers' parties, already mentioned, held in April 1967. By the end of the year, all of the socialist allies, except Romania, had reaffirmed their commitments to the GDR and Poland through a series of new bilateral treaties.[59]

Romania's reluctance to close ranks with the unified front was conspicuous.[60] It chose, for example, not to attend the Karlovy Vary conference. Although Soviet officials expressed their regret over Romania's decision, they did not force Romania to conform.[61] The USSR's tolerance of Romania's deviance can be explained a number of ways. First, one could argue that the Soviets were incapable of insisting on Romanian compliance, but this seems implausible. A more likely explanation might be that the Soviets did not feel that they needed to bring Romania into line. The domestic scene in Romania was tightly controlled and its real threat to any Soviet military position was low. Enforcing discipline would have been too expensive. This explanation, while generally consistent with a containment strategy, does not conform to the strategy's ideal formulation. Theoretically, as Soviet policy is driven by an increasingly intense perceived threat, the importance of the Warsaw Pact alliance and its solidarity should grow. What the Romanian case may indicate is that while the USSR's behavior generally resembled a policy of containment, its level of commitment to that policy, while high, fell short of that generated by the intense threat that they perceived during earlier periods of the cold war.

Soviet spokesmen worked hard to isolate West Germany. They drew a sharp distinction between the FRG and the other West European countries and called on the other Europeans to break with the "Washington-Bonn axis." This could be done best, they suggested, by recognizing the preconditions for peace in Europe, which they said were East German sovereignty and the newly defined Polish frontiers.[62] As would be expected of a nation following a containment policy, the Soviets expressed an interest in limiting American and West German influence and worked to broaden the base of political support that endorsed its conditions for peace.

Leaders in Moscow, for example, opposed West German acquisition of nuclear weapons. Secretary Brezhnev responded positively to Chancellor Kiesinger's December 1966 announcement that the FRG would not acquire unilateral control of nuclear weapons and agreed to negotiate the mutual renunciation of force. Negotiations began in February 1967. The Soviet Union broke off the talks in July, concluding that despite the "clever tactical maneuvers" of the Grand Coalition, West Germany was still unwilling to recognize the two absolute preconditions of European security: the acceptance of the existing boundaries in Europe, and the existence of two German states.

Soviet efforts to limit West German power also included attempts to establish political contacts with a number of other West European countries. President Podgorny visited Italy and Austria and Premier Kosygin traveled to London in February 1967. More noticeably, the

USSR improved its relations with France. In return for President de Gaulle's celebrated visit to Moscow in mid-1966, Soviet Premier Kosygin traveled to Paris in December. Throughout the next year, Soviet-French relations improved. They expanded ties in aviation, electronics, and food processing. More significantly, France withdrew its troops from NATO, and NATO forces left French territory. In April the USSR received the French chief of staff, General Charles Ailleret, in Moscow for May Day in a symbolic gesture—all the more significant because of General Ailleret's association with France's "all-azimuth" doctrine. Later in October, the head of the Soviet general staff returned Ailleret's visit by traveling to France after Premier Kosygin had made two stops in Paris for consultations en route to New York during the Middle East crisis.

The diplomatic activity simply complemented the Soviet Union's efforts to organize a European Security Conference that would pledge all its participants to the preservation of current boundaries and the existence of two German states. The conference would thus provide a multilateral endorsement of the territorial and political conditions. For the most part, the conference idea followed the expectations of a containment model. These efforts, however, could also be the foundation of a rollback strategy and relevant to the revisionist proposition.[63]

If the Soviets had been following a revisionist strategy in Central Europe because they believed they saw an opportunity for political expansion, their behavior would have included commitments to compelling a reduction in American or West German influence there. In the 1967 period it is difficult to find evidence of Soviet behavior that conforms to these expectations. The Soviets did not issue ultimatums demanding Western acceptance of its preconditions for peace such as Khrushchev had done in 1958 and 1961, nor did it unilaterally abandon its obligations in Eastern Germany, thus forcing the United States to acknowledge the GDR. While a great deal of effort went into propaganda and diplomacy exhorting the United States to retreat from its position on the GDR and Poland, the commitment the USSR exhibited to this change remained minimal. There is little evidence of unusual pressure on West Berlin or effective subversion in the FRG, much less overt coercive action directed at Bonn.

Although it is difficult to find evidence supporting the revisionist proposition regarding Soviet foreign policy in Central Europe during 1967, the expansionist theory may nevertheless be relevant. The lack of actions consistent with a revisionist strategy indicates that the prevailing Soviet view of Central Europe did not include perceptions of opportunity. Their inaction can be attributed to lack of capability and effective Western deterrence. The deterrent argument, given the strategic nuclear balance and the force deployments of NATO, is quite credible in this case. Additionally, while the USSR could have brought greater pressure to bear upon Berlin, it is difficult to imagine successful subversion short of overt military interference. Consequently, Soviet behavior in Central Europe in 1967, which closely resembles what one might predict of a nation following a containment strategy, does not necessarily disprove the claim that the Kremlin also had an expansionist motive. Obviously, it does not support the expansionist claim either, and full understanding of the situation depends on a consideration of the other regional cases.

The Middle East

When war in the Middle East broke out in June 1967, Secretary Brezhnev blamed Israel and held the United States responsible. "American imperialism" was said to be the cause of the Arab-Israeli clash:

> As for the chief cause of Israel's anti-Arab aggression, this was the desire of the American and British imperialists to strike a blow at the national-liberation movement in the Near East, to halt at any cost the movement of peoples along the path of social progress, to restore to bondage countries that had won freedom and independence at so dear a price, and rob them of their wealth.[64]

The Soviet spokesmen interpreted the crisis as evolving from threats to the relatively new government in Syria.[65] The status quo included the constituted governments and frontiers of Syria, Egypt, Jordan, and Israel, as well as Israel's right to existence and to naval transit. The containment and revisionist propositions can be evaluated in light of Soviet commitments to this political situation or its alteration.

The Soviet Union reportedly told Israel in 1967 that threats against Syria would "result in serious consequences," and that Israeli actions amounted to a "dangerous playing with fire on the part of Israel in an area near the borders of the Soviet Union."[66] The threat complemented other Soviet diplomatic moves designed to mobilize Arab support for Syria. Efforts to persuade Egypt to signal its solidarity with Syria contributed to the escalation of tensions and the eruption of war. When war did come, the Soviet government sided with Syria and Egypt, pledging to help in the defense of their regimes and territories. Activating the "hot line," it called on the United States to restrain Israel.[67]

Soviet support was not enough. The Arabs suffered a devastating loss. Israel quickly won the military contest and occupied Syrian, Egyptian, and Jordanian territory.[68] The magnitude of the Arab loss represented a severe test of the USSR's commitment. Given Israeli military supremacy and the destruction of Arab air forces, the protection of the territorial integrity of the Soviet Union's allies would have required rapid and large-scale resupply of essential war materials such as aircraft, and perhaps even direct Soviet intervention. To the frustration of Arab leaders, the USSR delayed the delivery of replacement supplies until after a cease-fire had been achieved and significant Arab territory lost. Soviet officials objected to the territorial revision, but took few risks to prevent this development.[69] They broke relations with Israel during the crisis but did not join with their Arab allies in breaking relations with the United States. In the UN they abandoned the Arab demands for a prior Israeli withdrawal and accepted the cease-fire resolution.

After the war, the USSR consistently supported Arab demands for Israeli withdrawal, but did not commit itself militarily or politically to a return to the prewar territorial status. The Soviet government made clear that its sympathy for the Arab cause would not lead to committed action. Rather than agreeing to a mutual-defense agreement with Egypt, and thus bolstering Arab leverage, it declined Nasser's appeal and refused to support any Arab use of force.[70] When endorsing UN Resolution 242, the Soviets made it clear that their commitment to their Arab allies was real but would not involve risks of war or high-cost adventures by what they criticized as Arab "extremists."[71]

Although the Soviet Union did not prevent territorial revision, it acted forcefully to preserve allied regimes. On June 10, with the cease-fire failing and Israel threatening Damascus, the Soviet Union threatened to intervene militarily.[72] It was perhaps willing to accept a regional defeat but was not ready to abandon its allies. The threat to use troops identified the limits on Soviet willingness to disengage themselves from the Middle East. Even though the Soviets' failure to preserve the territorial status quo indicated that they would go only so far, the threat of force reaffirmed a basic Soviet commitment to policies resembling a containment strategy.

It is possible that the USSR's encouragement of Egyptian mobilization led to Nasser's closing of the Strait of Tirana in the Gulf of Aqaba and the initiation of the war. If this Soviet behavior is seen as prompting a challenge to Israel, it could be consistent with a revisionist strategy. If revisionism had been the Soviets' aim, they would have backed demands for an Israeli retreat from its pre-1967 boundaries or supported forces opposed to Israel's existence. In early 1967 the Soviet Union did not call for a revision of Israel's frontiers nor endorse the Arabs' refusal to recognize Israel's right to exist. It did, however, provide military assistance to Arab regimes that called for the elimination of Israel. The amount of this aid, relative to the amount required to credibly coerce Israel, is an essential variable in the determination of whether or not this action is consistent with a strategy of revisionism.

Between 1963 and 1967, the Soviet Union provided Egypt and Syria with relatively modern military equipment (for example, MiG-21 interceptors and SAM-2s). This was in contrast to the obsolete weaponry it had previously supplied.[73] At the same time, it refused to give the Egyptians an offensive aerial capability and, much to Nasser's displeasure, did not provide medium-range missiles nor aircraft capable of ground support and battlefield interdiction. The Arabs continued to be dependent on relatively old MiG-15's and MiG-17s and a few modern SU-7s. As Jon Glassman concludes, by refusing to deliver specialized ground attack aircraft or tactical rockets in significant numbers, the Soviet Union provided its Arab allies with barely the capability to defend themselves and certainly not the ability to mount a major assault on Israel.[74] The outcome of the brief war and the USSR's failure to resupply aircraft during the fighting seem to bear out Glassman's conclusions.

The USSR's diplomatic efforts in 1967 also did not support an Arab military attack on Israel, nor did it engage its forces to protect Syrian and Egyptian frontiers, much less enforce a revision of Israel's. While encouraging Egyptian support for Syria, the Soviet Union told the Egyptians to seek a political compromise and not press militarily.[75] It also did not endorse the Egyptian closing of the Strait of Tirana and, through the Soviet ambassador in Cairo, directly "requested" that Nasser not initiate hostilities.[76] Additionally, the Soviets were reported to have told the Egyptians that they would not support an Arab attack on Israel but would respond to American escalation only in an effort to neutralize and contain U.S. involvement.[77]

The actual behavior of the Soviet Union in the Middle East in 1967 resembled a pattern of commitment consistent with a containment strategy. Whether or not its support for the Arabs went beyond what is easily explained in a containment model is more difficult to say. Certainly it did not insist on an American or Israeli retreat from the pre-June status and did not arm the Arabs with enough force to defend their own boundaries, much less coerce Israel.

An argument can be made, just the same, that the USSR provided all the assistance that it could, and that the lack of actions supporting the revisionist hypothesis and expansionist theory is attributable to lack of Soviet capability, lack of Arab ability, and the effective strength of Israel and the United States. This argument, however, is far less credible in the Middle East than in Central Europe. The USSR's impressive resupply of Egypt and Syria weeks after the cease-fire revealed the capacity to do far more, as did its June 10 threat to intervene. The Arab military disadvantage was also not a given but partially a product of unequal Soviet and American weapons deliveries to their allies. The Soviet Union, as it did in East Germany and would do in Egypt in 1970, had the capacity to affect this balance.

A second argument that can be raised in defense of the revisionist model might be called the "no-war-no-peace" proposition. This line of reasoning would suggest that the Soviet Union's lack of commitment to either the territorial defense of her allies or the Arabs' rejection of Israel, reflected a Soviet interest in perpetuating the conflict. This theory would suggest that the Soviets believed that the expansion of their influence in the region was enhanced by continuing turmoil and Arab dependence on the USSR.

The "no-war-no-peace" proposition, which might allow the expansionist theory to stand, despite a lack of observable revisionist behavior on the USSR's part, is not particularly convincing. First, it imputes to

Soviet decision making a rationality and confidence in the USSR's ability to control an escalation of conflict that seems unlikely. Second, it is not borne out by Moscow's actual behavior in not supporting the Egyptian military alternatives prior to the outbreak of hostilities, and failing to resupply essential weapons during the war. Third, the proposition is inconsistent with the USSR's behavior with respect to peace talks. The Soviet Union did not support the Arabs' maximal positions and accepted frontier adjustments, timed withdrawals, and demilitarized zones. It also was willing to cooperate with the United States to achieve a stabilized regional arrangement and to support Israel's right to peace and naval transit.[78]

There were, of course, real limits to Soviet accommodation, but this was to be expected if the USSR were following a policy of containment. The Soviet Union's actual behavior supported a Middle East peace that was based on a return to the territorial status quo with minor adjustments unfavorable to its allies. As the containment model predicted, Soviet leaders would not accept a settlement forcing a major territorial revision on their allies nor abandon their political influence in the region. If the prevailing Soviet view of the United States evoked a defensive response on the Soviets' part, which includes intense perception of threat, certainly leaders in Moscow would draw the line at accommodation, convinced that "appeasement" would not produce peace. In the Middle East case, actual Soviet behavior in 1967 resembled what might be expected in a containment strategy and fell far short of the type of commitment expected in a revisionist enterprise.

Southeast Asia

A fourth arena of Soviet-American contest during 1967 was Southeast Asia, where the central case was Vietnam. Defining the situation in any region is difficult, but the character of the Vietnam conflict was and remains unusually controversial. There are at least two fundamentally different perspectives regarding the status quo in 1967. The first would insist that there were two sovereign countries, North Vietnam and South Vietnam. This perspective would argue—in a fashion analogous to what Soviet leaders said about East Germany—that both should be recognized as legitimate and should recognize each other. From this perspective, revisionism in Vietnam would be defined as either a change in the boundaries or independence of either state, or a demand that each recognize the other. The status quo would include the North's refusal to recognize the regime in the South. Revisionism as in the German case, would include coercive actions to change this situation.

The second perspective would argue that one nation existed in Vietnam. In this view, Vietnam was partially successful in achieving independence from Western colonialism. It had created an independent government in the North and was fighting a civil war in the South. Thus the war in the South would be seen as part of the status quo, with both parties receiving external support. The Thieu regime received help from the United States while the National Liberation Front (NLF) received help from the Democratic Republic of Vietnam (DRV) and the Soviet Union. In this second perspective, revisionism imposed by the Soviets would be defined as fostering either a change in the status of the North or the complete defeat of either party to the civil war in the South.

The two perspectives have radically different implications for the analysis of Soviet international behavior in 1967. For example, in the first perspective Soviet support, either direct or indirect, for the NLF would be defined as consistent with a revisionist strategy. The NLF would be defined as an agent of the North. The same act, according to the second perspective, could be consistent with containment. The NLF would be defined as an existing actor under the threat of elimination.

This study cannot settle the Vietnam debate nor can it pretend that any consensus exists on the subject, yet before evaluating the containment and revisionist models we must define the situation in some way. Consequently, the study will operate within the context of the first perspective, according to which North and South Vietnam were two separate countries in 1967 and the NLF was not an acknowledged actor. Additionally, the status quo is assumed to include North Vietnam's refusal to recognize the legitimacy of the Thieu regime.[79] In a containment strategy I would, therefore, expect Soviet commitment to the defense of North Vietnam's sovereignty and territory, and also to the defense of its refusal to recognize the Thieu government.

Although Soviet protection for the North can be consistent with a containment policy, it certainly requires careful evaluation. Such protection can in effect provide an umbrella facilitating the North's attacks on the South. In this case protection would follow the main lines of a revisionist strategy. The context of Soviet assistance and the USSR's support for North Vietnamese and National Liberation Front programs, consequently, is important. In its ideal form the revisionist model would also predict Soviet commitments to forcing an American retreat through aid to the North's offensive potential, the direct interdiction of U.S. sea and air supply lines, and even direct military involvement.

Soviet propaganda offered steady and enthusiastic support for North Vietnam and the "forces of national liberation." They tied the Soviet Union's political prestige and credibility to the defense of the North. Leading Soviet spokesmen assured the world that the DRV would not be defeated or forced to accept "imperialism's puppet" regime.[80] The government backed up these pronouncements with substantial but not terribly impressive material aid. In this period it totaled roughly $700 million, with $505 million of this in military supplies.[81] Soviet leaders also lent diplomatic support to the DRV's cause, "linking" arms control and negotiations on detente to American involvement in Vietnam and the Middle East. The commitment, however, was far from what the ideal containment model would predict. The USSR did not act militarily to protect the North from escalating American bombing and was unwilling to commit Soviet personnel to the defense of allied territory. The assistance, although important, was not comparable to Soviet commitments in Europe or the Middle East and did not constitute an effective umbrella, as might be expected if the USSR had been pursuing a revisionist strategy.

The Soviet government endorsed three aspects of the North Vietnamese program including an unconditional cessation of U.S. bombing, U.S. withdrawal from South Vietnam, and the inclusion of the NLF in any settlement.[82] The insistence on a bombing halt is consistent with a containment policy while support for the latter two demands is consistent with revisionism. The commitment to American withdrawal, however, was unimpressive.

Although the Soviet government showered the DRV's program with verbal support, it did not complement this propaganda with material aid. It did not encourage the leaders in Hanoi to pursue military victory and instead urged them to enter into negotiations.[83] In January 1967 it succeeded in persuading Hanoi to consider talks if the United States agreed to a permanent and unconditional halt to the bombing. Ho Chi Minh, conceding to Soviet pressure, dropped his previous preconditions for talks: U.S. withdrawal and recognition of the NLF. He put aside the call for a permanent cessation of bombing, demanding only an unconditional halt. Soviet Premier Kosygin also worked with the United Kingdom in an unsuccessful effort to start talks. The Soviet endorsement of Vietnamese demands that the United States withdraw and recognize the NLF did not receive much material commitment. Moreover, the USSR's support of direct negotiations undermined North Vietnam's refusal to recognize Thieu. If the Soviets had allowed Hanoi to be coerced into recognizing Thieu's regime, this of course would have been inconsistent not only with revisionism but also with containment.

Ideally, if the Soviet Union were attempting to force changes in Vietnam, it might have provided the DRV with offensive military equipment and blocked U.S. supply lines. The Soviet Union did not commit itself to either of these programs. While it provided the DRV with a variety of weapons such as MiG-21 interceptors, antiaircraft batteries, ground-to-air missiles, and dispatched Soviet advisers to North Vietnam, these actions were barely sufficient to counteract the U.S. bombing, much less cover an offensive. The Soviet Union did provide the North with ground weapons such as tanks, armored personnel carriers (APC), and artillery that were used in offensives, but refrained from delivering complementary aerial support. For example, it did not send ground-to-ground missiles and sophisticated bombers or ground support aircraft. It also never issued ultimatums regarding American bombings, much less ultimatums demanding U.S. retreat from Southeast Asia. Moreover, it did not block or interrupt American supply lines to South Vietnam, challenge access to sea lines, or mine South Vietnamese harbors.

Actual Soviet behavior in Vietnam during 1967 can be seen as consistent with a containment strategy. Its level of commitment, however, was only moderate. Although the Soviets never abandoned the NLF's cause or tired of demanding U.S. withdrawal, they did not exhibit impressive commitment to these objectives. They also had an additional reason for supporting the NLF and North Vietnam that derived from the Sino-Soviet dispute and Soviet interests in encircling China.

The failure of Soviet policy in 1967 to conform to what might be expected of a revisionist strategy could be explained by arguing that the USSR lacked the resources to supply any more and by arguing that the American deterrent was effective. The first explanation is not very convincing. Despite Soviet economic dilemmas, weapons have generally been in surplus. It does not seem likely that the USSR lacked the spare missiles or aircraft that could have provided air support to North Vietnam's offensives. The second explanation is more plausible, but not wholly credible. The extended U.S. deterrent may have provided protection against direct Soviet actions against American supply lines but does not sufficiently account for the USSR's willingness to press for negotiations. The U.S. nuclear edge was not likely to have been a credible compelling force, since the use of nuclear weapons threatened greater costs than those at stake in Vietnam.

A third explanation for the lack of Soviet commitment to the North suggests that Brezhnev's interest in detente deterred him from pursuing the conflict in Vietnam more aggressively. At base, however, this argument claims that the USSR valued detente more than success in Vietnam and suggests that the commitments to revisionism were marginal at best. After all, it is the willingness "to pay" for policies, as explained in chapter 2, that is the measure of value and the basis for an analysis of motives.

Conclusion

The purpose of this chapter has been to determine the prevailing Soviet perceptions of the United States in 1967 and from this analysis to draw the most useful conclusions regarding Soviet foreign policy motives. Two streams of evidence, verbal statements and concrete actions, were reviewed. With respect to the verbal data, two key questions were considered: (1) to what extent did the image of the United States put forward by authoritative Soviet spokesmen resemble the "enemy" stereotype, and (2) to what extent did that image resemble the "degenerate" one? Little in the Soviet spokesmen's image of the United States resembled the "degenerate" stereotype; it was very similar to the "enemy" stereotype. This would suggest that prevailing Soviet perceptions in 1967 would be described best as following a defensive pattern and as

Figure 4. The Prevailing Soviet Image of the United States, 1967

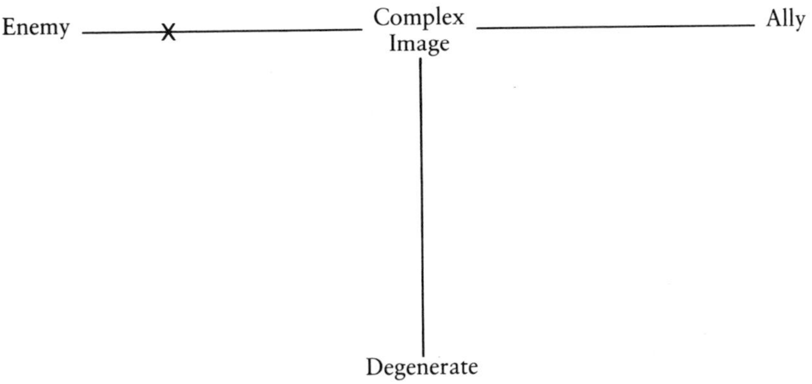

Enemy ———————×————————— Complex —————————————————— Ally
                                    Image

                              Degenerate

Summary of Evidence by Dimension	Degree of Resemblance to Stereotypes	
	Enemy	Degenerate
Motivation	High	Low
Capabilities and Power	Moderate to High	Low
Decisional Process	Moderate	Low

indicating considerable fear of the United States as a threat to the USSR's security.

The study of actual Soviet behavior considered two strategic possibilities, containment and revisionism, in four different arenas of Soviet-American interaction. In all four arenas the study focused on the resemblance of Soviet actions to the ideal formulation of these strategies and tried to evaluate the Soviets' commitment to these policies. When the evidence did not conform to what might be expected of a nation following a revisionist strategy, I tried to consider alternative arguments that might nevertheless support the expansionist theory. The findings and judgments related to all four arenas are summarized in figure 4 and table 4.

Support for the containment model as a description of Soviet behavior in 1967 was found in all four arenas. The Soviet Union appeared to be following a revisionist strategy only in Vietnam, and there with a low commitment. Alternative explanations that could sustain the expansionist theory seemed plausible in European affairs but not in the other regions. The study would suggest that a policy of containment is a more accurate explanation for Soviet strategic behavior than is a policy of revisionism.

Table 4. Soviet Foreign Policy Behavior, 1967: Degree of Resemblance to Two Strategic Models

	Containment		Revisionism		
	Degree of Resemblance to Model	Degree of Commitment	Degree of Resemblance to Model	Degree of Commitment	Credibility of U.S. Deterrent
Nuclear Weapons	High	High	—	—	High
Central Europe	High	High	Low	Low	Moderate
Middle East	High	Moderate	Low	Low	Moderate to Low
Southeast Asia	High	Moderate	Moderate	Low	Moderate to Low

This analysis of the Soviet Union's strategic behavior in 1967 leads to inferences parallel to those suggested by the analysis of verbal imagery. They both indicate a concern for security and self-defense, as spelled out in the defensive pattern, and suggest that the prevailing Soviet view in 1967 was that the United States represented a serious threat and was not only equal in power capabilities but also comparable in culture. Neither stream of evidence lends much weight to claims that prevailing leaders in Moscow perceived opportunities for expansion or self-aggrandizement deriving from perceived American weakness. Every indication is that in 1967 Soviet policy was dominated by a fear of the United States, and that consequently it would be logical to attribute its behavior to motives of self-protection and security.

Chapter 4

Soviet Perceptions and Foreign Policy, 1972

BY 1972 the bitter animosity that characterized Sino-American relations in 1967 had dissipated and had been replaced by an emerging spirit of rapprochement. The warnings of war were replaced by a new cordiality symbolized by President Nixon's reception in China and the Shanghai Communique. The communique outlined five principles of coexistence and accepted a formula acknowledging the existence of but one China, of which Taiwan was a part. As President Nixon recalls, the "most vitally important" aspect of the communique was the Chinese-American pledge to jointly oppose any country seeking "hegemony," a well-recognized code word referring to the Soviet Union.[1]

China's interest in the United States appeared to derive from a concern about Soviet ambitions. The "enemy" image that dominated official Chinese descriptions of the Soviet Union became ever more stereotypical. The Soviet invasion of Czechoslovakia with the declaration of the Brezhnev Doctrine, the eruption of military action on the Sino-Soviet frontier, and Soviet threats of nuclear strikes stimulated a Chinese willingness to deal with the United States.[2] By 1972 the Chinese had not only received Henry Kissinger but also welcomed President Nixon. In addition, they eliminated Lin Piao who reportedly opposed the rapprochement and explained to Kissinger that the primary strategic task they envisioned was the joint opposition to the "hegemonic aspirations" of the Soviet Union.[3] In September the Chinese normalized relations with Japan, again pledging mutual opposition to allowing any other nation to strive for hegemony in Asia. They evidently hoped to reach a detente that would allow them to concentrate fully on the Soviet threat. Perhaps they even hoped to raise the United States as a strategic asset vis-à-vis the USSR.[4]

The prevailing American view of China changed very quickly. Henry Kissinger recalls that well into March 1969 he and President Nixon still thought that the PRC was more aggressive than the USSR.[5] The Sino-Soviet border clashes apparently stimulated a reevaluation. Kissinger became convinced that the deepening split presented an important strategic opportunity for the United States. He decided that

Sino-American tensions were rooted in mutual suspicions and un-founded fears and that China was essentially defensive. The shift in American perceptions was evident in the relaxation of U.S. efforts to contain China. The United States reduced its troops in Vietnam, halted its naval patrols in the Taiwan Straits, reduced restrictions on trade and travel to China, and finally sided with China in the 1971 Indo-Pakistani war.

President Nixon and Secretary Kissinger were well known for their concerns about Soviet expansion, and in Nixon's first term in office both acted as if the basic "enemy" image still prevailed.[6] They exhibited open concern about the development of West German ostpolitik and worked to ensure the modernization of NATO. Moreover, despite ad-vice from experts in and out of government, they interpreted the Jor-danian-Palestinian-Syrian clash in September 1970,[7] the Pakistani-Bengali-Indian clash in 1971,[8] and the continuing struggle in Southeast Asia in classic cold war fashion. Despite its efforts to stabilize the nuclear relationship, the Nixon administration remained committed to a containment strategy and consequently saw China's growing concerns with the USSR as a geostrategic opportunity for the United States. Convinced that China was a "neuralgic point" for Moscow, Kissinger concluded that Sino-American rapprochement could curb Soviet adven-turism. According to Kissinger, such rapprochement would reinforce incentives for more accommodating Soviet behavior toward the West and would strengthen U.S. containment efforts.[9]

The geostrategic triangle had changed. U.S.-Soviet relations re-mained basically adversarial, despite the beginnings of detente. Hind-sight suggests that these symbolic beginnings such as the Basic Princi-ples Agreement and SALT I may also have represented a zenith in the relaxation of tensions. Sino-Soviet interaction had become even more hostile. Although not equal in rhetorical intensity, Chinese and Ameri-can leaders both spoke of the USSR as an "enemy," and increasingly saw themselves as joined by parallel interests and the common cause of containing the Soviet Union. The "collusion" between the United States and China that some Soviet journalists described in 1967 was in 1972 emerging as a tacit cooperative relationship.

Soviet Images of the United States in 1972

Images of Sino-American Relations

Soviet images of Sino-American relations changed substantially be-tween 1967 and 1972. China was now described as using the United States as much as the United States was using China. The image of China increasingly resembled the "enemy" stereotype, especially regard-ing the motivations behind its foreign policy.[10] It emphasized expan-sionist and great-power ambitions and highlighted the "nationalistic" and "chauvinistic" "war psychosis" that was said to be sweeping the country. Picturing the regime as "bonapartist" and "conspiratorial," Soviet spokesmen argued that China was using "imperial grandeur" to divert domestic opposition to the Chinese leadership and to fuel full-scale militarization.[11]

Leaders in Moscow claimed that the Maoists were bent on Asian domination and expansion but would not be able to achieve these aims. The regime was pictured as inherently weak and unpopular and as deficient in technological capacity and economic power. Spokesmen were openly contemptuous of Maoist organizational efforts and alleged parochialism. They concluded that the Maoists' only hope for expansion rested on American scientific, economic, and diplomatic support. The Maoists were described as trying to win American favor by betraying the cause of Third World liberation.[12]

Maoist collusion with imperialism, according to Soviet images, was designed to replace American influence in Asia with Chinese domination. "Playing on the contradictions between the two world systems," the Chinese were said to be promoting Soviet-American confrontations, especially in Europe. In the view of Soviet observers, they believed that this would force the United States to accelerate its withdrawal from Asia and leave the area open to Chinese hegemony. Soviet-American conflicts would weaken them both and allow China to become the dominant world power.

"Anti-Sovietism" was seen as the primary line in Maoist policy. Secretary Brezhnev argued:

> Speaking bluntly, what does Peking's foreign policy amount to today? It amounts to absurd claims to Soviet territory, to malicious slander of the Soviet political system, of our peaceloving foreign policy. It is outright sabotage of the efforts to limit the arms race, of the efforts to bring about disarmament and a relaxation of international tension. . . . Lastly, it amounts to unprincipled alignment on anti-Soviet grounds with any, even the most reactionary forces—the most rabid haters of the Soviet Union. . . . In substance, the purpose of doing the greatest possible harm to the U.S.S.R., of impairing the interests of the Socialist community, is now the sole criterion determining the Chinese leaders' approach to any major international problem.[13]

Journalists described the "unprincipled alignments" that the general secretary spoke of as "well-synchronized" coordination in a Maoist-imperialist alliance.[14]

Soviet images of China as an "enemy" were matched by active efforts to encircle the PRC. The USSR reinforced its forces on the Chinese frontier, courted North Korea, and stepped up negotiations with Japan.[15] At the same time the prevailing Soviet images of the United States became more complicated. In March, for example, Secretary Brezhnev explained that he remained uncertain as to the motives behind President Nixon's journey to Peking:

> In general, it should be noted that there are various views and guesses concerning the Peking meeting. But views aside, I repeat that the decisive word remains to be spoken by facts and actions. This is why we do not hurry to make our final assessment. The future, probably the near future, will show how things really stand, and then it will be time for us to draw the appropriate conclusions.[16]

The general secretary began drawing conclusions in the fall, arguing that "the imperialists are placing hopes on the Chinese leaders' openly hostile attitude to the Soviet Union and other socialist countries."[17]

Images of the United States

Motivation. In 1972, the authoritative Soviet spokesmen continued to describe the United States as imperialist and presented an image that resembled the "enemy" stereotype. The United States was pictured as seeking to maintain its domination over Western Europe and its neo-colonial control in much of the Third World.[18] Because it was concerned that a relaxation of tensions might undermine its control, the United States was said to be resisting detente, enforcing cohesion in NATO, and attempting to subvert the Warsaw Pact. Secretary Brezhnev argued:

> The methods by which imperialism seeks to influence the socialist world are diverse, varying from overt aggression, as in the DRV, to the most subtle flattery calculated to revive nationalistic prejudices and encouraging any departure from the international solidarity of the socialist countries. Sometimes the imperialists try to entice one socialist country or another by promises of economic gain. . . . Our class positions are diametrically opposed, and our antagonists, therefore, spare no efforts to hinder the successful development of our countries and impair our unity.[19]

"Neocolonial exploitation" through military aggression and "mercenary puppet regimes" was another central theme in Soviet denunciations of the United States.[20] Vietnam was the most often cited example, but the alliance of "puppet regimes" also included members in South Asia, Africa, the Middle East, and Latin America.[21] The American strategy, the Soviets said, was to fuel regional tensions and perpetuate civil wars because regional turmoil would provide opportunities for American intervention. The Indo-Pakistani crisis was described as an example of the United States "fanning the flames of conflict."[22] President Nixon's decision to reduce U.S. troops in Vietnam was also seen in this light as simply an American effort to pit "Asians against Asians." The policy of "Vietnamization" was pictured as nothing more than a cynical attempt to substitute Vietnamese for American casualties and to preserve American control by prolonging the civil war. Nixon's "Guam Doctrine," the Soviet press explained, was designed to secure American interests with Asian blood.

Although many of the motives the Soviet spokesmen attributed to the United States resembled the "enemy" stereotype, the image included important aspects that did not. Secretary Brezhnev, for example, argued that a new sense of realism prevailed in American decision making:

> Elements of realism in the policy of many capitalist countries are becoming evermore pronounced as the might and influence of the U.S.S.R. and the fraternal socialist countries increase, as our peace-loving policy becomes more active, and as other important progressive processes successfully unfold in the modern world. . . . This also applies to the United States of America in so far as it shows a willingness to depart from many of the coldwar dogmas that had for so long determined the orientation of all American foreign policy.[23]

In line with the general secretary's public pronouncements, Georgi Arbatov, a well-known Soviet observer of American affairs, described the shift in U.S. policy this way: "The international legal formulations essentially proclaim a shift on the U.S.A.'s part from 'Cold War' manifestations (including the 'positions of strength' policy and the striving for military superiority) to relations of peaceful coexistence and mutually advantageous cooperation."[24] Of course, Arbatov is often thought to express a somewhat more complex image of the United States than other leading officials. It is important to note that voices less optimistic about the shift in U.S. policy continued to reflect the "enemy" stereotype more clearly, and were more persistent regarding their perceptions of threat. The authoritative view, however, included a more complex reevaluation of U.S. behavior.

As is not true of "enemy" stereotype, the Soviet image in 1972 did not describe the United States as particularly expansionist but instead as imperialist, trying to preserve an already established position of world dominance. The metaphor of "guardian" was used by some Soviet journalists, while the authoritative spokesmen described the United States as attempting to block the forces of change and maintain its system of exploitation.[25] This shift in imagery may be subtle, but does seem to indicate a difference in intensity between the prevailing Soviet picture of the United States and the stereotype one might expect from a nation primarily concerned with security and self-defense in the face of an enemy.

Capabilities and Power. The most constant theme in the dominant image of the United States was that the development of the Soviet military and political power had forced a realistic shift in American foreign policy. All Soviet spokesmen stressed the importance of Soviet power in compelling the United States to accept peaceful coexistence. Academicians well known in the West like Nikolai Inozemtsev argued:

> Through the selfless efforts of science and industry and of scientists and the working class, the country created a first-class atomic and missile

industry that ensured the Soviet Armed Forces the most modern of weapons. This ended the U.S.A.'s "atomic diplomacy" and knocked the imperialist "policy of strength" off its very foundation. And the main thing is that a reliable barrier was raised against a world nuclear-missile war: Unleashing such a war would be suicidal.[26]

Arbatov concurred in this judgment that Soviet military strength had caused a change in the balance of forces:

> The C.P.S.U.'s most important documents stress that the balance of forces in the world arena is continuing to change in favor of socialism. Recent international events have provided practical confirmation of these conclusions and have shown that the change in the balance of forces is not some kind of abstract formula but a tangible reality that is making the imperialist powers adapt to the new situation and is making it possible to bring about major changes in the international arena. From this standpoint, the possibility of successful talks with the U.S.A. and of positive changes in Soviet-American relations is ensured by the activity of our party, the Soviet state and the entire Soviet people in strengthening the homeland's economic and defensive might, strengthening the ideological and political unity of our society and consolidating the Socialist Commonwealth.[27]

That Inozemtsev and Arbatov argued this theme is important. Their views were thought to be among the more complex and well-informed opinions in Moscow and could be expected to lead the prevailing image away from the "enemy" stereotype. However, the fact that their references to the United States continued to include this central theme indicates the limited degree of movement away from the stereotype in 1972. More hawkish views placed still greater emphasis on the importance of Soviet power in producing U.S. restraint.

The theme that prevailing spokesmen in Moscow advanced was the positive formulation of the "paper tiger" idea. That is, the United States is encouraged to aggression by Soviet weakness but can be compelled to exercise restraint if met with solid resolution and counterpower. As Arbatov argued, and more hawkish voices made even clearer, any change in the balance of forces favorable to the United States would be expected to lead to active American expansion.[28]

The emphasis on the importance of Soviet power corresponds to the "enemy" and not the "degenerate" stereotype. Soviet military strength was not described as deriving from a lack of American will or decadence. To the contrary, U.S. aspirations and will to dominate were seen as outstripping actual U.S. capacity to fulfill such ambitions. As Secretary Brezhnev explained, the United States w . no longer capable of sustaining its global advantage, not from lack of effort but rather from the development of counterpower: "No matter what senseless brutalities the modern colonialists may commit, imperialism no longer possesses its former ability to dispose of the destiny of the peoples unimpeded. The socialist cause, the national liberation movement are invincible. In our time, the international solidarity of the socialist states, of all revolutionaries, of all fighters for peace and progress, has become a tremendous force."[29]

The prevailing image of U.S.-Soviet relations described the correlation of forces as shifting in the favor of socialism, but did not claim that the Soviet Union was stronger than the United States. Rather, it claimed that the unusual American supremacy obtained after the Second World War no longer prevailed. The trends were unfavorable to the United States, but of course it had started with a great advantage. The press in Moscow did not argue that the United States was weak but that it could not sustain its previous hegemony. It was pictured as overextended in specific regions of the world. A rough balance was said to exist between Soviet and American forces. With a strong emphasis on the highly competitive and militaristic aspects of American society, the image did not resemble the "degenerate" stereotype.

Decisional Process.   The prevailing Soviet image in 1972 split American decision makers into "sober realists" and "reactionary cold warriors."[30] The image included substantially more complexity than would be expected from the "enemy" stereotype. Unlike the stereotype, it described the "sober" and "realistic" forces as prevailing in American foreign policy decisions. Secretary Brezhnev remarked:

> This is clear, among other things, from a marked change for the better recently registered in relations between the Soviet Union and the United States. In the last election campaign in the U.S.A.—as far as international issues were concerned—calls for a realistic foreign policy of peace were predominant. And this is in great contrast to the quarter of a century of cold war. The election results, in our view, speak of support for just such a policy.[31]

Soviet journalists, picking up the secretary's cue, identified the "realistic" forces as the majority of prominent American scholars, powerful business executives, government leaders, and indeed the majority of Americans.[32]

Brezhnev, however, cautioned that Soviet leaders remained "realists" who were "well aware that influential circles in the imperialist world have not yet abandoned attempts to conduct policy "from positions of strength."[33] Arbatov warned of "reactionary cold war hawks" among American leaders still dreaming of U.S. superiority and imperial control.[34] Some voices put even greater emphasis on the danger of persisting imperialist pressures in American policymaking and described a conspiratorial process much like that described in the "enemy" stereotype. No one saw U.S. leadership as vacillating, confused, or incompetent, as would be expected if they saw the United States as "degenerate." To the contrary, the descriptions outlined an "enemy." To the extent that the description of the decisional process had changed, it had gravitated toward more complexity rather than toward a "degenerate" stereotype.

If verbal imagery were the only basis for inferring prevailing Soviet perceptions of the United States, then the evidence would suggest that the dominant response was a defensive one, with a reduced but still strong perception of threat. While the resemblance between the spokesmen's image and the "enemy" stereotype is not perfect, it is far closer to the "enemy" than to the "degenerate" stereotype. Perceptions, however, should not be inferred from propaganda alone. The remainder of this chapter will analyze Soviet foreign policy behavior during 1972 in the following arenas of conflict: the development of strategic nuclear weapons, Central Europe, the Middle East, South Asia, and Southeast Asia.

Soviet Foreign Policy Behavior in 1972

Strategic Nuclear Weapons

Arms control and detente were popular ideas in 1972. Treaties were signed and agreements initialed. People were hopeful that a process of global stabilization and confidence building had begun. Public expectations may have been too high, for important disagreements remained. Hopes were encouraged, however, by a series of highly publicized diplomatic achievements. In strategic terms, these accomplishments may have been more a change in atmosphere or perhaps necessary first steps than a real sea change. Nevertheless, attention focused on three bilateral issues: the Basic Principles Agreement, trade, and strategic arms development.

The Basic Principles Agreement (BPA) signed at the Moscow Summit in May 1972 included twelve agreements that were to guide Soviet-American relations. Soviet commentators emphasized the importance of the first agreement, which read as follows:

> [The United States and the Soviet Union] will proceed from the common determination that in the nuclear age there is no alternative to conducting their mutual relations on the basis of peaceful coexistence. Differences in ideology and in the social systems of the U.S.A. and the U.S.S.R. are not obstacles to the bi-lateral development of normal relations based on the principles of sovereignty, equality, non-interference in internal affairs and mutual advantage.[35]

The second agreement pledged the parties to exercise restraint in their mutual relations and to forego efforts to obtain unilateral advantage. Because the security interests of both nations were based on equality and the renunciation of the use or threat of force, mutual restraint was recognized as the prerequisite for peaceful relations.[36]

The agreement's enthusiastic reception in Moscow could be expected in a nation following a containment strategy. The Americans had acknowledged the equality between the superpowers, a concession So-viet leaders had long sought.[37] However, the warm reception could also be interpreted as part of a strategy of forced revisionism toward other nations if the Soviets were seen as acting in bad faith and U.S. accep-tance of "peaceful coexistence" and equality were seen as a retreat. Leaders in Moscow could be said to be lulling the West into compla-cency and self-restraint while simultaneously persuading the United States to grant the USSR a measure of legitimacy it had previously withheld.

In terms of commitment, the 1972 BPA is relatively unimportant. Although it may have been critical in shaping Soviet expectations, in the United States it was overshadowed by SALT I. It involved very little risk or sacrifice on either side; its acceptance required no commitment of resources and constituted only a diplomatic pledge of uncertain priority. Very few Americans thought of the Soviet Union as equal to the United States. Moscow may have achieved nuclear parity but was not seen as equal according to any other criteria. Soviet involvement in third coun-tries was still called "penetration" and was thought to be best contained or prevented.

The increase in Soviet trade with the United States is also a rela-tively poor indicator of strategy.[38] The Soviet Union's willingness to purchase American grain might not have been expected if leaders in Moscow were greatly threatened by the United States, but their motives were not entirely clear. The grain purchases did not increase Soviet vulnerability, since the agricultural failures in the USSR were not a product of dependence on American imports.[39] Because Soviet agricul-tural problems were of long standing and were independent of Ameri-can policy, the grain purchases can be seen as simply providing short-term relief. Moreover, the deal stimulated Western interest in the USSR as a market and a potential energy supplier, and was negotiated on terms of mutual profit. Therefore it tells us little about commitment to either strategic model: containment or revisionism. Americans opposing both the BPA and increased trade with the Soviet Union described the arrangements as economically advantageous only to the USSR. They said such American "aid" facilitated the Soviet arms buildup. By pro-viding food, they argued, the United States allowed the Communists to ignore agriculture, and invest more resources in military production. It was the USSR's commitment to the development of nuclear forces that was seen as the real test of Soviet strategy.

The first Strategic Arms Limitation Treaty (SALT I) was presented by the Nixon administration as an achievement of detente. Its conclu-sion capped a long and arduous negotiating process.[40] Some argued that the process had been so difficult that what emerged was relatively meaningless. Others felt that it was of great symbolic importance. To evaluate its importance for this research, one must answer three ques-tions: First, did the limitation on antiballistic missile (ABM) systems, and the temporary freeze on the deployment of intercontinental ballistic missiles (ICBMs) and submarine-launched ballistic missiles (SLBMs) constitute an important test of Soviet commitments? Second, did the acceptance of SALT I indicate that the Soviets were following a containment strategy, or did it indicate a significant reducation in perceived threat? Did it signify the USSR's willingness to relax its vigilance and its resolve to deter U.S. aggression? Third, was the agreement consistent with what one might expect if the Soviets were pursuing a revisionist strategy?

Agreeing to forego further ABM deployments was not really a sacrifice for either side. In many ways it was simply a recognition of what was technologically feasible rather than a meaningful limit on available options. Neither power could deploy an effective ABM system that would reduce potential casualties below anything less than catastrophic numbers. No technical breakthrough was imminent and both sides would remain free to continue research and development—an opportunity that both took.[41]

The limit on ICBMs did not prescribe any reductions but did place a freeze on the deployment of new ICBM launchers and a cap on SLBM launchers. The effect on Soviet arms development would be rather minimal, and SALT I apparently did little to encourage confidence in arms control. In the 1970s strategic nuclear forces had not grown primarily in the deployment of additional launchers but rather in the modernization of missiles and reentry vehicles. SALT I did not proscribe multiple independently targeted reentry vehicles (MIRVs) or modernization of missiles to increase accuracy. Under the freeze, the USSR could still develop all of the major missile programs that observers in the West thought it contemplated.[42] Banned from deploying new "heavy missiles" (an option that was of questionable military value), the Soviet rocket forces were able to go ahead with the SS-17, SS-18, and SS-19 programs that by the end of the decade dramatically strengthened the Soviet arsenal. The SLBM limits were set higher than the forces either side already deployed. They also allowed for the modernization of SLBM and the introduction of MIRVs.

The Vladivostok Accords signed in 1974 set the upper limit on launchers at 2,400, requiring a reduction of between 50 and 90 Soviet launchers, but given the technical conversion to MIRV, this was an easy limit to meet. The accords set the limit on MIRVs at 1,320. At the time, the USSR had no MIRV systems deployed; consequently, it could add 1,320 launchers with MIRVs to its forces. If the USSR deployed this many ICBMs with MIRVs on them, it could theoretically put American land-based systems in jeopardy.[43] Liberal advocates for arms control urged the Nixon administration to join with the Soviets in banning MIRVs altogether.

As seen in figure 3, the 1973–1974 period records no break in the continuing escalation of strategic nuclear forces. Agreed limitations may have controlled growth below possible levels, but it is not clear that additional launchers would have been the optimal policy Soviet military planners would have chosen even in the absence of SALT I. The Soviets remained clearly committed to the development of improved strategic forces and exhibited little willingness to substitute arms control for unilateral deployment. Those who had hoped that detente would bring a relaxation of vigilance or a reduction in weapons development did not find these evident in Soviet nuclear policy. The Soviet Union continued to demonstrate an overriding commitment to deterrence that is so common in a containment strategy.

In 1972, the USSR's development of nuclear forces, while impressive, had not reached a level where it could claim compelling military superiority. Despite Soviet achievements, American strategic forces remained superior in the most important characteristics. The United States retained a substantial edge in warheads, in the number of targets it could threaten, and in countermilitary strength (a combination of accuracy and deliverable power). Moreover, the omissions of SALT I that allowed Soviet developments also allowed American modernization and even favored the United States, which had a monopoly on MIRV technology and was deploying it on both ICBMs and SLBMs. SALT I also did not cover bomber aircraft, where the United States had an advantage in numbers, quality, and deliverable payload. Additionally, the United States was actively increasing the number of targets a B-52 could hit by developing air-to-surface missiles. Each B-52 could potentially carry twenty. At the time of SALT I, the Defense Department was pressing Congress for the authorization of the MX missile, the Trident submarines, new SLBMs, 244 B-1 bombers, and a cruise missile program, all of which would be allowed under SALT I and which, at times, Secretary Laird suggested might be linked to the Pentagon's support of SALT.[44]

The Soviet Union's commitment to the development of strategic nuclear forces certainly superseded its confidence in arms control. The Soviet buildup, however, was not necessarily evidence of a drive for superiority or consistent with coercive and revisionist intentions toward other nations. U.S. strategic forces were still superior in those categories and characteristics that American military leaders considered most important. The Soviets may have been seeking parity and a guaranteed deterrent, as expected in a policy of containment. While the lack of limits on key technologies like MIRV allowed the deployment of systems that by 1979–1980 raised complicated new calculations, it was not the Soviet Union but the United States that refused to ban these developments. The Soviet commitment to nuclear military forces can be seen as consistent with either strategic model. As in 1967, competition in the development of nuclear weapons does not provide a good test of the Soviets' foreign policy behavior in other matters. The USSR's actions in specific geographical areas may be more telling and helpful in analyzing Soviet perceptions of the United States and strategic aims in 1972.

Central Europe

Central Europe was at the center of the cold war and was the setting for Soviet-American gestures toward detente. By 1972 West Germany had gone a long way toward satisfying the Soviets' insistence on the recognition of East Germany and the acceptance of Poland's current frontiers. Under the direction of Willy Brandt it had signed the nuclear nonproliferation treaty, acknowledged the existence of two states in the German nation, recognized the GDR as a sovereign and equal state, and accepted the "inviolability" of the existing Polish borders.[45] The Soviet "prerequisites for peace" had been met in treaties between Bonn and Moscow, Bonn and Warsaw, Bonn and East Germany, and the four powers responsible for Berlin.

As they had not done in 1967, authoritative Soviet voices acknowledged the change in West Germany as real, and described the FRG in much less stereotypical terms. The domestic balance in West Germany, they claimed, while still fluid, had shifted in favor of realistic and peaceable forces.[46] A policy of "realism" was said to be emerging and the chairman of the Presidium, Nikolai Podgorny, even argued that the realists among the West German elite had "cast aside" their traditional expansionist and revanchist ambitions and had committed themselves to peace and cooperation.[47]

Although encouraged, Soviet leaders certainly remained cautious. Secretary Brezhnev warned that reactionary and revanchist elements continued to exist in West Germany and, like their American partners, the West Germans still aspired to domination and hegemony in Europe.[48] Not even the more pessimistic, however, failed to recognize that West German policy had truly changed. Mikhail Suslov, for example, argued that the FRG displayed "realism" and "expressed its readiness to make a contribution to the cause of improving relations between our countries and to achieve detente in Europe."[49]

Soviet leaders attributed the change in West German policy to the USSR's strength. They said that the Soviet Union had compelled the West Germans to recognize the "realities" of Europe and abandon their "policy of strength."[50] If these grandiose claims have merit, and the nonrecognition of East Germany is defined as part of the status quo in 1967, then the change in West German policy toward recognizing East Germany may stand as evidence indicating a revisionist strategy. Most Western analysts, however, would resist such a simplified explanation.

Chancellor Brandt's image of the USSR did not fit the "enemy" stereotype. Rather than being intimidated, he gave every indication that he did not perceive as intense a Soviet threat as did his rivals in the Christian Democratic Union (CDU) or his counterparts in Washington. He did not describe the Soviet Union as an evil and expansionist state, nor did his defense minister, Helmut Schmidt. Instead, they characterized the Communist superpower as conservative, motivated by a desire to maintain and consolidate its sphere of influence.[51] Chancellor Brandt argued that Soviet leaders wanted detente, not as an avenue to hegemony in Europe, but rather for the freedom it would allow them in addressing social and economic problems at home.[52]

The chancellor concluded that the division of Germany was a "consequence" of the cold war rather than an outstanding cause.[53] He determined that to repair the tragedy that had befallen the German nation it was necessary to relax the fears that divided Europe. The division of Germany, he argued, could be surmounted only if the division of Europe were overcome. His strategy was designed to create a context of European cooperation in which German unity would be possible.[54] The first step in this ostpolitik was to reduce Soviet fears by accepting the territorial status quo. By recognizing the existing conditions, Brandt hoped to create a process leading to greater tolerance for real change and German reunification.

Chancellor Brandt did not question West Germany's membership in NATO nor did the Social Democratic leadership ignore the importance of a balance of power. They thought, however, that a balance of power already existed. Further Western efforts to reinforce containment, they feared, would only produce more repressive Soviet behavior in Eastern Europe and escalate the arms race. The chancellor, for example, opposed West German politicians like Franz Joseph Strauss of the Christian Social Union (CSU) who advocated replacing ostpolitik with a Far East policy. Brandt dismissed the notion as "foolish Machiavellianism," and argued that the FRG in union with China could not force concessions from Moscow but would only alienate and harden in opposition to Bonn the state that controlled East Germany and could affect the interests of the German nation.[55] Ostpolitik was designed to attack the legacy of mutual fear and begin a gradual process of deescalation and peaceful engagement.

Many Germans did not share Brandt's assessment of Soviet motives; nevertheless, a majority accepted the changes in West German policy. The failure of the "policy of strength" to produce favorable change in East Germany or to prevent the erection of the Berlin Wall certainly made Germans more receptive to an alternative approach. In this respect, Soviet strength in Eastern Europe probably did contribute to the strategic reevaluation in Bonn. There is no evidence that German leaders were intimidated by Soviet power, but Moscow's ability to preserve its grip on East Germany did convince many that a new strategy for reunification was necessary. Some Soviet leaders may have seen this as a retreat and thus perceived an opportunity to press for a revision of German policy. If the Soviet Union were following a revisionist strategy, one might expect that, sensing weakness, it would step up pressure and push for a German retreat beyond what could be expected of a nation committed only to containment. This the Soviet Union did not do.

Soviet leaders left no doubt that gaining Western acceptance of both the government in East Berlin and the postwar European boundaries was the precondition for detente in Europe. They insisted that the West accept the USSR's influence in Eastern Europe and formally renounce intentions to challenge forcefully what they defined as the postwar "realities." As Foreign Minister Gromyko explained, with respect to the Bonn-Moscow negotiations:

> A treaty whose contents would be reduced only to a commitment by the two sides on the renunciation of the use of force or the threat of its use, in conditions in which the inviolability of the existing borders in Europe would be jeopardized by the F.R.G., would be simply pointless for the Soviet Union. The normalization of the F.R.G.'s relations with other countries is possible only on the basis of the recognition of a respect for European realities.[56]

The Soviets insisted that the United States acknowledge the expansion in Soviet influence that followed World War II. The United States of course has made similar demands, insisting that Soviet leaders respect the globalization of U.S. interests. Because I have taken the situation in 1967 as the status quo, the Soviet demand conforms to a containment model. The pressure to change Western policy on recognition, however, suggests a strategy of revisionism.

As the West German government began to satisfy Soviet demands, the USSR did not step up pressure and insist on changes in the essential political and territorial status of Central Europe. Instead it accepted compromises. For example, the Soviets accepted de facto rather than de jure recognition of East Germany. They accepted the recognition of two equal states, but qualified by the West Germans' insistence that there was but one German nation and that its aim was eventual reunification. Additionally, they agreed to West Germany's demand that Poland's frontiers be considered currently inviolable, but as ultimately changeable and without legal basis.

The Soviets showed some willingness to compromise, but their concessions were basically limited to diplomatic language. However, this behavior was somewhat inconsistent with what one might expect from a revisionist strategy. Moreover, the Soviet Union's commitment to achieving a settlement in Central Europe was substantial. It not only accepted marginal diplomatic reformulations but also rejected East German opposition to the compromises. This rejection was most impressively demonstrated in the ouster of Walter Ulbricht when East Germany's party secretary resisted Moscow's decision.[57] Some leaders in Moscow also had to expend political capital to overcome domestic opposition to this policy. Secretary Brezhnev, alluding to this domestic concern, said:

> As for the Soviet Union, we are sincere and earnest in our approach to the question of improving our relations with the F.R.G., although for obvious reasons this is no simple question for our country. The hardships of the past war and suffering which Hitlerite aggression inflicted on our people are still alive in the memory of the Soviet people. But we believe that the grim past should not forever remain an insuperable obstacle to the development of our relations with West Germany.[58]

The Soviet Union went on to facilitate West German ratification of the treaty by accepting an accompanying letter that reaffirmed the nonforeclosure of long-range alteration in the German boundaries. It also agreed to a Joint Resolution that acknowledged the existing frontiers but denied them any legal basis, and defined the East and West as two parts of one Germany that would not abandon the aim of reunification through normalization.

As would be expected of a nation pursuing a containment strategy, the Soviet Union remained committed to the Warsaw Pact, socialist unity, and economic integration. Although the Soviets' actions indicated that containment was their objective, they did demonstrate some modest flexibility that might not have been expected, measured against the ideal strategy. The USSR, for example, continued to tolerate Romanian deviation from some Soviet foreign policies, accepted a modified schedule for integrating the Council for Mutual Economic Assistance (CMEA), and abandoned its policy of trying to isolate West Germany in Western Europe.[59]

The Soviet Union responded to the changes in West German policy not with increased demands, but rather with offers of economic opportunities and a preliminary opening of intra-German communication, travel, and family reunification. It threatened that if the West Germans failed to ratify the Bonn-Moscow Treaty, access to the East and trade relations would suffer. The warnings, however, were related to the loss of possible benefits rather than threats of new punishments. The leaders in the Kremlin seemed committed to inducing change by courting West German economic and national interests. This sort of behavior is, of course, precisely what one might predict if the Soviets were responding favorably to an ostpolitik strategy. Furthermore, it was consistent with the substance of any detente, and as might be expected, it alarmed the Nixon administration in Washington.

Secretary of State Kissinger expressed open concern that the Soviet Union was inflaming German nationalism in an effort to split NATO and roll back American influence.[60] He interpreted the Soviet commitment to rapprochement as consistent with a revisionist strategy, explaining that the USSR was trying to encourage German neutrality and produce the desired retreat by manipulating "carrots" rather than "sticks."[61] While Brandt felt the Soviet interest in detente coincided with what could be expected of a nation committed to a defensive strategy, Kissinger interpreted the behavior as consistent with a policy of revisionism.

Many Europeans in 1972 predicted that a genuine detente would increase the freedom of action for countries in both East and West, producing a less divided Europe. As seen in the Kissinger interpretation of the newly cordial Soviet-German relations and the Soviet reaction to American bridge-building aimed at East Europe, movements toward detente can alarm political leaders committed to a containment strategy. They may suspect the "enemy" of trying to manipulate nationalism among their allies, and split their security alliance. The critical test of the USSR's interest in detente, therefore, was its policy toward NATO. Was Moscow committed to splitting NATO? That is, did it pursue "selective detente," offering opportunities only to West Germany and not to the United States, or make Soviet rapprochement with West Germany contingent on its willingness to pull away from the Atlantic alliance?

In 1972 it was not clear that the Soviets were pursuing selective detente. Their commitment to splitting NATO appeared confined to propaganda advocating the dissolution of both NATO and the Warsaw Treaty Organization (WTO). The four-power negotiations over Berlin proceeded concurrently with the Bonn-Moscow talks and thus linked Soviet–West German and Soviet-American detente. The USSR increased its trade with the United States, just as Germany and the Soviets were becoming more economically dependent on each other, and the Soviet government included the United States as an unquestioned participant in the proposed Conference on Security and Cooperation in Europe.[62] With the signing of the U.S.-Soviet accords in May and the Soviet willingness to buy American agricultural products, the USSR exhibited as much interest in detente with the United States as with West Germany. Soviet leaders never made detente dependent on a reduction in the cohesion of NATO or on West Germany's commitment to the Atlantic alliance.

Soviet leaders were implacable in their demands for the equality of East Germany and the inviolability of Poland's frontiers. Once achieving some accommodation on these issues, however, they did not exhibit much interest in pressing for revision of West German policies or using selective detente to split NATO. The Soviet Union's behavior continued to reflect a containment strategy. Actions that might have been expected if the Soviets were following a strategy of revisionism were generally not evident. This of course could be explained by successful Western deterrence. Let us consider this possibility.

While in 1972 the USSR may have been deterred from forcefully challenging the West, this explanation does not explain the observed Soviet commitment to reaching a settlement and encouraging detente. To sustain the expansionist argument, one would have to interpret the Soviet interest in European detente as designed to split NATO. However, the evidence during this period is not persuasive. Another way one might interpret Soviet behavior as expansionist would be to assert that

Soviet leaders had deliberately obscured their interest in forcing revisionism in Central Europe so as to lull the West into complacency. Because the argument is teleological, it can only be addressed in light of the 1979–1980 period. A spinoff from this argument, however, might see the Soviet strategy in Europe as designed to reduce Western vigilance and open the way for adventures and expansion in Third World areas like the Middle East, South Asia, and Vietnam.

The Middle East: Egypt

Israel's occupation of Arab territories after 1967 created problems for the Soviet Union in 1972. Arab leaders refused to accept the situation and looked to Moscow for help. In strategic terms, the Soviet Union could have gone in several directions.

First, if Soviet leaders had perceived great threat from the United States and had seen the new alignments in the Middle East as an important cold war issue, they could be expected to reinforce their allies and try to recover their credibility there. A containment strategy would have caused the USSR to reject the post-1967 revisions and to support the territorial integrity of its Middle Eastern allies.

Second, if the prevailing Soviet view of the United States was moving away from the threatening "enemy" stereotype, then the Soviets could be expected to demonstrate less urgency in reinforcing their position in the Arab world. If Soviet commitment to containing the United States was relaxing because of detente, then one would predict a Soviet willingness to compromise and negotiate on the 1967 territorial changes. In a period of detente one would expect the USSR to preserve its Arab alliances but simultaneously to search for Soviet-American agreements instead of unilateral reinforcements.

Third, if leaders in Moscow interpreted American interest in detente as a sign of weakness and perceived the opportunity to press for Soviet expansion, then one could expect them to use their power not only to recover credibility in the Arab world but also to force an American retreat there. A revisionist model would predict a Soviet policy committed to the recovery of the internationally recognized territory of its friends and to the Arab demands against Israel in its pre-1967 frontiers. The Soviet Union would be expected to use its capabilities to return the status quo of 1967 and then force political and territorial revisions unfavorable to the United States.

The cornerstone of the Soviet Union's involvement in the Middle East was its relations with Egypt, Syria, and Iraq. These three countries were by far the most powerful Arab states and alliance with them was an essential component of a viable Soviet position in the Middle East. Soviet relations with small countries like South Yemen (PDRY) or Libya, or nonstate actors like the Palestine Liberation Organization (PLO) could not offset the trends established in ties to Cairo, Damascus, and Baghdad.[63] In this period Moscow's commitment would be put to the test by the Soviet Union's two most important allies, Egypt and Iraq.

Between 1969 and 1972 the Soviet Union's commitment to Egypt, its principal Arab ally, was tested repeatedly and found lacking by Egyptian leaders. President Nasser and later President Sadat refused to accept the results of the June war and urged the Soviets to help defend the internationally recognized pre-1967 frontiers of Egypt, Syria, and Jordan. Frustrated with the stalemate, Nasser proclaimed a "war of attrition" in 1969. The war went poorly for the Egyptians. Israel quickly destroyed Egyptian air defenses and by the end of January 1970 had declared all of Egypt a battlefield.[64] The debacle and the bombings of Cairo accelerated Egyptian requests for foreign support. Soviet leaders appealed to President Nixon, asking him to curtail the Israeli air strikes. In his appeal Premier Kosygin made it clear that the USSR would not leave Egypt defenseless in the face of continued Israeli bombing and occupation. For a variety of reasons the U.S. administration ignored the Soviet warning and sent new planes to Israel.[65] Some felt the situation was advantageous for Israel and others that it embarrassed the Soviet Union. Few apparently believed the USSR could or would actually move to defend its client.

The leaders in the Kremlin made good on Kosygin's pledge. They exercised a military option and reestablished for Egypt the situation that existed prior to the war of attrition.[66] They agreed that Egypt need not accept a plan for a general settlement while it was militarily prostrate, and along with Egypt and Israel rejected the proposals of Secretary Rogers. By July, however, with the bombing curtailed, they insisted that Nasser accept a cease-fire. Under the cease-fire and in violation of the agreement to hold forces in place and not to advance, the Soviets reinforced the Egyptian defense perimeter. They extended it back to the Suez Canal.

The Soviet Union's intervention had helped the Egyptian regime and prevented further losses, but had not liberated any occupied territories. Arab dissatisfaction would continue. The intervention demonstrated Soviet capability as well as, in the eyes of the Egyptians, the unwillingness of Soviet leaders to use it to change the post-1967 situation.

As Anwar Sadat assumed the presidency in Egypt, he declared that 1971 would be a "year of decision." The new president asked the Soviet Union to provide the aerial weapons necessary for offensive action. Expressing increasing frustration with the Soviets' refusal to provide advanced aircraft and long-range ground-to-ground missiles, Sadat began to put pressure on the Soviets.[67] In the spring of 1971 he purged an element of the Egyptian elite that he felt was too subservient to Moscow. He also agreed to entertain American envoy Joe Sisco and Secretary of State Rogers in Cairo.

The Soviet response was quick. In May the USSR agreed to sign the Treaty of Friendship and Cooperation with Egypt that it had previously declined. To placate Egyptian demands, the agreement pledged the Soviet Union to provide the material necessary for liquidating the "consequences of aggression." For Moscow it wedded Egypt to an "anti-imperialist front" and foiled what Soviet propaganda called an American effort to drive a wedge between the USSR and Egypt. Despite the treaty, repeated trips to Moscow by President Sadat, and verbal pledges from key Soviet officials, the USSR continued to withhold the weapons required for effective deterrence and air cover. Instead, it encouraged the Egyptians to seek Israeli withdrawal through negotiations.[68]

President Sadat's dissatisfaction with the Soviet commitment to the Egyptian cause came to a head following the U.S.-Soviet Summit in May 1972. At the meeting the Soviet Union endorsed a joint communique that advocated a military relaxation in the Middle East and seemed to accept the existing situation. For Sadat it showed Moscow's unwillingness to link the return of Egyptian territory to Soviet-American detente. Sadat attacked the Soviets for "selling out" the Arab cause and in June expelled their technicians, troops, and advisers from Egypt. The Egyptian decision presented a stark test of how much the USSR would pay to preserve its position in the Arab world. Sadat reported that he had three principal complaints:[69] First, the Soviets refused to support Arab military action to force Israeli withdrawal; second, they refused to supply Egypt with a "retaliation weapon" that could deter Israeli air strikes and allow for an Arab recovery of occupied territories; third, they sacrificed the territorial integrity and national dignity of their Arab allies to maintaining detente with the United States.

If the Soviets had been following a containment strategy, when faced with a major disruption in their alliance system, they would have acted to secure the cohesion and stability of its "anti-imperialist" front. At the time of the Egyptian decision there was no comparable threat of a reduction in American influence in the Middle East. The United States was continuing its special association with Israel and was increasing its ties to "moderate Arabs." Consequently, if Soviet behavior had been motivated by containment and perceived its enemies as posing a serious threat, then one would expect the USSR to work hard to preserve its position. However, the Soviet Union displayed little interest in either accommodating or coercing the Egyptians.

The Soviets accepted their expulsion from Egypt without much protest. Evidently they were unwilling either to court Sadat by responding to his complaints or to overthrow him.[70] They were not willing to violate detente in order to preserve their influence in Egypt. As one would expect in an era of detente, the USSR did not urgently commit itself to blocking the possible advantages for the United States that might accrue from these events. Rather, it acted as if the perceived threat of American aggressive action had substantially declined.

Even in a relaxed containment strategy (that is, in a detente model), one would not expect the Soviet Union to abandon its alliances. Instead, one would predict a willingness to relax vigilance and put detente ahead of unilateral reinforcement. Moscow moved to enhance its position in Syria and preserve the basic outlines of an alliance countering American influence, but could not compensate for the significance of what had occurred in Egypt. Although the Soviet Union withdrew its forces from Egypt, it did not abandon the Treaty of Friendship nor end its support for Egypt's basic position on Israeli withdrawal. In 1973 the USSR agreed to resume the supply of military equipment, but this reflected a change more on Egypt's part than on the Soviets'.[71] Throughout 1973 the USSR continued to show an interest in its alliance with Egypt; however, the commitment displayed fell far below what might be expected of a nation pursuing a containment strategy and was more consistent with a desire to foster detente. This behavior continued through the time of the Nixon-Brezhnev Summit in California and also throughout the war of October 1973.

Although the USSR provided Egypt with weapons, it continued to deny Sadat control over the deep-strike aerial capacity he demanded and left the Arab forces in a position that American, Soviet, and Israeli analysts agreed was incapable of challenging Israel. When Egypt and Syria did strike in October, the USSR did not support their decision, and moved immediately to engineer a cease-fire.[72] In the first few days of the war, a cease-fire proved impossible to coordinate. The Soviets called for an immediate cease-fire which the Arabs rejected because they had recovered so little of their territory. The United States, on the other hand, introduced plans for a return to the pre-fighting occupation boundaries as a tactic to stall until Israel gained a decisive upper hand. Despite their independent calls for a cease-fire, both superpowers quickly began to resupply their respective allies with consumables.[73] The Soviet Union significantly escalated its deliveries after Israel began to bomb population centers in Syria and Egypt.[74]

While the Soviets were not willing to force their allies to return to the post-1967 situation, they were at the same time not willing to endorse their military actions. After Egypt resisted the Soviet-American calls for a cease-fire, Soviet Premier Kosygin flew to Cairo and for several days put pressure on Sadat.[75] Following the visit, the Soviet government invited Henry Kissinger to Moscow and worked out a cease-fire arrangement.

The cease-fire did not hold. The battlefield situation had swung to the advantage of Israel, who now wanted to reverse the Arabs' psychological victory. Kissinger, determined to roll back Soviet influence, became concerned that the continuing Israeli encirclement of the Egyptian army would provoke Soviet action, drive Egypt back toward the USSR, and undermine U.S. efforts to woo Sadat away from Moscow. If these were his concerns, they were not unfounded. Following an American refusal to answer Sadat's urgent appeals, Secretary Brezhnev communicated to President Nixon that the USSR would not stand aside while

Egypt was humiliated. The Soviet threat of unilateral intervention if the United States refused to police the cease-fire produced a U.S. nuclear alert and American pressure on Israel to spare the Egyptian third army.[76] The war ended with President Sadat more convinced than ever that Soviet leaders would not sacrifice detente for the recovery of Arab territory and thus their influence in the region was substantially diminished.

Soviet policy toward Egypt did not indicate that the Soviet Union was following a revisionist strategy. It failed to reach the level of commitment required of a policy of vigilant containment, much less active involvement in Middle Eastern affairs. Even by the close of 1973, Soviet military intervention and aid simply prevented further losses. The USSR made no successful contribution to forcing an Israeli return to the 1967 status quo, much less did it threaten Israel's recognized frontiers. It did not challenge Israel's right to exist or support the Arabs' refusal to recognize Israel's existence. Nevertheless, one could argue that the Soviet Union was pursuing a policy of expansion by seeing its behavior as reflecting a lack of capability rather than an inclination to protect detente. Or one could argue that the Soviets wanted the Arabs to remain dissatisfied in order to perpetuate turmoil and to further Soviet penetration in the Arab world. Both of these arguments deserve consideration.

To enhance its influence, the USSR could have tried to either court or coerce Egypt. However, in an era of strong Egyptian nationalism, the Soviets' ability to manipulate the Egyptian elite or orchestrate a coup against Sadat was probably limited. They had tried to support a coup in the Sudan in 1971 and failed badly. After Sadat purged the Ali Sabri group, the USSR may have lacked many coercive options in domestic Egyptian affairs. Therefore, to keep the relationship it would have to court Sadat by responding to his three complaints. Moscow surely had the material capability to meet Sadat's demands. Despite its perennial economic failures, the USSR is able to produce weaponry and could have provided Egypt with the SCUD missiles and bombers that Sadat wanted. As they demonstrated in 1970, the Soviets also could have dispatched troops to recover Arab lands or at minimum to enhance Egypt's bargaining position. Moreover, the Soviets surely had the capacity to link detente to Israeli withdrawal and in effect to place a higher priority on its "anti-imperialist" alliances than on detente with the United States. Soviet leaders were apparently unwilling to run the risks associated with any of these options.

The risks entailed in American responses are difficult to calculate. U.S. officials had a vested interest in declaring that the risks were high. After all, they wanted to deter any potential Soviet aggression or expansion. Certainly if the USSR had challenged Israel's existence or 1967 frontiers, the cost would have been substantial. But such a challenge was not required for the Soviets to preserve their relationship with Egypt. All they needed to do was force an Israeli return to the 1967 status quo or, more pragmatically, a timed Israeli withdrawal from

Arab areas. The Soviets did not endorse the creation of a Palestinian state, or question Israel's right to exist. Their program lacked an immediate Arab recognition of Israel but was not dissimilar to the official American interpretation of UN Resolution 242. It is not clear that the United States would have taken great risks to refuse these terms. According to Henry Kissinger, President Nixon was inclined to force Israel to accept.[77]

A Soviet decision to meet Sadat's demands coupled with a Soviet determination to force Egypt to accept Israel's right to exist and make peace on what were essentially the 1967 frontiers probably would not have risked a nuclear confrontation with the United States. In an era of assured mutual destruction it seemed unlikely that the United States would risk a nuclear exchange to resist these terms. The 1973 alert does not undermine the argument. The U.S. threat in October was coupled with intense pressure on Israel to spare the Egyptian Third Army. It can be seen as covering American accommodation to Soviet demands as much as deterring Soviet behavior. Accounting for Soviet behavior on the basis of their inferior nuclear forces does not seem credible. A more plausible argument is that the Soviets refused to meet Sadat's terms because they felt confident that Israeli conventional superiority would ensure that a military conflict would not enhance Arab leverage but undermine it by still another defeat.

There is a problem with explaining the Soviets' refusal to meet Sadat's terms by arguing that they were deterred by Israeli military superiority. It is precisely Soviet supplies that could have offset the Israeli edge. The Israeli advantage was a variable the Soviets could have changed. Analyzing the military resources and potential leverage of the USSR and the Arab states, one finds no reason to believe that Israeli military superiority was invulnerable. The Israeli advantage was a product largely of unequal commitments by the United States and the Soviet Union to their allies. As demonstrated in Jordan in 1970 and again in October of 1973, the United States was determined to ensure that its allies never gave up political ground in the face of Soviet weapons.[78] The failure of the Soviets to demonstrate an equal commitment can hardly be explained by the regional military imbalance that resulted from this asymmetry in commitment.

Despite its potential ability to meet Egypt's demands, the USSR chose to provide Egypt with enough aid to resist aggression to some extent, but not enough to prevail in a conflict. The "no-war-no-peace" hypothesis would argue that the Soviet unwillingness to endorse an Arab option of war was coupled with a refusal to support viable plans for peace. It would fit them together into a clever strategy of penetration. The core of the argument rests on an evaluation of the plans for peace that the USSR accepted and refused, and on an assessment of what outcomes would resolve the regional disputes.

Soviet leaders were not willing to let Egypt be forced into accepting peace on Israel's terms. They rejected the first Rogers Plan in the midst of the war of attrition in 1969 and insisted that peace would require an Israeli withdrawal from nearly all of the occupied territories. Simultaneously, the Soviet government put forward proposals for resolution that in many respects were quite similar to official American preferences. Such proposals included timed withdrawal, talks to begin before complete withdrawal, peace negotiations between Arabs and Israel, recognition of Israel's right to exist within 1967 boundaries, and minor security alterations.[79] It was not the Soviets that lacked interest in peace negotiations. By Kissinger's account, it was the United States and Israel that had few incentives to open new initiatives.[80]

Secretary of State Kissinger felt that the continued stalemate in the Middle East would undermine the Soviet Union's position. He claims to have calculated that by blocking any further movement toward resolution, the United States could demonstrate to the Arabs that the Soviet connection was fruitless. It would not lead to the recovery of their territory. Convinced that the Soviet Union either would not run the risks or could not effect an Israeli withdrawal, Kissinger concluded that a "no-war-no-peace" situation would produce Arab defection from the USSR and a rollback of Soviet influence.[81] The United States, he reasoned, should forestall all Soviet withdrawal and peace initiatives until after the Arab-Soviet relationship had collapsed. The administration consequently deflected and ignored Soviet efforts to produce movement in negotiations and, in hindsight, underestimated Secretary Brezhnev's repeated warnings of an Arab-initiated war.[82] In light of Kissinger's logic, the "no-war-no-peace" hypothesis is particularly unconvincing because such a strategy on the Soviets' part would have produced Soviet rollback, not continued involvement.

The strategic imperative for Moscow, if it wished to perpetuate its influence in Egypt, was to exert pressure on the United States and Israel by beginning to meet Sadat's demands while simultaneously pressuring Egypt to endorse terms of withdrawal acceptable to the United States. Such a strategy could salvage the Soviet-Egyptian alliance by achieving Israeli withdrawal, even if upsetting Sadat by reissuing previously unacceptable terms such as the recognition of Israel. Kissinger reported that he was determined both to prevent any withdrawal that might be attributed by the Arabs to Soviet involvement and to forestall political settlements in the region until after the collapse of Soviet influence.[83]

Having failed to prevent the disruption of its alliance with Egypt, the Soviet Union was excluded from the American-mediated settlement talks. The USSR's behavior was consistent with what one would expect in a relaxed containment strategy. Its actions did not fit well with the predictions of a revisionist model. None of the various qualifying arguments is very persuasive. Because of Egypt's strength and leverage, the USSR's behavior toward it cannot be dismissed as an aberration in overall Soviet policy in the Middle East. This case was an important test of Soviet motives, and proves troublesome for those who claim that Soviet policy is expansionist and opportunistic. Of course, Soviet involvement in other countries in the region could cast a different light on the Egyptian case. During this same period, Iraq was testing the USSR's commitment to protecting its interests there. It may be useful to consider Soviet support for its other Arab ally confronting another friend of the United States, Iran.

The Middle East: Iraq

In the early 1970s the Kurds in Iraq mounted a major campaign for independence and posed a serious threat to the stability of the Baath regime. The government had tried to settle the Kurdish problem in March 1970 with a manifesto terminating hostilities and promising autonomy for the Kurds. In 1971 the implementation of the March manifesto was complicated by disputes over the distribution of oil revenues; nevertheless, it provided reasonable prospects for increasing stability.[84] By the middle of 1972, the March arrangements had collapsed completely. Heavy fighting broke out, and the Kurds demanded independence and control of the Kirkuk oilfields. A number of factors were responsible for the changed situation, including Kurdish concerns about the future of tribal structures and the strength of the Iraqi government. By far the most important variable was the introduction of substantial Iranian support for an armed Kurdish revolt.[85] The most active phase of the shah's plan to use the Kurds began in May 1972 when he enlisted American support during President Nixon's trip to Iran.[86] According to the Pike Commission's investigation of CIA activities, the United States, in conjunction with Iran and Israel, participated in a plan to use the Kurds to keep Iraq "off balance" and presumably to weaken the Soviet Union's influence with its Arab ally.

The Kurdish drive for independence represented a very real threat to the Iraqi government. In Iraqi eyes it represented an effort orchestrated by the United States to topple the "revolutionary" government and reestablish "imperialist" influence in Baghdad.[87] Iraq was already somewhat isolated in the Arab world because of its support for the July 1971 coup attempt in the Sudan. It sought help from its ally, the USSR.[88] As the Kurdish rebellion grew, Saddam Hussein signed a Treaty of Friendship with the USSR in April 1972. Later in the year, as U.S. and Israeli participation increased, Hussein sought stepped-up military assistance from the Soviets. He especially needed aircraft capable of slowing the infiltration of arms from Iran. Moscow was once again in a position where its credibility and commitments would be tested.

If the prevailing Soviet elites had perceived a threat from the United States and felt a containment strategy was necessary for defense, then they certainly would have responded forcefully to the Iraqi situation. Their alliance was in jeopardy, with the possibility that American-supported hostilities would produce a change in the Iraqi government. The leader of the Kurdish nationalists was openly pro-Western, promising that the United States would have a friend in OPEC once Kurdistan was free.[89] With the simultaneous disruption in Soviet-Egyptian relations and Syria's decision to align itself with Egypt, the USSR, if committed to serving as a counterweight to American influence in the Middle East, could only be expected to protect its relationship with Iraq. A revisionist strategy would have required a forceful Soviet response designed to stop the Iranian-American-Israeli involvement in Kurdistan and preserve the stability and good will of the government in Baghdad. Having forced Iran to accept the status quo, the Soviet Union, if pursuing a policy of forced revisionism in the Middle East, would have worked through Iraq to force an Iranian retreat either by giving up territory or by making concessions regarding its relationship with the United States.

The USSR did not act decisively to assist Iraq. In the early 1970s Moscow encouraged Iraq to distance itself from the West and provided Iraq with trade opportunities by bartering goods, but demonstrated little willingness to make sacrifices in Iraq's behalf. It endorsed Iraqi moves to nationalize the Iraqi Petroleum Corporation and encouraged the 1973 oil embargo. But these acts cost the Soviets nothing. They hardly demonstrated a serious commitment to preserving their Arab connections.

While providing plentiful verbal support and mutually advantageous trade opportunities, the Soviet Union was slow to assist the Baath regime against the Kurdish revolt. Until March 1974 it called on Baath leaders to exercise "patience" and "endurance" and to recapture the spirit of the March manifesto.[90] Although Soviet propaganda attacked the West for fueling the Kurdish problem, Soviet leaders did not link American behavior to their support for detente at either the 1972 or 1973 summits. Through January 1974 they tried to mediate an understanding between the Iraqi regime and the Kurdish Democratic party. The USSR allowed Iraq to buy weapons, although not in quantities comparable to those transferred to Iran by the United States.[91] They did not intervene with air cover or political leverage to ameliorate Iraq's dilemma. Especially frustrating for Iraq in this regard was the USSR's steadily improving relationship with Iran. Signaling improved relations was a state visit that the shah paid to the USSR in October 1972. In addition, Soviet-Iranian trade surpassed Soviet-Iraqi trade.[92]

In the spring of 1974, the USSR dropped all impartiality and turned its propaganda clearly against the Kurds.[93] The official imagery gravitated toward a "child" stereotype, dichotomizing the antagonists into benign progressives and right-wing feudal extremists. The Kurdish nationalists were depicted as an "interim tool" of imperialism that the United States would "doom to oblivion" once their involvement in the conflict had served its anti-Soviet purposes.[94] In January 1975 more Soviet weapons were sold to Iraq and reports of Soviet pilots flying missions against the Kurds were publicized as Iraq began to turn the tide militarily.[95] In March 1975 the shah and Saddam Hussein agreed in Algiers to a treaty ending hostilities and Iranian support for the Kurds. This was generally seen as favorable to Iran.

Soviet behavior in the Kurdish case did not conform to either the predictions of a containment or a revisionist strategy. In the face of the Kurdish conflict, the USSR was much more indecisive than the high-threat model would have predicted. Its willingness to pursue detente despite U.S. involvement in the Kurdish case was consistent with its recent behavior toward Egypt. In light of the disruption of Soviet-Egyptian ties, however, the Soviets' failure to respond forcefully to the weakening of Iraq is particularly good evidence that they were not following a strategy of containment with much commitment.

Since the Soviet Union's support for Iraq from 1972 to 1975 was less than what would be expected of a nation pursuing a vigilant containment strategy, it falls far short of the predictions of the revisionist model. The Soviets did not challenge the shah or U.S.-Iranian relations. Quite the contrary, they showed an interest in U.S.-Soviet and Soviet-Iranian detente despite continuing close Iranian-American ties.

The USSR's failure to act more decisively in the Kurdish case cannot be attributed to a lack of capability. Recently expelled from Egypt, the Soviets surely had the military supplies and forces necessary to close down the influx of weapons and Iranian troops, as demonstrated in 1975. Additionally, it is unlikely that U.S. nuclear forces compelled the USSR to tolerate the Kurdish operation. As noted, even Soviet propagandists correctly sensed that the United States and Iran were not committed to a Kurdish victory.

It might have been that the USSR was trying to expand its influence in the area by using Iraq's problem to extract concessions from Iraq as well as to court Iran. For example, the Iraqi regime accepted the Communist party into the National Front. The problem with this hypothesis is that it assumes that Soviet leaders would have risked alienating Iraq, thus jeopardizing their influence with their remaining Arab ally in the prospect of pulling the shah of Iran away from the United States. That leaders in the Kremlin thought they could persuade the shah in 1972–1973 to distance himself from the United States is unlikely, and their behavior hardly punished him for his Western associations. The threat to Soviet-Iraqi relations, on the other hand, was very real. Iraq, dissatisfied with the inadequacy of Soviet support in both the Kurdish and Arab-Israeli cases, began to rely on the USSR less and less.[96] With increased oil revenues, Iraq was able to buy weapons in Europe and reduce its ties to the USSR. Iraq did just that in the remaining half of the 1970s.

The Soviet Union's influence in the Middle East in 1972 was declining. Soviet behavior in both the Egyptian and Iraqi cases did not indicate any determination to contain U.S. power, much less to force revisionism in the area. It is difficult to argue that Soviet behavior in the

Middle East during this time demonstrated either a fear of enemy threat or a perception of opportunities for Soviet advancement there. The most plausible explanation for the Soviets' actions is that their fears had relaxed and they felt little compulsion to defend alliances needed for containment purposes. In South Asia, however, where Soviet support helped to dismember Pakistan and to "liberate" Bangladesh, the situation may have been different. Let us consider that case.

South Asia

The rise of Bengali nationalism and the political success of the Awami League in Pakistan created enormous pressure for change in that country. In the 1970 Pakistani elections, Sheikh Mujibar Rahman won both an overwhelming majority in the east and an absolute majority in the National Assembly of Pakistan. Traditional leaders and the army in West Pakistan refused to accept the Rahman victory. In March 1971 they arrested the Awami League leadership and began a program of repression in East Pakistan that, by the fall, many Western observers were comparing to genocide.[97] The Awami League declared the independence of Bangladesh on April 10, 1971, and looked to India for refuge and support. Pressure on India intensified as it absorbed some ten million Bengali refugees who threatened to overwhelm the resources of an already poor country. As the crisis in East Pakistan escalated and the United States announced President Nixon's decision to visit China, India looked for increasing support from the Soviet Union. India's concerns about Sino-American-Pakistani relations and the increasing refugee burden, along with the opportunities for enforced political revision that the Bengali nationalist movement presented, created a test of Soviet priorities and behavior.

If Soviet leaders had felt threatened by the developing Sino-American rapprochement, then certainly the USSR could have been expected to preserve its ties to India. If theirs was a strategy of containment, the Soviets might have been expected to commit themselves both to securing Indian cooperation and to alleviating the crisis in East Pakistan. They would not have been expected to prevent the creation of Bangladesh, since such an occurrence would have enhanced a Soviet containment strategy. At the same time, Soviet advocacy of such a change could have been part of a revisionist strategy. Defining the differences between the two models is particularly difficult in this case because the USSR's commitment to change can be seen within two contexts.

If an analyst assumes that the creation of an independent Bangladesh was the only way to reduce the violence and restore stability, then Soviet support for this outcome could be defined as consistent with a containment policy. In this view, one must assume that Bengali nationalism was strong and the prospects of any serious political resolution short of independence, remote. Consequently, they would see the creation of Bangladesh as having been the only viable policy for relieving the refugee pressure on India and in turn for securing a strong Indian-Soviet alliance.

A second picture of the situation might assume that a political settlement between the government of Pakistan and the Bengalis was possible and likely. In this case, Soviet support for the independence of Bangladesh could be defined as revisionist. Here one would have to assume that Bengali nationalism was weak enough to find adequate expression within the confines of an autonomy plan within Pakistan. One would also have to assume that the government of Pakistan was willing to deal with the Bengali leaders. Soviet or Indian support for Bengali independence could then be seen as unnecessary to relieve the pressure on India, and in turn defined as a revisionist act dismembering Pakistan. Since Pakistan was aligned with China at the time and had been historically linked to the United States, the action could also be defined as attempting to force a U.S. retreat.

The first definition of the situation is by far the most sensible and realistic. Soviet commitment to the creation of Bangladesh cannot automatically be considered consistent with a revisionist strategy and expansionist theory. Whether or not it reveals a containment strategy depends on the degree of commitment to this change and to other avenues for political settlement that existed in Bangladesh. Soviet suport for any Indian move against West Pakistan whatsoever may be considered inconsistent with a containment policy and indicative of a revisionist strategy.

The USSR did not endorse the Awami League's declaration of independence in April and throughout the first nine months of 1971 insisted that the crisis in the east was an internal affair of Pakistan.[98] Furthermore, it did not support the Indian desire to recognize Bangladesh and reportedly urged patience on India. Soviet leaders and propagandists alike urged Pakistani leader Yahya Khan to stop the bloodshed.

In August, following Secretary of State Kissinger's secret trip to China and the announcement of President Nixon's scheduled visit to Peking, the USSR concluded a twenty-year Treaty of Peace, Friendship, and Cooperation with India. This was to be expected if the Soviets were following a containment model. The agreement pledged Soviet support in the face of possible threats from a U.S.-Chinese-Pakistani alliance and promised Soviet assistance in reducing the burden of Bengali refugees.[99] The treaty made no mention of Bangladesh, and Soviet spokesmen continued to urge a political settlement within the existing Pakistani arrangement. Later in the fall, the USSR supported Indira Gandhi's tour of Western capitals as an effort to force restraint on Yahya Khan and to gain recognition of the Awami League's legitimacy. Still, they continued to call for a political settlement that respected Pakistani sovereignty.[100]

By December American envoys in New Delhi and Dacca as well as experts at the State Department and the CIA had concluded that the "reign of terror" in East Pakistan made secession inevitable and the independence of Bangladesh unavoidable.[101] Henry Kissinger recalls that a negotiated settlement was imminent but there is little evidence to support this view. Few area experts give it much credence. Christopher Van Hollen reflects the view of most:

> It is most improbable that any negotiations—which had not even begun at the time—would have succeeded, even if the imprisoned Mujib had been brought into the picture.... Since Mujib by late 1971 would not have settled for less than independence, a demand Yahya could not meet, any negotiations were doomed to failure—which helps explain why they never occurred.[102]

As it became clear to all that no political settlement was forthcoming, both Pakistan and India mobilized their forces. The Soviet Union increased its military deliveries to India as Pakistan continued to receive equipment from the United States and China.[103] By November India was providing arms and cover to the Bengali Liberation Army; the charismatic Bengali leader Mujibar Rahman remained in prison with Pakistani and American leaders determined not to negotiate with him. War was imminent.

Border skirmishes in East Pakistan engaged Indian troops in late November. When Pakistan bombed airfields in northwest India and launched a ground offensive into Jammu and Kashmir on December 3, the Indo-Pakistani War was begun in earnest. The following day India invaded East Pakistan with Bengali liberation forces. Within fourteen days they defeated the Pakistani army and unilaterally declared an unconditional cease-fire. During the fighting the Soviet Union fully supported India. It provided fighter aircraft, bombers, artillery, tanks, antiaircraft weapons, and leverage vis-à-vis China and the United States. Soviet envoys notified Peking that any Chinese action across the Himalayas, however unlikely, would be met with a Soviet attack on Sinkiang.[104] When the United States sent a task force toward the Bay of Bengal, the Soviets made clear with words and the display of ships that it would not be allowed to intervene without risk. The Soviet ambassador to the UN meantime vetoed three cease-fire proposals supported both by China and the United States. Soviet spokesmen insisted that the fighting would not end until the "root" of the crisis was resolved and the Bengalis achieved national self-determination.

Once the war began, the USSR exhibited a clear commitment to India and to the independence of Bangladesh. American efforts to persuade the Soviets to constrain India were fruitless. Secretary of State Kissinger tried to link the issue to the proposed May 1972 Summit and to detente in general. It was to no avail.[105] The Soviet Union did not, however, support any Indian move against West Pakistan. While its support for change in East Pakistan could be interpreted by Americans who were sympathetic to the Bengalis' plight as consistent with detente, any move against West Pakistan could not. The threat of an Indian-Soviet move against West Pakistan became the primary public justification for the dispatch of U.S. naval forces. Henry Kissinger has since claimed that an Indian move in the west was planned and that the U.S. show of force deterred this adventure. He, therefore, holds that the episode exhibited revisionist and expansionist behavior on the part of the Soviets. However, neither the evidence supporting this claim nor the logic on which it is based is necessarily convincing.

On December 8, 1971, the CIA reported that India intended to change the frontier in Azad Kashmir and attack the Pakistani armor and air force. The report was controversial and its reliability questioned. Experts who took it at face value were not surprised and concluded that it did *not* represent a design on West Pakistan. Kashmir was the subject of a long-standing dispute between Pakistan and India and was not identical to West Pakistan. The Pakistani armor and air force had led the attack on Indian Kashmir; that India intended to stop them hardly seemed surprising. Evidently, Kissinger took the report as evidence of an intent to attack West Pakistan. Christopher Van Hollen, the former deputy assistant secretary of state, reports, "Nixon and Kissinger were virtually alone in the U.S. Government in interpreting the report as they did." He continues, "There is no evidence for Kissinger's claim that India had a definite aim to dismember West Pakistan."[106]

During the crisis, the CIA gave low priority and little credibility to reports that India might be planning an attack on West Pakistan.[107] General Westmoreland and other military experts argued that India would face logistic problems in transferring its forces from east to west and concluded that, should India attempt such an act, the United States would have ample warning time and clear signals.[108] Since these military movements did not occur and since India instead declared a unilateral cease-fire as soon as it was successful in the east, the evidence of a planned attack to the west is scant. American intelligence reported from the outset of the crisis that Soviet envoys had said that the USSR would not support a move against West Pakistan and that Soviet leverage would be used only to deter Chinese and American interference in the creation of Bangladesh.[109] The Soviet Union endorsed the cease-fire immediately after the Indian success in the east. Given the local advantage of the Indian military and the doubtful credibility of American nuclear threats, the notion that the American task force deterred further moves or compelled the Indians and Soviets to accept the cease-fire is most implausible. The Soviet Union had been counseling caution from the outset. More likely, India and the USSR had no intention of moving against West Pakistan.[110]

The Soviet Union's support of India and the creation of Bangladesh did weaken Pakistan, force a retreat on the part of the United States and China, and therefore could be interpeted as consistent with a revisionist policy. In evaluating this argument, however, one must consider both the degree to which the change can be realistically attributed to the Soviet Union, and the degree to which support for the creation of Bangladesh necessarily indicates an expansionist motive. As discussed above, the Soviet support for Bengali independence was reluctant and directly connected to Soviet relations with India. It can fit easily within a containment interpretation. The importance of India in a Soviet defensive strategy is only heightened by the centrality of Sino-American relations in this case. Henry Kissinger has reported that U.S. policy in this instance was determined by the imperatives of demonstrating to China the value and reliability of American support. The specifics of Pakistan were surrendered to global strategy.[111] It is likely, in the face of Sino-American cooperation, that India (which is always important in Soviet relations with China) would have been perceived in Moscow as increasingly necessary not only for containing U.S. influence, but also containing the Chinese.

Soviet behavior in South Asia during the early 1970s can be seen as consistent with both a containment and a revisionist strategy, depending on how the situational context is defined. Because the USSR did demonstrate a commitment to change in the region, one could treat the evidence as moderate support for the revisionist proposition. However, the evidence can be treated—and this argument seems more sensible— as consistent with a containment proposition. The case in itself is clearly indeterminate and will have more significance when integrated with the findings in other arenas. Before we turn to a summary of strategic Soviet behavior across all arenas of conflict, we must examine events in Southeast Asia. It was in Vietnam, after all, that the United States was engaged in a hot conflict with Vietnamese Communist forces perceived by many as vehicles of Soviet revisionism in that country.

Southeast Asia

The political deadlock in Vietnam continued into 1972. The North and the Provisional Revolutionary Government (PRG) proclaimed by the NLF in 1969 refused to recognize the legitimacy of the Thieu regime. They demanded total American withdrawal and the creation of a coalition government in Saigon. The coalition would include representatives of the PRG and members of the Saigon government, excluding its top personalities, such as Thieu, Ky, and Huong. The United States rejected both of these demands and insisted on a "two-track" approach in which first a cease-fire would be sought and then the outstanding political issues discussed. It remained committed to both the Thieu government and the independence of South Vietnam.

Although the United States had withdrawn many combat personnel, it continued to prosecute the air war and support the Army of the Republic of Vietnam. The North continued to operate forces in the South and to transfer Soviet-supplied weapons to the PRG. In the spring of 1972 the North launched a ground offensive with Soviet-supplied tanks, artillery, and armored personnel carriers that put Soviet support to the test.

The spring offensive was met by American air power and sharp warnings that Soviet complicity would imperil detente. Secretary Kissinger threatened that if the Soviets did not withhold support from "that miserable little country" the United States would ensure the non-ratification of the Bonn-Moscow treaty and stall detente.[112] Soviet leaders evidently were not anxious to jeopardize detente. They did not provide North Vietnam with offensive aerial weapons capable of covering the ground assault, and, while offering verbal encouragement and SAMs, did not forcefully respond to the escalating American counterattacks. That spring, while in Moscow, Kissinger found the Soviet responses to American bombings and his "veiled threats," as "mild in the extreme."[113] Predicting that the Brezhnev leadership was dissociating itself from the DRV, the national security adviser returned to Washington to join the president in ordering the bombing of Hanoi and the mining of the harbors in Haiphong.[114]

The Soviet Union's lack of commitment to the spring offensive was dramatized by its failure to respond to the American bombing. These attacks went beyond stalling the offensive and presented a threat to the supply lines to North Vietnam. They not only provided a test of Soviet commitment to a revisionist policy (that is, the offensive) but also to its basic alliance with the DRV. In the face of escalating American pressure, many analysts, including Kissinger, expected the USSR to cancel the forthcoming summit meeting in a show of support for the DRV. They thought that the Soviets would link their pursuit of detente with U.S. behavior in Vietnam. This prediction, consistent with a containment model, was wrong. Soviet leaders not only went ahead with the Moscow Summit, but encouraged the DRV to resume negotiations without preconditions.[115]

The Soviet decision to not lend its diplomatic leverage to the North undermined the DRV's bargaining position. It also exhibited a commitment to detente that superseded the commitment to the cause of North Vietnam and the Provisional Revolutionary Government. Kissinger records that despite a private tongue-lashing the Soviet leaders adopted a position on Vietnam "void of any operational content," and in effect cut loose from "its obstreperous small ally."[116] This failure to "even approach the hint of a threat" with respect to the American bombings left the North with few options but to negotiate on American terms.[117]

In October 1972 Henry Kissinger announced that peace was at hand. The North Vietnamese had finally conceded to the "two-track approach" establishing first a cease-fire, and later a process leading to political change. The DRV and PRG gave in to American insistence that the Thieu regime remain in place and that reform be postponed until after the fighting stopped. On the other hand, the cease-fire was to leave the North Vietnamese forces in place in the South and the joint commissions would require President Thieu to negotiate with the PRG. Thieu found both of these conditions unacceptable. His objections frustrated President Nixon and Secretary Kissinger, who felt the proposal essentially represented an American success, but they were unwilling to force him to accept. The peace talks were reopened and Le Duc Tho, representing the DRV, was confronted with over sixty-five new American demands. By December the agreement unraveled and the peace that was at hand seemed to have been lost.

Frustrated with the tenacity of the North and the difficulty of designing a process that would promise change for the PRG and at the same time reassure Thieu that no change would be forthcoming, the Nixon administration decided to "go for broke." It would try to force the North to surrender. The "Christmas bombings" started on December 18 and ran for roughly two weeks. They dropped ten times the total tonnage dropped between 1969 and 1971. Like most of the world, the Soviet Union condemned the American policy. More significant, in the face of this challenge to the Vietnamese, it refrained from involvement and encouraged the DRV to sue for peace.

The restrained Soviet response to the escalation of American demands and to the December bombings is a significant indicator of a low level of commitment. North Vietnam's weakness and international vulnerability was clear after the May Summit, and in October, by accepting the "two-track" approach, the USSR's ally had exhibited flexibility. The American unwillingness to put equal pressure on Thieu, the escalation of demands, and the brutal bombings could easily be perceived in Moscow as a response to the North's demonstrated weakness. In fact, if the Soviet leaders felt threatened by American "imperialism," this would be precisely the interpretation one would predict. As a result, if the Soviet strategy had been aimed at containment, the USSR would have made a vigorous and committed effort to reestablish both the DRV's bargaining position and its own credibility as an ally. One would expect the Soviet Union not to let the DRV be forced into further retreat after having accepted initial compromises. This would be especially true in the face of American pressure. The Soviet Union, however, did not offer the DRV this type of support. Rather, it encouraged Hanoi to make additional concessions and settle on terms much the same as those accepted in October.

Soviet behavior demonstrated less of a commitment to the DRV than a containment model would have predicted, and far below what one might expect if it were following a revisionist strategy. It did not lend its full political leverage to enforcing the DRV's and PRG's demands and eventually let North Vietnam be forced into acceding to the American program. The refusal to accept the Thieu regime, a longstanding part of the status quo, would be sacrificed and direct negotiations begun. The cease-fire would be accepted before the political grievances that led to the fighting were addressed. The Soviet failure to threaten sea and air lanes or U.S. positions in Vietnam may be attributed to the American deterrent; however, the argument that Soviet leaders were intimidated by superior U.S. power or lacked the military capability to help the North resist cannot explain the USSR's decision to press, by withholding political support, North Vietnam into negotiations. In the early seventies, the Soviet Union's behavior in Southeast Asia was consistent with a detente model, which would predict relaxed vigilance regarding Soviet military commitments in the region.

While Soviet behavior did not indicate revisionist motives in 1972, the subsequent collapse of South Vietnam and the DRV's attack in 1975 require that the case be reexamined with hindsight. At least three hypotheses are possible. The first is that Moscow's failure to support North Vietnam was part of a long-range strategy to produce American withdrawal and clear the way for the North's attack. The second is that the USSR accepted the Paris Accords as a compromise plan that provided recognition for both the Thieu regime and the Provisional Revolutionary Government, and opened a process that would produce gradual change. The third is that Soviet leaders accepted the Paris Accords as a retreat on the part of the DRV, with a recognition of the Thieu regime and an abandonment of the PRG's aspirations for change. The USSR's support of the North Vietnamese attack in 1975 is not consistent with the third hypothesis, but the first two require further evaluation.

Although the fighting stopped briefly in 1973, the Paris Accords did very little to untangle the continuing political conflict. The PRG insisted that joint commissions fulfill the promise of negotiations and change agreed to in Paris. President Thieu called the accords a "sell-out," and rejected any notions of negotiating with the PRG or promises of change.[118] The PRG refused to surrender North Vietnamese troops in the south and its guerrilla forces—which were the source of what leverage they had. Thieu used his advantage to extend his control and to grant as little recognition to the PRG as possible. The CIA reported that by February 1974 Thieu's forces had taken 700 hamlets, 15 percent of the land, and 5 percent of the population controlled by the PRG at the time the accords were signed. In the meantime, the president himself refused to provide PRG delegates to the Joint Military Commission (JMC) with appropriate privileges and immunities, rejecting a PRG–South Vietnamese commission altogether. Disputes over the establishment of elections and civil freedoms also persisted. Thieu was not ready to surrender his power to a political process in which he might lose. The PRG was unprepared to surrender the military option until real political change seemed to be possible.[119]

Throughout 1973 the Soviet Union used its propaganda to blame Thieu for the persisting trouble and urged a respect for a negotiated process of change. Moscow's commitment, however, was declining. According to the Defense Intelligence Agency (DIA), the USSR in 1973 reduced its military assistance to North Vietnam by one-half and delivered the majority of its assistance in economic reconstruction and industrial aid.[120]

Despite continuing American aid, Thieu's difficulties escalated and by early 1974 he was opposed by a broad range of domestic opposition. He was criticized, for example, by Catholic Father Tran Hun Thanh for corruption, by General Doung Van Minh for tyranny, and by any number of labor and Buddhist leaders.[121] His image abroad also suffered from reports of political prisoners ranging from the official estimate of 32,000 to other estimates as high as 100,000, the figure accepted by most of the American media. President Thieu was inclined to blame his troubles on the activities of the PRG and DRV. But American intelligence concluded that until the spring of 1974 Thieu was on the offensive, seizing hamlets, and launching "preemptive" attacks, while DRV forces remained at a fairly constant level.[122] After conducting a charade at Tong Le Chan, President Thieu broke off the talks with PRG and North Vietnamese leaders, withdrew from any negotiated process of change, and returned to his position of fall 1972 when he initially rejected the Paris formula.[123]

In the spring of 1974, North Vietnamese forces began to retake the territory lost in 1973. By October they demanded the replacement of Thieu. The battlefield objectives initially were limited and designed to force a return to negotiations, but by December were expanded to include an assault on the South.[124] Soviet Chief of Staff Victor Kulikov visited Hanoi in December and reportedly took part in DRV deliberations. Judging from the subsequent fourfold increase in Soviet supplies, he evidently endorsed their decisions. Soviet support, however, remained far less than American aid to the South and seemed designed to improve the North's bargaining position.[125] When the North attacked, South Vietnamese forces were comparable to the North in nearly every equipment category, and in critically important areas, like helicopters, were vastly superior.[126] The attack consequently could have been intended in Moscow as a coercive effort to restart the process of negotiated change and not, as it turned out, a complete rout of the South. In any case, when the Communist forces captured Saigon in May, the Soviet leadership loudly applauded their victory.[127]

The 1973–1975 experience does not confirm the hypothesis that Soviet behavior in 1972 was simply part of a long-range master strategy. The failure of the Paris Accords was not simply the fault of Communist obstruction or subversion. Neither could the USSR be singled out as the only country encouraging its ally to seek unilateral advantage through the settlement. In light of the evidence, the second hypothesis—that Soviet leaders accepted the accords as a compromise with the promise of negotiated change—is more plausible. The Soviet Union certainly would not block the change desired by the North Vietnamese, but as it demonstrated in 1972 would not sacrifice much to enforce this revision. The 1975 experience does not contradict this conclusion. The success of the DRV is partially attributable to Soviet support, but is not a product of an impressive degree of commitment. After cutting aid in 1974, the USSR delivered to the North barely half of the assistance the United States gave to the South. Moreover, the collapse of the South Vietnamese army is as much a tribute to the weakness of Thieu as it is testimony to Soviet aid. The American reluctance to reengage forces in Southeast Asia was not a product of Soviet leverage. Rather, it reflected growing opposition to the war and the opinion that South Vietnam was not worth the cost of our involvement there precisely because the change occurring was not a product of Soviet expansion but rather of civil war.

In hindsight, the 1973–1975 experience does not alter the conclusions just drawn about Soviet behavior in 1972. The USSR exhibited little commitment to the DRV's hopes of ousting Thieu and conquering the South in 1972, and less commitment to North Vietnam's refusal to recognize Thieu than would be expected even if it were pursuing a containment strategy. By 1975 what had changed most was not the USSR's commitment to enforcing revision in Vietnam but rather the United States' growing unwillingness to secure President Thieu's reign, and his increasing inability to resist change. The USSR's endorsement and support of the North's victory was consistent with a revisionist strategy. It neither confirms this proposition, nor, given the context of the situation and the external variable of China, is it inconsistent with a relaxed containment model that in this study has been equated with support for detente. The case of Vietnam does not lead to clear-cut conclusions about Soviet strategy because the USSR's commitment was not great in the area. It evidenced a marginal commitment at best to either protecting North Vietnam in 1972 or ensuring its victory in 1975. This may reflect a relatively low priority placed on this arena of conflict and suggests that, as evidence bearing on the two propositions regarding Soviet foreign policy strategy, the Vietnamese case is not very useful unless it is considered with the evidence drawn from other arenas of interaction.

Conclusion

The purpose of this chapter has been to determine the prevailing Soviet perceptions of the United States at a time in which both Sino-American and Soviet-American relations reached significant benchmarks. The analysis is designed to provide a basis for conclusions about motivation and has been drawn from two streams of evidence: verbal and behavioral.

This chapter has considered three questions concerning the image of the United States presented by Soviet spokesmen in 1972: (1) To what extent did their image resemble the "enemy" stereotype? (2) To what extent did it resemble the "degenerate" stereotype? (3) As would be expected in a period of detente, in which the perception of threat is relaxed, to what extent did the image resemble an "enemy" stereotype, but with increasing awareness of complexity? The verbal evidence does not seem to fit the "degenerate" stereotype and suggests instead a more complex "enemy" image, consistent with an interest in detente. The evaluation of perceptions is presented in figure 5. Evidence drawn from the images presented in the Soviet media, however, is not persuasive and an assessment of Soviet foreign policy behavior is required before any meaningful conclusions can be drawn regarding perceptions and motivation.

This chapter has focused on Soviet actions during 1972 in five arenas: in the superpower competition over strategic nuclear weapons, foreign policy behavior in Central Europe, the Middle East, South Asia, and Southeast Asia. In each case, three strategic possibilities have been considered: (1) To what extent did Soviet behavior resemble a containment strategy and thus indicate a basic self-defense motive? (2) To what extent did it resemble a revisionist strategy and thus indicate an expansionist motive? (3) To what extent did Soviet behavior resemble a containment pattern, but with reduced commitment and urgency, as well as a willing-

Figure 5. The Prevailing Soviet Image of the United States, 1972

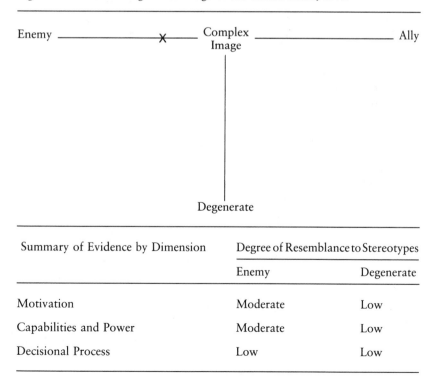

Summary of Evidence by Dimension	Degree of Resemblance to Stereotypes	
	Enemy	Degenerate
Motivation	Moderate	Low
Capabilities and Power	Moderate	Low
Decisional Process	Low	Low

ness to choose detente over unilateral self-reinforcement? The conclusions of the case studies, which attempt to analyze and not chronicle Soviet behavior, are summarized in table 5. This table reflects the degree of resemblance between Soviet behavior in 1972 and what might have been predicted by each strategic model; it also indicates the degree of commitment the USSR exhibited in carrying out these actions. In the cases where Soviet behavior did not resemble a revisionist pattern, the analysis considered whether these nonoccurrences could have been attributed to a lack of capability rather than to nonexpansionist aims. The table attempts to measure the effectiveness of deterrence in each instance.

The evidence in this chapter can support several propositions, but is most supportive of the detente model. In both words and deeds, the Soviets indicated in 1972 that their prevailing view of the United States included perceptions of threat, although substantially less than in 1967. The image of the United States that recurred in speeches and published statements was more complex than in 1967 and did not suggest a "degenerate" stereotype. The USSR's behavior suggested a policy of containment but with reduced commitment. Regarding nuclear weapons and the conflict in Central Europe, there was very little relaxation of Soviet commitment or willingness to trust in detente. This conclusion substantiates what many already know about Soviet security priorities. In the Middle East and Southeast Asia, however, the prevailing Soviet leaders were evidently willing to relax vigilance and substitute detente for the preservation and unilateral reinforcement of their own position. Neither in words nor in actions did the Soviets show an impressive commitment to imposing a revisionist policy on the United States or its allies. Depending

Table 5. Soviet Foreign Policy Behavior, 1972: Degree of Resemblance to Two Strategic Models

	Containment		Revisionism		
	Degree of Resemblance to Model	Degree of Commitment	Degree of Resemblance to Model	Degree of Commitment	Credibility of U.S. Deterrent
Nuclear Weapons	High	High	—	—	High
Central Europe	High	High	Low	Low	Moderate
Middle East	Moderate	Low	Low	Low	Moderate to low
South Asia	High	High	Moderate	Moderate	Moderate to low
Southeast Asia	Moderate	Low	Moderate	Low	Moderate to low

on one's definition of the situation in South Asia and Southeast Asia, one could see Soviet behavior in 1972 as moderately suggestive of a revisionist strategy, but backed by only low commitment.

It is difficult to disconfirm definitively any of the three hypotheses about prevailing Soviet perceptions of the United States in 1972, but it appears most plausible that the dominant Soviet leaders were at that time genuinely committed to preserving detente. Their actions and policy statements bear some resemblance to a containment strategy, but with a significant reduction in urgency. The evidence demonstrates a priority placed on detente that could not be expected if Soviet leaders had perceived an intense threat from the United States. Neither type of evidence supports the proposition that the Soviets saw at this time any opportunities for expansion. There is little resemblance between Soviet behavior and the predictions of a revisionist strategy, and Soviet restraint cannot be easily attributed to a lack of capability. Consequently, the USSR is probably best described as driven more by defensive than expansionist motives in 1972.

The research in this chapter finds that in 1972 the prevailing Soviet view was that the United States still posed a threat, but was less feared than in 1967. The USSR's general strategy toward the United States is best attributed to defensive aims, which remained preeminent. A relaxed sense of threat, however, allows other interests, such as economic gains from trade, to have an increased impact on policy because defensive considerations no longer completely bury secondary motivations. Yet while Soviet interests had become far more complex, self-defense was still a fundamental concern.

Chapter 5

Soviet Perceptions and Foreign Policy, 1979

IN JANUARY 1979 the United States and China normalized diplomatic relations. American images of a Chinese "bamboo curtain" and Chinese images of imperialism's "forces of darkness" were distant memories replaced with talk of military and economic cooperation. The Chinese press described the relationship as a "Peace Rose and Flower of Friendship," depicting the American involvement in Asia as a "powerful factor for maintaining Asian and world peace."[1] On the other side, prominent Americans well known for their vociferous concerns about the Chinese threat in 1967 were describing the PRC as a defensive state interested in modernization and worthy of U.S. friendship and military assistance.[2] Prior trade barriers were withdrawn and even commerce in sensitive areas such as military equipment was under way. At the beginning of the year, the Carter administration received a prior briefing on the PRC's decision to attack Vietnam by Deng himself.[3] By the year's end, the United States granted China most-favored-nation trade status and prepared to dispatch Secretary of Defense Harold Brown to explore how the United States might assist in China's military modernization. The Sino-American rapprochement had reached a new zenith and represented a political shift that many agreed was of great strategic significance. As might be expected, however, the wisdom of pursuing the new "alliance" was not agreed upon by all parties in either Washington or Peking.

Between 1972 and 1979 the leadership in both the United States and China changed, interrupting the steady development of relations. Late in 1975 as the presidential election campaigns gained momentum, conservative Republicans like former governor of California Ronald Reagan had pressed the Ford administration to reaffirm American ties to Taiwan. Reagan supported increasing cooperation with the PRC so as "to provide a barrier to Soviet expansionism," but argued that China at the same time must recognize Taiwanese and South Korean independence. He said that a tough approach that kept American commitments to Taiwan would demonstrate U.S. credibility and enhance China's view of American reliability. This he reasoned would make the United

States a more attractive partner for China, given Peking's concerns about the USSR. The 1976 Republican platform reflected this influence and reaffirmed the 1954 security pact with Taiwan.[4]

As intraparty politics reduced the U.S. administration's ability to pursue Sino-American rapprochement, the death of Chou En Lai in January 1976 brought to power a new group of Chinese leaders who believed that China should be more self-reliant and ideologically disciplined.[5] Following Mao's death in September, however, Chinese leaders like Deng, who favored a rapprochement with the United States, were able to reemerge. Within a year he revised the earlier emphasis on self-reliance and reaffirmed a geopolitical and economic interest in American-Chinese relations. In the United States, on the other hand, the lack of a consensus on foreign policy was not resolved and produced ambiguous signals from the Carter administration on both the urgency of containment and the strategic wisdom of playing the "China card."

There was much dissension in the United States regarding U.S. policy in Southeast Asia. The Vietnam War was not a unifying experience for Americans as "Munich" had been decades earlier.[6] The Vietnam episode was very important, but various observers drew sharply different lessons from the experience. As described in chapter 1, at least three competing schools of thought on Soviet behavior were prominent in the United States. Two of these were at loggerheads. Conservatives attributed the loss of U.S. control in Southeast Asia to U.S. passivity and weakness, and called for a substantially reinforced effort to contain what many saw as Soviet efforts at expansion.[7] In their view, the United States needed to reassert its strength and protect its friends like Israel. Further, the United States should mobilize its allies and potential partners like China in order to reduce the developing momentum of Soviet influence and global involvement.

Liberals, on the other hand, attacked the Kissinger legacy in foreign affairs for its strategic rigidity, political ignorance, and secretive abuse of authority and democratic governance.[8] They criticized the Nixon administration not for ignoring the Soviet threat but for being completely consumed by it. Fighting communism, they argued, had led to unwise and immoral policies in Pakistan, Jordan, Vietnam, Cambodia, Chile, Greece, Portugal, South Africa, and Angola. They attributed the declining American control in the Third World to the increasing level of political awareness in those countries and aspirations of self-determination and nationalism. To reassert American "control," they argued, would be wrong and probably impossible. They suggested that recognizing the limits to U.S. influence was not "defeatism" but "realism." Longing for an American-determined world order or stability was simply romantic nostalgia. For the liberals, containment had been overemphasized as had been the expansionist character of Soviet policy. Consequently, while they favored normalization with China, they opposed using China to further frighten the Soviets.

President Carter's policies reflected the lack of consensus among attentive members of his administration. Zbigniew Brzezinski, who had in the early 1970s found himself in closest substantive agreement with Senator Henry Jackson, represented a hawkish policy community deeply concerned about Soviet adventurism.[9] Andrew Young and Cyrus Vance represented the more liberal orientation interested in supporting policies that were less dependent on cold war assumptions.[10] The dichotomy in strategic advice was not well integrated and found expression in a dual-track strategy of firmness on the one hand and cooperation on the other. As if trying to satisfy two different strategic visions by following mutually contradictory prescriptions, the administration sent out initiatives both to reinforce containment and to relax cold war competition. It presented SALT proposals in March 1977 that pleased hard-line voices, like that of Henry Jackson, and engaged in an active human rights policy vis-à-vis the Soviet Union and Eastern Europe.[11] Additionally, the president initiated visits with two of the Soviet Union's most important allies, Poland and India, and spoke of the need to persuade Moscow that it "cannot impose its system of society upon another."

On the other hand, Carter declared that containment had been overemphasized and that there were new possibilities for arms control and international cooperation.[12] In this vein, the administration spoke of reducing forces in Korea and taking a new look at relations with black Africa. It criticized and stopped aid to friendly, "anticommunist" nations that violated human rights, like Argentina, Uruguay, and Brazil. Moreover, the president endorsed a movement toward a Soviet- and American-sponsored approach to Middle East negotiations, although he shortly abandoned this initiative. As might be expected, the ambiguity in the American commitment to reinforcing its policy of containment did not facilitate the Sino-American rapprochement. When Secretary of State Vance visited Peking in the fall of 1977, he reaffirmed the Carter administration's interest in Soviet-American detente. Deng Xiaoping called the meeting a "setback" in Sino-American relations, and there was negative publicity when no joint communique was issued.[13] U.S.-Chinese relations were after all based on a parallel strategic interest in countering potential Soviet expansion. The process did not gather significant new momentum until early 1978 as a more "enemy"-like image of the USSR gained ascendancy in the White House.

Brzezinski was very concerned about "Soviet adventurism" in the Third World, charging specifically that the USSR was carrying on a proxy war against China and using Cubans to enhance its influence in the horn of Africa.[14] The national security advisor was convinced that an improvement in Sino-American relations would reinforce the containment of the Soviet Union.[15] In the spring of 1978, despite State Department objections, President Carter decided to dispatch Brzezinski to China, instructing him to press for normalization of diplomatic relations.[16] The president's instructions, Brzezinski's accounts, and the public reporting of the visit itself, leave no doubt that in 1979 American leaders had made up their minds to develop ties with China.[17] Following the visit, relations developed quickly as the United States acceded to all three of China's major demands. It agreed to sever diplomatic ties to the Chiang regime in Taiwan, terminate the U.S.-Taiwan Security Pact of 1954, and withdraw the remaining U.S. troops from Taiwan.

By 1979 the image of the USSR prevailing in Washington had noticeably gravitated toward the "enemy" stereotype. President Carter spoke increasingly of Soviet expansionism and the "darker side of change."[18] In his memoirs the president explains: "The fact was that when violence occurred in almost any place on earth, the Soviets or their proxies were most likely to be at the center of it."[19] The United States' relationship with China became a major element in a broad policy of reinforcing efforts to contain the Soviet Union that included increased defense spending, new strategic systems, military facilities in the Middle East, new missiles in Europe, and encouragement of Japanese and Chinese opposition to "hegemonism." The relationship with the United States occupied an equally logical role in China's "united front against hegemonism."[20]

There was no ambivalence in official Chinese depictions of the USSR. The image approached the "enemy" stereotype.[21] The Chinese leadership, while announcing that scientific, industrial, and technological development would be the appropriate long-term strategy for strengthening China, decided that in the short term it needed to take advantage of every opportunity to gain an important ally, even if this allegiance might be temporary, unstable, and conditional.[22] The united front formed by closing ranks with possible partners and exploiting rifts among Soviet allies might allow China to meet what they saw as the Soviet threat and at the same time to proceed with economic development. Because of the emphasis Chinese leaders placed on economic and domestic modernization, it is difficult to determine the degree to which they perceived the Soviet Union as a threat. Although they painted stereotypical pictures in their propaganda, Chinese behavior toward the Soviet Union was less impressive. The PRC cut its defense budget yearly, reduced the army by 800,000, and converted a significant portion of its defense industry to civilian production.[23] Although it worked hard to establish a diplomatic united front by sending envoys to Japan, Western Europe, Eastern Europe, the ASEAN states, Iran, and North Korea, this enthusiasm for mobilizing others did not translate into clear sacrificial commitment on China's part. For example, China gave up very little to obtain trade and diplomatic relations with the United States. The motion toward normalization came largely from American compromises. The Chinese did agree, however, to establish relations despite the continued U.S. commercial and cultural ties to Taiwan and two unilateral declarations that the United States remained committed to a peaceful settlement with Taiwan and reserved the right to sell arms to Taiwan after 1980.[24]

In 1979 the United States and China had found common cause in cooperating to contain potential Soviet expansion. Voices in Washington felt increasingly threatened by the Soviet Union, lending a new urgency to the argument for using Sino-American relations to compel Soviet accommodation. Many opposed this argument. While liberals questioned the wisdom of increasing Soviet anxieties, some American conservatives thought the administration's "rush" to use China gave China undue leverage vis-à-vis the United States. The conservative critics calculated that if leaders in Peking truly perceived a great threat from Moscow, then given China's weakness and vulnerability it ought to be willing to "pay" more for American aid and military support than simply broadcasting ferocious propaganda and advising others to increase their commitment to resisting Soviet expansion. Whatever the depth and urgency of Peking's fears, China acknowledged the United States as an available asset from which both strategic leverage and economic and technological assistance could be derived.

The Sino-American cooperation that Soviet observers had seen in 1967 was by the close of the 1970s an openly advertised quasi-alliance. Various predictions about the effect this relationship would have on Soviet perceptions and policy had been publicly aired throughout the decade and continued to be discussed within the Carter administration. Let us examine once again Soviet leaders' perceptions of the United States in 1979, as derived from both verbal evidence and the Soviet Union's actual behavior.

Soviet Images of the United States in 1979

Images of Sino-American Relations

Soviet spokesmen in 1979 described a virtual alliance between the United States and China. Both the "hawk" and "dragon" were pictured as playing their partner's "card" and as collaborating to construct a "Pacific community" or anti-Soviet Beijing-Tokyo-Washington alliance. In these images China was a substantial "enemy" independent of the United States. It was described as expansionist and as aspiring for Asian and even worldwide domination. The authoritative spokesmen in Moscow presented a nearly stereotypical image of the PRC.[25] Attributing Chinese behavior to "rabid nationalism" and "Great-Han chauvinism," they painted China not only as highly militarized and despotic, bent on conquest and hegemony, but also as frustrated by the might of the Soviet Union.[26] China was said to be too weak to achieve its grandiose "great power" aims; consequently it schemed to organize an anti-Soviet front.[27] The intensity of the prevailing "enemy" image of China was evident not only in official propaganda but also in Moscow's efforts to secure alliances in Asia.

The Soviet Union made abundantly clear its commitment to the preservation of the present territorial boundaries in Asia. Its diplomatic advocacy of an Asian collective security system may have waned, but not its commitment to the Sino-Soviet frontier. It deployed forty-six military divisions along the border, three of them in Mongolia. Furthermore, it refused to discuss the issues China said were in dispute and would not agree to a process of military disengagement.[28] It also continued to court India despite the victory of Prime Minister Morarji Desai and his attempts to improve India's relations with China and the United States.[29] The PRC's attack on Vietnam in early 1979 stalled the progress in Sino-Indian talks and led to further increases in Soviet assistance to India.[30] When Indira Gandhi returned to power in January 1980, she softened India's criticism of the USSR's invasion of Afghanistan and by July established diplomatic relations with the Vietnamese-backed Heng Samrin government in Kampuchea. The USSR's commitment to India manifested itself in increased industrial and military aid and was climaxed by a state visit to New Delhi by Secretary Brezhnev in December.

Beyond India, the USSR supported Vietnam in its escalating conflict with China. The Soviets, never close to the Khmer Rouge, answered Vietnamese requests for aid as tensions mounted between Kampuchea and Vietnam.[31] Matching China's endorsement of Kampuchea, the USSR accepted Vietnam into the Council for Mutual Economic Assistance and in November 1978 signed a Twenty-Five Year Treaty of Friendship. The Soviet Union endorsed the Vietnamese invasion of Kampuchea and provided assistance when China retaliated in early 1979. In the face of the Chinese invasion, the Soviets lent full diplomatic support to Vietnam and engaged air and naval forces for intelligence, reconnaissance, and logistical support. During the fighting, the USSR mobilized its forces on China's frontiers and threatened China with harsh consequences if its attack did not end quickly.[32] Given the limited nature of China's assault and Vietnam's ability to defend itself, the USSR's actions seemed all that might be expected of a rather intense commitment.[33] While moving to secure its ties with India and Vietnam, the USSR apparently abandoned hope of completing the encirclement through Japan.[34] It attacked the 1978 Sino-Japanese Treaty and moved unilaterally to strengthen its forces in Far East Asia.[35]

Judging from rhetorical imagery in Soviet statements and from Soviet behavior, one must conclude that in 1979 the Soviets regarded China as a significant threat. Secretary Brezhnev, following China's attack on Vietnam, went so far as to describe China as the "most serious threat":

> The position of China's leaders is increasingly merging with the policy of imperialism.
> By their unprecedentedly brazen bandit attack on a small neighbouring country—Socialist Vietnam—the present Beijing rulers revealed fully to

the whole world the perfidious aggressive essence of the great-power policy pursued by them.

Now everybody sees that it is this policy that represents the most serious threat to peace in the world. The entire danger of any forms of connivance at that policy is more evident now than ever before.[36]

On the anniversary of the beginning of the Second World War, articles in *Pravda* and *Izvestia* compared China to Nazi Germany and the United States to prewar England. The common theme throughout these articles was that the United States was trying to use China as a weapon against socialism in a fashion they claimed was analogous to a British effort to use Hitler.[37] According to the spokesmen, the United States would not be able to control China's aggressiveness. Aleksandrov explained:

> Beijing's anti-Soviet policy is inflammatory and provocative. It is no secret to anyone that the open intention of pushing the Soviet Union and the United States into the abyss of thermonuclear war forms part of Beijing's strategic plans. After forcing the U.S.S.R. and the United States into military conflict, Beijing probably intends to remain outside the nuclear holocaust and to "exploit it to its advantage," watching what happens and channeling events in a direction of benefit to itself.[38]

While the historical metaphor designated China as a more radically expansionist enemy, Soviet imagery clearly described the American effort to "play the China card" as part of a larger actively imperialist policy.[39]

Images of the United States

Motivation. In 1979 the prevailing spokesmen in Moscow described the United States as bent on world supremacy.[40] The imagery of their speeches and statements evoked the "enemy" stereotype, depicting the United States as expansionist and striving through brute force to exercise worldwide control.[41] It was said to be seeking a "position of strength" from which to dictate to the Soviet Union and even challenge the security of socialism.[42] Its strategy, the Soviets explained, was to control NATO and cement a NATO-U.S.-Japanese-Chinese alliance against the USSR. On top of this, the United States was said to be committed to an unprecedented military arms buildup and to "knocking together" a system of puppet regimes that would facilitate American domination. According to Secretary Brezhnev, the primary American motives were economic and strategic:

> The intention has emerged to set up a network of U.S. military bases in the Indian Ocean, in countries of the Middle and Near East, and in African countries. The United States would like to subject these countries to its hegemony and, without hindrance, to pump out their natural resources, while at the same time using their territories for its strategic designs against

socialism and the national liberation movement. This is the essence of it all.[43]

As in the "enemy" stereotype, the objectives of the United States were described as imperialistic and sinister and were covered in great detail. Soviet leaders derived a simple motivational explanation for U.S. policy: the economic self-interest of "military-industrial circles." The largely monocausal explanation was made only slightly more complex by the claim that President Carter's desire for reelection and personal power also contributed to U.S. militancy. *Pravda* editorialized:

Having encountered the [U.S.] population's discontent and the decline in its prestige in the country, the present government found nothing better than to resort to the long-known device—to attempt to divert the Americans' attention from the obvious setbacks in the field of domestic policy and a number of serious failures in foreign policy. For these purposes a militarist, chauvinistic psychosis is being stirred up in the U.S.A. Acting as the initiator of a new flare-up of jingoism, the White House is hoping to win the backing of the most reactionary circles. At the same time it is counting on "neutralising" the other candidates from both bourgeois parties who in this situation will hardly be able to outdo the administration, criticising the present course of Washington's policy from rightwing positions, because it is impossible to go rightwards further than that.[44]

Although the Soviet spokesmen described the United States as determined to stop "progressive" change, they did not say that it was decadent, passive, or in retreat, which is consistent with the "degenerate" stereotype.[45] To the contrary, they presented the United States as actively aggressive and imperialistic. According to *Pravda,*

What is meant by the "leading role" is Washington's intention to dictate its orders in any region, to any state and, in those instances that the U.S. administration finds expedient, to use any means, including arms, to resist national-liberation, revolutionary, all progressive movements. What we have, thus, is a new claim to American world supremacy.[46]

Capabilities and Power. While in 1979 the prevailing spokesmen in Moscow attributed imperialist and aggressive motives to the United States, they simultaneously described a continuing shift in "the correlation of forces." The era of American supremacy was gone, they said. Current U.S. ambitions for control and imposed stability were therefore unachievable. Aspirations for change manifested in national liberation movements were said to be too powerful to suppress and the increasing might of the socialist world too formidable.

As in 1967 and 1972, Soviet spokesmen did not describe American successes as deriving from Soviet weakness, but rather made the similar point in a positive form by arguing that Soviet power prevented U.S. expansion. Secretary Brezhnev described the United States as repeatedly checking the Soviet Union's "mettle" and concluded that only Soviet power could reduce imperialist opportunities and deter American aggression.[47] He explained that the shift in the correlation of forces was not caused by, nor had resulted in, American resignation, but rather had produced mounting frustration in Washington and the need for increased Soviet resolve:

> As the opportunities for imperialism to dominate other countries and people are reduced, the reaction of its most aggressive and shortsighted representatives increase in fury. This aggressiveness can only be restrained by the might and the sensible policy of peaceloving states and the determination of peoples to foil the dangerous plans of the pretenders to world domination.[48]

Although the spokesmen depicted a relative decline in American influence, they did not describe the United States as weak either politically or militarily. They argued instead that an "approximate equivalence," "balance," or "parity" of military power existed between the United States and the USSR, and between NATO and the Warsaw Pact.[49] Some journalists explained that the shift in forces reduced the United States' previous supremacy. It was incapable of achieving its global objectives but was still the single most powerful nation in the world:

> Although the relative weight and influence of the major capitalist powers are steadily dwindling as the correlation of forces in the world changes, the President is gambling on its role as "the most powerful country in the world, with special obligations." The proclaimed intention is to "alter any course of events" in different areas (above all in the developing countries) which the U.S. ruling circles find undesirable. This is an overt claim to imperialist leadership. It is out of desire to exercise this claim, which smacks of a yen for world domination, and not because of an imaginary military lag, that the current administration is banking on force—above all military force—as the main way of implementing a hegemonist policy.[50]

Unlike the "degenerate" stereotype, the United States was not seen as weak. Nor was it pictured as lacking in will. To the contrary, *Pravda* editorialized that the ruling circles refused to abandon their aspiration of global supremacy,

> that the country's ruling circles, having encountered the realities of the present-day world and the objective growth of the forces of peace, progress and socialism, obviously are unwilling to make their policy in keeping with the United States' real weight in the present-day world. They apparently are unable to get rid of the imperial, hegemonistic mentality and do not want to reckon with the established alignment of forces in the international arena, are unwilling to see that mankind has entered the eighties of the twentieth century and that nowadays one cannot speak the cold war language and think in Truman's and Dulles' categories.[51]

Alexander Bovin described the United States as highly ambitious and full of the will to act, deficient not in resolve but in understanding:

> The United States has grown accustomed to impunity. It is strong—that means it can kill, it can plunder, it can stage coups and countercoups. But the times are changing. Truly those who sow the wind reap the whirlwind. People will not and cannot any longer tolerate cynical disregard for the peoples' rights and interests and support for tyrants and despots. And people are protesting. . . . Do people in America understand that? Many do understand. Many still do not understand. And many simply do not want to understand. So again we have the arrogant pose of some awesome judge. Again we have the aircraft carriers plying the oceans. The "big stick" is again being tried out for size. In a word, an obvious and dangerous return to "strong-arm methods" is taking place in U.S. foreign policy.[52]

Decisional Process. According to Soviet spokesmen, the American decisional process in 1979 was substantially less complex than it was in 1972. They described a fundamental struggle between realistic and militaristic voices and concluded that the Carter administration had succumbed to the pressure of the "rabid anti-Soviets."[53] The "hawks," who were said to be dominant, were described as relatively homogeneous and as uniting the interests of "big business and the Pentagon." As befits the "enemy" stereotype, the Soviets seemed to have an undifferentiated picture of a U.S. "military-industrial complex" ruled from a small center. The nucleus of the "business monopolists" and "militarists" was described as controlling a large segment of legislators, the mass media, most research programs, and private foundations.[54] As in the stereotype, these forces were said to be plotting various international intrigues and as capable of engineering a number of complex conspiracies and subversive operations.[55]

The image was more stereotypical than in 1972, but its simplicity resembled the "enemy" and not the "degenerate" stereotype. "Zigzags" were noted in U.S. policy, but were not described as vacillation. Rather, the decisional process was said to be torn between two sets of elites, with the most militant eventually prevailing. The United States was seen as suffering less from a lack of leadership than from strong leadership that was "unrealistic" and highly aggressive.

The prevailing Soviet perceptions of the United States in 1979 might be described as consistent with the defensive model emphasizing potential threat. This preliminary interpretation, however, is based on verbal evidence alone. Soviet-American relations had become far more tense in 1979–1980 than they were in 1972 and Soviet behavior alarmed many Americans. The rest of this chapter will examine Soviet actions during 1979 in four arenas: strategic nuclear weapons, Central Europe, the Middle East, and Southwest Asia.

Soviet Foreign Policy Behavior in 1979

Strategic Nuclear Weapons

In this study, a containment policy has been associated with a nuclear balance between the superpowers, whereas a revisionist policy has been associated with an effort to achieve nuclear superiority. I have assumed that a commitment to maintaining equivalent forces is essential for mutual deterrence, while a drive for nuclear superiority indicates a desire to dominate and control other nations. In 1967 and 1972 the quantitative and qualitative advantages the United States enjoyed made it impossible to discern whether the substantial Soviet weapons buildup indicated a commitment to achieving superiority or simply to maintaining equivalence. At the same time, it was never determined precisely what force levels actually indicated superiority. By 1979–1980, however, Soviet nuclear forces had so markedly improved (especially with the introduction of MIRVs after 1975) that the question of equivalence or superiority was far more acute. The Soviet buildup was often presented as incontrovertible evidence of a drive for superiority, confirming the warnings of those who saw Moscow's policies as expansionist. Because the USSR's commitment to strategic nuclear weapons has been so great and so often used in attributing motives for their behavior, we must analyze carefully its utility as evidence.

Strategic superiority is difficult to define in terms of one nation's weapon systems compared with those of another. Superiority generally refers to a psychological condition in which leaders of one nation might perceive the opportunity to compel another to act or retreat. Therefore, if the Soviet Union developed forces that could threaten the United States and simultaneously protect itself from American retaliation, that might constitute superiority. The U.S. deterrent might be undermined by a combination of capabilities for both disarming American retaliatory systems and protecting valued Soviet targets. It is nearly impossible to define what level of forces would be required to give the Soviet leaders adequate confidence for issuing threats and handling potential American responses to them. Obviously, what risks Soviet leaders might be willing to take and what costs they might bear become central variables in arguments over whether certain force levels might give them superiority rather than merely maintain mutual deterrence.

Defense Spending.   There can be no question about the Soviet commitment to the development of military forces. It is great. CIA analysts estimated that from 1976 to 1979 the USSR's defense budget constituted between 11 and 13 percent of its gross national product (GNP), with an increase in constant dollars of 3 percent each year.[56] These figures are of course controversial, with the former director of the Defense Intelligence Agency reporting the burden as closer to 17 percent of GNP, rising at not 3 percent but 8 percent per annum.[57] While defense spending as a percent of GNP provides an indication of commitment (that is, sacrifice), it is not a measure of superiority. Since the Soviet Union's GNP is roughly only 55 percent of that of the United States, the greater burden does not necessarily represent greater spending nor translate into superior forces.[58] Franklyn Holzman, an analyst independent of the U.S. government, argues that CIA procedures exaggerate Soviet defense spending and concludes that "it is possible and seems highly probable that alternative methodologies would indicate that the United States is spending as much or more on defense than the USSR."[59] He also points out that European NATO members spent $76 billion on defense during 1979 while Warsaw Treaty Organization (WTO) members spent only $17 billion, and that total NATO military expenditures substantially exceeded those of the WTO.

The tremendous differences between the Soviet and American economies make spending comparisons difficult and their utility as evidence related to strategic hypothesis unclear. It is the weapons that are deployed, however costly their acquisition (in terms of relative sacrifice), that are most directly related to inferences about a nation's capacity to deter aggression or to exert compelling influence.

Doctrines about Deterrence and the Conduct of War.   It is difficult to assess the Soviet and American nuclear arsenals, as we have said. The competing systems are multifaceted and asymmetrical, while the possible conditions of their use are exceedingly complex. We can estimate the number and characteristics of different weapons, but these tabulations reflect a static condition and not the relative usefulness of the systems.[60] Weapons are essentially instruments, and like tools, their utility is not measured simply by their numbers but according to the functions they are designed to perform. Because, until they are used, the function of strategic forces is primarily psychological, the analyst must conjecture what military missions—such as dominating escalation, prompt counterforce strikes, or massive population destruction—a country must be capable of performing in order to achieve the psychological effect necessary to force the enemy to act or to prevent its action. Consequently, assessments of Soviet forces as either equal or superior to those of the United States require not only a statement of static force levels but also a consideration of assumptions about the psychological and political effects of the relative capabilities.

American analysts have attempted to infer the military and concomitant political utility of Soviet strategic nuclear weapons from the publicly announced doctrines concerning their use. They contrast doctrines for fighting a war with those of deterrence, the former being associated with the use of strategic forces to defeat the enemy's forces. Doctrines about fighting a war conceive of nuclear forces as military instruments for disarming an adversary and protecting the homeland, and thereby compelling the adversary to surrender.[61]

The dichotomy between using forces to fight and using forces to deter the enemy is theoretically interesting, but somewhat artificial with regard to Soviet and American nuclear arsenals. For several decades strategists in both countries have argued that assured destruction is not sufficient to deter an adversary that can retaliate in kind. An ability to fight and threaten the use of weapons in a fashion that is not suicidal has long been accepted as the essential components of credible deterrence.

In Soviet strategic doctrine, nuclear weapons have been assigned various functions in the conduct of war. Soviet defense officials claim that should war come they intend to prosecute the conflict to the best of their ability in hopes that somehow Soviet forces might prevail.[62] The doctrine and contingent preparation to fight, however, does not necessarily support claims that Soviet leaders think that nuclear war can be "won," or that the USSR aims to win a war rather than deter aggression.[63] Western strategic planners have long since recognized that in order to effectively deter war, a country must clearly project to a potential adversary both the will and the ability to fight at various levels of violence.[64] As Raymond Garthoff has argued:

> Soviet military power, and the constant enhancement of its capability and readiness, is thus justified primarily for deterrence, as well as to wage a war if one should come despite Soviet efforts to prevent it. This view is held by the military and political leaders. It is not accurate, as some Western commentators have done, to counterpoise Soviet military interest in a "war-fighting" and "war-winning" capability to a "deterrent" capability; the Soviets see the former capabilities as providing the most credible deterrent, as well as serving as a contingent resort if war should nonetheless come.[65]

David Holloway explains that in Soviet thinking about nuclear war "no contradiction is seen between the prevention of war and the preparation for war; war can be prevented only if the Soviet Union prepares to wage it."[66]

Soviet "war-fighting" doctrine may be consistent with the intention to use weapons primarily for deterrence. It is also an unpersuasive form of evidence for several other reasons. First, it is essentially verbal rhetoric gleaned from the publicly available and censored Soviet media, and therefore may have little correspondence to how the USSR plans actually to prosecute a war. Second, the claims made in military writings on both sides about the possibilities of prevailing in nuclear war have obvious morale-sustaining functions domestically and deterrent purposes internationally.[67] Whatever purposes the doctrinal claims may have, they are constantly contradicted by more authoritative voices emphasizing the catastrophic and suicidal aspects of nuclear conflict.[68] In evaluating the likelihood that Soviet leaders intend to use their strategic forces to compel action and not to deter action, the focus on doctrine is not sufficient. It is necessary to consider the USSR's ability to disarm

American forces, shelter itself from unacceptable retaliation, and thus evade a U.S. deterrent.

Missile Deployments and Civil Defense.   The Soviet rocket forces followed the American lead and introduced MIRVs from 1975 to 1979. By 1980 this modernization of ICBMs gave the USSR a fleet of SS-17, SS-18, SS-19 missiles with enough warheads to threaten a strike on U.S. land-based missiles, particularly the 550 Minuteman IIIs. This development worried some Americans because it represented a Soviet ability to disarm that part of the U.S. triad capable of quickly responding against Soviet launchers. Should the United States lose the Minuteman-IIIs, they argued, it would be forced to retaliate against Soviet population centers, inviting attack against U.S. cities. In such a situation, they reasoned, an American president confronted with terrible losses from the collateral effects of strikes on U.S. missiles would not put many times more American lives in jeopardy by inviting attacks on cities. Instead, he would accommodate Soviet demands.[69] Presenting this scenario as plausible, these analysts concluded that the USSR's emphasis on ICBMs with MIRVs and its continuing program for civil defense was evidence of an intention to use nuclear forces to compel, not to deter, the United States.

The "window of vulnerability" argument has problems when it is used to defend the hypothesis that the Kremlin intends to use its weapons aggressively. First, as former director of the CIA Admiral Stansfield Turner has argued, it simply is not true that the United States is incapable of measured retaliation without Minuteman-IIIs.[70] Cruise missiles and bombers can attack with great accuracy, potency and reliability. The time-urgent aspect of retaliation is not vital. If the Soviets struck first, it is likely the remaining land-based and sea-based forces would be on station and on alert to launch on warning. Consequently, ICBMs, which give more than twenty minutes of warning, would be more likely to hit empty silos than to disarm residual forces. Other stationary targets such as communication centers, ports, bases, and depots would make more logical targets for retaliation and could be hit as effectively with cruise missiles as speedier ICBMs.

Second, the USSR's commitment to civil defense is not a measure of the effectiveness of its program against U.S. offensive measures. Consequently, it does not indicate Soviet confidence in sheltering valued areas. Soviet civil defense efforts are much greater than the minimal American plans and may be able to reduce casualties should war come. This is a far cry from suggesting they could reduce casualties to anything less than a horrific level. Although the effectiveness of Soviet civil defense is a controversial issue, the Arms Control and Disarmament Agency concluded in December 1978 that Soviet civil defense "could do little to mitigate the effects of a major attack."[71] American weapons after a first strike would still be capable of destroying tens of millions of Soviet citizens, most

Soviet population centers and industrial facilities, and any selection of major military installations, regardless of Soviet defenses.

A number of studies have develped different scenarios for U.S. retaliation after a hypothetical Soviet first strike. One must assume that the Soviets would be willing to take staggering risks. The Congressional Budget Office estimated that roughly 5,000 U.S. weapons might survive a Soviet strike. If 1,000 were held in reserve, the remainder could be expected "to destroy 80 percent of the Soviet industrial target base and 90 percent of military facilities other than missile silos." The report recognizes that "Soviet civil defense efforts might erode the destructive potential of current U.S. forces." It estimated 95 million deaths without an effective system. With an effective system, it estimated 20 million immediate deaths. Longer-range effects are difficult to gauge. It cautioned, "There is, however, a tradeoff between Soviet civil defense programs and the capability of the Soviet Union to launch a surprise attack; that is, it is unlikely that the Soviet Union could implement an effective civil defense program without alerting the United States to a pending attack."[72] Arthur Katz's analysis suggests that between 3,000 and 4,260 U.S. warheads would be likely to survive a Soviet attack, and that 1,014 warheads would be needed to threaten 204 Soviet cities, 74 percent of the USSR's population, and 62 percent of its industrial capacity. He concludes, "It should be evident that both countries possess substantially greater numbers of weapons and equivalent megatonnage than would be required for an extremely damaging retaliatory attack, even when only the immediate, direct, and easily quantified nuclear effects are considered."[73]

In the related area of antimissile systems, the Soviets, like the Americans, are incapable of deploying an ABM system that can reliably deflect American attacks. While antiair and antimissile technologies have been developed and can intercept cooperative targets, they still can be defeated easily by determined attackers. The more advanced technologies can intercept missiles that are not trying to "fool" the defense but can be rather easily defeated by several available countermeasures.

Third, the Soviet development of ICBMs as the principal component of its strategic forces can be attributed to factors other than first-strike intentions. The USSR has little access to the sea and its technological sophistication in sea-based weapons has lagged. Additionally, land-based forces simplify command and communication problems and may reflect the bureaucratic power of the strategic rocket forces. Moreover, one may draw a biased inference in treating Soviet decisions to mount MIRVs on ICBMs and to enhance accuracy as indicative of an intention to compel the enemy while not drawing a similar inference from American capabilities. By some estimates, U.S. forces could inflict a more disarming first strike on Soviet forces than vice versa.[74] If a hundred MX and the Trident D-5 missiles are deployed, this American threat will become more severe for the Soviet Union.[75]

The vulnerability argument is not technically convincing because of alternatives to ICBM retaliation. Neither is it politically convincing because to disarm the Minuteman IIIs the Soviets must strike unexpectedly. The threat to attack the Minuteman IIIs could not be used in an escalating political crisis because in this situation the U.S. could put these forces on alert or launch on warning. Consequently, Soviet leaders could not expect to benefit from the vulnerability of U.S. ICBMs until after the attack. Given the range of possible American responses, one must make some very radical assumptions about the willingness of Soviet leaders to take risks and accept casualities.

To claim that Soviet strategic forces have meaningful superiority and can be used aggressively, Richard Pipes and Colin Gray assume that Soviet leaders would risk tremendous civilian losses. Pipes contends that because of their "instrumental view of the value of lives" Soviet leaders might not consider 150 million casualties "intolerable."[76] The argument at this point becomes fully circular. The central proposition under investigation here is whether expansionist motives can be reasonably attributed to the Soviets. To explore the hypothesis, I have examined strategic weapons development. In this arena, the operational issue is whether Soviet forces surpass deterrent uses and could be used for compellence. To argue that the USSR seeks military superiority, one must asume that the Soviet leaders are so bent on expansion and power that they would run fantastic risks and accept massive losses to gain them. If circular logic is rejected, the Soviet forces deployed do not indicate a desire for military superiority. They do not have the ability to compel other nations at controllable costs and their behavior can more reasonably be explained as consistent with seeking equivalence and maintaining deterrence.

Arms Control and Negotiated Limits.   After long and tough bargaining, the SALT II Treaty was finally accepted by Presidents Carter and Brezhnev in June 1979. It established a set of equal limits on strategic launchers.[77] Because experts disagreed on which missions the forces needed to be able to perform and on which weapons could guarantee this capability, they reached different conclusions about the merits of the treaty. The most important debates focused on whether or not the treaty would enhance stable mutual deterrence and be adequately verifiable. Both sides in the debate understood that the simple equality in the number of weapons set by common ceilings was an inadequate indicator of the strategic implications of the treaty. The Carter administration argued that the limits on ICBMs with MIRVs and a "fractionation freeze" (a limit on the number of warheads in missile launchers) managed the threat to U.S. land-based forces while allowing the United States to modernize all three legs of its triad, including the B-1 bombers and cruise missiles, Trident and D-5, and MX missiles. Critics such as Paul Nitze, on the other hand, complained that the treaty in practice would leave the Soviet Union more ICBM warheads and not be verifiable within narrow enough parameters of risk.[78]

Many tactical complexities of SALT II received great attention. For the purposes of this study, the central question is whether the USSR's acceptance of the treaty is evidence of a drive for superiority or, at the other extreme, an indication of a willingness to rely on negotiations and relax its commitment to deterrence. The answer to these questions is no on both counts. The force levels accepted in the treaty did not assure the USSR clearly superior capability and did not undermine U.S. systems. Most concerns centered on the treaty's failure to guarantee against the Soviets' gaining advantages in the future or cheating. These concerns did not prove an aggressive motive, they simply assumed Soviet bad faith and the intent to achieve superiority. Certainly Moscow's acceptance of SALT II is not necessarily inconsistent with an aspiration toward nuclear superiority. However, on the surface SALT II is at least equally consistent with the proposition that Soviet leaders will accept a nuclear balance. Their rejection of earlier American proposals (like those offered in March 1977) does not contradict this interpretation.[79]

SALT II did not require the Soviet Union to reduce its reliance on its nuclear arsenal for deterrence. It also revealed little confidence in negotiations as opposed to unilaterally deployed weapons. At best, it might have contributed to the stability of the continuing relationship of mutual deterrence. Possibly the treaty prohibited Soviet developments that otherwise would have been pursued, but in the main it allowed the Soviets, like the Americans, to continue all of their modernization programs as well as a new system yet undeveloped. As liberal and conservative critics of SALT II agreed, it represented little arms control and indicated very little willingness on either side to relax its vigilance in reinforcing deterrent systems.

Summary.   The USSR's commitment to strategic nuclear forces in 1979 is difficult to evaluate as consistent with either a revisionist or a containment model. It is difficult to define superiority, and many analysts would challenge the logic of even measuring revisionism in this way. Many consider military superiority and offensive military capability to be consistent with defense. American conservatives, for example, argue that U.S. superiority would be consistent with a containment strategy, as would be the development of a "war-winning capability." Moreover, there is no reason to think that the Soviet Union could develop superiority in the nuclear field even if it wanted to. American technical, economic, and military resources are simply too great. The development of military capability is consequently a very imperfect measure by which to evaluate hypotheses about strategies and motives.

Analysts who describe the USSR as expansionist and seeking strategic superiority argue that the real evidence of this development is to be found not in the weapons competition but in geopolitical adventurism.[80]

They suggest that the Soviets, confident in their nuclear umbrella, would use this strategic leverage to paralyze the West and pursue a policy of revisionism in the Third World. Consequently, to consider the competing hypotheses about the aims motivating Soviet international behavior in 1979, we must examine Soviet actions in Central Europe, the Middle East, and Southwest Asia.

Central Europe

Developing reasoned arguments that can apply the general strategic models of containment and revisionism to specific cases is always difficult. The complexities introduced by different ideas about detente make the task particularly complicated in Central Europe. The West German strategy of ostpolitik was designed to produce change. We must differentiate, therefore, between commitments to different types of change, not simply distinguish between supporting the existing security systems and forcefully pushing for political revision.

The strategic models translate into three major propositions regarding Soviet actions in Central Europe during the late 1970s. The first is that the USSR opposed change and committed itself to the modernization of the Warsaw Pact and to the polarization of Europe. The second is that the USSR committed itself to the strength of the WTO but was willing to relax its vigilance in this enterprise. That is, it would accept cautious modifications in the Eastern system in a reciprocal fashion with a relaxation in NATO defenses. It would engage in new relations with both the United States and West Germany, allowing new interdependencies between the NATO countries and the nations of Eastern Europe. The third is that the USSR committed itself to producing a change in the Atlantic Alliance while preventing any relaxation in the Warsaw Pact, thereby rolling back U.S. influence, dividing it from its Western allies, and creating preconditions for Soviet European hegemony. This final hypothesis would expect the Soviet Union to emphasize relations with Western Europe while denying the Americans and West Europeans similar access to its East European allies.

Maintaining the Warsaw Pact. Whether the USSR's interest in change was consistent with detente or represented a preliminary effort to split NATO is a controversial matter. The Soviet commitment to the Warsaw Pact is not. In terms of diplomatic, military, and economic commitment, Moscow's maintenance of the WTO and insistence on the 1972 status quo received highest priority. In 1976 the Political Consultative Committee of the WTO met for the first time in two years and established a Foreign Ministers' Committee to further integrate bloc-wide foreign policy. The meeting attracted special attention because it convened in Romania for the first time since 1966. The committee met again in 1978. At the alliance-wide summit meeting celebrating the twenty-fifth anniversary of the pact in May 1980, Soviet leaders left no doubt about their commitment to the political status of the alliance.[81] They backed up their pledges with massive military forces and in October 1975 East Germany and the Soviet Union agreed to a new Treaty of Friendship and Cooperation. In this treaty all references to German reunification were eliminated and the eventual fusion of all socialist nations highlighted as a goal.[82] Visiting East Berlin in October 1979 on East Germany's "national day," Secretary Brezhnev reaffirmed the USSR's commitment and signaled its insistence that U.S. recognition of the status quo in Eastern Europe remain a precondition of detente.

Splitting NATO.   As might be expected of a nation pursuing a containment strategy, in 1979 the USSR not only demonstrated an enormous commitment to the strength and coherence of its own security system but also was happy to see divisions within NATO. One could expect the Soviet Union to encourage differences in NATO and to be pleased by political trends weakening its primary adversary. While no one could expect the Soviet Union to help strengthen the Atlantic Alliance, one might expect limits on its effort to exploit NATO's differences. Taking advantage of them might be expected in a containment strategy, but an actual commitment to undermining the alliance would indicate revisionism.

American analysts understand a containment strategy to include programs designed to weaken alliances, such as encouraging East European independence from the USSR. They take advantage of pent-up nationalism and anger because of domestic repression and mismanagement. In the Carter administration, Security Adviser Brzezinski enunciated the policy of selective detente explicitly aimed at encouraging Romanian, Hungarian, and Polish independence from Moscow.[83] Such programs tread a fine line between containment and a rollback strategy. If they are undertaken with relatively low level of commitment such as verbal propaganda and symbolism, economic aid, and without exerting any real pressure, then they can be treated as part of a containment policy. In the mid-1970s two such opportunities opened for the USSR: Portugal and Turkey.

Political Change in Portugal and Turkey.   In late April 1974 Premier Marcelo Caetano's regime collapsed, giving way within a month to an armed forces movement. The pressures for change in Portugal had their roots in the previous dictatorship and quickly led to a broadening of the political spectrum. The new regime led by Generals Gomes and Gonçalves tolerated the participation of the Portuguese Communist party (PCP) in national politics and indicated a new willingness to negotiate with the Soviet Union. As might be expected, the change was seen as threatening in the Nixon White House. American responses and the ill-fated coup attempted by General Spinola only intensified anti-American sentiment and further divided NATO allies.[84]

While the USSR was not responsible for the changes in Portugal,

Portuguese sentiments, or the U.S. decision to isolate Portugal in NATO, it did offer substantial encouragement for the PCP and Portuguese independence from the American policy.[85] This support, however, had strict limits, with the Soviets unwilling to confront the United States or to back a communist seizure of power.[86] Late in the summer of 1975 some elements of the PCP made a bid for power but failed badly.[87] Later that year the Portuguese government, with U.S. and European aid, reduced the role of the PCP. Moscow offered little more than verbal sympathy to the left and, as expected in a period of detente, pursued ties with the government.[88]

The U.S. embargo on arms sales to Turkey that followed from the 1974 Cyprus crisis also provided an opportunity for the USSR to improve relations with a NATO member. As in Portugal, the Soviets did not cause the division and cannot be blamed for having driven the original wedge between the United States and Turkey. However, they did respond to Turkey's frustration and provided greatly increased assistance and trade.[89] Moreover, they concluded a nonaggression agreement with Turkey and moved to accommodate Turkey's position on Cyprus. Although Turkey's displeasure with the United States facilitated Soviet-Turkish detente, Moscow's behavior did not prolong or complicate the rift in Turkish-American relations. The remedy lay in U.S. and Turkish moderation and the problem was substantially mitigated in the fall of 1978 after the United States lifted its arms embargo and Turkey reopened U.S. bases to American personnel. Soviet courtship of Turkey was obviously selective, and might have surpassed the sort of policies one could expect in a containment strategy. It certainly was in a gray area between what is often part of containment and what is consistent with the preliminary stages of a revisionist strategy. The Turkish-Soviet detente, however, was not rigidly dependent on Turkish independence from NATO and continued as West Germany, and later the United States, assured Turkish participation in the Western alliance.

As developed above, the Soviet support for nongovernmental forces that are hostile to the United States, like the PCP, and for NATO governments in Turkey that have been offended by U.S. policy, could constitute a rollback strategy. The same can, of course, be argued about American support for nongovernmental groups in Poland that are anti-Soviet or about U.S. relations with the Romanian government. The level of commitment to actually dismembering the alliance rather than simply reducing the power arrayed against one's own alliance is all that identifies these acts as designed to roll back the enemy's influence rather than to contain it. There is no precise demarcation separating one pattern from the other. Governments on both sides are certain to charge the other with rollback behavior and insist that their own behavior is consistent with detente. Given the history of this sort of interaction during the 1970s, the USSR's actions in Portugal and Turkey demonstrate a level of commitment that I find consistent with containment. In these cases most analysts agreed that the divisions in NATO were not of the Soviets' making. The widening gap in American–West German policy, on the other hand, aroused deeper fears and suspicions. For many, the USSR's enormous commitment to theater forces in Europe and its rapprochement with West Germany suggested an active effort to produce German neutralism. In this case, the actual divisions between the NATO partners were attributed to Soviet efforts to both intimidate and court West Germany.

Courting West Germany and Limiting Political Reform in Eastern Europe. Willy Brandt's strategy of ostpolitik was designed to relax competing alliances and ultimately to bring about domestic liberalization in Eastern Europe. The hope was that change and the relaxation of bloc solidity would occur in both Eastern and Western Europe in some reciprocal fashion. Just what would constitute reciprocity, however, was never agreed upon. There were two broad expectations that served as general scales, but the evaluation of specific actions remained controversial. First, many expected that the Soviets would relax their suppression of domestic voices in Eastern Europe who were opposed to the conditions of their alliances with the Soviet Union. Many Americans anticipated a liberalization of East European regimes and, at a minimum, respect for civil liberties and human rights in those countries. Second, most anticipated an increased interdependence between East and West Europe and increased access to Eastern Europe. It was clear to all that the USSR was pursuing an active rapprochement with the West Europeans and encouraging a new interdependency with West Germany. This could be consistent with either detente or a rollback policy, depending not on Moscow's overtures to the West, but on its willingness to tolerate reciprocal penetration and change in Eastern Europe. Consequently, the USSR's behavior in Eastern Europe became a central variable in strategic analyses of Soviet policy toward West Germany.

There is no question that in the years associated with detente the ability of the West to contact East Europeans improved dramatically. This was most evident in trade relations: ties to Hungary, Romania, and Poland developed quickly. As seen in the case of Poland, Eastern countries amassing large debts accepted new dependencies on Western concerns.[90] This trade, like bilateral U.S.-Soviet trade, may reflect little sacrifice or risk on the side of the Soviet Union if it is assumed that Western capital and supplies represent no real dependencies and are simply a "bailout" of inefficient and corrupt socialism. Moreover, many argued that the increase in East-West government-to-government contact was not a sufficient criterion for evaluating the relaxation and reciprocal change expected of the USSR. In fact, the argument could be made that such government-to-government interaction strengthens the USSR's position by providing needed capital and undermining the pressure for liberalization. Consequently, for some the Soviet Union's tolerance of trade diversification was not an adequate indicator of Soviet relaxation. They required concrete progress in respect for human rights and domestic reforms both in economic rationalization and political liberalization.

No doubt many German families and Polish citizens benefited greatly from detente. At the same time, the level of this "success" was far below the hopes and expectations of American politicians. Certainly some domestic relaxation was evident in Hungary and especially in Poland. Although Poland's Solidarity movement did not achieve success until August 1980, the socioeconomic decline and political conditions that both propelled its cause and allowed for its organization were visible in 1977–1980.[91] The Soviets never encouraged the latitude given to reformist and opposition voices in Poland. They expressed constant apprehensions about the dangers of uncontrollable change but did not preempt the trend. The "renewal experience" in Poland achieved a number of successes in winning greater freedom of expression, assembly, and organization, and access to the information media. Solidarity was, however, unsuccessful in actually producing a change in the structures of power or in reforming Poland's decision-making system. Its efforts to participate in the economic management of the workplace perhaps drew a final line testing the limits of reform.[92] The USSR would not accept a process that might challenge the structure of power and undermine the alliance. It is difficult to tell how much change was really possible even after the imposition of martial law. Opinions in Poland and elsewhere on this question vary widely. The case demonstrates how difficult it would be to measure political change in the East and West and establish any agreed-upon definition of reciprocal and roughly comparable relaxation.

Given the nature of the Soviet empire, true liberalization in East European countries would most likely produce a collapse of the Warsaw Pact. A similar situation does not exist in the West. Soviet spokesmen, evidently agreeing with this estimate, described Western insistence on domestic liberalization as the instrument of an American attempt at rollback and not as part of a reciprocal process linking U.S. and Soviet behavior. The ostpolitik strategy never accepted the Soviet empire on normative grounds but analytically attributed its maintenance to Soviet security concerns. Consequently, it would not expect the USSR to accept a process that could unleash an uncontrollable disintegration of the WTO unless there were some reciprocal dissolution of NATO. Soviet conservatism in Eastern Europe was widely recognized. This, however, is not inconsistent with a cautious containment policy allowing only safely controlled relaxation of its alliances. Determining if this conservatism is consistent with a cautious detente model or with a rollback strategy requires a comparison with United States–West German relations. If the coherence and strength of NATO were declining more quickly than changes in the Warsaw Pact, then Soviet conservatism regarding East Europe could be seen as consistent with a revisionist policy.

American administrations had never been enthusiastic about West Germany's ostpolitik and from Henry Kissinger through Zbigniew Brzezinski, national security advisers had harbored concerns about German neutralism. As the Carter administration moved to reinforce and modernize NATO, its strategic differences with the Schmidt government became more public and acute.[93] At a time when the prevailing view in the United States called for a rejuvenation and strengthening of containment, the West German government remained committed to detente. The differences between Washington and Bonn came into clear focus on at least three issues: reinforcement and modernization of NATO forces, reactions to the Soviet invasion of Afghanistan, and relations with China.

West Germany accepted American initiatives to increase NATO defense budgets and deploy new missiles in Europe but without enthusiasm and only after significant pressure. The pledged spending increase of 3 percent was very ambiguously implemented, while the plan to deploy modernized land-based intermediate-range nuclear missiles (INF) was tied tightly to arms control.[94] In May 1978, for example, when the decision to deploy new missiles in Europe was made in Washington, the FRG received Soviet President Brezhnev and agreed to negotiate controls on "gray area" weapons.[95] The West German priority on arms control and interest in negotiating before deployment continually frustrated American officials. This was particularly true when the chancellor proposed a freeze on deployment just months after the Soviets invaded Afghanistan.[96]

The invasion of Afghanistan led to another disagreement between Washington and Bonn. The United States pressed West Germany to punish the USSR while the Germans worked to salvage detente. Although the Schmidt government agreed to follow some of the American sanctions, the chancellor simultaneously called for a calm examination of "German interests" and "crisis management."[97] He argued that "whoever wants peace must resolve conflicts through negotiations" and reaffirmed his intention to meet President Brezhnev that year. Rejecting as "thoughtless" any suggestions that NATO "extend its geographical commitments," the chancellor dissociated West Germany from the newly enunciated American pledge to defend Southwest Asia (the Carter Doctrine) and proceeded to visit Moscow in July 1980.[98] Prior to the Soviet–West German summit meeting, he suggested that with regard to Afghanistan the United States ought to couple pressure on the USSR with political arrangements satisfying Soviet security and prestige concerns.

The West German reluctance to join the United States in reinforcing its containment policy also applied to the use of the "China card."

Chancellor Schmidt cautioned against West European arms sales to China and argued that German interests "will not be defended on the Mekong or the Ussuri," but are secured in Europe.[99] Defense Minister Hans Apel presented the calculation well:

> I am not one of those, though, who expect something good to come from the present rivalry between the People's Republic of China and the Soviet Union neither for Europe nor Asia. On the contrary, the Germans are urgently interested in detente making progress all over the world. We want to continue this policy which has scored visible advantages for us Germans, for our allies and partners in the West, as well as for the states of Eastern Europe, including the Soviet Union; this policy promises advantages in the future as well.
>
> The Federal Republic does not know any such thing as a China card. We will supply no arms to China. Our position in this matter is very obvious. Our policy is not aimed at postponing World War III but at preventing it.[100]

The Soviet Union worked hard to persuade the West Germans not to follow the American lead on reinforcing NATO missiles or imposing sanctions because of the Afghanistan invasion. Prior to the NATO missile decision, President Brezhnev suggested that the West had a choice between the benefits of detente and the costs of escalating military and political tensions in Europe.[101] To forestall the NATO decision, he proposed negotiations, unilateral reductions, and new confidence-building measures. All this climaxed with a 1979 media event advertising the withdrawal of some Soviet troops from East Germany.[102]

At the same time, the Soviets made it clear that German acceptance of the American plan would produce stern consequences.[103] After the positive NATO decision and the Soviet invasion of Afghanistan, Moscow moved quickly to remind the FRG of some of these costs. It rejected talks on intermediate-range nuclear forces, canceled the meeting of the Soviet–West German Joint Economic Development Commission, and postponed Erich Honecker's planned summit meeting with Helmut Schmidt. Additionally, it announced that if West Germany did not join in the U.S. plans, then new possibilities for trade and intra-German relations would be opened. During the spring of 1980 the Soviets courted West Germany anew, offering political, economic, and diplomatic opportunities, never failing to connect these "advantages of detente" to resisting plans to reinforce NATO or to impose sanctions on Moscow.

Intimidating West Germany—Theater Nuclear Forces and German Perceptions. The Soviet opposition to new NATO missiles or Western-imposed sanctions is not surprising. Nor is such opposition necessarily an attempt to split NATO. There can be a large difference between opposing the reinforcements sought by the Carter administration and opposing NATO in general. This certainly was true in the case of West

German public opinion which overwhelmingly supported NATO but not necessarily the decision to deploy new missiles.[104] Soviet pressure on West Germany was linked to plans for the reinforcement of NATO, not to its participation in NATO. Likewise, the costs the Soviets threatened were related to the benefits of detente and not to the basic status established in 1970–1972. It was more often Americans, frustrated with the lack of West German vigilance, who perceived opposition to reinforcement as equivalent with opposition to NATO. For these analysts, the USSR was attempting to prevent modernization in the West while building superiority in the East. If this were allowed, they argued, West Germany could be "Finlandized" and American influence diminished there. Consequently, the reinforcement issue was perceived as vital for NATO and functionally equivalent to support for the alliance itself. Estimating the existing balance of power in Europe became basic to evaluating Soviet behavior as either an attempt to split NATO or to secure detente.

Comparing conventional and theater nuclear forces is a complicated task and cannot be done with any precision or certainty.[105] A multitude of variables and assumptions are involved for which persuasive data is not publicly available or simply does not exist. Numerical comparisons across dimensions for which data is available in terms of equipment stocks, weapons deployed, and military divisions are only marginally useful and can be misleading if taken as an index of the military balance.[106] In Europe the analytic difficulties are compounded by the connection between theater and strategic forces (for example, American SLBMs, and Soviet ICBMs), as well as the inequalities in geographic proximity and alliance solidarity. Because of the many different ways to measure military forces and the variety of assumptions and scenarios that can be conjectured, evaluations of the balance run the gamut from emphasizing NATO's vulnerability and inferiority to highlighting Western advantages and strength. I will not attempt to make yet another estimate here, nor to settle the ongoing technical-military debate. For my purposes this is not necessary.

The reason for evaluating the military balance at this point is to consider the wisdom of treating the Soviet Union's opposition to the reinforcement of NATO as an effort to gain intimidating superiority. For this objective it is probably sufficient to note that prominent Western analysts concluded that parity existed and that an overall balance continued "to make military aggression appear unattractive" to the Soviets.[107] These analysts may be wrong. But if in their net assessments a rough parity was in place, it does not seem unreasonable to believe that Soviet planners reached similar conclusions as their spokesmen consistently claimed. One would expect Soviet defense planners to exaggerate Western forces and see them as more threatening than Western observers did. However, Soviet leaders, while arguing that existing forces were roughly balanced, continued to modernize their weaponry and perpetuate trends that were unfavorable to the West. American observers were especially concerned about the development of intermediate-range nuclear forces.

Perceptions of the enemy's available power can often be more important politically than its actual military capacity to perform specific missions. Given the importance of public opinion in West European democracies, the USSR's deployment of highly visible and threatening weapons systems, such as the SS-20, could give it significant power of intimidation even if in a technical military assessment they did not represent a usable advantage. The psychological impact of Soviet theater nuclear ("gray area") weapons (the SS-20, MiG 27, Backfire bomber) became a central point of controversy in debates over the NATO decision to deploy new land-based INFs. It was argued that Moscow's deployments indicated a commitment to intimidation irrespective of technical arguments about NATO's strength. These weapons might shake West German confidence in American protection and produce a German interest in accommodation with the Soviet Union. Those who observed a military balance between the superpowers felt that a rapid and determined mobilization by NATO was necessary for the balance to be maintained in a conflict. The deployment of new Soviet weapons was seen as possibly leading to a psychological paralysis in the West and in turn Soviet superiority.

As with the "window of vulnerability" argument, it is problematic to interpret the USSR's deployments of theater nuclear weapons as necessarily indicating aggressive aims rather than self-defense. First, the Soviet decision to modernize SS-4 and SS-5 missiles did not occur in a vacuum, but rather in the context of NATO's decisions to upgrade its Polaris missile fleet (three MRVs per missile) to Poseidons (ten MIRVs per missile); to develop ground-, sea-, and air-launched cruise missiles; and to begin an impressive modernization of its tactical aircraft.[108] Simultaneously, modernization plans for the British and French nuclear forces were announced. Such plans would increase the number of warheads on these systems in excess of the increase in warheads the USSR gained from the SS-20s. In light of these Western programs, the Soviet decision to deploy the SS-20s could be attributed to easily understood military modernization. Additionally, some argue that the main objective of the SS-20 deployment was to protect Soviet hegemony in Eastern Europe, not to intimidate Western Europe.[109]

Second, in the opinion of prominent Western analysis, the unequal advantages in certain weapon characteristics that the modernization programs were producing could best be addressed by negotiations and arms control and were not so large as to indicate clearly aggressive intentions on the part of the Soviets.[110] Furthermore, there were technical and bureaucratic explanations for the Soviet decision to deploy the SS-20. The SS-4 and SS-5 missiles were aging systems with outdated technology. They were vulnerable to attack and required eight to

twenty hours to prepare for firing.[111] Gregory Treverton describes the
Soviet decision this way:

> The SS-4 and SS-5 are obsolete; they take a day or more to prepare for
> firing. Simple logic, military necessity and bureaucratic momentum could
> all have suggested that they be modernized. . . . A final decision to deploy
> the SS-20 would have been taken in the early 1970s, or about the time that
> it became clear such systems, along with American foward-based systems
> (F.B.S.) would not be limited by SALT I. At that point the military argu-
> ment for proceeding would have been straightforward and compelling; a
> new system was ready, old systems needed replacing and SALT left the
> issue unconstrained.[112]

Raymond Garthoff concludes: "There is a perfectly understandable
Soviet military rationale for modernization, without resort to speculation on intentions for a first strike or political pressure. Moreover,
what evidence there is argues *against* the explanation of political
intimidation."[113] The deployment of SS-20s beyond the limits Soviet
spokesmen recognized as balanced in 1979–1980 can be attributed to
"bargaining chip" tactics as easily as to a commitment to Soviet
superiority.

Third and finally, the argument requires an assumption that Soviet
leaders would expose their nation to potentially devastating military
consequences on the chance that NATO countries might be paralyzed
by the fear of nuclear attack. However, this assumption is circular. To
make the case, one must assume that Soviet leaders are so bent on
military superiority and expansion that they would run tremendous
risks to achieve them. Moreover, the argument rests on a questionable
interpretation of West German politics that attributes the antimissile
peace movement to defeatism and appeasement.

Deciphering the psychological roots of people's perceptions of foreign countries is difficult, but there is no obvious reason to attribute
West German differences with the United States to rampant pacifism
and overwhelming fear of the Soviet Union. Also, there is no reason to
assume that Soviet leaders perceive a lack of will or susceptibility to
nuclear blackmail in West Germany. Social Democratic leaders that
opposed American initiatives gave every indication that they feared the
USSR less than did the Christian Democrats who favored the NATO
deployment. The opposition to deployment is more easily attributed to
a less threatening strategic assessment than to successful Soviet intimidation.[114] Chancellor Schmidt, for example, argued, "On our side the
firm conviction exists that the leadership in Moscow is pursuing a
responsible policy and does not intend to wage a war of aggression in
Europe."[115] One of the Social Democratic party's most visible leaders,
Herbert Wehner, went further, explaining, "There is a philosophy, say,
in the context with this 1979 winter maneuver, that some threat is
emanating from the Soviet Union. I deny that. It is necessary to debate,

calculate, and argue with the Soviet Union over what it has, but what it has is defensive and not aggressive."[116]

At the same time, the chancellor dismissed talk of German neutralism as nonsense and solidly anchored the FRG in the Atlantic Alliance:

> Rapallo would mean turning away from the West and toward the East; putting it bluntly, that would be an absurd idea. All our friends in the Atlantic Alliance know that our policy aimed at an arrangement with East European countries was successful only because we could act from a position that was firmly anchored in the Western Alliance. The U.S.S.R. leadership knows very well that the Federal Government firmly adheres to its basic positions and that our country is and remains a most significant part of the Western Alliance.[117]

Most survey data indicated that the chancellor's views were widely shared and that neither neutralism nor realignment were very popular ideas. Many West Germans favored more cooperation with the USSR but in the context of detente, not realignment. One survey in July 1981 found 50 percent favoring closer ties to both the United States and the Soviet Union equally, and only 2 percent favoring closer ties to the USSR.[118] In other surveys 82 percent of SPD leaders continued to favor close ties to the United States on defense matters, while the support for neutralist sympathies continued to be less than in the 1950s.[119]

Rather than a result of intimidation, West German resistance to U.S. initiatives can be seen as a product of confidence in the possibility of detente with the USSR.[120] For example, Chancellor Schmidt argued that the Soviets would accept a balance of forces and that while asymmetries existed, they might be addressed through arms control:

> A gigantic power such as the Soviet Union will always try to fill a vacuum with its influence if you let it have leeway. This is why a peace policy requires a policy of balance of political forces. The Soviet Union recognizes this today; just take a look at the remarkable formula in the joint declaration which we signed, the formula of parity relating to military forces. . . . I am very satisfied with this.[121]

Defense capabilities and a balance of power were never minimized by Schmidt, but he argued that armaments alone were not sufficient to guarantee peace:

> Our security is based on two principles, on two elements, which fundamentally are equally important: Defense capability on the one hand, arms limitation on the other, both of them merging to a balance. Balance alone is not a peace guarantee. If you want to base peace exclusively on military balance it would remain a highly precarious peace. Much depends on a correct psychological approach to the concern and problems of the other side. This includes the economic field as well as purely psychological fields.[122]

The reluctance of West Germans to endorse American policy did not seem to derive from a sense of intimidation or desire to appease Moscow. It grew from a deeply felt concern that American leaders exaggerated Soviet expansionist ambitions and failed to appreciate Soviet security concerns. Chancellor Schmidt drew analogies between an unintended slide into World War I and the existing Soviet-American rivalry. He concluded that at present neither superpower had a convincing strategy for preventing war or developing a lasting detente.[123]

Summary. The Soviet Union's committed opposition to NATO modernization fits well with the expectations of both the containment and detente models. The case for interpreting this behavior as designed to split NATO and enforce revisionism in Western Europe is less clear-cut. It requires the acceptance of a number of doubtful political assumptions. The absence of clearly revisionist behavior in Europe can be attributed to the credibility of the Western deterrent and therefore does not necessarily disconfirm the expansionist theory. Many analysts recognized that a strong Soviet interest in detente in Europe was tied to revisionist efforts in other regions. For American officials concerned with global Soviet policy, the USSR's commitment to "business as usual" in Europe was "indivisibly" connected to Soviet intervention in the Third World. The Soviet Union's acceptance of the status quo in Europe was seen as a result of effective Western power and as a tactical decision to concentrate on other areas for expansion. Supporting detente in Europe was interpreted as a ploy to undermine West European resistance to Soviet expansion in the Third World. Because Soviet influence could imperil European oil supplies, European detente was perceived as part of a larger Soviet revisionist plan to dominate Europe through the Middle East and Persian Gulf. Even if Soviet behavior in Europe indicated a cautious adherence to detente, many Americans argued, Soviet adventurism in Third World areas was not. It is particularly important in this period, therefore, to analyze Soviet behavior in the Middle East and Southwest Asia.

The Middle East

In 1979 the Middle East evoked special concern among makers of U.S. foreign policy. Soviet involvement in the horn of Africa and southern Arabian peninsula alarmed many Americans. They interpreted Soviet policy as designed to undermine American influence and establish leverage over Western oil supplies. Soviet support for Arab regimes that refused to recognize Israel's right to exist was also seen as part of a growing challenge. As the view of the USSR prevailing in Washington gravitated toward the "enemy" stereotype, Soviet involvement was increasingly identified as revisionist, and the strategic alternatives were often not considered. It is therefore imperative that, before turning to the analysis of Soviet behavior, we should consider the expectations of the containment and detente models.

Arab-Israeli Conflicts. If prevailing Soviet leaders saw the United States as increasingly threatening, as is suggested by an analysis of verbal imagery, then the USSR could be expected to strengthen its Arab relations. Moscow could be expected to renew efforts to recover countervailing positions in Egypt, Syria, and Iraq. If this proved impossible, the USSR could also be expected to seek new allies, offsetting the deterioration of its influence with the major Arab powers.

On the other hand, if the sense of threat in Moscow was relaxing, and thus leaders were interested in promoting detente, then the USSR could be expected to grant less priority to the reinforcement of its political-security system. It might offer support to Arab friends but not at a level likely to interrupt Soviet-American detente. Its support would not be enough to allow a successful Arab recovery of occupied territory, much less a challenge to Israel proper, and thus would fall far short of Arab demands. Although the Soviets would not be expected to forego opportunities for making new allies, they would be unwilling to sacrifice much for their development. Likewise, Soviet leaders would not be expected to accept significant Israeli occupation of Arab territory, but instead endorse negotiations that reaffirmed the 1967 status quo including Israel's legitimacy, UN resolutions 242 and 338. As indications of Soviet behavior in the region in 1979, Soviet relations with the major Arab powers, Egypt, Syria, and Iraq, are most important.

Soviet Relations with Egypt. In the second half of the 1970s, Soviet-Egyptian relations collapsed into bitter acrimony. The chronicle of the disintegration is well known, as is the American mediation of the post-1973 disengagement.[124] By August 1975 when the second Sinai Agreement between Egypt and Israel was signed, the USSR had stopped military deliveries to Egypt and was demanding payment for outstanding debts. President Sadat refused to pay, and in March 1976 canceled Soviet access to Egyptian naval facilities and abrogated the Soviet-Egyptian Treaty of Friendship. In November of 1977 he agreed to go to Jerusalem, which culminated in the Camp David Accords. U.S. and Egyptian forces were practicing joint military exercises by late 1979. After the Soviet Union invaded Afghanistan, President Sadat publicly agreed to make Egyptian facilities available to the United States.[125]

Although the deterioration of Soviet-Egyptian relations and rise of American-Egyptian relations is common knowledge, it is less clear why this collapse occurred. More important, it is unclear why the Soviet Union did so little to prevent it. President Sadat's frustration with the USSR's unwillingness or inability to help the Arabs recover their territories was clear in 1972 and remained evident throughout the decade. Charging the leaders in Moscow with selling out the Arab cause to detente, Sadat attributed their reluctance to match American involvement to "unfaithfulness" and an interest in keeping the Arabs weak.[126]

Whatever the reasons, the USSR exhibited little interest in courting Sadat. They refused to meet his demands for weapons and did not link Soviet-American detente to Israeli withdrawal. Rather than competing for Egyptian favor, the Soviets criticized President Sadat and cut off aid in 1975. Thereafter they attacked his leadership and seemed preoccupied with the conclusion of the Conference on Security and Cooperation in Europe. At the same time, there is very little evidence that they tried to regain their influence in Egypt by overthrowing Sadat or compelling his compliance. Although Soviet propaganda attacked the regime and the Egyptian-U.S.-Israeli "collaboration," the USSR evidently did not commit itself seriously to Sadat's ouster.[127]

The acceptance of the Camp David process dramatically eroded Sadat's standing among Arab and Egyptian nationalists, transforming his image from that of a hero in 1973–1974 to traitor in 1978–1980. After his decision to go to Jerusalem, Foreign Minister Ismail Fahmy resigned in protest, as did Deputy Foreign Minister Muhammad Riad. Fahmy's chief adviser, Osama el-Baz, also resigned, but stayed in the president's service at Camp David. Following the Camp David Summit, Foreign Minister Mohammed Ibrahim Kamel and Egypt's ambassador to the United States, Ashraf Ghorbal, also resigned.[128] These resignations were only the defections from within the leadership. Other opponents were even more dissatisfied and perfectly willing to seek Soviet help. The result was a situation of domestic vulnerability that the Soviets might have exploited.

The USSR's failure to interfere heavily in Egyptian politics and work to reestablish influence in Egypt is not easily attributed to lack of opportunity. Although there were unconfirmed charges of Libyan plots against Sadat in the summer of 1980, the connection, if any, to the Soviet Union was unclear. Egypt certainly continued to field a far more powerful army than Libya's.[129] More significantly, if the Soviets had been aiming to topple Sadat, it is unlikely they would have moved through Libya. There were any number of disaffected Egyptian elites that had a much better chance of success than Quaddafi. Former Chief of Staff General Saad Eddin al-Shazli, for example, was committed to Sadat's ouster and promised to reestablish the Soviet connection. He was already recognized as the legitimate opposition to Sadat by Syria, Libya, South Yemen, and the PLO. Soviet support for Shazli was unimpressive as the USSR's propaganda came out in favor of the Egyptian National Progressive Union, a legal opposition group originally authorized by Sadat.[130] The commitment to Sadat's removal and the reemergence of Soviet ties seemed to remain mostly at the level of propaganda.[131]

Soviet Relations with Syria.   As Soviet relations with Egypt collapsed, the USSR moved to enhance its relations with the PLO and Libya, but these smaller actors could not compensate for the strategic loss.[132] If the USSR were to recoup its countervailing influence, as would be expected if it were following a containment pattern, it would need to reinforce its ties to Syria. Instead of courting Syria, however, the USSR allowed the relationship to deteriorate. In June 1976, Syria reestablished relations with Egypt three months after Egypt had abrogated its treaty with the Soviet Union. In the fall of 1976, Syria and Egypt settled on a plan for political union and by the spring of 1977 Secretary Brezhnev was describing Syria as aligned with Egypt, Saudi Arabia, Israel, and the United States.[133] The war in Lebanon had presented both opportunities and dilemmas for the Soviet Union, whose inaction resulted in a still greater diminution of influence in the region.

When the conflicts in Lebanon exploded into full-scale civil war, the Syrian regime harbored a number of fears and aspirations, one of which was that a National Movement–PLO victory might invite either an Israeli occupation of Lebanon or a division of Lebanon and the creation of an independent Maronite state aligned with Israel.[134] Either possibility would have been detrimental to both Syrian security and Syrian attachments to Lebanon. When Lebanese President Franjieh and other Maronite leaders asked the Assad government to prevent an imminent National Movement victory, it agreed and intervened militarily. The Syrian army quickly came into battle against the National Movement and Palestinian forces. The crisis created yet another test of Soviet commitment. Resolute and possibly costly action was demanded by Soviet clients in both Lebanon and Syria.

The Soviet Union refused to support Syria's intervention and condemned the military engagement as a "knife in the back of the Palestinians."[135] At the same time, it refused to project its own influence into Lebanon to reduce Syrian anxieties about a divided Lebanon and an Israeli-Maronite alliance.[136] Unwilling to relieve Syrian concerns by involving itself in the conflict and unwilling to support Syrian action in Lebanon, the USSR alienated Syria. Because the Syrian army was fighting the PLO and National Movement forces, Moscow's condemnation of President Assad's decision may be seen as an effort to protect the Soviets' image as a loyal friend of the Palestinian cause. However, the USSR's failure to deliver meaningful supply to PLO–National Movement forces did little to bolster its credibility.[137] Other than propaganda, the lack of Soviet commitment to either side or to resolving the conflict showed that the Soviet Union had little interest in recovering its declining influence in the region or in countering growing American leverage there.

Despite American mediation attempts and obvious U.S. concern with excluding the Soviet Union from negotiations, the Camp David Accords created perhaps the best opportunity for the USSR to recoup its losses. Calculating that President Sadat's move destroyed the Arab bargaining position and believing that the United States would never pressure Israel to withdraw from the West Bank or accept Palestinian self-determination, President Assad denounced the accords and President

Sadat as traitorous. The immediate effect was to destroy the Syrian-Egyptian alliance and stimulate an intensified interest among Arabs in making a strategic response enjoying Soviet support. The Soviet Union had the opportunity to rebuild its relations with Syria and Iraq by responding to their increased need for Soviet leverage. Given the strategic advantages the Egyptian-Israeli accords represented for the United States, even assuming that the Soviets were upholding detente, one could predict Soviet interest in restoring a regional balance of power.

The Soviet Union condemned the Sadat initiative and applauded the Tripoli and Algiers Conferences (held in December 1977 and January 1978) as efforts to mobilize Arab opposition.[138] Endorsing the Steadfastness Front, the USSR used its diplomacy and propaganda to encourage Arab resistance and to organize a united Arab response with an Iraqi-Syrian alliance at its core.[139] Shortly after the Camp David Summit in September 1978, the USSR in October received President Assad in Moscow and supported Syria's position in Lebanon. Jointly they assailed the Israeli attack on Lebanon that had reached invasion proportions in the spring.[140] It is difficult to assess the USSR's role, but less than three weeks later a Syrian-Iraqi summit took place. The summit resulted in a joint communique establishing a bilateral committee of Syrian and Iraqi foreign and defense ministers and military chiefs. After the Egyptian-Israeli Accords were signed in March 1979, Syria and Iraq announced in June the formation of a joint political command.

Because it entailed Saudi and Jordanian participation, the cooperation between Iraq and Syria represented a credible strategic response to Egypt's defection. The Baghdad agreements represented a vital dimension of any potential Soviet effort to secure a countervailing position.[141] Although the USSR was generous with verbal encouragement for Arab unity and restored arms deliveries to Syria and continued to sell arms to Iraq, when the Baghdad arrangement collapsed in August–September 1979, Moscow committed few resources to its preservation. Since the Iraqi-Syrian tie was imperative for a credible Soviet and Arab response to Camp David, one might predict a vigorous Soviet campaign to "ensure" its success if the Soviet Union were following a containment policy. One might expect a Soviet-sponsored summit meeting in Moscow, for example, where Iraqi and Syrian leaders would feel the pressure of inducements and threats somewhat similar to the level of American involvement at Camp David. However, no "Camp Ivan" materialized, as the USSR was evidently unwilling to invest major resources to "make" the Baghdad arrangement work. Contrary to the expectations of either the containment or revisionist models, the USSR did not seize the opportunity to recover its influence in the region. Instead, it limited its commitment to applause and encouragement. The active involvement necessary to make the Arab strategic response succeed was not forthcoming.

Nowhere was Moscow's unwillingness to court Arab allies clearer than in Lebanon. President Assad found the Camp David Accords, signed in March 1979, particularly traitorous because Israel was bombing Lebanon at the time. During 1978–1979 when the USSR had the opportunity to exploit Arab anger with the United States and prove itself as a useful and credible superpower ally, it did little to help Syria, the PLO, or the Arabs in Lebanon. As Israel invaded and bombed Lebanon, the USSR did not respond vigorously, as it had done for Egypt in 1970.[142] The failure to provide the Syrians and Lebanese with air defense became more significant after the Baghdad arrangement collapsed. Syria was the only remaining Soviet friend among the Arab big three. Iraq, always uncomfortable with Soviet "appeasement" of Israel and the East European interest in Iranian oil, moved steadily toward nonalignment and by 1979 opposed the Soviet government's policies toward Ethiopia, Afghanistan, South Yemen, Vietnam, Cambodia, and presented itself to key American officials as a possible ally.[143] By the fall of 1980, Iraq received most of its support for its war against Iran from Jordan and Saudi Arabia, traditional friends of the United States. Soviet influence in the area depended primarily on the Steadfastness Front of Syria, Libya, Algeria, South Yemen, the PLO, and Lebanon.

Responding to Syria's request, in October 1980 the USSR agreed to a Treaty of Friendship.[144] The limits of this commitment to Syria were made dramatically clear in 1982, however, as the USSR failed to act in the face of Israel's occupation of much of Lebanon and the subsequent creation of a Phalange-led government. Following a somewhat typical pattern, the Soviets allowed the Syrians to be humiliated and then once the fighting stopped, resupplied their allies, this time with more advanced air defense systems.

Relations with Egypt and Syria—Summary.   The urgency with which the USSR pursued the reestablishment of countervailing power in the region is below what might be expected in a containment strategy. Leaders in the Kremlin could have done much more to compete for influence in Egypt, to encourage Iraqi-Syrian cooperation, or to protect Lebanon. The collapse of the Soviet position among the major Arab powers is a function of many political and cultural differences, but foremost among these variables is the USSR's failure to prove itself a useful ally. Soviet support, although generous in propaganda and arms sales for profit, fell far short of Arab desires and was insufficient to recover occupied territories and protect Syrian forces in Lebanon, much less to challenge Israel proper. Most Western analysts gave the Israeli military a significant edge.[145] Dennis Ross, who in 1983 was deputy director of the Office of Net Assessments, U.S. Department of Defense, concluded that the Israeli edge was so impressive that any forces that even the Soviet Union could introduce quickly would be no match for the IDF (Israeli Defense Forces). He went on to argue, however, that the USSR could dramatically change this situation by prepositioning forces in Syria or in the longer term by introducing new forces.[146] Evidently

Soviet leaders were unwilling to expend these resources to recoup their losses. Passing up opportunities to regain credibility with the Arabs, they demonstrated only a moderate interest in preserving Soviet influence and did not seem terribly anxious about American diplomacy. U.S. officials may have been inclined to attribute the USSR's "exclusion" to resolute American acts and lack of Soviet opportunities. To do so, however, seems to underestimate Soviet capabilities and discount Moscow's lack of willingness to spend its resources.

While most observers recognized the decline in Soviet influence among key Arab powers, the USSR's activities in Ethiopia and South Yemen deeply alarmed American analysts. Many interpreted the behavior as an effort to improve Soviet abilities to interdict Western oil supplies.

The Ethiopian-Somali Conflict. The USSR's activity in the horn of Africa contrasted with its reluctance to compete for influence in Egypt, Iraq, and Lebanon. The Soviet airlift to Ethiopia that accelerated in December 1977 was massive and shocked Western analysts who had underestimated Soviet power and attributed its previous five years of relative decline to lack of capability.[147] The unpleasant reminder that the USSR was a superpower capable of large-scale regional intervention in the Middle East so alarmed many Americans that a great deal of attention was riveted on the level of activity which indicated a substantial Soviet commitment. Less time seemed to be devoted to strategic analysis—that is, determining whether the activity that indicated an urgency unexpected in detente was consistent with a containment or revisionist strategy.

The forces for change in eastern Africa, like revolution in Ethiopia and irredentism in Somalia, developed independently of Soviet behavior. The USSR did not instigate the Ethiopian revolution, nor did the revolution cause an immediate break in U.S.-Ethiopian relations.[148] Despite increasing radicalism in Ethiopia, the United States continued to provide Ethiopia with military aid for several years after the revolution. Once Major Mengistu Haile Mariam announced in February 1977 that he would seek aid from the Soviet Union, U.S. aid stopped.[149] The Ethiopians' decision to escalate the revolutionary tenor of their Marxist-Leninist rhetoric and the Americans' decision to dissociate themselves from the Mengistu regime created an opportunity for Soviet involvement.

In early 1977 the Soviet Union attempted to construct a new socialist alliance joining Ethiopia, Somalia, South Yemen, and soon-to-be-independent Djibouti. It sponsored trips to the region by both Fidel Castro and President Podgorny in an effort to persuade Somalia and Ethiopia to align with each other and with the Soviet Union.[150] While promising arms to Ethiopia, it withheld deliveries in the spring and early summer as it worked to produce Somali acceptance and restraint. On May 6, Moscow received the Ethiopian head of state, Mengistu Haile

Mariam, and signed a Treaty of Friendship and Cooperation; it also announced that the USSR supported the territorial status quo in the horn of Africa and denounced foreign efforts to dismember Ethiopia. Somalia, however, continued to support armed forces in the Ogaden region, with major fighting beginning in May. In July the United States indicated it was willing to supply Somalia but quickly qualified the offer, refusing aid while Somali-backed forces were in the Ogaden.[151] Somalia, nevertheless, received arms and money from a variety of regional countries including Egypt, Saudi Arabia, Iraq, Syria, and Iran.[152] By August the Soviet effort was widely seen as a failure, as deliveries to Ethiopia escalated and Soviet newspapers like *Izvestia* accused Somalia of invasion.[153]

After ten months of trying to construct a federation, the USSR evidently gave up the effort, stopped deliveries to Somalia, accepted the Somali decision of November 13 which was to abrogate the Soviet-Somali Treaty and expel Soviet personnel, and then threw its full weight behind Ethiopia. With a massive airlift of arms and Cuban troops in December and January, the USSR was able to help Ethiopia reverse the battlefield trends and force a Somali withdrawal to the internationally recognized territorial status quo.

The Soviet interest in a socialist federation in the horn of Africa and the Gulf of Aden became clear in early 1977 and coincided with a low point in the USSR's relations with the major Arab powers. Egypt had already abrogated its treaty with the Soviet Union and had formed a defense pact with the Sudan and Saudi Arabia. Syria was in a political-military union with Egypt. Soviet relations with Libya had only just begun. At the same time, the United States was pressing its human rights campaign in Eastern Europe and suggesting SALT proposals that the Soviets refused even to discuss. Saudi Arabia with American backing was working to construct an agreement between the Sudan, North Yemen, and Somalia. In June, President Carter declared his intention to "aggressively challenge" the Soviet Union's influence in Somalia.[154] Consequently, a containment model would expect a determined Soviet effort to offset some of the regional leverage lost in Egypt and Syria by striving to reinforce its countervailing influence in eastern Africa. The USSR's attempt to complement its Somali and South Yemeni ties with a relationship to Ethiopia posed real risks for the Soviets, as President Carter's overtures to Somalia made clear.

The Soviets' decision to court Ethiopia jeopardized not only their alliance with Somalia but also their alliance with Iraq, which was the only major Arab power the USSR was still supplying with weapons. When the Somalis expelled the Soviets in November, it appeared that the Soviet Union's position in the horn of Africa might be lost. On the Ogaden plateau, the Somalis were meeting with military success and enjoyed U.S. support for an autonomy plan. The Eritreans, who were backed by the Sudan, Egypt, and other Arabs, including Iraq, were gaining control in the north.[155] The attempt at *pax Sovietica* had gone bust, with the USSR losing its facilities in Somalia and inheriting a disintegrating Ethiopia in dire straits.

At this point, leaders in Moscow evidently saw great risks in not moving decisively. The USSR launched its massive airlift in December and moved quickly to secure first the Ogaden, and then Eritrea. The support of Ethiopia against Somalia, an Arab League member, further alienated the Soviet Union from major Arab powers. Even more costly, however, was the USSR's role in attacks on the Eritreans. At a time when the Soviet Union might have been able to capitalize on Arab reactions to Sadat's initiative and regain its regional leverage in the Arab world, the crushing of Eritrean resistance brought about universal Arab and Islamic condemnation of the USSR.[156] Moshe Dayan's announcement that Israeli advisers were also aiding the Ethiopian attacks on the Eritreans only further illustrated how incompatible the Soviet position in Ethiopia was with plans to win back Arab confidence.[157]

Many Americans saw the Soviet airlift not as a determined effort to salvage regional influence after a strategic near-fiasco but rather as part of a calculated plan to increase the threat to Western oil supplies. The USSR's behavior was often described as improving the Soviet Union's regional leverage and consistent with a revisionist strategy. While it is unlikely that Soviet decision making is as rational and nonincumbered by bureaucratic momentum as this argument would imply, the greatest weakness of this position is that it ignores the regional context of the Soviet move and the other options open to the USSR. The most obvious way for Soviet leaders to enhance their leverage in the area was to support Somalia and the Eritreans, not Ethiopia. In mid-1977 the Western Somali Liberation Front and the Eritrean Liberation Front were achieving success and Ethiopia was incapable of reversing the military tide. By backing these liberation fronts, the USSR could have retained its traditional allies and put itself on the same side as the primary Arab powers. Moreover, given Ethiopia's weakness, it is possible the Soviets could have forced an Ethiopian concession to a new federation with Eritrean and West Somali autonomy, or left a landlocked rump Ethiopia militarily defeated and economically destroyed. Rather than sponsoring these changes, the USSR intervened to prevent territorial and political revision and thus further damaged its reputation in powerful Arab capitals.

If the USSR had been committed to dominating the horn of Africa, then its failure to press the advantage over Somalia is also difficult to explain. In March 1978 President Barre was forced to announce Somali withdrawal from the Ogaden, as Ethiopia, with Soviet aid, had captured a decisive upper hand. The Soviet Union guaranteed safe passage for Somali withdrawal. It did not use the opportunity to intimidate Barre and force a Somali acceptance of the original federation plan of the previous March. It also repeatedly promised that Ethiopian forces would not cross Somali frontiers.[158]

There may be a number of reasons why the USSR did not push the

Ethiopian advantage either to compel Barre's acquiescence or to produce his ouster, but the restraint is not easily attributed to lack of
opportunity. The Ethiopian military edge was substantial, and American threats to aid Somalia largely incredible. Somali forces were not
trained to use American weapons, and the supply of surplus Soviet
weapons from U.S. clients like Egypt, Saudi Arabia, and the Sudan
could not match Soviet supplies to Ethiopia. Moreover, the United
States had no proxy forces to offer Somalia to match the Cubans and
instead confronted strong opposition from its regional friends such as
Israel and Kenya. Additionally, there were significant domestic constraints, as Congress expressed considerable reservation. In Somalia
President Barre was vulnerable to domestic opposition and could have
possibly been overthrown if the Soviets had been so inclined. In April
1978, for example, there was a coup attempt against Barre evidently led
by elements in the armed forces and by Ogaden clans angry at Barre's
defeat and his inability to sustain weapon deliveries from the Soviet
Union or elsewhere.[159] There were no reports of Soviet involvement in
this attempt, nor were there any open efforts to support it.

A final problem with describing the Soviet commitment to Ethiopia
as part of a calculated effort to enhance Moscow's regional leverage is
its effect on South Yemen. The Soviet decision to back Ethiopian rather
than Somali and Eritrean forces strained relations with even its smallest
and most dependent Arab client. During the airlift Aden became a
staging ground for Soviet deliveries to Addis Abba, further complicating
already difficult internal South Yemeni politics. Reportedly, President
Salem Robea Ali, although traditionally aligned with the Soviet Union,
opposed its role in eastern Africa, especially in Eritrea.[160] These South
Yemeni concerns had little effect, as Ali was overthrown and killed in
June 1978. Succeeding him was Abdul Fatah Ismail.

Ismail and Ali reportedly disagreed on a number of issues such as
the degree of centralized organization, relations with Saudi Arabia, and
ties to North Yemen. They also reflected personal, factional, and tribal
differences. Although both expressed strong interest in relations with
the USSR, it was reported that they disagreed on South Yemen's role in
facilitating Soviet aid to Ethiopia.[161] What role this issue played in the
back-to-back murders of the presidents of North and South Yemen is
hard to assess. What role the Soviets might have played is also a controversial issue about which there are more conjectures and assumptions
available than there is evidence.[162] In any case, the struggle itself highlighted the difficulties the Ethiopian adventure was causing in Soviet-
Arab relations. Iraqi leaders, for example, blamed and condemned the
USSR for the events in Yemen, tying them to the April coup in Afghanistan and Communist party activity in Iraq. Since the USSR at the time
was diplomatically encouraging Iraqi-Syrian cooperation and trying to
capitalize on Arab reaction to "Sadat's defection," its behavior in Ethiopia hardly seemed part of a calculated plan for regional advantage.

Conflict Between North and South Yemen.   Following the Soviets' expulsion from Somalia, access to facilities in the Gulf of Aden became more important for Soviet naval and air reconnaissance in the Indian Ocean. As could be expected if it were pursuing a containment strategy, the USSR moved to upgrade South Yemeni facilities. This aroused special concern in Washington in late 1978 and early 1979 when fighting broke out between North and South Yemen, and more significantly, when the shah of Iran was overthrown by revolution. The Carter administration charged the Soviet Union with trying to destabilize North Yemen and in turn threatening Saudi Arabia and Western oil supplies. To counter the perceived threats and to reassure Saudi Arabia of American resolve after the events in Iran, it committed $200 million to the Yemen Arab Republic.[163] When the fighting intensified, the United States, in conjunction with Saudi Arabia, sent forces to the area and through emergency legislation committed another $390 million to the Yemen Arab Republic.[164] While much of the alarm in Washington was fueled by events in Iran, the conflict in Yemen was widely perceived as part of a Soviet strategy begun in Ethiopia. As in the Ethiopian case, however, making a strategic assessment of the USSR's activity in South Yemen is not so easy.

The conflicts on the southern Arabian peninsula derive from a complex set of tribal and political differences. It is difficult to decipher the exact dynamic of the fighting that erupted in early 1979, and it is not clear who initiated the violent episode. The reports on Soviet involvement are also confused. Analysts close to the scene, who generally suspect Soviet mischief, argued that the USSR appeared to be "surprised" at the outbreak of fighting.[165] Saudi Arabia, widely rumored to have orchestrated the assassination of North Yemeni President Ibrahim al-Hamdi in October 1977 and known to keep South Yemeni tribal dissidents on retainer, may also have been instrumental in the border war.[166] It clearly worked to persuade the Carter administration to subsidize the Saudi involvement in North Yemen which for many North Yemenis was seen as patronizing and unpopular interference.

Because the episode coincided with the collapse of the shah in Iran, American officials were anxious to demonstrate a continuing U.S. commitment to the region and to reestablish credibility with Saudi Arabia. One official called it "the proving ground" of the U.S. commitment to the Middle East and Persian Gulf.[167] The impulse to show strength was strong, independent of Soviet behavior. The actual evidence that the USSR was responsible for the fighting or was trying to intimidate Saudi Arabia was quite unclear.

The Soviet Union did not provide South Yemen with a military edge over North Yemen, as might be expected in a revisionist strategy. While U.S. government estimates of the Soviet aid to South Yemen were not made public, independent observers of the military balance described a rough parity between the two Yemens and a rather impressive advantage

Table 6. Military Forces in the Yemen Conflict, 1978–1981

	South Yemen	North Yemen	Saudi Arabia
1978–1979			
Army	19,000	36,000	45,000
Tanks	260	220	75
Aircraft	34	26	171
1980–1981			
Army	22,000	30,000	31,000
Tanks	375	860	100
Aircraft	111	49	136

Sources: *The Military Balance 1978–1979* (London: IISS), pp. 41–44; *The Military Balance 1980–1981*, pp. 47–50.

to the Yemen Arab Republic if Saudi forces were considered.[168] Table 6 provides a rough illustration of the forces.

Not only is there little evidence of a Soviet move to amass an intimidating military force, but also prominent American analysts were arguing that at the time the USSR was trying to court the Saudis, not intimidate them.[169] In early 1979 the Soviet Union was encouraging the Baghdad Arrangement that included Saudi Arabia. While the Soviets might have conceived of the Yemeni conflict as a source of leverage vis-à-vis Riyadh, sponsoring such an affair risked further alienation of Iraq and thus jeopardizing the core Syrian-Iraqi relationship producing Saudi participation. Moreover, Soviet leaders did not encourage South Yemen to persist, as might be expected if it had been trying to unnerve Saudi Arabia, but rather applauded the March cease-fire and the subsequent Yemeni plans for union.[170] Instead of subverting North Yemen, the USSR offered it aid and, much to the Carter administration's frustration, the government in Sana accepted. The United States rushed $540 million of security assistance to stop "Soviet-sponsored aggression" but within a year North Yemen was receiving more military assistance from the USSR than from the United States.[171] While the Soviet aid undermined simplistic interpretations of the previous fighting, the ouster and arrest of President Ismail in April 1980 reemphasized the importance of internal determinants and the danger of interpreting South Yemeni politics exclusively as a function of Soviet decisions. President Ali Nasser Mohammed, while remaining closely aligned to the Soviet Union, actively sought to reinforce South Yemen's regional relations, making early overtures to Saudi Arabia.[172]

The publicly available evidence concerning Soviet behavior in southern Arabia, while not conforming to the expectations of a revisionist model, is consistent with what could be predicted by a containment model. The Soviet Union had maintained positive relations with South Yemen throughout the 1970s and after the expulsion from Somalia could be expected to reinforce its facilities in the area and access to them. It is not known how much aid the USSR provided South Yemen before violence erupted in early 1979, but the major escalation of support occurred after this time in the fall when South Yemen was admitted as a honorary member of the Warsaw Pact and was given observer status in the CMEA.[173] By October when the Soviet government signed a twenty-year Treaty of Friendship with South Yemen, the Baghdad arrangement had collapsed and the U.S. regional position had been substantially improved by the signing of the Camp David Accords. U.S. weapons and financial aid were arriving in Egypt in greatly increased quantities and the American search for military facilities in the region was reaching fruition.[174] At the same time, the estrangement between the USSR and Iraq grew wider as Iraq increasingly aligned with Saudi Arabia, and American officials entertained the possibilities of declaring common cause with Iraq.

Active Soviet involvement is not identical to revisionism. To treat it as such is simply to abandon the serious analysis of strategy. In 1979 the Soviet Union was certainly involved in the Middle East and at times actively committed, but its behavior did not conform to the predictions of a revisionist model. The pattern of Soviet behavior across the region to the contrary, was more consistent with plausible expectations of a containment model. The Soviet Union exhibited a low-to-moderate commitment to the preservation of its relations with the major Arab powers, as would be expected of a relaxed containment or detente model. As it demonstrated in Ethiopia and South Yemen, however, the USSR would not accept its exclusion from the region and would commit itself to maintaining countervailing power. The activity in the southern Arabian peninsula particularly alarmed Americans because of its proximity to oil supplies and the collapse of the shah. When the USSR's active support of Ethiopia and South Yemen was coupled with the revolutionary changes in Iran and the Soviet invasion of Afghanistan, many were convinced that the Soviets were committed to a strategy of revisionism in the area. Consequently, Soviet behavior in Southwest Asia requires special consideration: does it corroborate this interpretation?

Southwest Asia

In late December 1979 the Soviet Union invaded Afghanistan, sending 100,000 troops and five military divisions to occupy the country. The commitment evidenced in the Soviet act stood in stark contrast to the "relaxation" hoped for in a decade begun with talk of detente. Although the invasion provoked widespread condemnation, it did not affect fundamentally the American debate over Soviet policy.[175] Two interpretations regarding motivation were advanced, each with a clear strategic proposition. For some, the invasion was part of a larger Soviet design to gain leverage over the oil supplies in the Persian Gulf. Control of Afghanistan was seen as another step, along with those in Ethiopia and South Yemen, toward securing control of the flow of oil and in turn decisive influence vis-à-vis Western Europe and Japan. The invasion, in this picture, was described as indicative of the revisionist model reflecting the preliminary stages in an attempt to force a U.S. retreat.[176]

Another explanation of the invasion emphasized defensive motives. It said the attack was consistent with what could be expected of a nation following a containment strategy.[177] In this analysis, the Soviet application of "the Brezhnev Doctrine" to Asia prevented a loss of Soviet influence in Kabul and secured Afghanistan as a continuing Soviet client. Observers taking this view put the invasion in the context of Sino-American rapprochement and argued that a containment strategy would entail decisive Soviet commitments to preserving the USSR's influence in Southwest Asia and particularly in Afghanistan and India. As with proponents of the first view, however, these analysts agreed that Soviet efforts to control Iran or the Persian Gulf would go beyond the limits of containment and reveal a revisionist strategy. Consequently, to evaluate the relevance of the competing strategic models, we must consider Soviet behavior vis-à-vis both Afghanistan and Iran.

The Invasion of Afghanistan. The Soviet invasion imposed significant changes on Afghanistan but did not force the United States to retreat from a previous position of influence. The USSR had enjoyed a preeminent place in Afghan foreign policy throughout most of the postwar period. The relationship became noticeably closer after the rise of Prince Daoud in 1973, although it waned somewhat in 1976–1978 as Daoud accepted greater Iranian involvement and reduced Parchami participation.[178] When the Khalq seized power in April 1978, they quickly reinforced Afghani-Soviet ties and signed a Treaty of Friendship in December.

Although the April coup interrupted the Iranian-Afghani rapprochement and led to a stronger strategic and ideological relationship between Afghanistan and the USSR, analysts close to the scene doubted that the Soviet Union was involved.[179] The circumstantial evidence weighs heavily against the conclusion that there was a significant Soviet role in the Khalq's seizure of power. First, Daoud's regime was domestically vulnerable not so much because of improving contact with the shah but rather because of repression, corruption, and economic failure. For some time after the coup there was a degree of tolerance and hopefulness for the new regime, reflecting the lack of regret for the passing of Daoud's rule.[180] Second, the coup was led by the Khalq, which had minimal ties to the USSR, and not by the Parcham which had historically received Moscow's favor. The Soviets seemed surprised by the Khalq's success. In the fall the Khalq began to purge the Parcham elite and arrested many for treason, including Babrak Karmal, who chose to remain in Eastern Europe rather than return for trial. Third, the U.S. government continued to provide substantial aid to Afghanistan, stopping assistance not because of the coup but rather as a result of the murder of U.S. Ambassador Dubs in February 1979 at the hands of Shiite fundamentalists. The seizure coincided with the peak of the Shiite-led revolution in Iran. The ambassador was killed in a rescue attempt launched by Afghani security forces. Spokesmen in Washington accused the Khalq regime and its Soviet advisers of prematurely resorting to force, whereas U.S. officials in Kabul reportedly believed that the Soviets had counseled patience. They attributed the tragedy to confusion among the Afghani leadership.[181]

Whether or not the April coup was caused by Soviet machinations, the USSR welcomed the change and responded favorably to Khalq requests for aid. Initially the "revolution" in Afghanistan may have presented Soviet leaders with an easy decision. A neighboring government showing an affinity for "progressive ideologies" and friendship for the Soviet Union presented itself as an ally in a region where the United States and China supported powers in Iran and Pakistan. If Soviet leaders were concerned about increasing Sino-American cooperation and wanted to develop a security system on their southern frontiers, the inclination to support the new Afghan government would be natural. As the Khalq imposed a "revolution from above," however, the costs of ensuring the regime's survival grew dramatically. Pushing for reforms in landownership, marriage payments, and education, the "revolutionary" regime provoked intense domestic resistance, thus requiring increasing dependence on repression and Soviet assistance.[182] In the face of mounting domestic violence in Afghanistan (as for example among Shiites in Herat in March 1979), the Soviet Union pledged its commitment to resisting alleged "interference" by the United States, China, Pakistan, and now-revolutionary Iran. At the same time, the USSR urged the Khalq to moderate the tempo of change and to seek a broader base of support.[183] By September, what may have appeared in April 1978 as an irresistible opportunity to secure an ally had become a far more expensive and complex decision for leaders in Moscow.

Despite the heavy investment of material aid and political prestige that the USSR had sunk in Afghanistan, it was unable to persuade the Khalq regime to moderate its policies and reach out to opposition elements. Indeed, it was partially because of the visible Soviet aid that the Communist regime was unable to establish its domestic legitimacy. In September the Soviets evidently tried to orchestrate the removal of Vice-President Amin, who was described as the main engine of change. They failed. Amin forces murdered President Taraki and kept up the pace of revolutionary violence.[184] In the following months, Amin resisted Soviet direction in domestic and foreign policy. By the end of the year, internal resistance had become so intense that Western analysts were predicting the imminent collapse of the Amin regime. Soviet decision makers faced the prospect of either a revolution against the Khalq, by forces which would blame the USSR for its previous support of the "Afghan revolution," or a massive increase in Soviet interference. After a failed effort designed either to persuade Amin to follow Soviet advice or to oust him in a coup, leaders in Moscow apparently decided to eliminate the falling Khalq regime and secure the USSR's influence through a Parcham government established on the back of military occupation.[185]

At various moments throughout the postwar era, the leaders of both superpowers have concluded that their influence in a third country can be secured by the use of force. The logic that compels military intervention in the face of a disintegrating alliance is not mysterious nor incompatible with defensive and security concerns. Having risked Soviet prestige in its commitment to Afghanistan, "hawks" in Moscow may well have argued that Soviet credibility was at stake, and that if resolve was not demonstrated on their frontiers, the USSR's respect would be diminished internationally. They could have envisioned uncontrolled change in a narrow bipolar image of the world that defined superpower involvement in zero-sum terms and thus regarded indigenous nationalists as agents of the "enemy."[186] Holding a "child" image of "progressive modernizers" versus "agitating bandits," a faction of Soviet leaders evidently convinced themselves that politics in Afghanistan could be manipulated by decisive military action and that a potential outpost of "American and Chinese" subversion closed.[187]

The Soviet invasion reflects an imperialistic attitude vis-à-vis Afghanistan but does not necessarily prove that the Soviet Union was pursuing a revisionist strategy. The failure to appreciate nationalism in Third World countries and overconfidence in the legitimacy of regimes owing their existence to foreign powers are not unique to Soviet leaders nor to revisionist behavior. Given the context of Afghani politics in late 1979, Soviet calculations most likely concentrated on the strategic risks of not moving and of "losing" Afghanistan, however imperialistic and misplaced these security concerns may have been. Although reinforcing its control of Afghanistan was clearly an aggressive act, the Soviet move in itself could easily be explained by the containment model.

Analysis of the motives behind the Soviet act, however, is not what alarmed U.S. officials. Rather, as Brzezinski reports, "The issue was not what might have been Brezhnev's subjective motives in going into Afghanistan, but the objective consequences of a Soviet military presence so much closer to the Persian Gulf."[188] The Carter administration interpreted the USSR's invasion as establishing the preconditions for a revisionist challenge. It imposed sanctions not to produce a Soviet withdrawal from Afghanistan but instead to deter future Soviet moves toward the Persian Gulf or Indian Ocean. The interpretation of the act became intricately connected to Soviet behavior toward Iran.

Revolution in Iran. Certainly the most significant strategic change in the Persian Gulf during this period was the Iranian revolution and the collapse of the United States' "pillar."[189] This mass revolution from below was quite different from the reforms in Afghanistan imposed from above, and presented enormous opportunities for the Soviet Union. While the force of change was profoundly indigenous and beyond the control of either of the superpowers, the revisionist model would predict active Soviet efforts to ensure the collapse of "America's" shah, and most significantly, to project the influence of the USSR. Actual Soviet behavior during the revolution, however, was more ambiguous than the revisionist model predicted.

Once the Iranian revolution appeared likely to succeed, the Soviet Union applauded its "anti-imperialist" and "anti-American" dimensions. It did little, however, to cause the uprising or perpetuate it. Soviet propaganda was relatively late in recognizing the significance of the mounting opposition in Iran and until late in 1978 refrained from attacking the shah.[190] After all, Moscow enjoyed rather significant economic relations with the shah's regime and even minimal military ties.[191] Moreover, the East European countries, along with the USSR, had courted the shah in the mid-1970s, offering him and his wife honorary degrees and warm receptions in the hope of securing oil supplies. As the revolution mounted, Soviet propagandists initially attributed its force to many of the same factors as did the Western media. They emphasized the dilemmas of "modernizing" a traditional society, unwise investment choices, and widespread corruption. It was quite late into the process before Soviet voices began to highlight the evils of the shah's regime that the revolutionaries had pointed out, such as its despotism, torture, stilted and corrupt economic programs, and dependence on the United States.[192]

Not surprisingly, Soviet propaganda responded favorably to the collapse of U.S. influence in Iran and supported Iranian inclinations to distance themselves from the previous American connection. In mid-November, the Carter administration consistently reaffirmed its commitment to Iran and with increased vigor made it clear that the United States wanted to ensure the shah's tenure.[193] Secretary Brezhnev responded by warning that "any interference, especially military, in the affairs of Iran—a state directly bordering on the Soviet Union—would be regarded by the U.S.S.R. as a matter affecting its security interests."[194] The Soviet media in early 1979 reiterated concern about American interference and warned against a U.S.-orchestrated military coup.[195] Like U.S. warnings against Soviet interference in Afghanistan, and later in Poland, the USSR through its propaganda and diplomacy made clear its interest in change.[196] Its actual role in defending the revolution is uncertain. Although the United States did not attempt the coup that Brzezinski advised, it is unlikely that this decision or Iranian anger at U.S. interference can be wisely attributed to the USSR's self-proclaimed role as the revolution's protector.

The Soviet Union has demonstrated its willingness to support movements that are not communist if they espouse an "anti-imperialist" line and oppose the projection of U.S. influence. In Iran the USSR lent propaganda and some diplomatic support to the revolution, but found it very difficult to court the leaders of the Islamic Republic. Iran's political leaders, following the religious direction of the Ayatollah Khomeini, displayed an open distrust of communism and a commitment to self-reliance that was based on a denunciation of both superpowers.[197] Moreover, they seemed unimpressed by the USSR's self-serving encouragement of Iranian independence from the United States. They insisted on changes in Soviet policy toward Afghanistan and toward Moslems in Central Asia. On these issues the USSR was intransigent. It rejected Iranian requests for a consulate in Dushanbe, and reinforced its aid to the Khalq regime which was intensely hostile to the Khomeini-led government.[198] Soviet policy welcomed the collapse of American influence in Iran but remained uncertain about its attitude toward the religious revolutionaries.

The Soviet Union was not an important cause of the Iranian revolution. As might be expected in either a containment or revisionist strategy, it was happy to see the expulsion of American involvement. When in the fall of 1979 Iran and the United States entertained preliminary efforts to reestablish contacts, Soviet journalists expressed their disappointment with the revolution.[199] While anxious to define itself as a protector of Iran, a role it again claimed after the U.S. hostages were seized in November, the USSR found it difficult to win Iranian sympathy.[200] Its late support for the revolution, its relations with the shah, its influence in Afghanistan, and its policies in Central Asia created enormous obstacles to courting the Islamic government. The proposition that the USSR was committed to expanding its influence in the Persian Gulf by courting revolutionary Iran became more untenable after the Soviets invaded Afghanistan and failed to protect Iran from Iraq's invasion the following year. However, if courting it were not possible, then, according to some observers, the USSR could be committed to intimidating Iran and to projecting its control through coercion.

The revolution presented many opportunities for the USSR to exert a coercive or intimidating influence in Iran. Perhaps the most obvious avenue for Soviet penetration was through ethnic separatism. In 1979 the Turkomen, Kurds, and Arabs (three peoples who are mostly Sunni) all launched efforts to achieve greater regional autonomy and mounted violent resistance to the new government dominated by Shiite fundamentalists.[201] In December 1979 the Azerbaijanis also rose in rebellion, producing serious violence in Tabriz. A revisionist model of Soviet behavior might expect the USSR to exploit these opportunities to weaken Iran and to expand its influence by supporting ethnic disintegration. However, the USSR did not offer aid to any of these movements and refrained from lending even propaganda encouragement. Instead, the Soviet press consistently endorsed a unified Iran and blasted the "instigators" of nationality problems as CIA agents, pro-shah elements, and SAVAK provocateurs.[202]

In the fall of 1979 the Soviets offered a more sympathetic picture of the Kurdish case, depicting Kurdish leaders as representing legitimate, historically rooted national concerns and the government troops as remnants of the shah's "immortal guard."[203] At this time Iranian officials were exploring the reestablishment of trade and military contacts with the United States and the Soviets may have been using the Kurds to exert leverage against Tehran. There are Iranian claims that the USSR delivered material aid to the Kurds but little reliable evidence. Once the hostage crisis began and U.S.-Iranian relations soured drastically, even this propaganda support diminished and the USSR again championed a unified state. In December, when the Azerbaijani movement peaked, the Soviets offered no sympathy. They praised the virtues of a cohesive Iran, and certainly did not encourage the notion of an independent Azerbaijan, especially not adjacent to the Soviet Republic of Azerbaijan.[204]

Although the Kurds, Arabs, or Turkomen, if not the Azerbaijani, all presented inexpensive wedges for Soviet mischief, the national movement that received the greatest Western attention was that of the Baluch. Because the Baluch occupy territory adjacent to the sea, the notion of a pro-Soviet Baluchistan became part of scenarios that connected the USSR's control of Afghanistan to aspirations for a warm-water port. The best organized movements for Baluch independence are in Pakistan, but they also have traditionally been active in Iran, receiving Iraqi support between 1969 and 1975.[205] The Baluch can be seen as an especially inviting ally for the Soviets because of their animosity toward traditional U.S. support of Pakistan and Iran, as well as their subsequent interest in Soviet assistance. Moreover, there is no shortage of Baluch activists that are pro-Soviet and willing to serve as Soviet allies.[206] Additionally, the Baluch are mostly Sunni, and some claim that they share a historical relation with the Arabs. In any case they can be expected to find common cause with many Arabs against the Shiite and Persian regime led by Ayatollah Khomeini. Consequently, a Soviet commitment to Baluch independence might not only enhance Soviet leverage over Iran and Pakistan, but also improve its credibility in the Arab world.

The potential opportunity for Soviet domination of Southwest Asia made the Baluch scenario frightening, even though somewhat implausible. The Baluch in Iran after all were badly outnumbered and could be quickly suppressed by Iranian forces. Perhaps major Soviet aid could make a difference, but the USSR did not support Baluch independence. The Soviets instead consistently called for a solution to Baluch concerns within the existing state frameworks and moved to eliminate one of the strongest voices inflaming the cause of Baluch separatism, Hafizullah Amin.[207] Contrary to Soviet policy, Amin vociforously promoted the notion of a Greater Afghanistan and fueled the sentiments for Pushtun

and Baluch separatism. One of Babark Karmal's first and most noticeable changes upon coming to power was a sharp deescalation in this
rhetoric and a dissociation of Afghanistan from the Baluch issue in
Pakistan.[208] Rather than coinciding with a Soviet effort to foster an
independent Baluchistan, the occupation of Afghanistan, quite the contrary, was at loggerheads with support for Baluch nationalism.

The invasion of Afghanistan created alarm in Washington irrespective of the Soviets' failure to exploit Iran's ethnic vulnerabilities, because of their military ability to act unilaterally. The Soviet Union does
not need Persian Gulf oil, at least not in the short term, but could derive
substantial leverage by denying the oil to the West. By moving forcefully, the USSR could intimidate not only Iran but also Iraq and Saudi
Arabia. In the words of one Defense Department report, they could
"destroy NATO and the American Japanese Alliance without recourse
to war."[209] To implement a strategy of denial, the Soviet Union would
not need to occupy Iran or the oil fields, but simply prevent the flow of
oil from reaching the West. Perhaps the quickest way to achieve this
objective would be to destroy key oil facilities in the gulf. For this task,
the USSR has more than adequate military force with or without the
control of Afghanistan.[210] Air strikes launched from within the Soviet
Union might stop a majority of the flow, send an intimidating signal to
regional parties, and leave no Soviet ground forces in the area. This type
of option might place the United States in the difficult position of
deciding between retaliating directly against the Soviet homeland or
against some innocent third party that happened to be allied to the
USSR. In either case the United States could not defend the oil flow and
at best could only threaten to use questionable deterrents.

Summary. Some analysts have argued that the USSR's failure to move
militarily toward the Persian Gulf is attributable to U.S. deterrence. The
case, however, is not fully convincing. There is no doubt that a Soviet
land invasion of Iran would be a massive endeavor risking great cost,
but the occupation of Iran is not necessary to deny the oil to the
West.[211] It is through the denial that the Soviet Union would derive
leverage. Even the arguments that contend that the United States could
deter this unlikely land attack are not compelling. The Soviets' conventional and logistic advantages in the area are tremendous. While it is
true that the Iranian mountains are formidable and airlift would be
necessary, Iran nevertheless borders on the USSR, while American
forces would need to travel 8,000 miles.[212] Moreover, U.S. forces would
require uninterrupted air and sea lanes, neither of which could be assured if the USSR had determined to fight American forces.[213]

Recognizing the Soviets' conventional and logistic edge, some analysts have argued that the United States could reduce the Soviet opportunity by placing American forces in Iran as a "tripwire."[214] The logic
seems to argue that Soviet forces would be reluctant to kill Americans

because of the probable tie to nuclear escalation. The nuclear option for the United States, however, is not fully credible. For more than twenty years Western deterrence theorists have argued that in an era of mutual assured destruction the resort to nuclear weapons in a contest where the United States has no significant conventional capacity would be suspect. While the dangers associated with killing American troops may truly weigh heavily on the minds of leaders in the Kremlin, the risks of dropping nuclear weapons on Soviet soldiers could be expected to give Washington leaders serious pause. This ought to be especially true for those who perceive Soviet strategic forces as "superior." The credibility problem would be more severe if the USSR were to attack first with rockets and aircraft, which is more likely considering Soviet military doctrine, and U.S. officials after the fact contemplated initiating a nuclear exchange.

Because of the importance that U.S. officials attach to the free flow of oil, Soviet planners would face uncertain risks in attacking the Gulf regardless of the conventional imbalance.[215] Vulnerability and public definitions of "vital interests," however, do not insure a credible extension of deterrence. Comparisons between the Truman and Carter Doctrines are not appropriate, not so much because of dissimilar regional capabilities, but because of the changed strategic environment in which the USSR has achieved nuclear parity.[216] If the United States through nuclear engagement is required to put at stake interests more dear than those in the Persian Gulf, the credibility of this option is likely to be diminished. It might be noted that if the USSR is unwilling to risk the dangers associated with attacking a U.S. 'tripwire," it seems unlikely that it might risk a direct strike on the American mainland as postulated in the "window of vulnerability" argument.

The Soviet Union may be waiting for still greater opportunities to exert its influence in Iran; future Soviet policy may be more active. (Of course, this teleological argument cannot really be tested.) This sound precaution makes good sense in policy terms, but is not an adequate explanation for current behavior. Speculation on future possibilities should not be used to dismiss the behavioral evidence to date. The USSR's failure to seize the advantages already at hand reflects a rather low commitment to policies that might be expected in a revisionist strategy. It has not demonstrated a significant commitment to courting or to intimidating Iran, even when offered a number of opportunities to do both.

For example, while failing to defend Iran against Iraq in late 1980, the Soviet Union at the same time refused to support Iraq. The Iraqi attack on Khuzistan presented an opportunity for the USSR to coerce Iran and project its influence into the Persian Gulf. Because of Arab concerns about the Khomeini-led government, such support might both smooth the troubled relationship with Iraq and simultaneously please and intimidate Saudi Arabia and the smaller gulf states. The USSR, however, did not seriously involve itself in this conflict and instead simply lamented the turmoil that invited "U.S. manipulation."[217] Its behavior seemed to show a concern with the containment or reduction of U.S. influence more than with the expansion of Soviet power.

The USSR exhibited great commitment to enhancing its influence in Afghanistan, but the invasion was not correlated with significant efforts to gain control of Western access to Persian Gulf oil. Soviet behavior toward Iran may in the future demonstrate revisionist motives, but in the 1979–1980 period it can more plausibly be described as conforming to the containment model. The USSR, while always applauding and encouraging the decline of U.S. influence, failed to exploit any number of political or military opportunities to expand its own. Attributing Soviet inaction to U.S. deterrence may not be a compelling argument in this case. The potential strategic gains of acting were significant, while the costs in terms of U.S. threats of retaliation were uncertain. Resistance by regional powers, although a credible possibility, could be mitigated by moving through Iraq or deterred by an awesome display of Soviet power. In any case, the Soviet Union's unwillingness to take the possible risks or expend significant resources in order to exploit opportunities in Iran seems to indicate a rather marginal commitment to revisionism and stands in contrast to its aggressive determination to control Afghanistan. The behavior of the USSR in Southwest Asia conforms more easily to the predictions of a containment model than revisionism. This suggests that active Soviet involvement in Afghanistan, as well as in South Yemen and Ethiopia, may be more adequately explained as driven by defensive concerns than expansionist aspirations.

Conclusion

Both verbal and behavioral evidence suggests that the perceptions of the United States prevailing in Moscow had changed substantially between 1972 and 1979. The predominant image of the United States resembled the "enemy" stereotype in 1979 more closely than in 1972 and revealed a heightened sense of threat. Although the imagery had become noticeably less complex, especially in the description of U.S. motives and decisional process, it still included more differentiation than in 1967, suggesting that the perceived threat had increased, but was still less intense than in 1967. As in the other two periods, the picture of the United States prevailing in the Soviet media had little in common with the "degenerate" stereotype. Contrary to the pessimistic conclusions of some American analysts, it did not depict the United States as weak of will. Figure 6 summarizes the analysis of imagery.

Through its strategic behavior, the Soviet Union demonstrated in 1979 that it too had the will and capacity to act. The relaxed atmosphere in which geopolitical competition might take less priority had not

Figure 6. The Prevailing Soviet Image of the United States, 1979

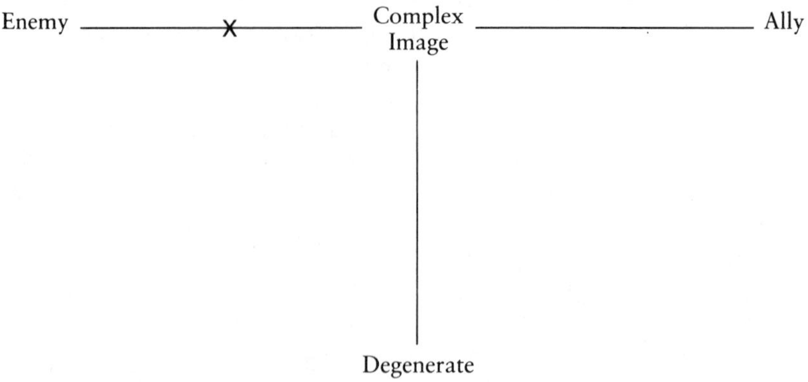

Enemy ——————×—————— Complex ——————————— Ally
                                    Image

                                      |
                                      |
                                      |
                                      |
                                      |
                                      |

                              Degenerate

Summary of Evidence by Dimension	Degree of Resemblance to Stereotypes	
	Enemy	Degenerate
Motivation	Moderate to High	Low
Capabilities and Power	Moderate	Low
Decisional Process	Moderate	Low

been achieved as the advocates of detente and ostpolitik had hoped. Rather, the Soviet Union demonstrated a major commitment to weapons development, diplomacy in Europe, involvement in the horn of Africa, and intervention in Afghanistan. The simple recognition of Soviet commitment, however, does not constitute analysis of strategy. When considering Soviet behavior in four arenas of conflict—the development of strategic nuclear weapons, Central Europe, the Middle East, and Southwest Asia,—I have tried to evaluate the resemblance between the USSR's actions and the plausible expectations of the containment and the revisionist strategic models. The conclusions of the relevant case studies are summarized in table 7.

In none of the four arenas was the evidence consistent with predictions of the revisionist model; instead, it fulfilled the expectations of the containment hypothesis. In the area of nuclear weapons, the USSR's high commitment did not translate into a clear drive for superiority. Because Western strategists argue that superiority can be linked to defensive aims, the nuclear arms race itself must be discounted as a base for drawing inferences about motivation. In Europe, Soviet diplomacy was actively committed to carrying on "business as usual" and to preservation of detente, although reluctant to accept change in Eastern Eu-

Table 7. Soviet Foreign Policy Behavior, 1979: Degree of Resemblance to Two Strategic Models

	Containment		Revisionism		
	Degree of Resemblance to Model	Degree of Commitment	Degree of Resemblance to Model	Degree of Commitment	Credibility of Deterrent
Nuclear Weapons	High	High	—	—	High
Central Europe	High	High	Moderate	Low	Moderate
Middle East	Moderate	Moderate	Low	Low	Moderate to Low
Southeast Asia	Moderate	Moderate	Moderate	Low	Moderate to Low

rope. While consistent with the containment hypothesis, the USSR's interest in preserving the status quo in Europe could be connected to its behavior in the Middle East and Persian Gulf. The rationale for seeing this connection is that in the revisionist model Soviet efforts in Europe could be interpreted as a "holding action" while the USSR expands its influence and gains decisive leverage in the Third World. However, a consideration of the USSR's behavior in the Arab Middle East, the horn of Africa, South Yemen, Afghanistan, and Iran, does not sustain the revisionist proposition. In both the Middle East and Southwest Asia, the containment model provides a more plausible description of Soviet behavior.

The evidence from words and deeds suggests that prevailing Soviet perceptions of the United States in 1979 may be described best as defensive and Soviet policy as committed to containment. These conclusions indicate that in 1979 the Soviets regarded the United States with fear and concluded that U.S. capability was roughly comparable to their own. There is no evidence that prevailing leaders perceived opportunities in American weakness or were motivated by expansionism. To the contrary, an intensified sense of threat may have stimulated Soviet commitments to self-defense; this possibility lends support to the interpretation that emphasizes security motives.

Chapter 6

Theories of Motivation and Soviet Foreign Policy

THIS BOOK began by arguing that attributing motives is essential to political analysis and pointed out the importance of theories concerning Soviet aims in U.S. foreign policy. It has had two purposes: first, to contribute to the empirical study of the motives underlying foreign policy behavior in general, and second, to evaluate the plausibility of contending theories regarding Soviet foreign policy over the past two decades. This last chapter will try to speak to both objectives. First, it will summarize the empirical study of images in Soviet speeches and documents and measure them against actual strategic behavior; then, in light of this evidence, it will evaluate the three competing perspectives on Soviet foreign policy outlined in chapter 1: communist expansionism, realpolitik expansionism, and realpolitik self-defense. By attempting to draw the implications from the empirical findings for each perspective, I will try to reflect on the possible lessons of this study.

The prevailing image of the United States that was described in all three periods resembled the "enemy" stereotype more than it did the "degenerate" stereotype. In 1967 the imagery in Soviet statements was found to be rather simplistic and extreme. In 1972 it became noticeably more complex and less stereotypical. In 1979–1980 it again took on more characteristics of a stereotype. The trend in the Communist spokesmen's imagery of the United States is summarized in figure 7.

Chapter 2 introduced the problem of sampling the Soviet media as well as the difficulty of treating different voices as a common source. The first problem concerns the reliability of published statements, while the second concerns the dangers of simplification and distortion. The problem of reliability is particularly worrisome. Because so much is written in the Soviet press, it is possible to find contradictory passages and different quotations to support both the "enemy" and "degenerate" stereotypes. An analyst with a preconceived viewpoint might be inclined to see only those passages that support one view or another, and might select quotations that give a misleading impression because they represent exceptions, not the rule. To be more confident that the analysis of Soviet images presented above is reliable and reflects the prevailing

Figure 7. Prevailing Soviet Perceptions of the United States, 1967–1979

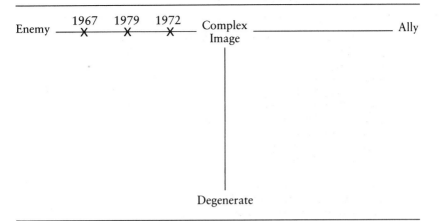

Soviet view of the 1970s, I consulted a study of how members of the Politburo saw the United States during that period. The data base for this study included every speech or article that a Politburo member delivered or signed from 1970 to 1978.[1] The speeches were broken down and coded into subjects or themes by three independent coders who achieved better than 75 percent intercoder reliability. Because this data was not collected by the author and is organized according to items that can be combined to resemble images, it provides an excellent basis for testing the reliability of my conclusions about the prevailing image of the United States among Soviet leaders during the 1970s.

Politburo members do not speak very often about the decisional process in the United States, and when they do, they concentrate mostly on objectives and motives. This creates something of a problem in testing and measuring the stereotypes. The data base does not tell us about Soviet views of U.S. decision making; it is confined primarily to the motivational aspect of the stereotype. Because the theory of perception underpinning this approach assumes that attributions about motives are at the center of one nation's leaders' perception of another nation, this limitation, while regrettable, may be tolerated. Table 8 lists the subjects and themes identified in Politburo speeches and statements from which the study drew its conclusions about the stereotypes dominating the perceptions of Soviet leaders.

Of all the Politburo members, those who had the most to say about the United States and Soviet foreign policy were First Secretary Brezhnev, Defense Minister Grechko, Foreign Minister Gromyko, Secretary Kirilenko, Chairman of the Council of Ministers Kosygin, Boris Ponomarev (chief of the International Department), Secretary Suslov, and Defense Minister Ustinov. To focus the analysis, the study treated these members as a subgroup whose views on foreign policy would reflect

Table 8. Themes and Subjects in Politburo Statements That Refer to the United States as an Enemy or Degenerate Nation, 1971–1978

Items Contributing to the "Enemy" Stereotype
    Imperialism
    Imperialists
    Imperialist aggression
    Imperialist forces
    Imperialist foreign policy
    Imperialist intervention in other nations
    Imperialist policies
    Imperialist subversion
    Bankruptcy of imperialism
    Neocolonialism
    Capitalist exploitation
    Capitalist exploitaton of the Third World
    Antisocialist behavior by West
    Attempts to drive a wedge between socialist nations
    U.S. espionage
    U.S. violation of Basic Principles
    U.S. violation of 1972 agreements
    U.S. policy of peace through strength
    U.S. military strategy as drive for superiority
    U.S. feeling of superiority to other nations
    Anti-Soviet feeling in the United States
    Anticommunist tendencies in the United States
    Reactionary forces in the United States

Items Contributing to the "Degenerate" Stereotype
    Corruption in the United States and the West
    Economic problems in the United States and the West
    Moral crises in the United States and the West
    Political problems in the United States and the West
    Racial conflicts in the United States and the West
    Social problems in the United States and the West
    Spiritual disintegration of the United States
    Weakness and declining military effectiveness of the United States
    Economic upheavals in the West
    Internal problems in the West
    Soviet military superiority
    Soviet moral superiority

Source: Philip Stewart, "Foreign Policy Perceptions of the Soviet Politburo in the 1970s: Analysis and Data for Final Report," unpublished, Department of Political Science, Ohio State University, 1981.

prevailing images.[2] To determine which stereotype would best capture the images of the United States, the study considered all the references by these members to any of the items contributing to either stereotype. Taking all items pertaining to the United States, whether defined as "enemy" or "degenerate," as 100 percent, tables 9 and 10 present the

Table 9. Image of the United States as an Enemy Nation Held by Politburo Members, 1971–1978 (in percent)

	1971	1972	1973	1974	1975	1976	1977	1978	WX[a]	X[b]
Brezhnev	100	100	98	80	83	93	79	79	89	89
Grechko	100	97	97	93	33	—	—	—	97	84
Gromyko	—	67	—	93	100	94	68	78	83	83
Kirilenko	100	97	100	89	100	88	80	100	94	95
Kosygin	100	95	100	83	92	57	100	83	87	89
Ponomarev	100	100	81	—	96	100	100	100	97	97
Suslov	100	100	77	100	81	100	90	91	90	92
Ustinov	—	—	100	100	100	88	96	93	92	96
Andropov[c]	—	—	100	—	—	—	100	—	100	100
WX	100	98	93	90	88	92	87	87		
X	100	94	94	91	86	89	89	89		
Total N[d]	121	107	223	151	112	148	129	136		

Source: Philip Stewart, "Foreign Policy Perceptions of the Soviet Politburo in the 1970s: Analysis and Data for Final Report," unpublished, Department of Political Science, Ohio State University, 1981.

a. WX includes only those scores for any member or year that are based on an N of 6 or more.

b. X includes the scores of all in the sample who spoke.

c. Andropov is listed although his participation was limited during the decade.

d. Total N for all members = 1,127. N by member: Brezhnev, 228; Grechko, 210; Gromyko, 116; Kirilenko, 56; Kosygin, 109; Ponomarev, 170; Suslov, 97; Ustinov, 70; Andropov, 11.

percentage of each member's image that resembled the "enemy" and "degenerate" stereotypes.

Although the data are not so precise as to justify major inferences from slight variations (such as 5 percent or less), the results suggest at least three findings. First, the preponderant image of the United States offered by all the members in all eight years is that of an enemy. Second, across the decade the "enemy" imagery became less intense, although it was still dominant throughout. Third, items related to the "degenerate" stereotype, while never dominating Politburo attitudes, became more common in the later 1970s. This last observation demands further investigation.

The trend in the direction of the "degenerate" stereotype may simply reflect an increasingly complex view of the United States as the "diabolical enemy" picture relaxes. On the other hand, it may indicate a tendency to discount U.S. capabilities and be related to opportunities perceived by Soviet leaders. The issue will be explored more fully below. Before we turn to a discussion of the relative emphasis given to various foreign policy issues by members of the Politburo during the 1970s, a few words about differences within that body are in order.

Table 10. Image of the United States as a Degenerate Nation Held by Politburo Members, 1971–1978 (in percent)

	1971	1972	1973	1974	1975	1976	1977	1978	WX[a]	X[b]
Brezhnev	0	0	2	20	17	7	21	21	11	11
Grechko	0	3	3	7	67	—	—	—	3	16
Gromyko	—	33	—	8	0	6	32	22	17	17
Kirilenko	0	0	0	11	0	13	20	0	6	6
Kosygin	0	5	0	17	8	43	0	17	13	11
Ponomarev	0	0	19	—	4	0	0	0	3	3
Suslov	0	0	23	0	19	0	10	9	9	8
Ustinov	—	—	0	0	0	13	4	7	8	4
Andropov	—	—	0	—	—	—	0	—	0	0
WX	0	4	12	13	12	10	17	15		
X	0	14	12	13	23	16	17	15		
Total N[d]	121	107	223	151	112	148	129	136		

Source: Philip Stewart, "Foreign Policy Perceptions of the Soviet Politburo in the 1970s: Analysis and Data for Final Report," unpublished, Department of Political Science, Ohio State University, 1981.

    a. WX includes only those scores for any member or year that are based on an N of 6 or more.
    b. X includes the scores of all in the sample who spoke.
    c. Andropov is listed although his participation was limited during the decade.
    d. Total N for all members = 1,127. N by member: Brezhnev, 228; Grechko, 210; Gromyko, 116; Kirilenko, 56; Kosygin, 109; Ponomarev, 170; Suslov, 97; Ustinov, 70; Andropov, 11.

The data suggest some variation in views among Politburo members, but at the same time highlights the sameness. The range across the members with respect to the intensity of the "enemy" imagery, for example, is never as great as the distance between the whole set of "enemy" images and the set of "degenerate" images. If the mean of each member (excluding Andropov because of a small N) across the eight years is rank-ordered, the total spread is 14 percentage points, suggesting probable differences between the likes of Grechko and Brezhnev but simultaneously defining rather narrow parameters. The rank orderings suggest conclusions that are consistent with other research efforts uncovering at least two levels of perceived threat, one observably more intense than the other.[3]

At the same time, the results of this analysis support the decision to focus on a single prevailing Soviet view. At the level of shared images, the "enemy" picture is certainly common. Although differences are evident, they are not so great as to make it impossible to infer a prevailing image from the Politburo spokesmen.

Politburo images of the United States differ in degree, not in direction. The "enemy" image is "shared." These results suggest that it would be wrong either to deny important differences or to exaggerate their character. Just as it is important to recognize differences among Americans who share an "enemy" conception of the USSR, but to different degrees, it may be useful to explore differences among Soviet politicians. At the same time, the range evident within the Politburo is not similar to that encompassed by U.S. groups such as the Committee on the Present Danger and the Committee on East-West Accord. The range is more similar to the variation between recent secretaries of state and national security advisers. Debates are over the intensity of the perceived threat and over the preferred policy options.

Although Politburo members may differ somewhat as to the seriousness of the U.S. threat, the "enemy" image is clearly predominant. The increase in references to the "degeneracy" of the United States toward the end of the period, however, requires further exploration. It runs counter to the imagery presented in the case study which is described as gravitating back toward the "enemy" stereotype. To investigate the explanation for this increasing "degenerate" score, we may find it useful to focus not only on imagery but also on the policies advocated by various Politburo members. The "degenerate" scores may simply reflect the analysts' statistical decision to divide the total image into two categories, leaving out the possibility of complex views. If this is the case, one would not expect a correlation between the "degenerate" image of the United States and a concentration on the development of Soviet armed might. To the contrary, a positive relationship between the "enemy" image and a concentration on an arms policy would be expected. Furthermore, one could expect an inverse relationship between an "enemy" image and an emphasis on detente.

To explore Politburo members' interest in various foreign policy strategies, we will focus on three related policy dimensions: detente, Soviet arms development, and support for liberation movements in "oppressed" nations. The three are not mutually exclusive; it is likely that Soviet leaders conceive of these policies as mutually reinforcing. Differences in emphasis, however, can be expected. A member who regards the United States as a serious threat may be less sanguine about the viability of detente and more confident of the deterrent power of Soviet military might. This member may see detente as a product of the emphasis on Soviet arms. On the other hand, another member may feel less threatened and may favor detente as a means for stabilizing the deterrent relationship. In this perspective, arms development may receive less emphasis, especially when armed conflict between the superpowers is seen as assuring mutual destruction. For this member, reducing the U.S. threat should be accomplished not through bilateral arms competition but by supporting anti-imperialist forces in national liberation movements. Another member may perceive opportunity in American weakness, in which case a "degenerate" image of the United States ought to correlate with a continuing high emphasis on Soviet militariza-

Table 11. Themes and Subjects in Politburo Statements, 1971–1978

Detente
 International detente
 International cooperation
 International security
 Peace in specific countries
 Peaceful competition
 Peaceful coexistence
 Principles of peaceful coexistence
 Cooperation with West
 Detente with West
 Trade with West
 Military detente

Arms Development
 Soviet armed forces
 Soviet defensive capability
 Potential Soviet defense capabilities
 Combat readiness of Soviet troops
 Nuclear war capability
 Conventional war capability

Support for National Liberation Movements
 Anti-imperialist struggle
 Class struggle
 Anti-colonial struggle
 National liberation struggle
 Liquidation of colonialism
 Wars of national liberation

Source: Philip Stewart, "Foreign Policy Perceptions of the Soviet Politburo in the 1970s: Analysis and Data for Final Report," unpublished, Department of Political Science, Ohio State University, 1981.

tion. Other hypothetical combinations are possible, but the pattern in relative emphasis is essentially an empirical question.

The themes and subjects appearing in Politburo members' statements that were used to define the three policy dimensions are summarized in table 11. Considering the total number of references to all three policy areas as 100 percent, table 12 summarizes the proportion of each member's emphasis on detente. Similarly, tables 13 and 14 reflect the relative emphasis upon Soviet arms development and support for national liberation movements, respectively. Table 15 gives the total number of references given in tables 12–14. Figure 8 plots these trends in policy emphasis against the prevalence of the "enemy" and "degenerate" stereotypes during the period.

The data suggest a number of patterns. First, an interest in detente is foremost if the mean score for Politburo responses is plotted for all

Table 12. Emphasis on Detente as a Percentage of Politburo Members' References to Three Foreign Policy Areas, 1971–1978

	1971	1972	1973	1974	1975	1976	1977	1978	WX[a]	X[b]
Brezhnev	88	97	96	93	90	97	90	90	93	93
Grechko	13	30	17	25	23	—	—	—	22	22
Gromyko	—	94	76	88	71	95	99	100	89	89
Kirilenko	70	71	86	92	94	82	100	95	84	86
Kosygin	87	55	91	98	93	100	93	93	89	89
Ponomarev	89	91	81	86	82	96	90	98	89	89
Suslov	85	78	85	90	80	100	81	82	85	85
Ustinov	—	38	70	95	43	34	24	40	49	49
Andropov[c]	71	—	96	89	—	—	67	—	81	81
WX	72	69	78	84	72	86	78	85		
X	72	69	78	84	72	86	81	85		

Source: Philip Stewart, "Foreign Policy Perceptions of the Soviet Politburo in the 1970s: Analysis and Data for Final Report," unpublished, Department of Political Science, Ohio State University, 1981.

a. WX includes only those scores for any member or year that are based on an N of 6 or more. For total N, see table 15.

b. X includes the scores of all in the sample who spoke.

c. Andropov is listed although his participation was limited during the decade.

Table 13. Emphasis on Soviet Arms Development as a Percentage of Politburo Members' References to Three Foreign Policy Areas, 1971–1978

	1971	1972	1973	1974	1975	1976	1977	1978	WX[a]	X[b]
Brezhnev	6	3	2	7	3	2	7	3	4	4
Grechko	85	66	81	72	75	—	—	—	76	76
Gromyko	—	0	24	5	29	0	1	0	10	10
Kirilenko	27	14	9	6	2	0	0	5	9	8
Kosygin	13	41	3	2	3	0	0	6	9	9
Ponomarev	11	0	12	14	0	1	8	0	6	6
Suslov	15	10	5	10	0	0	7	11	7	7
Ustinov	—	63	30	33	52	65	75	60	54	54
Andropov[c]	29	—	0	11	—	—	0	—	10	10
WX	27	28	21	18	21	110	16	12		
X	27	28	21	18	21	10	114	12		

Source: Philip Stewart, "Foreign Policy Perceptions of the Soviet Politburo in the 1970s: Analysis and Data for Final Report," unpublished, Department of Political Science, Ohio State University, 1981.

a. WX includes only those scores for any member or year that are based on an N of 6 or more. For total N, see table 15.

b. X includes the scores of all in the sample who spoke.

c. Andropov is listed although his partipication was limited during the decade.

Table 14. Emphasis on Support for National Liberation Movements as a Percentage of Politburo Members' References to Three Foreign Policy Areas, 1971–1978

	1971	1972	1973	1974	1975	1976	1977	1978	WX[a]	X[b]
Brezhnev	6	0	2	0	7	2	3	6	3	3
Grechko	2	4	2	3	3	—	—	—	3	3
Gromyko	—	6	0	7	0	4	0	0	2	2
Kirilenko	3	14	6	2	6	18	0	0	7	6
Kosygin	0	5	6	0	3	0	7	1	3	3
Ponomarev	0	9	8	0	18	4	2	2	5	5
Suslov	0	12	10	0	20	0	12	7	8	8
Ustinov	—	0	0	3	5	2	0	1	2	2
Andropov[c]	0	—	4	0	—	—	33	—	9	9
WX	2	6	4	2	8	4	8	2		
X	2	6	4	2	8	4	7	2		

Source: Philip Stewart, "Foreign Policy Perceptions of the Soviet Politburo in the 1970s: Analysis and Data for Final Report," unpublished, Department of Political Science, Ohio State University, 1981.

a. WX includes only those scores for any member or year that are based on an N of 6 or more. For total N, see table 15.

b. X includes the scores of all in the sample who spoke.

c. Andropov is listed although his participation was limited during the decade.

Table 15. Total Number of References by Politburo Members to Detente, Soviet Arms Development, and Support for National Liberation Movements, 1971–1978

	1971	1972	1973	1974	1975	1976	1977	1978	Total
Brezhnev	156	152	571	266	320	242	276	290	2,273
Grechko	159	143	335	322	40	0	0	0	999
Gromyko	0	35	21	193	7	44	162	223	685
Kirilenko	30	7	125	88	17	11	6	22	306
Kosygin	45	106	282	109	69	50	86	161	908
Ponomarev	18	33	103	22	62	200	49	53	540
Suslov	27	60	67	59	90	17	57	45	422
Ustinov	0	8	20	39	21	271	354	149	862
Total	442	544	1,549	1,107	626	835	999	943	7,045

Source: Philip Stewart, "Foreign Policy Perceptions of the Soviet Politburo in the 1970s: Analysis and Data for Final Report," unpublished, Department of Political Science, Ohio State University, 1981.

Note: Totals for Andropov are not given because of his limited participation during the decade.

Figure 8. Trends in Soviet Policy Emphasis and References to the "Enemy" and "Degenerate" Stereotypes of the United States, 1971–1978 (in percent)

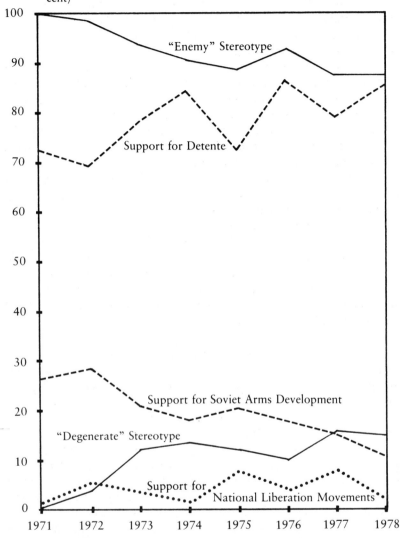

Source: Philip Stewart, "Foreign Policy Perceptions of the Soviet Politburo in the 1970s: Analysis and Data for Final Report," unpublished, Department of Political Science, Ohio State University, 1981.

eight years, and, despite vacillation, it receives increasing emphasis over the period—with the exception of Grechko and Ustinov. Second, the emphasis on arms development is more frequent than the focus on aiding wars of national liberation, and declines, although not evenly, across the decade. Third, endorsements of national liberation movements are not as frequent as positive references to detente and the necessity to build up Soviet arms, and such endorsements follow a rather sporadic path across the decade.

Comparing the studies of images and policy emphasis is not easy. Although the data base is relatively large, the cumulation by year provides only eight observation points, which reduces the utility of a number of techniques for assessing covariation. While statistical conclusions might be inappropriate, the data do lead to a number of observations. If Politburo means are considered, the "enemy" image is highest when the emphasis upon Soviet weapons development is likewise high. The decline in the emphasis on military strength in rough terms corresponds with the decline in references to the United States as an enemy. An inverse relation between "enemy" imagery and the emphasis on detente may prevail. This possibility runs counter to the hypothesis that Soviet inclinations to emphasize arms development derives from an image of the United States as "degenerate" or from a perception of declining American power. The emphasis on arms seems more likely to correspond with heightened perceptions of threat.[4]

The different policy emphasis within the Politburo can be seen when the members are rank-ordered by policy dimension. Table 16 presents the mean across the eight years for each member. The ordering at both ends of the scale remains basically the same for all eight years, with Brezhnev and Ponomarev leaders in support for detente and Ustinov and Grechko always lowest on the detente issue and leaders in emphasizing arms development.

Comparing Soviet Politburo members' relative emphasis on the "enemy" and "degenerate" stereotypes with their policy priorities has interesting implications for this study's basic hypotheses regarding Soviet leaders' perceptions of the United States. First, those members who most emphasize U.S. "degeneracy" are also those who stress the importance of detente. Second, those who most stress Soviet arms development are least likely to regard the United States as "degenerate." This pattern suggests that the growth of the "degenerate" stereotype is more likely to represent a movement toward greater complexity in Soviet perceptions of the United States than an inclination to discount American will power. The emphasis on building up Soviet arms is not related to references to U.S. "degeneracy" and does not support the hypothesis that the Soviets' emphasis on weapons development results from a perception of American weakness. To the contrary, the patterns suggest that those members who emphasize Soviet arms most are least sensitive to the vulnerabilities and weaknesses in the United States. Those who do hold a more complex picture recognizing both America's strengths and weaknesses are most inclined to emphasize detente.[5]

Comparing the Politburo members' emphasis on supporting national liberation movements with their images of the United States bolsters the previous arguments. Those most apt to see the United States as "degenerate," such as Gromyko and Kosygin, put the least emphasis

Table 16. Rank Ordering of Politburo Members' Scores on Imagery and Policy
Emphasis, 1971–1978

Stereotyped Images of the United States		Policy Emphasis	
"Enemy"		**Support for Detente**	
Grechko	97	Brezhnev	93
Ponomarev	97	Kosygin	89
Kirilenko	94	Gromyko	89
Ustinov	92	Ponomarev	89
Suslov	90	Suslov	85
Brezhnev	89	Kirilenko	84
Kosygin	87	Ustinov	49
Gromyko	83	Grechko	22
		Support for Soviet	
"Degenerate"		**Arms Development**	
Gromyko	17	Grechko	76
Kosygin	13	Ustinov	54
Brezhnev	11	Gromyko	10
Suslov	9	Kirilenko	9
Ustinov	8	Kosygin	7
Kirilenko	6	Suslov	7
Ponomarev	3	Ponomarev	6
Grechko	3	Brezhnev	4
		Support for National	
		Liberation Movements	
		Suslov	8
		Kirilenko	7
		Ponomarev	5
		Brezhnev	3
		Kosygin	3
		Grechko	3
		Gromyko	2
		Ustinov	2

Source: Philip Stewart, "Foreign Policy Perceptions of the Soviet Politburo in the 1970s:
Analysis and Data for Final Report," unpublished, Department of Political Science, Ohio
State University, 1981.

Note: Scores reflect the mean for each member across the decade. Andropov is not
included because of his limited participation during the period.

on aiding the liberation of third countries. Ponomarev and Kirilenko,
who trail in "degenerate" scores, lead in their support for national
liberation struggles. The implication may be that support for interference in other nations is a result of fear of the U.S. threat and, along
with arms development, constitutes a strategy for self-defense. Grechko's
and Suslov's scores suggest that there is a difference of opinion on the
importance of U.S.-Soviet competition in the Third World. Suslov, like
Brezhnev, places equal emphasis on building up arms and supporting

national liberation, while Grechko clearly prefers Soviet arms development. This may reflect only role obligations but could also reflect a more complex picture of the U.S. "enemy" held by Suslov and Brezhnev and a more sophisticated appreciation of the competition between the superpowers for influence in the Third World as being political as well as military.[6]

Stewart's data on Politburo images and policy emphasis generally supports the reliability of the conclusions regarding prevailing Soviet images of the United States described throughout this study. Nevertheless, it is necessary to consider several differences between his analysis and the conclusions outlined in earlier chapters. First, although the Politburo study supports the conclusion that the prevailing Soviet view of the United States conformed to the "enemy" stereotype, it suggests a different trend from that found in the case study. Because Stewart's data base does not include speeches or articles appearing in 1967, it is impossible to confirm the 1967 view described in chapter 3, or to evaluate the change between 1967 and 1972. The scores for the "enemy" image in 1972 must be understood as reflecting the statistical decision to represent only two possibilities: "enemy" and "degenerate." More complex perceptions were not considered. Consequently, the very high "enemy" scores are partially a product of the very low "degenerate" scores. The results show that the view of the United States held by Soviet leaders does not resemble the "degenerate" stereotype, but is not inconsistent with the claim that their views were less stereotypical in 1972 than in 1967.

Second, the trend from 1972 to 1979 toward a less stereotypical view, indicated by the Politburo analysis, contradicts the results of the case study discussed in chapter 5. Two factors might explain this variation. First, the coded data base is complete only through June 30, 1979. Consequently, the imagery found in Politburo statements for late 1979 and early 1980 is not included. It is possible, even plausible given the events of this period, that the trend toward simplification and stereotyping in the Soviet view of the United States came into full force after mid-1979. Second, the coded data base does not include references to the U.S. decisional process. It is in this aspect of the stereotype that the first signs of simplification are likely to be evident. This category was partially responsible for the judgments I reached regarding the 1979 period and explain another portion of the difference between the Politburo data and my study of the period.

Third, although the differences in images illuminated by these two studies are confined to rather narrow parameters, the differences in policy emphases are not. My decision to present a single prevailing image as a "shared image" is supported by the Politburo study, but questioned by its results on variation among members in policies advocated. These differences, however, do not discredit the notion of a prevailing view. The policy differences may be related to disagreements over what instruments to use and to the various roles played by Politburo members. Because the coding procedure recorded the frequency of a member's advocacy of a particular policy, it is especially sensitive to the effect of role responsibilities. Given that only Grechko and Ustinov are the true anomalies in the group, one can conclude that role has an important effect on the members' images of the United States. The instrumental differences, while significant, can be understood within the parameters of the variation in imagery and do argue for internal differentiation. As already argued in the case of the Stewart study, however, the general sameness can be usefully represented in a single prevailing view.

According to the perceptual theory introduced in chapter 2, the "enemy" imagery indicates that Soviet leaders are presenting a defensive response. This finding would suggest that prevailing Soviet perceptions are best described with a model that emphasizes perceived threats, not perceived opportunities. These conclusions, while perhaps important, are not sufficient for a judgment about motivation. They are based solely on the Soviet media and may reflect conscious deception, expected propaganda, and standard operating procedures among Soviet censors.

Consequently, chapters 3–5 have examined Soviet foreign policy behavior during each period. After defining the situation in each arena, I have compared the USSR's actions with behavior that could be expected of a nation following either the containment or the revisionist model. The results of this analysis of Soviet strategy are summarized in tables 17–19.

Table 17. Soviet Foreign Policy Behavior, 1967: Degree of Resemblance to Two Strategic Models

	Containment		Revisionism		
	Degree of Resemblance to Model	Degree of Commitment	Degree of Resemblance to Model	Degree of Commitment	Credibility of Deterrent
Nuclear Weapons	High	High	—	—	High
Central Europe	High	High	Low	Low	Moderate
Middle East	Moderate	Low	Low	Moderate to Low	High
Southeast Asia	Moderate	Moderate	Low	Moderate to Low	High

Table 18. Soviet Foreign Policy Behavior, 1972: Degree of Resemblance to Two Strategic Models

	Containment		Revisionism		
	Degree of Resemblance to Model	Degree of Commitment	Degree of Resemblance Model	Degree of Commitment	Credibility of Deterrent
Nuclear Weapons	High	High	—	—	High
Central Europe	High	High	Low	Low	Moderate
Middle East	Moderate	Low	Low	Low	Moderate to Low
South Asia	High	High	Moderate	Moderate	Moderate to Low
Southeast Asia	Moderate	Low	Moderate	Low	Moderate to Low

Conclusion

Chapter 1 discussed three contending perspectives on Soviet foreign policy, each labeled with its central motivational concept. They were Communist expansionism, realpolitik expansionism, and realpolitik self-defense. Because these theories are usually presented in a nonfalsifiable form, this study has adopted a method that translates the core claims about motivation into more testable propositions. The hypotheses derived this way represent only a part of each competing theory, but my hope is to capture the central differences in the interpretation of Soviet motives. Let us consider the implications for each of these perspectives that may be derived from the preceding study.

Theory 1: Communist Expansionism

The first theory attributes Soviet behavior to a drive to enlarge the area of the world controlled by the USSR. This theory is difficult to test because it simultaneously argues that the USSR will not be willing to pay a high price for this expansion. Advancing a "paper tiger" image, the theory suggests that the Soviets will constantly be searching for easy conquests but will retreat in the face of resistance and rising costs. The Communists are described as desirous of world domination, but not war, and as waiting for the unilateral surrender of their foes. Their objective is said to be global hegemony without great cost. The expansionist hypothesis consequently does not rest upon observable commitment and is impossible to test or to disprove.

Table 19. Soviet Foreign Policy Behavior, 1979: Degree of Resemblance to Two Strategic Models

	Containment		Revisionism		
	Degree of Resemblance to Model	Degree of Commitment	Degree of Resemblance to Model	Degree of Commitment	Credibility of Deterrent
Nuclear Weapons	High	High	—	—	High
Central Europe	High	High	Moderate	Low	Moderate
Middle East	Moderate	Moderate	Low	Low	Moderate to Low
Southeast Asia	Moderate	Moderate	Moderate	Low	Moderate to Low

This study considers only the claim about motivation. I have connected the expansionist proposition theoretically to an "enemy" image and a revisionist strategy. Soviet commitment to revisionist actions, in terms of sacrifice and investment, has been defined as a critical indicator of expansionist motives; thus, it differentiates the test from the "paper tiger" assumption and the comprehensive theory. In this examination, the expansionist hypothesis is not supported by either the verbal behavior of Communist spokesmen or the foreign policy choices of the USSR.

In none of the three periods did the image of the United States prevailing in the Soviet media resemble a "degenerate" stereotype or indicate that Soviet leaders regarded the United States as presenting an opportunity. In 1967 the imagery on all major dimensions indicated an "enemy" stereotype and, according to the theory advanced in chapter 2, reflected intense perceived threat on the part of the prevailing leaders in Moscow. The shift in 1972 reflected less of a sense of threat, as would be predicted in an era of detente. It did not reveal an ascendance of perceived opportunity as a result of seeing the United States as relatively weak.

The changes in imagery between 1972 and 1979 suggest that the comparative security of detente gave way to heightened anxiety in Moscow and greater fear of the United States. This finding is contrary to assertions that Soviet leaders were increasingly willing to take bold risks in the later half of the 1970s. The analysis of imagery suggests that Soviet activity in the Third World during this period was not correlated with a declining respect for American will; quite the opposite, it indicates a growing concern about an escalating American threat. In other words, the opportunities Soviet leaders perceived in third countries were not correlated with perceptions of American weakness, or opportunities vis-à-vis the United States, as they would regarding a "degenerate" state, but to the contrary were related to intensified fear of a still powerful adversary. Additionally, the "enemy" imagery indicates that in the prevailing Soviet view the United States was still regarded as either comparable in capabilities and power or stronger than the USSR and as striving for continued superiority.

The imagery suggests that prevailing Soviet perceptions between 1967 and 1979 are better described as defensive rather than expansionist or imperialist. The case studies of foreign policy behavior complement this finding, lending little support to the expansionist theory. In most of the arenas considered, Soviet behavior could be more plausibly seen as indicating a containment strategy rather than revisionism. Although in a number of arenas the evidence was inconclusive, the USSR's commitment to revisionist actions was never strong, and the revisionist proposition was rarely compelling. This of course is not inconsistent with the expansionist theory which predicts a low commitment to expansion. It does, however, suggest the Soviet Union, in functional terms, does not value expansion very highly.

Because the expansionist theory is nonfalsifiable, the evidence from concrete foreign policy behavior cannot disconfirm its accuracy. However, we can evaluate the evidence often used to defend the expansionist hypothesis. This study suggests a number of important lessons on this point.

First, the Soviet military buildup is not incontrovertible evidence of a drive for superiority and does not substantiate charges of revisionist or expansionist aims. The analysis of strategic weaponry demands exceptional technical and psychological complexity and does not lend itself to such simple and clear-cut interpretations. Evaluating a nation's capability to deter aggression and compel other nations, the core issue, is too often surrendered to the comparison of weapon systems in the abstract without considering their assigned missions and political purpose. Meaningful measures are difficult to construct, and many comparisons do more to obfuscate the fundamental assumptions about the defense requirements than to clarify the net evaluations. Estimates of "superiority" and "equivalence" are based on assumptions about the psychological effect of various weapon systems on both sides. They inherently include critical political assumptions about the "will" of the adversaries and their tolerance for risk and damage. Consequently, such simplistic comparisons are inadequate for understanding motivation and lead quickly to circular arguments and a technical emphasis that overlooks the fundamental assumptions.

Second, the USSR's involvement in a region and its support for various regimes is not equivalent to revisionism or a drive for expansion. To regard the development of influence as necessarily indicative of expansionism is to commit a cardinal error of political analysis. This mistake treats power as an absolute rather than a relative phenomenon.[7] The exercise of Soviet influence in Syria, Libya, Ethiopia, and South Yemen, for example, does not of itself indicate a nation committed to enforcing political change in those countries. Instead, it must be analyzed in the context of international competition in the Middle East. Too often Soviet activities are seized upon as the exclusive focus of study and not integrated into a political context that includes other events unfavorable to the USSR or Soviet options not taken.

When Soviet activity and influence in the Middle East is placed in a regional and relative perspective, the expansionist hypothesis is not convincing. The lack of Soviet involvement in Egypt and Iraq in 1972 is starkly obvious. Likewise, the Soviet Union's potential friends in Tripoli, Damascus, and Aden appear rather unimpressive in comparison to those lost in Cairo and Baghdad or those aligned with the United States in Tel Aviv and Riyadh. Moreover, Soviet support for the Steadfastness Front seems less of an effort to court "Arab radicalism" when the important differences between the Soviet and Arab positions on peace terms and the USSR's reluctance to back Arab concerns in Lebanon are considered. Soviet intervention in Ethiopia and Afghanistan, likewise, reflect a disregard for Arab allies and represent rather mixed payoffs in terms of regional influence.

Third, movements and events in third countries that may reduce U.S. influence are not necessarily evidence of Soviet revisionism even if the USSR endorses their aims and refuses to prevent their success. Soviet applause and even encouragement for forces seen as "anti-imperialist" is not necessarily inconsistent with containment any more than is the United States' enthusiasm for Poland's Solidarity movement. Welcoming an indigenous movement is not the same as causing it. It is imperative that domestic movements and revolutions that run counter to U.S policy be analyzed carefully and not inappropriately attributed to Soviet instigation. For example, this study regards Bengali grievances as so immense that the independence of Bangladesh was considered a change induced more by regional forces than by Soviet orchestration. The importance of indigenous grievances also makes it unwise to attribute to the Soviet Union the struggles of the NLF and the PLO. In these cases Soviet support was obvious, but with a rather marginal commitment to change. The USSR was willing to compromise the cause of either to preserve detente with the United States.

The communist expansionism theory logically leads to a policy of active containment and even rollback of Soviet influence. If the United States were to deny the "totalitarians" international success, the weakness of the "paper tiger" would be revealed and in turn internal change would occur in the USSR. The logic of this theory derives from George Kennan's analysis of nearly forty years ago: "The United States has it in its power to increase enormously the strains under which the Soviet policy must operate, to force upon the Kremlin a far greater degree of moderation and circumspection than it has had to observe in recent years, and in this way to promote tendencies which must eventually find their outlet in either the breakup or the gradual mellowing of Soviet power."[8] The results of this study, which do not support the expansionist diagnosis, have at least three general implications for such a strategy.

First, the USSR's commitment to unilaterally assured nuclear deterrence is supreme. U.S. efforts to compel the Soviets to accept U.S. domination or "margins of security" are likely to fail. The USSR has demonstrated little confidence in arms control agreements and no willingness to trade its forces for "bargaining chips." This study's analysis of Soviet perceptions and foreign policy strategy suggests that Soviet leaders perceive a basic parity between the superpowers' strategic military power and not a Soviet advantage. Consequently, they are likely to perceive U.S. "bargaining chips" as efforts to achieve superiority and as evidence of bad faith vis-à-vis detente. In this atmosphere, one-sided proposals or associated weapons procurements meant as bargaining ploys are likely to reinforce the Soviets' skepticism both about the value of arms control and the prospects of protecting their security through negotiations with the United States.

To the extent that Soviet weapons development is a symptom of security calculations and bureaucratic momentum, the strategy of reinforced containment will stimulate further growth in the arms race. Although the Soviets demonstrated some interest in stabilizing the deterrent relationship, they remained throughout the 1970s first and foremost committed to unilateral strength. It is unlikely they will reduce the heart of their strategic force (that is, ICBMs) to achieve more stability until they achieve the technical capacity to match U.S. forces in other systems. This is particularly likely as the U.S. deploys cruise missiles in Europe and attempts to extend its deterrent power from its strategic forces into the Persian Gulf. Concerned about credibility, Soviet leaders are likely to preserve the limited and accurate options that ICBMs represent and refuse agreements that reduce the range of options and hence the credibility of their nuclear responses. Because in submarine-based missiles, long-range aircraft, and cruise missile programs the Soviet Union lags behind the United States in terms of quantity, quality, and accuracy, it is not likely the Soviets will surrender their advantage in ICBMs. Their interest in stability has not superseded a commitment to credible deterrence both bilaterally and in an extended case.

Second, the USSR has demonstrated its capacity to enforce its imperial control over other socialist countries and to project its influence. Notions of rolling back Soviet involvement or compelling its expulsion from third countries are romantic. Although the USSR reduced its participation in the Middle East and Southeast Asia in 1972, it demonstrated later in the decade that it retained the capability to interfere in those regions. The proposition that detente could be used to exclude the

USSR from contests in the Third World and thereby secure American alliances for containment seems to be disconfirmed by Soviet actions in Ethiopia, Afghanistan, and Vietnam.

The cases in this study suggest that the "paper tiger" theme underpinning the logic of reinforced containment leads to both an overestimation of the relative Soviet military capabilities and a dangerous underestimation of Soviet power. While not recognizing the range of possible options available to the USSR to counter American pressure, the diagnosis assumes too much latitude for Soviet retreat.[9] As demonstrated, in strategic arms development, Ethiopia, and the Middle East (for example, Syria in 1967, Egypt in 1970 and 1973), the USSR can compete with the United States and use its might to set limits on retreat. Its logistic and military advantages in the Persian Gulf present contemporary opportunities to counter U.S. containment efforts. Before surrendering to American pressure and accepting the disintegration of its regime and empire, the USSR could be expected to exploit all of its options in the Persian Gulf. At the same time, given the predominance of the "enemy" image among Soviet leaders, it is likely to be reluctant to show weakness or retreat, especially in the face of U.S. pressure. Prevailing Soviet leaders perceive the United States as contained by Soviet might and seem to express a "paper tiger" theme of their own. They probably reason that Soviet power is all that American leaders understand and respect, and they will respond accordingly. Because of the importance of credibility in nuclear deterrence and the priority of strategic deterrence in Soviet behavior, it is most unlikely that Soviet leaders will perceive much latitude for retreat under pressure without jeopardizing Soviet security.

Third, American intervention in third countries, which is designed to reinforce a containment strategy by supressing internal disaffection, may be counterproductive if deep-seated grievances in those countries are not alleviated. Associated with the inclination to attribute too much importance to the USSR as a cause of political change in other nations is a tendency to minimize the power generated by internal grievances and resentment of U.S interference. While advocates of reinforced containment understand instantly the USSR's problem with indigenous nationalism in East bloc countries and resistance to repression in Poland and Afghanistan, they often fail to recognize similar limits on U.S. policy in Vietnam, Bangladesh, or Iran. Rising mass participation and ascendant aspirations for self-determination make intervention by outsiders exceedingly complex and difficult to effect successfully. Abstract generalities about the utility of force cannot be substituted for concrete political diagnoses in specific cases. If the citizenry of a country reject the ruling regime as a foreign creation, then forceful intervention by another nation to protect that regime is unlikely to enhance its legitimacy or stability. Long-term suppression, as the USSR has demonstrated, may be one option, but the maintenance of imperial control will probably fail to secure an independently reliable ally necessary for containment. An excessive commitment to containment may produce not only Soviet aggression and repression that otherwise could have been avoided, but also an unwise American reliance on deterrence in third countries where such coercive tactics are both inappropriate and counterproductive.[10]

Theory 2: Realpolitik Expansionism

According to a second theory, the Soviet Union is driven by a fundamental commitment to self-defense, and once securing this, it will opportunistically seek to expand its area of domination. The commitment to defense can be tested, but the expansionist claim is not so easily proved. Because according to this theory the USSR will seize low-risk, low-cost opportunities, theory 2, like the Communist expansionism theory, does not predict a high commitment to revisionist acts. This study finds that Soviet behavior in all three time periods did reveal a major commitment to defense and rather marginal sacrifices for expansion; however, we cannot conclusively determine whether this indicates a lack of expansionist ambition or the lack of opportunity. Because of the difficulty of measuring the extent to which opportunities exist in concrete situations, I was forced simply to assess whether or not the lack of revisionist behavior can be plausibly explained by lack of opportunity. For the most part, I was not persuaded by the proposition that the Soviet Union, no matter how opportunistic, is dedicated to forcing revisionism in other nations.

Theory 2 suggests that the USSR is both defensive and expansionist. The Soviet Union's recognition of the nuclear stalemate and the status quo in Europe is described as a holding action complementing its expansionist activities in the Third World. To capture this complexity I focused on a set of arenas including strategic arms and Europe as well as critical regions in the Third World. I sought to make independent judgments regarding Soviet strategy in each arena and in each period to allow for possible inconsistencies, mixed motives, or trends across regions and time. I concluded my discussion of each period with a net assessment. This aggregate picture obviously ignores lower-level complexity, but is useful in analyzing general strategy. Such a broad picture is necessary in strategy formation and seems appropriate to the global nature of Soviet-American competition.

While the USSR's commitment to nuclear deterrence and the status quo in Europe was found to be high, its inclination to exploit opportunities in the Middle East and South Asia was less clear. In 1967, and especially in 1972, the USSR's commitment to its allies in Egypt, Iraq, and North Vietnam failed to resemble even a containment strategy, much less a revisionist one. In 1979, opportunities for strategic involvement in Lebanon and Iran also provoked little Soviet action. At the same time, the USSR's behavior in Syria in 1967, Egypt in 1970 and 1973, Iraq in 1974, Ethiopia in 1977, and Afghanistan in 1979 indicated that it was neither unable nor unwilling to threaten and use force in the region, despite the risks of potential U.S.-Soviet confrontation.

The failure of the USSR to seize plausible opportunities, coupled with its willingness to act vigorously in Third World areas, casts doubt on the accuracy of the "opportunistic" explanation for Soviet policy. A more convincing hypothesis would be that tough Soviet action in the Middle East and southern Asia is stimulated not by perceptions of opportunity for expansionist gain but by perceived threats of imminent loss.[11] The concern about possible setbacks and U.S. advantage also cast doubt on the notion that the USSR has a proclivity to fuel local conflicts.

The realpolitik expansionist perspective claims that the USSR encourages regional turmoil in the Third World. Regional conflict, however, has been found in this study not only to present opportunities for Soviet penetration but also to create expensive tests of Soviet reliability; in turn, such conflicts threaten or actually undermine Soviet alliances such as in Egypt, Iraq, and Somalia. The Soviet interest in fueling turmoil, consequently, is not always great. Moreover, the definition of what constitutes encouraging turmoil is impossible to determine without invoking assumptions about the causes of regional conflicts. For U.S. government officials it may be reasonable to argue that any aid to forces resisting American interests abroad is abetting conflict. For independent scholars, however, the task is exceedingly more difficult. The ethnocentric assumption that the capability of parties to resist the will of the United States or its allies is the "cause" of conflict is unacceptable. To assume that the successful suppression of regional opposition to U.S. interests and exclusion of the USSR from an area will produce stability is to take a very narrow and short-sighted approach to peace.

All parties to a conflict want peace, but on their terms. For world powers, peace is one of many objectives and is not generally the highest in priority. Protecting territory, maintaining independence, defending certain conceptions of justice, and gaining strategic advantage often supersede an interest in peace. Take, for example, the United States' aid to the Kurds. Both superpowers provide weapons and support to regional combatants, allowing them to defend their terms and usually to resist defeat. Whether or not this constitutes fanning the flames of turmoil depends on a number of controversial assumptions, not the least of which relate to the "legitimacy" of the competing terms and the "fairness" of the proposed settlements. Many would consider the Soviet Union's effort to compel the Afghan resistance forces to surrender, and the severe repression in Afghanistan, as more important "causes" of the ongoing turmoil than the aid given by the United States and others to the rebel groups. Likewise, in the Ogaden region the Ethiopian policy toward ethnic Somalis contributed to conflict, along with Somalia's irredentist ambitions and armed invasion. Determining the cause of violence requires the examination of both the outstanding grievances and the relative balance of power in any region. It is extraordinarily difficult to determine how various acts such as the U.S. support for Somali aspirations or the USSR's aid to the Ethiopian government will affect the prospects for resolution of the conflict. Fighting can be ended in many ways, including total victory by either side. At the same time, the infusion of foreign aid may create a more equitable balance between the contenders, forcing mutual compromise and possibly a more secure settlement.

The USSR has often rejected peace terms endorced by the United States, but this is not the same as aggravating instability. In some cases the USSR has advocated terms of settlement no more one-sided than those advanced by the United States and at least equally likely, or no more unlikely, to produce possible compromise. For example, in Vietnam the Soviets, like many in the United States and around the world, attributed the turmoil as much to Thieu and the U.S. presence there as to the NLF's resistance. While rejecting Thieu, they did advocate negotiations and a process of reform to ameliorate the intense internal sources of discord. The process failed, but not only because of the USSR's involvement. U.S. encouragement of Thieu's efforts to press his advantage in 1973–1974, and Thieu's own refusal to accept change, contributed to the impasse as did North Vietnam's refusal to accept a cease-fire without real political change.

In East Pakistan, the U.S. efforts to protect Pakistani control were not likely to resolve conflict there. The turmoil was not a product of Soviet mischief but Pakistani repression. For months the USSR pressed for compromise and none was imminent. To attribute the turmoil to Bengali resistance, one must adopt a bias that is unwarranted. The Soviets did little to encourage the Bengalis and endorsed what was perhaps the most credible formula for stability.

The Soviet Union has refused to accept Israeli occupation of the West Bank, Gaza, and the Golan Heights, and has spurned any peace plans that fail to deal directly with these issues. It has also provided the Arab Steadfastness Front with the capability to resist Israeli terms for peace that do not surrender the West Bank to Palestinian self-determination. It will also not legitimate any Israeli efforts to settle the issues unilaterally through Lebanon and the elimination of the PLO. However, it has not refused to negotiate for peace. George Breslauer has concluded: "It is not that the Soviets do not want a settlement that will defuse the constant threat of war in the region; it is rather that the Soviets have been consistenly committed to the realization of *a particular kind of settlement*, one that is based on the four terms outlined above."[12] The four terms Breslauer outlines are: (1) U.S.-Soviet co-mediation of the settlement process, (2) Israeli withdrawal from territories occupied in 1967, (3) establishment of a Palestinian homeland, and (4) U.S. and Soviet guarantees of the security of all states in the region, including Israel. It has consistently supported Israel's right to exist in peace with secure boundaries along roughly the 1967 frontiers. Its proposals, while unacceptable in Israel, are not radically different from formulas advocated by the United States, although they include Soviet participation and PLO representation.[13]

The causes of turmoil in Arab-Israeli relations are many and are not exclusively the product of Arab intransigence. Israeli reluctance to accommodate Palestinian nationalism is significant. The USSR has not allowed its allies to be forced into surrender (although it did little to help them in Lebanon), but it has not backed their efforts to impose unilateral terms to the extent that the United States has supported Israel. U.S. preoccupation with excluding the Soviet Union has not led to a more compromising attitude in Israel. Moreover, it is not clear whether or not Israeli efforts to retain the West Bank and decide the issue by force in Lebanon, or Palestinian and Syrian efforts to resist the Israeli terms, are fueling the persistent turmoil more.

To conclude that the USSR encourages regional turmoil, one must accept a number of contentious and politically loaded assumptions. That it vigorously and deliberately fuels anti-Americanism, on the other hand, is clear. As in Iran, the Soviet Union may have nothing to do with the origins of anti-American sentiments, but it will encourage those that exist. This interest in "anti-imperialist" forces and reducing U.S influence, however, is not necessarily evidence of expansionist motives. The United States is likewise energetically committed to anti-Soviet propaganda and minimizing Soviet involvement in third countries. The interest in relative power, as all Realists agree, is a universal concern integral to self-defense and expansion. By itself it is indicative of neither.

The logic of the realpolitik expansionist theory leads to a dual-track strategy of containment that mixes deterrence and detente. Proponents of theory 2 prescribe a complex integration of firmness and cooperation as a response to both defensive and expansionist Soviet motives. Granting first priority to deterrence, the dual-track strategy aims to modify Soviet behavior by punishing it for resisting U.S terms and offering incentives for cooperative behavior. The intent of the strategy is to eliminate Soviet perceptions of opportunity for expansion while not provoking intensified perceptions of threat. The results of this study present three implications for this strategy.

First, it is likely that Soviet leaders will perceive the dual strategy just outlined as a uniform strategy of containment and interpret offers of cooperation as either dangerous ploys or attempts at subversion. The predominance of the "enemy" image in Soviet statements and their obvious fear of an American threat suggests that Soviet leaders could translate the U.S. plan into a consistent plot.[14] For the strategy to succeed, a tremendously efficient mode of communication between the superpowers would be necessary, which is rare in international relations, especially between adversaries. Soviet leaders with an "enemy" image of the United States are likely to seize upon evidence of U.S. firmness and deterrence and dismiss offers of cooperation as insincere.[15]

Their attitudes are likely to resemble the reactions of American conservatives when confronted with Soviet offers of good will simultaneously with larger Soviet programs of arms development, regional power projection, and firm deterrence. Not even brilliant implementation and excellent communication would be likely to persuade prevailing Soviet leaders that a relaxation of vigilance was safe and that U.S. gestures of cooperation sincere if the United States is simultaneously deploying B-1 bombers, and new Trident, MX, and cruise missiles, excluding the USSR from Middle East negotiations, developing facilities in Egypt, Oman, Kenya, and Somalia, enlarging and strengthening NATO, and playing the "China card."

Second, U.S. efforts to raise the cost of action and thereby deter Soviet behavior in third areas may, in Soviet calculations, simply raise the risks of not moving. In this study I found that aggressive Soviet behavior is often associated with fear of loss, not perceived opportunities for gain. This was probably the case in Czechoslovakia (1968), Egypt (1970, 1973), Ethiopia (1977–1978), Afghanistan (1979), and Poland (1981). The risks associated with losing a position in these areas, as it is perceived in Moscow, are greater than the costs the United States can credibly threaten should the USSR act to prevent the setback. U.S. efforts to deter a given Soviet act, therefore, are likely to be ineffective and probably counterproductive. First, U.S warnings and diplomatic efforts to deter the Soviet Union are likely to heighten perceived threats in Moscow and raise the apparent security value of the endangered position. Second, escalating U.S. deterrent efforts force Soviet leaders to calculate that "inevitable" and "necessary" moves to protect their influence are better taken sooner rather than later. Third, U.S. efforts at deterrence are likely to convince Soviet policymakers with an "enemy" image of the United States that not moving decisively would signal weakness and invite further U.S. pressure for rollback. They would be reluctant to risk setbacks in any case. In the face of American threats or in a situation where U.S. leaders may claim credit for having compelled Soviet restraint, the incentive to move would probably be irresistible. U.S. deterrent attempts, while incapable of raising costs any higher than those already at stake, may have the effect of destroying U.S. credibility and ensuring the very outcome that the United States sought to deter.

U.S. deterrence and coercive diplomacy in circumstances where Soviet leaders perceive threats from pending setbacks and exclusion from certain areas, such as in Poland, the Middle East, and Afghanistan, may expose Soviet imperialism and reflect American outrage, but are unlikely to have a positive effect on the situation. The USSR would most likely answer the perceived challenge with tougher policy of its own. It might, for example, bolster its own commitments and enforce greater solidarity and obedience from its allies. Rather than enhancing containment, American pressure is likely to narrow the latitude vis-à-vis Moscow that regional parties such as Poland have in which to maneuver. The prospects for independent movements like Solidarity in those countries will be dimmed, not brightened.

Furthermore, in efforts to deter Soviet involvement in the Middle East and Southwest Asia, the United States may engage in counterproductive interference. Based on a Pavlovian analogy, the strategy assumes that the United States can "teach" the USSR to accommodate American concerns. This, however, requires a substantial degree of control over the political environment. In areas like Southwest Asia this is increasingly beyond the reach of either superpower. The advocates of this strategy generally recognize the importance of local nationalism and indigenous grievances and argue that the Soviet Union fosters rather than causes turmoil. Ironically, the strategic prescription, which emphasizes excluding the Soviet Union from Southwest Asia, leads to a projection of U.S. power there that, rather than fostering regional resolution and stability, is likely to fuel "anti-imperialist" sentiment. Such a strategy would further associate the United States with repressive and inherently unstable regimes and deepens its dependence on projected force such as with the Rapid Deployment Force now in the Central Command. The net result may be to diminish U.S. leverage and enhance the USSR's ability to encourage anti-Americanism.

Third, the assumption that the Soviet Union seizes available opportunities can lead to an underestimation of Soviet power and overextension of American commitment. "Opportunity" is often tautologically defined: if the USSR takes action, this is proof that it saw the opportunity; when it does not, this proves that no opportunity existed. Naturally, this type of definition leaves no room for evidence of Soviet self-restraint. This reasoning is dangerous because it allows an assumption about motives to interfere with the analysis of the exercise of power. I have tried to measure the concept of opportunity independently of Soviet behavior and evaluate the plausibility of attributing inaction to lack of opportunity. In a number of critical cases such as the Persian Gulf I found the deterrent caveat less than compelling. This suggests that the realpolitik diagnosis might underestimate both Soviet leverage and the expected costs of U.S. actions. Moreover, it may lead to misplaced confidence in the United States' ability to deter Soviet acts and unfounded expectations of success when defeat is probable.

Theory 3: Realpolitik Defense

Imperialist and aggressive Soviet behavior toward many third countries is, according to a third theory, attributed to an increased sense of threat from the United States, China, or both. The USSR is described as defensive and driven by paramount security concerns, even if they are exaggerated. This study has tested the defensive theory by means of two hypotheses regarding behavior: first, that the prevailing Soviet image of the United States resembles the "enemy" stereotype; and second, that the USSR's behavior in many world arenas indicates a strategy of containment. In 1967 and 1979 the verbal and behavioral evidence weighed most heavily in favor of these hypotheses. In 1972 Soviet defensiveness seemed to have relaxed somewhat, as was appropriate during an era of detente. Although this study has not disproved the defensive hypotheses, it obviously cannot prove their accuracy either. It does argue that, of the general theories considered, the defensive explanation of Soviet international behavior is more plausible than the other two interpretations, at least in the arenas examined.

The defensive interpretation is certain to be controversial. In a survey of American leaders conducted in 1976 and 1980 by Ole Holsti and James Rosenau, the issue on which they found the greatest consensus was the belief that the Soviet Union is generally expansionist rather than defensive in its foreign policy goals. In 1976, 83 percent either agreed strongly or agreed somewhat that the USSR was expansionist. In 1980, 85 percent agreed.[16] The results of this study, as with Gamson's and Modigliani's earlier test of rival theories, do not support this widely shared perspective. These results may, however, be more consistent with other research than might appear from this conclusion alone.

In my study of Soviet motives I have assumed a hierarchy of inclusiveness, beginning with self-defense. Consequently, all three theories agree that the USSR is driven by defensive aims and security concerns. The two expansionist perspectives, however, claim that Soviet behavior goes beyond mere self-protection and is also driven by expansionist motives. Quite often the argument is nonfalsifiable because its proponents do not expect the USSR to run great risks or sacrifice very much in order to achieve these aims. Sometimes a teleological qualification is introduced, suggesting that Soviet leaders take a long view of history and therefore one cannot trust current behavior that shows patience and restraint: they are bent on expansion. As mentioned in the case of Southwest Asia, these concerns are important precautions and underlie sound reservations in policy planning, but can make contemporary analysis impossible. Without rejecting these future possibilities, I tested a part of the expansionist argument by seeking evidence of the "degenerate" stereotype and revisionist strategy. I evaluated actual Soviet behavior in terms of commitment to the policies a revisionist model might predict. This is essential to empirically based research, but does not provide a direct test of the competing perspectives. After all, they are driven as much by theory as evidence and are nonfalsifiable. The expansionist theories can account for the lack of observable commitment to revisionism. In fact, in the short run they predict it.

While Soviet leaders verbally described the U.S. threat as global, their behavioral commitments in different regions indicated substantial variation in their sense of threat. As might be expected, the USSR granted highest priority, in terms of relative commitment, to maintaining a nuclear deterrent and dominating Eastern Europe. In these arenas it demonstrated little faith in diplomacy and no willingness to relax its security systems. In the Middle East, on the other hand, the Soviets exhibited less concern than might be expected if they saw the United States as a serious threat. Their behavior in Egypt, Kurdistan, and Lebanon was less vigorous than a containment model would predict. They exhibited, for example, a substantial willingness to sacrifice Soviet credibility in the Middle East and Southeast Asia in order to pursue detente. As demonstrated in Ethiopia in 1977–1978, in South Yemen in 1979, and in Syria in 1980, however, there remained a basic commitment to preserving regional influence that caused the Soviets to resist exclusion, particularly as talk of detente disappeared.

The three periods chosen for this study were selected to span the development of Sino-American relations. One reason for this choice was to consider whether the United States' playing the "China card" would correlate with more accomodating Soviet behavior. The results suggest that the answer is no. Increased U.S.-Chinese cooperation coincided with intensified perceptions of threat in Moscow and led not to capitulation but to reinforced Soviet commitments in Afghanistan, India, and Vietnam. U.S. efforts to join with China in common cause against the USSR were seen in Moscow as incompatible with detente. While the Sino-American rapprochement coincided with an increasing Soviet interest in detente with Bonn, the USSR linked the prospects for improved Soviet–West German relations to the West Germans' reluctance to endorse the United States' reinforcement of containment efforts. By 1979 the Soviet interest in detente with West Germany was perceived by many Americans as an effort to undermine NATO and hardly the kind of "accommodation" they had hoped the pressure of Chinese-American cooperation would produce.

A strategy of disengagement or detente is associated with the logic of realpolitik self-defense. Although the results of this study support the general thrust of such a strategy, they also point out obstacles to its success. First, Soviet leaders have been very conservative with respect to the USSR's security and inclined to trust only unilateral military power. To persuade such conservatives to accept a relaxation in vigilance would be no mean task. No confidence in arms control can be expected. With the deployment of weapons like the cruise missle that complicate if not defy verification, arms control as a device for building confidence may no longer be viable.

Confidence-building measures and economic interdependence could foster relaxation in Europe and reduce the likelihood of confrontation. While this would be no small achievement, the long-term success of any military detente will be limited by the persisting Soviet domination of Eastern Europe. Western public opinion will insist that the process of detente include the relaxation of domestic repression in Eastern Europe and this in turn will threaten the survival both of the Communist regimes and of the Warsaw Pact. Soviet leaders may never accept this and will certainly not tolerate such change if no comparable dissolution is occurring in NATO. It would require strong positive incentives such as economic cooperation and a forthright Western commitment to reducing Soviet perceptions of threat to convince enough leaders in Moscow that the risks of change are worthwhile.

Second, U.S. efforts to allay Soviet fears may be read in Moscow as evidence of weakness. The paradox of the "enemy" stereotype is that the "paper tiger" image interprets accommodating behavior as capitulation. Because the prevailing Soviet elite accept the "enemy" image of the United States, they are likely to interpret U.S. efforts to revive detente as reflecting the successful application of Soviet might. Rather than understanding an American gesture toward detente as indicative of peaceful intent, Soviet "hawks" are likely to attribute the move to fear of Soviet strength and advocate pressing still harder. An initiative intended to persuade Soviet leaders who hold a moderate "enemy" picture of the United States that detente is possible, may instead convince the hawks in Moscow that a hard-line policy is working. At the same time, a strong signal of American resolve may discourage the enthusiasm of Soviet hawks, yet only convince them as well as those with less intense fears that their worst estimates of American intentions were correct.

Designing diplomatic strategies to reduce enemy images is a perplexing task. Neither accommodation nor strength will be effective independently. At the same time, a dual-track strategy that reinforces containment and aims to compel Soviet acceptance of American terms is likely only to intensify Soviet resistance. Detente, which by definition means relaxation, will not be easily combined with efforts to reinforce Western containment either through NATO, China, or Soviet exclusion from Third World events. The results of this study suggest that the USSR will not relax its vigilance in return for trade or negotiated arms control if the primary focus of U.S. policy is the strengthening of containment. For a dual-track strategy to work effectively, the United States will need to demonstrate a commitment to change in its own security arrangements commensurate with those expected from the USSR. As seen in the case studies, reciprocal trust and mutual relaxation are very difficult to manage. Well-established suspicions in both Washington and Moscow will incline analysts to perceive an asymmetrical pace of change. Each side is likely to be more sensitive to the potential alterations in its own systems and will see only the "enemy's" persisting strength, not its restraint.

The "enemy" stereotype inherently assumes bad faith. The perceptions of those holding this image are independent of the behavior of the observed country. Its restraint is not perceived, nor are its accommodating overtures taken seriously. Challenges are seen irrespective of the country's efforts to reassure and even these efforts are likely to be interpreted as disingenuous and manipulative. The "enemy" stereotype sets up self-fulfilling predictions and interprets whatever is going on in light of prior expectations. Regardless of the actual pattern of events, the enemy will be seen as probing and retreating, as responsive to the carrot only if the stick is ever present. Definitions of the situation will be derived from the general stereotypes and will reaffirm its predictions. A psychological theory may argue that the stereotype reflects great fear of an enemy, but this does not tell how to transcend stereotypical thinking. Because the stereotype cannot be empirically disconfirmed, it greatly complicates any attempts at conflict management, much less peacemaking.

Given the "enemy" images that leaders in Washington and Moscow have of each other, neither nation is likely to respond appropriately to the behavior of the other. Both may be motivated by security concerns, but the dynamics of competition will probably not follow a neatly spiraling stimulus-response pattern. Neither side will see the restraint of the other. Both will interpret the actions in the worst possible light, assuming bad faith. Initiatives intended as signals of flexibility will be missed, dismissed, or misinterpreted. Actions seen as benign and ordinary by the initiator will be read by the other as threatening and probably malevolent. Efforts to stimulate relaxation are, therefore, not likely to produce quick and clear counteroffers. Communication is likely to be so imperfect that behavior may not even appear to be related to the adversary's previous actions except to the initiator of each act. The clear processes of escalation and deescalation expected in an action-reaction model may never appear.

In the 1970s Soviet perceptions of the United States resembled the "enemy" stereotype but did not fit the ideal case, as assumed in the argument above. Nevertheless, the "enemy" image, as expected, made communication and signaling very difficult and the action-reaction model quite inadequate. These results create problems not only for deterrence advocates but also for those who promote a strategy of "graduated and reciprocated initiatives in tension reduction." Several critiques of deterrence policy have demonstrated that the degree of rationality and level of effective communication it assumes is not compatible with international reality. The tension-reducing strategy is also dependent on accurate communication. In fact, it assumes that not only threats will be understood but also flexibility and gestures of compromise will be perceived and correctly deciphered. Unfortunately, in an atmosphere dominated by "enemy" images, this is not likely to be the case.

My results suggest that communicating with the Soviet Union is certain to be complicated. Ironically, they suggest that the task the United States has put the most energy into, signaling resolve and credibility, is likely to be the easiest. Soviet leaders are predisposed to see American threats. The much more difficult task of signaling flexibility and relaxing Soviet fears has received less attention. Soviet insecurity has led to a number of imperialist and brutal policies. The United

States, therefore, must act to reduce Soviet perceptions of threat while simultaneously registering strong opposition to authoritarianism. Because communication with the USSR is likely to be distorted, there will probably be a significant lag between flexible initiatives and positive responses. Moreover, in many cases perceptions of the situation are so different that completely incompatible definitions of reciprocity are certain to exist. Any search for greater detente will be a very imperfect process for a long time. Powerful leaders on both sides who operate with stereotypical images will never be convinced that their relaxation of military vigilance is reciprocated. The fits and starts and inconsistent behavior that are to be expected will certainly complicate the strategy and provoke domestic and bureaucratic pressures that may undermine its viability at home. The problems derived from the predominance of "enemy" images may not be insurmountable, but they surely reduce the prospects for a mutual disengagement strategy.

Monitoring the effects and appropriateness of any strategy is an ongoing endeavor that is particularly difficult in foreign policy. In a dual strategy that emphasizes detente and a willingness to allay rather than exacerbate or manipulate Soviet fears, positive change will be long in coming and is not likely to be achieved smoothly. The process, for example, is likely to facilitate change in third regions such as the Middle East that may appear threatening to different groups in the United States, regardless of their concern about the Soviet Union. The multiple effects of such a strategy on many relationships will make it hard to access the strategy's effect on the USSR. It may produce intense lobbying from regimes dependent on American aid and in danger of domestic or regional challenges if U.S. support should wane, as U.S. commitment to containment relaxes. This will only heighten concerns about the costs of detente and fuel concerns about Soviet involvement in those nations.

This book was stimulated by a concern that U.S. policy prescriptions toward the USSR are often based on rigidly accepted yet largely unexamined theories of Soviet international behavior. Its main aim has been to explicate such unquestioned assumptions about motivation and treat them as propositions. Therefore, although my results support the interpretation that the Soviets are primarily concerned with self-defense, I will not conclude by outlining and advocating a disengagement policy. A greater emphasis on detente may be called for, but no strategy is likely to be a panacea that quickly and effectively reduces undesirable Soviet behavior. More important, my purpose in this book is not prescriptive but diagnostic.

Political analysis, like medical analysis, is time-bound, uncertain, and limited by imperfect information. Political actors can change. A single diagnosis of Soviet policy is not wisely translated into a general theory assumed to have permanent utility. An analysis can yield a temporary logic for treatment, but it must be continually revised and questioned as the effects of the preliminary probes are evaluated. Analysis of motivation is both an essential and ongoing process that should never be assumed to render definitive final interpretations. Although this study has offered substantive findings, its more fundamental purpose has been to draw attention to unexamined assumptions about motivation. While certain assumptions about motives and perceptions are unavoidable in intelligent strategy formulation, their analysis needs both theoretical and methodological refinement. The essential role of theory in strategic diagnosis ensures that heated debate will continue even if our access to evidence improves.

Analysis of Motivation and Foreign Policy Theory

I have focused on Soviet leaders' verbal images of the United States found both in public statements and in foreign policy commitments. I organized my search for evidence and its analysis on two theoretical conceptions: first, a theory of perceptions and images, and second, a theory of strategic models applied to specific arenas of competition. In my application of the conceptual framework, I found that the two streams of evidence led to similar conclusions. Both suggested that prevailing Soviet perceptions of the United States are dominated by a sense of threat and that it is plausible to attribute Soviet foreign policy behavior primarily to a concern for self-defense. This does not suggest that the Soviets always express their views in the public media. However, perceptions might be determined in a less direct way. This study finds that verbal imagery indicates an "enemy" stereotype of the United States and that this image can be usefully integrated with a theory of perception.

Because I have stressed behavior at the state level and international behavior of the USSR, I have sought to describe only prevailing Soviet perceptions of the United States. Much internal complexity has been missed, and it might prove very informative to compare various patterns of perception to different voices within the USSR. This task would require more rigorous coding definitions for each stereotype and substantial access to Soviet propaganda. If coupled with an analysis of the prevailing view, such a study might offer insight into probable influence patterns and possible associations between various roles and perceptions of the United States.[17]

Policy debates surely go on in Moscow, but I did not design this study to examine the policy formulation process. Instead I sought to address fundamental motivational theories at the strategic level of Soviet international behavior. As with the understanding of motives, interpretation of strategy also needs theoretical refinement. The discipline has accepted concepts about motives such as expansion and self-defense that are not easy to define or measure. It is as if diseases central in medical diagnoses were not connected to identifiable symptoms. Analysts grasp the concepts in the abstract, but understand less about the consequences they might be associated with in concrete arenas. Testing the usefulness or appropriateness of these concepts is not simple. It requires a set of assumptions about each situation and theoretical deductions that translate the general conception into context specific options.

Deriving concrete hypotheses to represent general theories of motivation requires an assessment of the USSR's capabilities and opportunities. This is a project burdened with probable attributional biases and contextual complexity.[18] The probable leverage and expected costs are impossible to calculate except in terms of probability and plausibility. The task of estimation is made still more difficult because of the cross-cutting biases of governments that have vested interests in both over-selling the likely retaliation for deterrent purposes and understating their ability to retaliate for reasons of budget politics. Moreover, the analysis must be tailored to each region under examination; it must be sensitive to the concerns of third countries and the USSR's ability to court and intimidate them.

Defining what could be expected of a world power following various strategies in particular arenas is not a mechanical process. It demands the development of a thoughtful logic that explicitly reveals its assumptions regarding each situation and argument. This situational theorizing will define the "meaning" of whatever evidence is collected in both actions and nonoccurrences and must be at the center of scholarly dispute. In this study the logic in each arena is made explicit. My intention is not to win the polemic of the day, but rather to identify where intellectual and situational definitions may differ and where further evidence might alter existing evaluations.

Nothing in this study suggests that analyzing motivation is a simple task or one likely to avoid controversy. Arguments will rage over definitions, theories, and evidence. It is easy to understand why scholars such as Hans Morgenthau sought to cricumvent the endeavor, and others like J. David Singer decided to concentrate at a different level of analysis.[19] The retreat to Realism, however, will not suffice. Strategic prescription must be based on a political diagnosis that provides a logic explaining why the prescription is likely to have a desired effect. This will require an assessment of not only the relative capabilities but also the motivating factors producing the USSR's undesirable behavior. Attribution of motives will, consequently, remain at the center of prescriptions for strategy and will be a necessary target for research.

Concepts about motivation and perception serve as core variables in many foreign policy models. Efforts to avoid them have not been successful in producing important and convincing explanations for international behavior. Often these attempts have not circumvented claims about motivation but simply incorporated them as either implicit assumptions or explicit, yet undefined, assertions. Moreover, frequently employed concepts such as defense, expansion, perception of threat, and perception of opportunity imply certain judgments about motives. The careful consideration of the relevance and accuracy of these concepts in specific cases, however, has not received the necessary attention. Deduced logic and explicit theories are required to connect these powerful analytical concepts to empirical evidence drawn both from what leaders say and what they do. Broader-level theories of international relations cannot be empirically tested and thus will remain premature if the root assumptions on which they are based are not examined. Unless we tackle the basic problems inherent in generating the data about aims, values, motives, or perceptions, a good deal of research in international relations will suffer from a lack of meaningful evidence.

I have attempted to devise an empirically based approach to the study of foreign policy motivation. While the scheme was applied in the case of only one country, the framework should also be useful in comparative research. The complexity of defining the situation and the difficulty of inferring the perceptions of national leaders in a single case, however, highlight the magnitude of the challenge for cross-national comparison and theory-building in international relations.

The results of this study cast doubt on the accuracy of current theories of Soviet foreign policy that assume that the USSR's primary motive is to expand its domination over others. Moreover, they suggest that U.S. efforts to reinforce the containment of Soviet influence may be counterproductive: they are not likely to reduce undesirable Soviet behavior or to enhance American security or prospects of peace. These are disturbing possibilities.

My aim in this study, however, is not to settle a political debate but rather to press the academic debate into areas where assumptions about motivation must be defended explicitly and empirically. Such assumptions must be treated as hypotheses and not as matters of faith, ideology, or national patriotism. This fundamental question in foreign policy analysis should not be surrendered to untested assumptions, shared images, bureaucratic vested interests, or—worse still—government doctrine. Attributions about motives provide a logic for the prescriptions of strategy. If they are in error, then they can doom the prospect for policies derived from them, however well applied. The study of foreign policy motivation, therefore, is essential not only for academic understanding but also for national defense and effective peacemaking.

Notes
Bibliography
Index

Notes

Chapter 1
American Views of Soviet Foreign Policy

1. Glen Snyder and Paul Diesing, *Conflict Among Nations: Bargaining, Decision Making, and System Structure in International Crises* (Princeton, N.J.: Princeton University Press, 1977), p. 254.

2. Hans Morgenthau, *Politics Among Nations: The Struggle for Power and Peace*, 5th ed. (New York: Knopf, 1973), pp. 4–7.

3. For a recent critique, see John A. Vasquez, *The Power of Power Politics: A Critique* (New Brunswick, N.J.: Rutgers University Press, 1983).

4. Morgenthau, *Politics Among Nations*, p. 64.

5. Harvard Nuclear Study Group: Albert Carnesale, Paul Doty, Stanley Hoffmann, Samuel Huntington, Joseph Nye, Jr., and Scott Sagen, *Living with Nuclear Weapons* (New York: Bantam, 1983), p. 36.

6. A significant premise is one that "constitutes a ground for a decision." Information is significant when it "opens up a range of decisions that otherwise would be ignored." When motivational assumptions change entire strategies are called into question (Morton Kaplan, *System and Process in International Politics* [New York: Krieger, 1975], pp. 103–05).

7. For this approach to the philosophy of science, see Larry Laudan, *Progress and Its Problems Toward a Theory of Scientific Growth* (Berkeley and Los Angeles: University of California Press, 1977).

8. Laudan argues, "The first and essential acid test for any theory is whether it provides acceptable answers to interesting questions: whether, in other words, it provides satisfactory solutions to important problems" (ibid., p. 13).

9. See Richard Cottam, *Foreign Policy Motivation: A General Theory and A Case Study* (Pittsburgh, Pa.: University of Pittsburgh Press, 1977), pp. 31–53.

10. See Walter Mischel, "Toward a Cognitive Social Learning Reconceptualization of Personality," *Psychological Review* 80 (1973), 252–83. Also see Bernard Weiner, *Theories of Motivation: From Mechanism to Cognition* (Chicago: Rand McNally, 1972).

11. For a development of the logic of concepts and the limits of empiricism, see F.S.C. Northrop, *The Logic of the Sciences and Humanities* (New York: World Publishing, 1959).

12. Max Weber defined sociology as "a science which attempts the interpretive understanding of social action in order thereby to arrive at a casual explanation of its course and effects" (*The Theory of Social and Economic Organization*, trans. A. M. Henderson and Talcott Parsons [New York: Free Press, 1964], p. 88).

13. The debate between explanations focused on environmental determinants of behavior and explanations focused on internal variables is long standing in social psychology. Some of this debate has led to a conceptualization of the interaction of the subject and the environment. This conception of environmental conditions as perceived and mediated by Soviet leaders will be the orientation of this research. See L. J. Cronbach, "The Two Disciplines of Scientific Psychology," *American Psychologist* 12 (1957), 671–84; and L. J. Cronbach, "Beyond the Two Disciplines of Scientific Psychology," *American Psychologist* 30 (1975), 116–27. Also see K. S. Bowers, "Situationism in Psychology: An Analysis and a Critique," *Psychological Review* 80 (1973), 307–36; and D. J. Bem and A. Allen, "On Predicting Some of the People Some of the Time: The Search for Cross-situational Consistencies in Behavior," *Psychological Review* 81 (1974), 506–20.

14. Wayne Ferris, *The Power Capabilities of Nation-States* (Lexington, Mass.: D. C. Heath, 1973).

15. See J. D. Singer, "The Levels of Analysis Problem in International Relations," in *The International System: Theoretical Essays*, ed. Klaus Knorr and Sidney Verba (Princeton, N.J.: Princeton University Press, 1961), pp. 77–92.

16. See Kenneth Waltz, *Theory of International Politics* (Reading, Mass.: Addison-Wesley, 1979), pp. 71–72, 120–22; and *Man, the State and War* (New York: Columbia University Press, 1954), pp. 230–34.

17. Morgenthau, *Politics Among Nations,* pp. 207–21.

18. On leverage and bargaining, see Richard Cottam and Gerard Galluci, *The Rehabilitation of Power in International Relations* (Pittsburgh: University Center for International Studies, 1978); and Snyder and Diesing, *Conflict Among Nations,* pp. 183–281.

19. The argument in favor of a perceptual focus is put forward by Robert Jervis, *Perception and Misperception in International Politics* (Princeton, N.J.: Princeton University Press, 1976), pp. 13–31.

20. This perspective differs from that of Morton Kaplan, who argues that national interests can be objectively determined (*System and Process,* pp. 164–65). It begins from the premise that needs are related to values. Western economies, for example, need certain resources to maintain a certain standard of living. The standard of living is a value, one that is essentially a preference, not a biological requirement. Because needs are related to values they are difficult to treat as objective conditions. Hitler, after all, argued that Germany needed living space in order to sustain its national sustenance, a claim many found unpersuasive both politically and morally.

21. Edward Jones and Richard Nisbett find that observers tend to attribute their own behavior to internal factors and the behavior of others to environmental conditions. See "The Actor and the Observer: Divergent Perceptions of the Causes of Behavior," in *Attribution: Perceiving the Causes of Behavior* ed. Edward Jones et al. (Morristown, N.J.: General Learning Press, 1971), pp. 79–94. Also see E. J. Phares, *Locus of Control in Personality* (Morristown, N.J.: General Learning Press, 1976).

22. See, for example, William Welch, *American Images of Soviet Foreign Policy: An Inquiry into Recent Appraisals from the Academic Community* (New Haven, Conn.: Yale University Press, 1970).

23. Ole Holsti and James Rosenau, *American Leadership in World Affairs: Vietnam and the Breakdown of Consensus* (Boston: Allen and Unwin, 1984), pp. 108–39.

24. These labels correspond to what William Gamson and Andre Modigliani called "destructionist," "expansionist," and "consolidationist," in *Untangling the Cold War: A Strategy for Testing Rival Theories* (Boston: Little, Brown, 1971).

25. This summary is meant to describe an abstract or ideal version of the theory, but is based on the following works: Richard Pipes, *U.S.-Soviet Relations in the Era of Detente: A Tragedy of Errors* (Boulder, Colo.: Westview Press, 1981), and Richard Pipes, ed. *Soviet Strategy in Europe* (New York: Crane, Russak, 1976); Walter Laqueur, "Containment for the 80s," *Commentary* 70 (Oct. 1980), 33–42; and "Pity the Poor Russians?" *Commentary* 71 (Feb. 1981), 32–41; Colin Gray, "Nuclear Strategy: The Case for a Theory of Victory," *International Security* 4 (Summer 1979), 54–87; and Robert Conquest, *Present Danger: Towards a Foreign Policy* (Stanford, Calif.: Hoover Institution Press, 1979).

26. The core logic of the "operational art" or probe and retreat is spelled out by Nathan Leites in *The Operational Code of the Politburo* (New York: McGraw-Hill, 1951). For a recent study that concludes that such "operational principles" usefully describe Soviet behavior, see Hannes Adomeit, *Soviet Risk-Taking and Crisis Behavior: A Theoretical and Empirical Analysis* (London: Allen and Unwin, 1982), pp. 51–62, 315–25.

27. For a discussion of the independence of this theory from observable data see Ole R. Holsti, "Cognitive Dynamics and Images of the Enemy," in David J. Finlay, Ole R. Holsti, and Richard R. Fagen, *Enemies in Politics* (Chicago: Rand McNally, 1967), pp. 25–96. Also see Douglas Stuart and Harvey Starr, "Inherent Bad Faith Reconsidered: Dulles, Kennedy, and Kissinger," *Political Psychology* 3 (1982), 1–33.

28. The notion of contemporaneity argued for by Kurt Lewin is applicable in foreign policy analysis. Lewin argued that casual claims about human behavior in a particular period require an empirical defense drawn on evidence from that same period. Lewin's rigor does not minimize historical data, but guards against the substitution of historical determinism for contemporary diagnosis. For a review of Lewin's notion see Morton Deutsch, "Field Theory in Social Psychology," in *The Handbook of Social Psychology*, 2d ed., ed. Gardner Lindzey and Elliot Aronson (Reading, Mass: Addison-Wesley, 1968), pp. 412–87, 418–19.

29. See Richard Pipes, "Why the Soviet Union Thinks It Could Fight and Win a Nuclear War," *Commentary* 64 (July 1977), 26–29. Also see Richard Pipes, "Militarism and the Soviet State," *Daedalus* 109 (Fall 1980), 1–12; and "A Reply," *Encounter* 54 (April 1980), 72–75. For the resonse of a Russian nationalist, see Alexander Solzhenitsyn, "Misconceptions About Russia Are a Threat to America," *Foreign Affairs* 58 (Spring 1980), 797–834. Also see Wladislaw Krasnow, "Richard Pipes' Foreign Strategy: Anti-Soviet or Anti-Russian?" and Pipes's response in the *Russian Review* 38 (April 1979), 180–97.

30. See, for example, Jerry Hough, *Soviet Leadership in Transition* (Washington, D.C.: Brookings, 1980).

31. One excellent study that illustrates how difficult this is even for the first secretary is George W. Breslauer, *Khrushchev and Brezhnev as Leaders: Building Authority in Soviet Politics* (London: Allen and Unwin, 1982).

32. This summary is an ideal type, but is based on the following works: Seweryn Bialer, *Stalin's Successors: Leadership, Stability, and Change in the Soviet Union* (Cambridge: Cambridge University Press, 1980); "Poland and the Soviet Imperium," *Foreign Affairs* 59 (1980), 522–39; "The International and Internal Contexts of the 26th Party Congress," in *Russia at the Crossroads: The 26th Congress of the C.P.S.U.*, ed. Seweryn Bialer and Thane Gustafson (London: Allen and Unwin, 1982), pp. 7–38; and Seweryn Bialer and Joan Afferica, "Reagan and Russia," *Foreign Affairs* 61 (Winter 1982/83), 249–71. The notion of "opportunistic expansion" is a theme running throughout the articles in *The Soviet Union in the Third World: Successes and Failures*, ed. Robert Donaldson (Boulder, Colo.: Westview, 1981). Also see Robert Legvold, "The 26th

Party Congress and Soviet Foreign Policy," in *Russia at the Crossroads,* ed. Bialer and Gustafson, pp. 156–77; and "Containment Without Confrontation," *Foreign Policy* 40 (Fall 1980), 74–98. William Hyland, "U.S.-Soviet Relations: The Long Road Back," *Foreign Affairs* 60 (1981), 525–50; Dimitri Simes, "The Death of Detente," *International Security* 5 (Summer 1980), 4–25; "Disciplining Soviet Power," *Foreign Policy* 43 (Summer 1981), 33–52; "Deterrence and Coercion in Soviet Policy," *International Security* 5 (Winter 1980/81), 80–103; and "The Clash Over Poland," *Foreign Policy* 46 (Spring 1982), 49–66.

33. There have been very few efforts to study Soviet risk-taking. In their study, Jan Triska and David Finley asked five experts to estimate risk and accepted their subjective estimates (*Soviet Foreign Policy* [New York: Macmillan, 1968], pp. 310–49). Hannes Adomeit takes exception to the judgments of the Triska and Finley panel and argues for a different ordering of high-risk situations (*Soviet Risk-Taking,* pp. 51–55). The problem of identifying the environmental circumstances and probable reactions of other states in any objective fashion has not been adequately addressed. Because the task often requires speculation, it may be impossible to defend with tools other than logic and argument and thus never be reduced to an "objective" category.

34. For one effort to deal with this case, see Hyland, "U.S.-Soviet Relations," pp. 538–39.

35. See, for example, Kenneth Arrow, *Social Choice and Individual Values* (New Haven, Conn.: Yale University Press, 1963). Robert Jervis develops a similar argument linking the concept of "basic intentions" to demonstrated risk taking and sacrifice (*Perception and Misperception in International Politics,* pp. 48–52).

36. This summary is an ideal type, but is based on the following works: George Kennan, *The Cloud of Danger: Current Realities of American Foreign Policy* (Boston: Atlantic Monthly Press, and Little, Brown, 1977); and *The Nuclear Delusion: Soviet-American Relations in the Atomic Age* (New York: Pantheon, 1982). Stephen Cohen, "Common and Uncommon Sense About the Soviet Union and American Policy," in House Committee on International Relations, *The Soviet Union Internal Dynamics of Foreign Policy: Present and Future,* 95th Cong., 2d sess. (Washington, D.C.: GPO, 1978); Fred Warner Neal, ed., *Detente or Debacle: Common Sense in U.S.-Soviet Relations* (New York: Norton, 1979). Also see Richard Barnet, "U.S.-Soviet Relations: The Need for a Comprehensive Approach," *Foreign Affairs* 57 (Spring 1979), 779–95; and Richard Barnet, *The Giants: Russia and America* (New York: Simon and Schuster, 1977).

37. Jervis, *Perception and Misperception,* p. 63.

38. See, for example, Ernst Haas, "Why Collaborate? Issue Linkage and International Regimes," *World Politics* 32 (1980) 357–405.

39. Cottam, *Foreign Policy Motivation,* pp. 157–257.

40. See Phares, *Locus of Control in Personality;* also see Kelley G. Shaver, *An Introduction to Attribution Processes* (Cambridge, Mass.: Winthrop, 1975).

41. Alexander George, *Managing U.S.-Soviet Rivalry: Problems of Crisis Prevention* (Boulder, Colo.: Westview, 1983), p. 4.

42. In theories concerning foreign policy, attributions of motivation often define the essential "understanding," and at a lower level of abstraction, are analogous to what Thomas Kuhn might identify as the central theory defining a scientific paradigm (*The Structure of Scientific Revolutions,* 2d ed. [Chicago: University of Chicago Press, 1970]).

43. See Snyder and Diesing, *Conflict Among Nations,* pp. 66–68.

44. Ibid., pp. 24, 44, 85, 156–57.

45. Snyder and Diesing discuss this problem but offer no method for inferring motives or perceptions (ibid., pp. 6–21). In their case studies they refer to

an area expert (pp. 103, 105, 115). Richard Ned Lebow also recognizes the problem in *Between Peace and War: The Nature of International Crisis* (Baltimore: Johns Hopkins University Press, 1981), pp. 224–25, 30–37, 206–11, 243–45, 278.

46. See Alexander George and Richard Smoke, *Deterrence in American Foreign Policy: Theory and Practice* (New York: Columbia University Press, 1974). In the case studies presented by George and Smoke, the key judgments about motivation are offered on pp. 397–403, 418–21, 459–66. In *The Limits of Coercive Diplomacy: Laos, Cuba, Vietnam,* ed. Alexander George, D. Hall, and W. Simons (Boston: Little, Brown, 1971), p. 216, George concludes that there are eight conditions required for the success of deterrence. The first three include: 1. strength of U.S. motivation, 2. asymmetry of motivation favoring the United States, and 3. clarity of American objectives.

47. Fritz Heider, *The Psychology of Interpersonal Relations* (New York: John Wiley, 1958), pp. 79–124. Also see Jones et al., *Attribution: Perceiving the Causes of Behavior.*

48. The inescapable need for motivational and political diagnosis in strategy formulation is a central theme developed by Ken Booth in *Strategy and Ethnocentrism* (New York: Holmes and Meier, 1979). George and Smoke conclude that what is necessary in policy science is the development of "empirical theory" concerning "how things work" in order to derive policy-related predictions on the probable effects of various prescriptions (*Deterrence in American Foreign Policy,* p. 618).

49. On the issue of shared images, see John Steinbruner, *The Cybernetic Theory of Decision: New Dimensions of Political Analysis,* (Princeton, N.J.: Princeton University Press, 1974), pp. 88–139; and Morton Halperin, *Bureaucratic Politics and Foreign Policy* (Washington D.C.: Brookings, 1974), pp. 11–16.

50. Alexander George, *Presidential Decisionmaking in Foreign Policy: The Effective Use of Information and Advice* (Boulder, Colo.: Westview Press, 1982), p. 242.

51. Robert Jervis, "Beliefs About Soviet Behavior," in *Containment, Soviet Behavior, and Grand Strategy,* ed. Robert Osgood (Berkeley, Calif.: University of California Institute of International Studies, 1981), pp. 56–59.

Chapter 2
Inferring Perceptions in Foreign Policy Research: A Theoretical Approach

1. See, for example, Rajan Menon, "Military Power, Intervention, and Soviet Policy in the Third World," in *Soviet Foreign Policy in the 1980s,* ed. Roger Kanet (New York: Praeger, 1982), p. 275. Also see Dimitri Simes, "The Death of Detente," *International Security* 5 (1980), 3–25.

2. Menon, "Military Power," p. 275.

3. Aryeh Yodfat, *The Soviet Union and the Arabian Peninsula: Soviet Policy Toward The Persian Gulf and Arabia* (London: Croom Helm, 1983), p. 50.

4. Dennis Ross, "Considering Threats to the Persian Gulf," (Washington, D.C.: Woodrow Wilson Center for International Security Studies, 1981), paper 29, pp. 7–8, emphasis in original.

5. Mark Katz, *The Third World in Soviet Military Thought* (London: Croom Helm, 1982), p. 138.

6. Arthur Stein, "When Misperceptions Matter," *World Politics* 34 (1982), 505–26.

7. Ibid., pp. 511–14.

8. See Robert Jervis, *Perception and Misperception in International Politics* (Princeton, N.J.: Princeton University Press, 1976), pp. 217–87. For how different the lessons were that various American leaders learned from the Vietnam experience, see Ole Holsti and James Rosenau, *American Leadership in World Affairs: Vietnam and the Breakdown of Consensus* (Boston: Allen and Unwin, 1984), pp. 58–78.

9. John L. Gaddis, *Strategies of Containment: A Critical Appraisal of Postwar American National Security Policy* (Oxford: Oxford University Press, 1982), p. 274–357.

10. Fred Halliday, *The Making of the Second Cold War* (London: Verso and NLB, 1983).

11. Stein, "When Misperceptions Matter," p. 510.

12. Holsti and Rosenau, *American Leadership in World Affairs*, p. 281.

13. See Jervis, *Perception and Misperception;* Alexander George, *Presidential Decisionmaking in Foreign Policy: The Effective Use of Information and Advice* (Boulder, Colo.: Westview, 1980); John Steinbruner, *The Cybernetic Theory of Decision: New Dimensions of Political Analysis* (Princeton, N.J.: Princeton University Press, 1974).

14. See Jack Levy, "Misperception and the Cause of War: Theoretical Linkages and Analytical Problems," *World Politics* 36 (October 1983), 76–99.

15. For a review of decision making and perceptual studies, see Glenn Snyder and Paul Diesing, *Conflict Among Nations: Bargaining, Decision Making, and System Structure in International Crises* (Princeton, N.J.: Princeton University Press, 1977), pp. 282–418. For a review of efforts to apply decision-making approaches to the Soviet case, see Arnold Horelick, A. Ross Johnson, and John Steinbruner, *The Study of Soviet Foreign Policy: Decision Theory–Related Approaches,* Sage Professional Papers in International Studies, vol. 4, no. 02–039. (Beverly Hills, Calif., and London: Sage, 1975). Also see Jervis, *Perception and Misperception,* pp. 13–57; Ole Holsti, "Foreign Policy Viewed Cognitively," in *The Structure of Decision: The Cognitive Maps of Political Elites,* ed. Robert Axelrod (Princeton, N.J.: Princeton University Press, 1976), pp. 18–54; and Amitai Etzioni, "Social-Psychological Aspects of International Relations," in vol. 5 of *The Handbook of Social Psychology,* 2d ed., ed. Gardner Linzey and Elliot Aronson (Reading, Mass.: Addison-Wesley, 1968).

16. See, for example, John Armstrong, "The Domestic Roots of Soviet Foreign Policy." in *The Conduct of Soviet Foreign Policy,* ed. Erik Hoffman and Frederic Fleron (Chicago: Aldine Atherton, 1971), pp. 50–60. Jiri Valenta has refined this basic idea, using William Riker's theory of coalitions including actors committed to "winning" more than policy, in "The Bureaucratic Politics Paradigm and the Soviet Invasion of Czechoslovakia," *Political Science Quarterly* 94 (Spring 1979), 55–76.

17. This model was developed by Carl Linden, *Khrushchev and the Soviet Leadership: 1957–1964* (Baltimore: Johns Hopkins Press, 1966).

18. The bureaucratic approach, which assumes perceptions and attitudes are role-determined, is best illustrated by Vernon Aspaturian, *Process and Power in Soviet Foreign Policy* (Boston: Little, Brown, 1971), pp. 491–551. This model has been refined and the emphasis on role determination softened in H. Gordon Skillings, "Groups in Soviet Politics: Some Hypotheses," in *Interest Groups in Soviet Politics,* ed. H. G. Skillings and Franklyn Griffiths (Princeton, N.J.: Princeton University Press, 1971), pp. 19–45.

19. For the models that strive to identify actors by values, see Alexander Dallin, "Soviet Foreign Policy and Domestic Politics: A Framework for Analy-

sis," in *The Conduct of Soviet Foreign Policy,* ed. Hoffmann and Fleron, pp. 36–49; Franklyn Griffiths, *Genoa Plus 51: Changing Soviet Objectives in Europe,* Wellesley paper 4 (Toronto: Canadian Institute of International Affairs, 1974); Roy Medvedev, *On Socialist Democracy,* trans. Ellen de Kadt (New York: Norton, 1975), pp. 48–90; and Alexander Yanov, *Detente After Brezhnev: The Domestic Roots of Soviet Foreign Policy* (Berkeley: University of California Institute of International Studies, 1977). Also see Stephen Cohen, "Common and Uncommon Sense About the Soviet Union and American Policy," in U.S. Congress, House, Committee on International Relations, *The Soviet Union—Internal Dynamics of Foreign Policy: Present and Future,* 95th Cong., 2d sess. (Washington, D.C.: GPO, 1978).

20. Many scholars have written on Soviet perceptions. Some, like Seweryn Bialer in *Stalin's Successors: Leadership, Stability and Change in the Soviet Union* (Cambridge: Cambridge University Press, 1980), have drawn general pictures based on a body of Soviet writings without specific footnoting. Others, such as John Lenczowski in *Soviet Perceptions of U.S. Foreign Policy: A Study of Ideology, Power and Consensus* (Ithaca, N.Y.: Cornell University Press, 1982), have reviewed the themes of the censored media with careful referencing. Stephen Gibert in *Soviet Images of America* (New York: Crane, Russak, 1977) has summarized some themes in Soviet propaganda with specific citations, while Morton Schwartz in *Soviet Perceptions of the United States* (Berkeley and Los Angeles: University of California Press, 1978) has recounted the images he found in the writings of the Institute of the U.S.A. and Canada, of the Soviet Academy of Sciences. Ilana Kass in *Soviet Involvement in the Middle East: Policy Formulation, 1966–1973* (Boulder, Colo.: Westview Press, 1978), has tried to summarize differences in various Soviet voices by citing specific newspapers while controlling the time frame and regional focus. For a study based on second-hand interviews, see Gregory Guroff and Steven Grant, "Soviet Elite: World View and Perceptions of the U.S.," U.S. International Communication Agency, June 1980 and Sept. 1981.

21. Many themes are present in Soviet statements. Consequently, analysts claiming that "the Soviets must indeed mean what they say" (Lenczowski, *Soviet Perceptions,* p. 23) must select a portion of the contradictory statements that are to be taken literally. The result is a competition between studies, like Lenczowski's and Gibert's *Soviet Images,* filled with statements stressing Soviet military might and confrontation, and others, like Morton Schwartz's *Soviet Perceptions,* that reproduce statements supportive of detente. Some of these problems can be handled by keeping track of many competing issues and by reporting the frequency with which each one is evident. Philip Stewart, for example, has found that among Politburo speeches during the 1970s, detente as an issue appeared in 42.6 percent, while Soviet military forces were mentioned in only 28.4 percent, and class struggle appeared in only 1.3 percent ("Foreign Policy Perceptions of the Soviet Politburo in the 1970s: Analysis and Data for Final Report," unpublished, Department of Political Science, Ohio State University, 1981, p. 7). See also Philip Stewart, James Warhola, and Roger Blough, "Issue Salience and Foreign Policy Role Specialization in the Soviet Politburo of the 1970s," *American Journal of Political Science* 28 (1984): 1–22.

22. For the results of two systematic studies, see William Zimmerman and Robert Axelrod, "The 'Lessons' of Vietnam and Soviet Foreign Policy," *World Politics* 34 (Oct. 1981), 1–24; and Philip Stewart, "Elite Perceptions and the Study of Soviet Decision-Making," presented at the Conference on Soviet Decision-Making, National Security Affairs Center, Naval Postgraduate School, Monterey, August 1980; "Peripheral and Central Issues in Soviet Foreign Policy," presented at the Midwest American Political Science Association, April

1982; and "Conflict and Consensus in Soviet Foreign Policy," presented at the annual meeting of the International Society of Political Psychology, June 1982.

23. Given the nature of politics, leaders are likely to exaggerate their perceived threats and minimize their perceived opportunities. See Grant Hugo, *Appearance and Reality in International Relations* (New York: Columbia University Press, 1970).

24. John Lenczowski claims that "the material that appears in their press is largely an index of real perceptions, real desires, or real policy priorities" (*Soviet Perceptions,* p. 23). Philip Stewart defines perceptions "as the attributes that a person associates with a specific issue, person, or object," and measures perception as the appearance of discrete themes and words used by Politburo members in their public speeches ("Conflict and Consensus in Soviet Foreign Policy," pp. 12–15). In Zimmerman and Axelrod, "The 'Lessons' of Vietnam" statements in the different Soviet presses are coded as direct evidence of "lessons" about Vietnam that Soviet leaders learned. These efforts are in line with other studies that rely on verbal statements as direct reflections of perceptions. See also Robert Axelrod, ed., *The Structure of Decision,* pp. 291–332; and Thomas Hart, *The Cognitive World of Swedish Security Elites* (Stockholm: Esselte Stadium, 1976).

25. William Zimmerman and Glen Palmer, "Words and Deeds in Soviet Foreign Policy: The Case of Soviet Military Expenditures," *American Political Science Review* 77 (1983), 358–67; and William Zimmerman and Robert Axelrod, "The Soviet Press on Soviet Foreign Policy: A Usually Reliable Source," *British Journal of Political Science* 11 (1981), 183–200.

26. Zimmerman and Palmer, "Words and Deeds."

27. Using indirect indicators is not uncommon in the social sciences. In studying anxiety psychologists postulate symptoms and then use these symptoms as indicators. The same type of logic underpins the Thematic Apperception Test. One effort to study the motives of U.S. presidents with an indirect set of indicators is Richard Donley and David Winter, "Measuring the Motives of Public Officials at a Distance: An Exploratory Study of American Presidents," *Behavioral Science* 15 (1970), 227–36.

28. William Gamson and Andre Modigliani, *Untangling the Cold War: A Strategy for Testing Rival Theories* (Boston: Little, Brown, 1971).

29. David Bobrow, "Uncoordinated Giants," in *Foreign Policy U.S.A./ U.S.S.R.,* ed. Charles W. Kegley, Jr., and Pat McGowan, vol. 7 of *International Yearbook of Foreign Policy Studies* (Beverly Hills, Calif.: Sage, 1982), pp. 23–49.

30. Ibid., p. 30. Also see Alexander George and Richard Smoke, *Deterrence in American Foreign Policy: Theory and Practice* (New York: Columbia University Press, 1974); and Alexander George, ed., *Managing U.S.-Soviet Rivalry: Problems of Crisis Prevention* (Boulder, Colo.: Westview, 1983).

31. Gamson and Modigliani, *Untangling the Cold War,* pp. 152–68.

32. Ibid., pp. 127–51.

33. On the problems of quantified coding, see Horelick, Johnson, and Steinbruner, *Study of Soviet Foreign Policy,* pp. 31–36.

34. R. J. Rummel, *Peace Endangered: The Reality of Detente* (Beverly Hills, Calif.: Sage, 1976), for example, draws confident conclusions from the quantitative analysis of data which itself is enormously controversial.

35. Even when an event is agreed upon, for example, the USSR sent troops into Afghanistan, whether to code this as an action or reaction, remains in dispute. See, for examples, Vernon Aspaturian, Alexander Dallin, and Jiri Valenta, *The Soviet Invasion of Afghanistan: Three Perspectives* (Los Angeles: University of California Center for International and Strategic Affairs, 1980); Robert Donaldson, "Soviet Policy in South Asia," in *Soviet Policy in the Third World,* ed. W. R. Duncan (New York: Pergamon Press, 1980), pp. 212–38;

Alfred Monks, *The Soviet Invasion in Afghanistan* (Washington, D.C.: AEI, 1981); Anthony Arnold, *Afghanistan: The Soviet Invasion in Perspective* (Stanford, Calif.: Hoover Institution, 1981); and N. P. Newell and R. S. Newell, *The Struggle for Afghanistan* (Ithaca, N.Y.: Cornell University Press, 1981).

36. George, ed., *Managing U.S.-Soviet Rivalry*; and Stephen Kaplan, *Diplomacy of Power: Soviet Armed Forces as a Political Instrument* (Washington, D.C.: Brookings, 1981).

37. See, for example, Kaplan, *Diplomacy of Power*, pt. 1, pp. 27–204. Also see Robert O. Freedman, "Soviet Policy Toward the Ba'athist Iraq," in *The Soviet Union in the Third World: Successes and Failures*, ed. R. Donaldson (Boulder, Colo.: Westview, 1981), pp. 161–64. Also Freedman, *Soviet Policy Toward the Middle East Since 1970* (New York: Praeger, 1978), pp. 7–8; and Jiri Valenta, *Soviet Intervention in Czechoslovakia, 1968: Anatomy of a Decision* (Baltimore: Johns Hopkins University Press, 1979), p. 44, 136, 156.

38. Stephen Gibert, for example, assumes "the reality of a confident and expansionist Soviet Union, determined to become the dominant world power," and uses this assumption to determine which statements "simply serve the immediate interests of the Soviets" and which are genuine reflections of perceptions (*Soviet Images*, pp. 8, 153). For other examples of studies that use a motivational claim to guide the selection of statements, see Lenczowski, *Soviet Perceptions*; and R. Judson Mitchell, "A New Brezhnev Doctrine: The Restructuring of International Relations," *World Politics* 30 (Apr. 1978), 366–90.

39. For two case studies that do consider rival hypotheses, see George A. Breslauer, "Soviet Policy in the Middle East, 1967–1972: Unalterable Antagonism or Collaborative Competition," in *Managing U.S.-Soviet Rivalry*, ed. George, pp. 65–106; and Arthur J. Klinghoffer, *The Angolan War: A Study in Soviet Foreign Policy in the Third World* (Boulder, Colo.: Westview, 1980).

40. See Zimmerman and Palmer, "Words and Deeds." Also see Michael Sullivan, "Foreign Policy Articulation and U.S. Conflict Behavior," in *To Augur Well: Early Warning Indicators in World Politics*, ed. J. D. Singer and M. D. Wallace (Beverly Hills, Calif.: Sage, 1979), pp. 215–35.

41. For studies that have considered perceptions of opportunity and threat, see Gamson and Modigliani, *Untangling the Cold War*; and Jan. F. Triska and David Finley, *Soviet Foreign Policy* (New York: Macmillan, 1968), pp. 137–48. On the importance of considering perceptions of opportunity and threat, see Richard Herrmann, "Perceptions and Foreign Policy Analysis," in *Foreign Policy Decision Making: Perception, Cognition, and Artifical Intelligence*, ed. D. Sylvan and S. Chan (New York: Praeger, 1984), pp. 25–52.

42. On the concept of cognitive structures, see James Bieri, "Cognitive Structures in Personality," in *Personality Theory and Information Processing*, ed. Harold Schroder and Peter Sudefeld (New York: Ronald, 1971), pp. 178–208. Also see Harold Kelly, "Causal Schemata and the Attribution Process," in *Attribution: Perceiving the Causes of Behavior*, ed. Edward Jones et al. (Morristown, N.J.: General Learning Press, 1971), pp. 151–74.

43. See Solomon Asch, *Social Psychology* (Englewood Cliffs, N.J.: Prentice-Hall, 1952), pp. 215–17. For a review of gestalt and other approaches to impression formation such as N. J. Anderson's additive models, see Albert H. Hastorf, David J. Schneider, and Judith Polefka, *Person Perception* (Reading, Mass.: Addison-Wesley, 1970), pp. 35–60. For an application of this argument in international relations, see Kenneth Boulding, "National Images and International Systems," *Journal of Conflict Resolution* 3 (1959), 120–31; and *The Image* (Ann Arbor: University of Michigan Press, 1956). For preliminary empirical validity, note the higher interitem correlations and mutually exclusive character of the belief systems found by Holsti and Rosenau, *American Leadership in World Affairs*, pp. 128–33.

44. Robert Jervis, "Beliefs About Soviet Behavior," in *Containment, Soviet Behavior, and Grand Strategy,* ed. Robert Osgood (Berkeley: University of California Institute of International Studies, 1981), pp. 55–59.

45. See Jervis, *Perception and Misperception,* J. Levy, "Misperception and the Cause of War"; George, *Presidential Decisionmaking in Foreign Policy;* and Steinbruner, *The Cybernetic Theory of Decision.*

46. See Fritz Heider, *The Psychology of Interpersonal Relations* (New York: John Wiley, 1958). For two efforts to use balance theory in foreign policy analysis, see Richard Cottam, *Foreign Policy Motivation: A General Theory and a Case Study* (Pittsburgh, Pa.: University of Pittsburgh Press, 1977); and Daniel Heradstveit, *The Arab-Israeli Conflict: Psychological Obstacles to Peace* (Oslo: Universitetsforlaget, 1981).

47. See Steinbruner, *The Cybernetic Theory of Decision,* pp. 103–09.

48. See C. A. Kiesler, B. E. Collins, and N. Miller, *Attitude Change: A Critical Analysis of Theoretical Approahces* (New York: Wiley, 1969).

49. See Susan Fiske and Shelley Taylor, *Social Cognition* (Menlo Park, Calif.: Addison-Wesley, 1984); and Richard Nisbett and Lee Ross, *Human Inferences: Strategies and Shortcomings of Social Judgment* (Englewood Cliffs, N.J.: Prentice-Hall, 1980), pp. 33–35. The stereotypes might also be thought of as "scripts" that place the observer in a role that is morally justified and balanced with a positive self-image. On "scripts," see Robert Abelson, "Script Processing in Attitude Formation and Decision Making," in *Cognition and Social Behavior,* ed. John Carroll and John Payne (Hillsdale, N.J.: Lawrence Erlbaum, 1976), pp. 33–45.

50. Cottam, *Foreign Policy Motivation,* p. 64.

51. For a theoretical derivation of the "enemy" stereotype, see Murray Edelman, "The Need for Enemies," presented at the annual meeting of the International Society of Political Psychology, 1983.

52. Cottam, *Foreign Policy Motivation,* p. 65. To determine if a subject perceives threat from a foreign country, this approach compares the resemblance between the subject's description of the country and the "enemy" stereotype.

53. Because much of Jervis's work is focused on great-power conflicts, the common misperceptions he finds are most often related to this stereotype. Overestimating one's influence and effectiveness, for example, is similar to the simplification noted here under capability. The notions of overcentralization and planning are included under decisional process. See Jervis, *Perception and Misperception,* pp. 319–81.

54. See Ralph K. White, *Nobody Wanted War: Misperceptions in Vietnam and Other Wars* (New York: Anchor, 1970), David J. Finlay, Ole Holsti, and Richard Fagan, *Enemies in Politics* (Chicago: Rand McNally Co., 1967).

55. Cottam, *Foreign Policy Motivation,* pp. 151–310.

56. See Morton Halperin, *Bureaucratic Politics and Foreign Policy* (Washington, D.C.: Brookings, 1974), pp. 11–16; and Jiri Valenta, *The Soviet Invasion in Czechosolvakia, 1968: Anatomy of a Decision* (Baltimore: Johns Hopkins University Press, 1979), pp. 5, 44, 136, 156. For both Halperin and Valenta, the questions pertaining to basic perceptions of the adversary are assumed as "shared images." Valenta assumes that Soviet leaders share a perception of opportunity in the Third World and perception of threat from the United States. Substantiating these basic propositions will be the focus of this research; they will not be assumed at the outset. The research operates at a level similar to that of the "operational code." See Alexander George, "The Causal Nexus Between Cognitive Beliefs and Decision-Making Behavior: The 'Operational Code' Belief System" in *Psychological Models in International Politics,* ed. Lawrence S. Falkowski (Boulder, Colo.: Westview, 1979), pp. 95–124.

57. See Stephen Krasner, "Are Bureaucracies Important? (or Allison Wonderland)?" *Foreign Policy* 7 (Summer 1972), 157–79.

58. The Communist spokesmen's image will be drawn from a data base that includes collections of Brezhnev's speeches—*Following Lenin's Course* (Moscow: Progress, 1972); *Our Course: Peace and Socialism* (Moscow: Novosti, 1973, 1974, 1975, 1977)—and every article on the United States that appeared in *Pravda* or *Izvestia* in any of the three periods and was translated in either the *Current Digest of the Soviet Press* (*CDSP*) or the *Foreign Broadcast Information Service: Daily Report, Soviet Union* (*FBIS*). Additionally, the data will include all related articles published during each period in *International Affairs* (*Moscow*). These translated sources provide an excellent data base. First, I am searching for basic images reflecting Soviet views of U.S. motivation, capabilities and power, and decisional process. At this level these sources are reliable and disputes over the translation of specific words or phrases are unlikely to affect the general image. Second, the base includes a large sample of authoritative statements and related Soviet articles. Third, the core of the study will be based on international behavior for which the Soviet media is not the best source.

59. See, for example, Zimmerman and Axelrod, "The Lessons of Vietnam and Soviet Foreign Policy"; Franklyn Griffiths, "The Sources of American Conduct: Soviet Perspectives and Their Policy Implications," *International Security* 9 (Fall 1984), 3–50; William Jackson, "Soviet Images of the U.S. as Nuclear Adversary, 1969–1979," *World Politics* 33 (1981), 614–38. Robert Cutler, "The Soviet Union in the 1974 Cyprus Affair," presented at the 15th National Convention of the American Association for the Advancement of Slavic Studies, 1983).

60. The tendency to apply a double standard when drawing inferences from Soviet and American actions has been found among American observers. See Stuart Oskamp, "Attitudes Toward U.S. and Russian Actions: A Double Standard," *Psychological Reports* 16 (1965), 43–46; and Stuart Oskamp and A. Harty, "A Factor-Analytic Study of the Double Standard in Attitudes Toward U.S. and Russian Actions," *Behavioral Science* 13 (1968), 178–88.

61. Henry Kissinger, *Nuclear Weapons and Foreign Policy*, abr. ed. (New York: Norton, 1969), pp. 43–80.

62. For an example of how Hitler described a revisionist strategy, see *Hitler's Secret Conversations 1941–1944*, trans. Norman Cameron and R. H. Stevens (New York: Farrar, Straus and Young, 1953); and *Hitler's Secret Book*, intro. Telford Taylor, trans. Salvator Attanasio (New York: Alliance, Longmans Green, 1939), pp. 190–97.

63. See Gamson and Modigliani, *Untangling the Cold War*, p. 23.

64. This method for considering the predictions of each model and comparing them to actual Soviet behavior is parallel to the method employed by John Steinbruner to evaluate his decisional models at a different level of analysis (*The Cybernetic Theory of Decision*, pp. 191–98, 239–47, 311–26).

65. On the utility of "focused comparison," see Alexander George, "Case Studies and Theory Development: The Method of Structured, Focused Comparisons," in *Diplomacy: New Approaches in History, Theory, and Policy*, ed. Paul Gordon Lauren (New York: Free Press, 1979), pp. 43–68.

66. McClelland also reviews the difficulties in applying events data to Soviet-American interaction, stressing the difficulty of capturing the indirect character of competition through "proxies" (Charles A. McClelland, "Let the User Beware," *International Studies Quarterly* 27 [June 1983], 174). For one study that uses events data, see A. Hybel and D. B. Robertson, "Assessing the Dynamic Reaction of the U.S.S.R. to American and Chinese Actions and to its Nuclear Gap with the U.S.A.," *International Interactions* 4 (1978), 125–54.

67. On the usefulness of studying nonoccurrences, see George, *Presidential Decisionmaking in Foreign Policy*, pp. 59–61. McClelland, "Let the User Beware," p. 174, argues that missing nonoccurrences is a problem for most sets of events data.

68. E. Jones and Richard Nisbett, "The Actor and Observer: Divergent Perceptions of the Causes of Behavior," in *Attribution: Perceiving the Causes of Behavior,* ed. Jones et al. (Morristown, N.J.: General Learning Press, 1971), pp. 79–94; and Jervis, *Perception and Misperception in International Politics,* pp. 35–48.

69. Without an assumption about motivation, the analyst cannot confirm that deterrence worked. The analyst can, however, tell when it fails. See George and Smoke, *Deterrence in American Foreign Policy,* for a typology of deterrence failures in American foreign policy. Also see B. Blechman and S. Kaplan, *Force Without War: U.S. Armed Forces as a Political Instrument* (Washington, D.C.: Brookings, 1978).

Chapter 3
Soviet Perceptions and Foreign Policy, 1967

1. See Secretary Rusk's testimony in *United States Policy Toward Asia,* U.S. Congress, House Subcommittee on the Far East and the Pacific of the Committee on Foreign Affairs, 89th Cong., 2d sess. (Washington, D.C.: GPO, 1966), pp. 523–34. Also see U.S. Congress, Senate Committee on Foreign Relations, *U.S Policy with Respect to Mainland China,* 89th Cong., 2d sess. (Washington, D.C.: GPO, 1966).

2. See "Transcript of Secretary Rusk's News Conference on Foreign Affairs," *New York Times,* Oct. 13, 1967, pp. 14–15. The alliances included Japan, South Korea, Taiwan, Thailand, the Philippines, Pakistan, and South Vietnam.

3. See Kwan Ha Yim, ed., *China and the U.S., 1964–1972* (New York: Facts on File, 1975). Also see the *New York Times,* Aug. 14, 1967, p. 1; and Aug. 22, 1967, p. 1. In May 1967 Chou En Lai warned the PRC would send its army into North Vietnam if the North were threatened by either an invasion or a "sellout" peace (*New York Times,* May 15, 1967, p. 1).

4. See Yim, ed., *China and the U.S.,* pp. 147–58.

5. See, for example, Editorial, "Smash the Big U.S.-Soviet Conspiracy!" *Peking Review,* Feb. 24, 1967, 6–7; "Chairman Mao Tse-tung on People's War"; and Lin Piao, "Long Live the Victory of People's War," in *Peking Review,* Aug. 4, 1967, 5–35. Lin Piao's article was a reprint of his famous 1965 article. Many felt the Chinese considered Americans as simply the current agents of the hated legacy of Western and Japanese intervention. See Doak Barnett, *China and the Major Powers in East Asia* (Washington, D.C.: Brookings, 1977).

6. For a study of the Chinese media, see Alfred Low, *The Sino-Soviet Dispute: An Analysis of the Polemics* (Rutherford, N.J.: Fairleigh Dickinson University Press, 1976).

7. See, for example, Editorial, "Hit Back Hard at the Rabid Provocations of the Filthy Soviet Revisionist Swine!" *Renmin Ribao* in *Peking Review* 10 (Feb. 3, 1967), 23–24. For development of this idea, see the testimony of both A. Doak Barnett and Donald Zagoria in *U.S Policy with Respect to Mainland China,* pp. 32–33; 396. Also see William Griffith, *Sino-Soviet Relations, 1964–*

1965 (Cambridge, Mass.: MIT Press, 1967). The Chinese opposition to "peaceful coexistence" as a Soviet policy became clear in the late 1950s. See Donald Zagoria, *The Sino-Soviet Conflict, 1956–1961* (Princeton, N.J.: Princeton University Press, 1962), pp. 39–65; 152–71; and William Griffith, *The Sino-Soviet Rift* (Cambridge, Mass.: MIT Press, 1964), pp. 16–18.

8. June T. Dreyer, *China's Forty Millions* (Cambridge, Mass.: Harvard University Press, 1976), pp. 210–11.

9. The PRC had recalled its ambassador from Moscow in 1962 and at that time insisted that the USSR close all of its consulates in China. In 1967 the Chinese mounted mass demonstrations against the remaining Soviet embassy in Peking and in February held the compound and the Soviet personnel under siege for eighteen days (*New York Times*, Jan. 30, 1967, p. 3, Feb. 8, 1967, p. 4, and Feb. 14, 1967, p. 9).

10. Low, *Sino-Soviet Dispute*, pp. 126–36; and Griffith, *Sino-Soviet Relations 1964–1965*, pp. 114–18.

11. See Dean Rusk, in U.S. Congress, House, Subcommittee on the Far East, and the Pacific of the Committee on Foreign Affairs, *Sino-Soviet Conflict*, 89th Cong., 1st sess. (Washington, D.C.: GPO, 1965), pp. 353–66.

12. Ibid., pp. 364–65. Also see the testimony of A. Doak Barnett, Donald Zagoria, and John Lindbeck in *U.S. Policy with Respect to Mainland China*, pp. 32–35; 79–82; 214–15; 369–70; 396; and President Johnson's comments, in Roderick MacFarquhar, *Sino-American Relations, 1949–1971* (New York: Praeger, 1972), pp. 210–11.

13. See W. W. Rostow, *The Diffusion of Power: An Essay in Recent History* (New York: Macmillan, 1972), pp. 222–50; 264–95; 391–406. Also see Dean Rusk, *The Winds of Freedom* (Boston: Beacon, 1963).

14. A. N. Kosygin (chairman of the Council of Ministers, and member of the Politburo of the Central Committee of the CPSU), "On a Leninist Course," *Pravda*, Mar. 7, 1967, pp. 1–2; "Toward Great New Accomplishments," *Izvestia*, Mar. 7, 1967, *CDSP* 19 (Mar. 29, 1967), 3–4. Brezhnev makes a similar charge: see "In the Name of the Triumph of Communism," *Pravda*, Mar. 11, 1967, pp. 1–3, *CDSP* 19 (Mar. 29, 1967), 5–7, 29.

15. "Communique of Plenary Session of the Central Committee of the C.P.S.U.," *Pravda* and *Izvestia*, Dec. 13, 1966, p. 1, *CDSP* 18 (Jan. 4, 1967). Also see F. Burlatsky, and Y. Kuskov, "In Struggle for Solidarity of Communist Forces," *Pravda*, Jan. 20, 1967, pp. 4–5, *CDSP* 19 (Feb. 8, 1967), 16–18.

16. Editorial, "On the Anti-Soviet Policy of Mao Tse-tung and his Group," *Pravda*, Feb. 16, 1967, p. 3. This article also appeared as a similarly titled editorial in *Izvestia*, Feb. 17, 1967, pp. 2–3, *CDSP* 19 (Mar. 8, 1967), 8. Also see N. Kapchenko, "Whence the C.P.C. Leadership's Political Line?" *International Affairs* (*Moscow*), Mar. 1967, p. 19.

17. Editorial, "On the Anti-Soviet Policy of Mao Tse-tung and His Group," p. 9. Also see L. Sergeyev, "Whom Does Culture Impede?" *Izvestia*, Feb. 21, 1967, p. 2, *CDSP* 19 (Mar. 15, 1967), 17–18.

18. Editorial, "On the Anti-Soviet Policy of Mao Tse-tung and His Group," p. 7. Brezhnev makes a similar point: see "In the Name of the Triumph of Communism," p. 7.

19. Editorial, "On the Anti-Soviet Policy of Mao Tse-tung," p. 8.

20. Brezhnev, "In the Name of the Triumph of Communism," p. 7.

21. Editorial, "On the Anti-Soviet Policy of Mao Tse-tung," p. 7. Also see L. Delyusin and L. Kyuzadzhyan, "A Threat to Socialism in China," *Izvestia*, July 4, 1967, pp. 2–3, *CDSP* 19 (July 26, 1967), p. 7.

22. Brezhnev, "In the Name of the Triumph of Communism," p. 7; Delyusin and Kyuzadzhyan, "A Threat to Socialism," p. 9. Also see Editorial, "On the Anti-Soviet Policy of Mao Tse-tung," p. 7.

23. Delyusin and Kyuzadzhyan, "A Threat to Socialism," p. 8–9, and Editorial, "On the Anti-Soviet Policy of Mao Tse-tung," p. 8.

24. The USSR increased divisions deployed in Central Asia from twenty-two to thirty, between 1965 and 1967 (*The Military Balance 1967–1968* [London: ISS, 1967], p. 6). Also see *The Military Balance 1965–1966* (London: ISS, 1966); Robert H. Donaldson, *Soviet Policy Toward India: Ideology and Strategy* (Cambridge, Mass.: Harvard University Press, 1974), pp. 204–10; Raymond L. McGovern, "Moscow and Hanoi," *Problems of Communism* 16 (May–June 1967), 64–71; and Marshall D. Shulman, "Recent Soviet Foreign Policy: Some Patterns in Retrospect," *Journal of International Affairs* 22 (1968), 26–47; Chin O. Chung, *P'yongyang Between Peking and Moscow: North Korea's Involvement in the Sino-Soviet Dispute 1958–1975* (University, Ala.: University of Alabama Press, 1978), pp. 81–126.

25. Maury Lisann, "Moscow and the Chinese Power Struggle," *Problems of Communism* 18 (Nov.–Dec. 1969), pp. 32–41. Also see Franz Michael, "Moscow and the Current Chinese Crisis," *Current History* 53 (Sept. 1967), 141–47; 179–80; and Marian Kirsh, "Soviet Security Objectives in Asia," *International Organization* 24 (Summer 1970), 454.

26. Kosygin, "On a Leninist Course"; "Toward Great New Accomplishments." General Secretary Brezhnev struck a similar theme although generally related his description of "U.S. imperialism" to specific conflicts. See L. I. Brezhnev, "Speech at Reception in Honor of Graduates of Military Academies," *Pravda* and *Izvestia*, July 6, 1967, pp. 1–2, *CDSP* 19 (July 26, 1967), 4–5.

27. L. I. Brezhnev, "Fifty Years of Great Achievements of Socialism," report and concluding speech delivered at the Joint Jubilee Meeting of the Central Committee of the CPSU, the Supreme Soviet of the USSR, and the Supreme Soviet of the RSFSR in the Kremlin Palace of Congresses, Nov. 3–4, 1967, in Brezhnev, *Following Lenin's Course* (Moscow: Progress, 1972), p. 57.

28. "Resolution of the CPSU Central Committee: On Preparations for the 50th Anniversary of the Great October Socialist Revolution," in *Pravda* and *Izvestia*, Jan. 8, 1967, pp. 1–2, *CDSP* 19 (Jan. 25, 1967), pp. 11–14.

29. Editorial, "Crimes of American Aggressors," *Pravda*, Mar. 2, 1967, p. 1, *CDSP* 19 (Mar. 22, 1967), 16–17.

30. For journalistic expressions of the dominant theme, see K. Vishnevetsky, "International Commentary: Common Link of Tension," *Izvestia*, May 23, 1967, p. 3, *CDSP* 19 (June 14, 1967), 26; V. Kudryavtsev, "The Aggressor's Cynicism," *Izvestia*, May 6, 1967, p. 2, *CDSP* 19 (May 24, 1967), 12–13; I. Shatalov, "South-East Asia in the Military Strategic Plans of Imperialism," *International Affairs (Moscow)*, Apr. 1967, p. 53.

31. Editorial, "The Aggressors Will Answer for His Crimes," *Izvestia*, June 16, 1967, p. 1, *CDSP* 19 (July 5, 1967), 9–10. Also see Yury Zhukov, "Self-Exposure of the Restorers of Colonialism," *Pravda*, June 12, 1967, p. 5, *CDSP* 19 (July 5, 1967), 6–7; and V. Petrov, "Criminal Collusion," *Izvestia*, June 13, 1967, p. 5, *CDSP* 19 (July 5, 1967), 7–8.

32. "Resolution of Plenary Session of C.P.S.U. Central Committee, Adopted June 21, 1967: On the Policy of the Soviet Union in Connection with the Aggression of Israel in the Near East," *Pravda* and *Izvestia*, June 22, 1967, p. 1, *CDSP* 19 (July 12, 1967), 11, 19. Also see Brezhnev, "Fifty Years of Great Achievements of Socialism," p. 59.

33. A. P. Kirilenko (Politburo member and secretary of the Central Committee), "Under the Banner of Leninism Toward New Victories for the Causes of October," *Pravda* and *Izvestia*, Apr. 23, 1967, pp. 1–2, *CDSP* 19 (May 10, 1967), 9–11. Also see Brezhnev, "Speech . . . in Honor of Graduates of Military Academies."

34. See Brezhnev, "Fifty Years of Great Achievements of Socialism," pp.

40–41. Also see L. I. Brezhnev, "Speech at Karlovy Vary," *Pravda*, Apr. 25, 1967, pp. 1–3, *CDSP* 19 (May 17, 1967), 6.

35. Shatalov, "South East Asia in Plans of Imperialism," pp. 53–54.

36. Y. Melnikov, "U.S. Foreign Policy: A Threat to Peace," *International Affairs (Moscow)*, Jan. 1967, p. 65.

37. Brezhnev, for example, in "Fifty Years of Great Achievements of Socialism," p. 57, said that U.S. intervention was responsible for the war in Vietnam, developments in Laos, and the Middle East, as well as "reactionary coups engineered" in "Asian, African, European and Latin American countries." The United States was also blamed for the military coup in Greece, the Arab-Israeli War, and African adventures. Also see S. Samoilov, "Shadow of the C.I.A. Over Greece," *Pravda*, June 5, 1967, p. 4, *CDSP* 19 (June 28, 1967), 25–27; and "Resolution of Plenary Session of C.P.S.U. Central Committee."

38. Y. Rakhmaninov, "Alternative to a Divided Europe," *International Affairs (Moscow)*, Apr. 1967, p. 44; and Brezhnev, "Speech at Karlovy Vary," pp. 6–7.

39. V. Matveyev, "Sober and Raving Voices," *Izvestia*, Feb. 24, 1967, p. 2, *CDSP* 19 (Mar. 15, 1967), 21–22.

40. See I. Geyevsky, "The Aggressor's Uneasy Home Front," *Izvestia*, Feb. 26, 1967, p. 5, *CDSP* 19 (Mar. 15, 1967), 22. Also see V. Matveyev, "Stagnation and Progress in the U.S.A.," *Izvestia*, Dec. 25, 1966, p. 3, *CDSP* 18 (Jan. 18, 1967), 19, 21.

41. Lawrence Freedman, *U.S. Intelligence and the Soviet Strategic Threat* (Boulder: Westview, 1977), pp. 101–17, esp. 114. Also see *Strategic Survey 1967* (London: ISS, 1968), pp. 22–23; and *The Military Balance 1967–1968* (London: ISS, 1968), p. 45.

42. While early studies failed to fully understand the USSR's determination to match the United States' nuclear edge, there was little doubt that in 1967 the latter still enjoyed a substantial numerical advantage. See John Prados, *The Soviet Estimate: U.S. Intelligence Analysis and Russian Military Strength* (New York: Dial Press, 1982), p. 183–99.

43. Lyndon B. Johnson, *The Vantage Point: Perspectives of the Presidency, 1963–1969* (New York: Holt, Rinehart and Winston, 1971), pp. 483–84. Also see Thomas A. Wolfe, *Soviet Power and Europe 1945–1970* (Baltimore: Johns Hopkins Press, 1970), pp. 267, 269–71.

44. Brezhnev, "Speech at Karlovy Vary." Also see L. I. Brezhnev, "Rally of Brotherhood," *Pravda*, Oct. 16, 1966, pp. 1–3, *CDSP* 18 (Nov. 9, 1966), p. 4.

45. Brezhnev, "Speech at Karlovy Vary," p. 8.

46. Ibid., p. 3.

47. Academicians V. M. Khvostov and Leo Stern, "Commonwealth of Class Brothers," published as an editor's note, *Pravda*, Mar. 17, 1967, p. 5, *CDSP* 19 (Apr. 5, 1967), 21–22.

48. See Jack M. Schick, *The Berlin Crisis, 1958–1962* (Philadelphia: University of Pennsylvania Press, 1971); Jean E. Smith, *The Defense of Berlin* (Baltimore: Johns Hopkins Press, 1963); and Robert Slusser, *The Berlin Crisis of 1961: Soviet American Relations and the Struggle for Power in the Kremlin, June–November 1961* (Baltimore: Johns Hopkins University Press, 1973).

49. See James P. Warburg, *Germany Key to Peace* (Cambridge, Mass.: Harvard University Press, 1953); and Keesing's Research Report, *Germany and Eastern Europe Since 1945: From the Potsdam Agreement to Chancellor Brandt's "Ostpolitik"* (New York: Charles Scribner's Sons, 1973).

50. President Johnson introduced the notion of "bridge-building" as a third program in U.S. general policy. The first two programs, granted higher priority, continued to be the modernization of NATO and the strengthening of a "United West European community." The president simultaneously recog-

nized the reunification of Germany as "a vital purpose of American policy," and explained that a united Germany could exist within the Western community without frightening other Europeans. For a text of Johnson's speech, see the *New York Times*, Oct. 8, 1966, p. 12.

51. Khvostov and Stern, "Commonwealth of Class Brothers."

52. Brezhnev, "Speech at Karlovy Vary," p. 7.

53. L. I. Brezhnev, "Speech at the Seventh Congress of Socialist Unity Party of Germany: For the Unity of Communists of the World," *Pravda*, Apr. 19, 1967, pp. 1–2, *CDSP* 19 (May 10, 1967), 3–6.

54. The central question is whether the USSR is expansionist vis-à-vis Western Europe, not Eastern Europe. Its imperial control of Eastern Europe is taken as a given in 1967. This follows Morgenthau's concept of imperialism (see *Politics Among Nations: The Struggle for Power and Peace*, 5th ed. [New York: Knopf, 1973], pp. 45–48).

55. "Soviet Government Statement, *Pravda*, Jan. 29, 1967, pp. 1, 4, *CDSP* 19 (Feb. 15, 1967), 11–13.

56. Ibid. Also see Brezhnev, "Speech at the Seventh Congress . . . for the Unity of Communists," and "Speech . . . in Honor of Graduates of Military Academies."

57. *The Military Balance 1967–1968* (London: ISS, 1967), p. 6.

58. See R. Pyadyshev and R. Sergeyev, "Problems of European Security," *Pravda*, Feb. 24, 1967, p. 4, *CDSP* 19 (Mar. 15, 1967), 16.

59. *Strategic Survey 1967*, p. 18.

60. See Robin Alison Remington, *The Warsaw Pact: Case Studies in Communist Conflict Resolution* (Cambridge, Mass.: MIT Press, 1971), pp. 87–93.

61. See Wolfe, *Soviet Power*, p. 351.

62. Brezhnev, "In the Name of the Triumph of Communism," p. 6, and "Speech at the Seventh Congress of Socialist Unity Party of Germany," p. 4. Gerhard Wettig argues that after the SPD's Dortmund Party Congress, the USSR came to the conclusion that there was no significant West German group worth appealing to. He concludes that they adopted a strategy of isolating the FRG rather than trying to bring about domestic change or loosening ties to the United States (*Community and Conflict in the Socialist Camp: The Soviet Union, East Germany and the German Problem 1965–1972*, trans. E. Moreton and H. Adomeit [New York: St. Martin's Press, 1975], pp. 27–28). Brezhnev, somewhat in contradiction to Wettig's proposition in his speech at Karlovy Vary, did appeal to the SPD to articulate and press for a new foreign policy in the FRG, but for the most part, as Wettig's argument would suggest, he criticized the SPD and directed his appeals to other West European countries.

63. Generally, the idea of a security conference was presented by the Soviets in a context including only European states and with its main aim being the reduction of foreign military bases in Europe (i.e., U.S. military bases). However, the Soviet Union was ambiguous on whether or not the United States should attend the proposed conference, and at times major Soviet spokesmen, like the editors of *International Affairs* (*Moscow*), explicitly announced that the United States and West Germany certainly should attend such a conference as long as they first accepted the "two key prerequisites" of peace in Europe (Editorial, "On the Threshold of 1967," *International Affairs* (*Moscow*), Jan. 1967, p. 6). Thomas Wolfe discusses the ambiguity of the Soviet position and concludes that the USSR was vague on whether or not the United States should participate in the proposed conference (*Soviet Power*, p. 311).

64. Brezhnev, "Speech at Reception in Honor of Graduates of Military Academies,"

65. "Resolution of the Plenary Session . . . : On the Policy of the Soviet Union in Connection with the Aggression of Israel in the Near East."

66. See Jon D. Glassman, *Arms for the Arabs: The Soviet Union in War in the Middle East* (Baltimore: Johns Hopkins University Press, 1975), pp. 37–41. The Soviet message to Israel was communicated to the Israeli Ambassador by Soviet Deputy Foreign Minister Malik on April 21, 1967, quoted in Avigdor Dagan, *Moscow and Jerusalem* (New York: Abdlard-Schuman, 1970), pp. 202–03.

67. Lyndon B. Johnson, *The Vantage Point: Perspectives of the Presidency 1963–1969* (New York: Holt, Rinehart and Winston, 1971), p. 298.

68. This territory was acquired by Jordan during the war of 1948. It can be considered Palestinian. For purposes of this study it is treated as Jordanian since Jordan controlled it in 1967.

69. The Soviet Union in the UN pressed for immediate Israeli withdrawal. See V. Mayevsky and B. Strelnikov, "In U.N. and Outside Its Walls," *Pravda*, June 26, 1967, p. 4, *CDSP* 19 (July 19, 1967), 10. In July TASS issued a warning to Israel and the United States to withdraw, saying the "imperialists" were "playing with fire," and "making a serious mistake in their evaluation of the determination of the Arab states and their friends" but did not threaten either nation with any specific consequences. See Tass Statement, "Risky Playing with Fire," *Pravda*, July 21, 1967, p. 4; and *Izvestia*, July 21, 1967, p. 1, *CDSP* 19 (Aug. 9, 1967), 11.

70. Glassman, *Arms for the Arabs*, pp. 65–69; and Nadav Safran, *From War to War: The Arab-Israeli Confrontation 1948–1967* (Indianapolis: Pegasus, Bobbs-Merrill, 1969), p. 411.

71. Glassman, Arms for the Arabs, pp. 43–44. Also see Ilana Kass, *Soviet Involvement in the Middle East: Policy Formulation 1966–1973* (Boulder, Colo.: Westview Press, 1978), pp. 50–51; and Alvin Rubinstein, *Red Star on the Nile: The Soviet-Egyptian Influence Relationship Since the June War* (Princeton, N.J.: Princeton University Press, 1970), pp. 41–42.

72. Johnson, *Vantage Point*, p. 302.

73. Glassman, *Arms for the Arabs*, pp. 26–33. Also see Stockholm International Peace Research Institute, *Arms Trade Registers: The Arms Trade with the Third World* (Cambridge: MIT Press, 1975), pp. 43–46; 63–65; *The Military Balance 1967–1968*, pp. 40–41.

74. Glassman, *Arms for the Arabs*, pp. 26–33.

75. Mohamed Heikal, *The Cairo Documents* (Garden City, N.Y.: Doubleday, 1973), p. 242. According to Heikal, Premier Kosygin in late May told Egyptian Minister of War Shams el Din Badran to seek a "compromise" and to "work politically."

76. Ibid., p. 244.

77. Glassman, *Arms for the Arabs*, pp. 33–36.

78. See George Breslauer, "Soviet Policy in the Middle East, 1967–1972: Unalterable Antagonism or Collaborative Competition?" in *Managing U.S.-Soviet Rivalry: Problems of Crisis Prevention* ed. Alexander George (Boulder, Colo.: Westview, 1983), pp. 65–106.

79. This is consistent with this study's treatment of the national issues in Germany. In that case, the origin of Soviet control in Eastern Europe was not at issue but taken as a given. Here the creation of the government in the South is not at issue but is taken as already in existence. The DRV's nonrecognition of the government in the South is accepted as part of the status quo, just as Western nonrecognition of the regime in East Germany was treated as part of the status quo in Central Europe.

80. Editorial, "Crimes of American Aggressors," *Pravda*, Mar. 2, 1967, p. 1, *CDSP* (Mar. 22, 1967), 16–17. Brezhnev also made this explicit. See "Fifty Years of Great Achievements of Socialism."

81. See Justus M. Van der Kroef, "The Soviet Union and South East Asia,"

in *The Soviet Union and the Developing Nations*, ed. Roger E. Kanet (Baltimore: Johns Hopkins University Press, 1974), pp. 79–118. Also see Stockholm International Peace Research Institute, *The Arms Trade with the Third World* (Stockholm: Almquist and Wiksell, 1971), pp. 429–30.

82. See Editorial, "Crimes of American Aggressors"; and Brezhnev, "Fifty Years of Great Achievements." Also see Donald S. Zagoria, *Vietnam Triangle: Moscow, Peking, Hanoi* (New York: Pegasus, 1967), p. 52.

83. In 1964, when military victory for the DRV appeared near, the Soviet Union urged the North to seek a political settlement in the UN rather than final victory. See Zagoria, *Vietnam Triangle*, pp. 42–45; Raymond L. McGovern, "Moscow and Hanoi"; and Marshall D. Shulman, "Recent Soviet Foreign Policy." Also see Kurt L. London, "Vietnam: A Sino-Soviet Dilemma," *Russian Review* 26 (Jan. 1967) 26–37.

Chapter 4
Soviet Perceptions and Foreign Policy, 1972

1. Richard M. Nixon, *The Memoirs of Richard Nixon* (New York: Grosset and Dunlap, 1978), p. 577.

2. Soviet voices raised the prospects of a nuclear strike on China; first in a *Pravda* editorial, and later through Victor Louis in the *London Evening News*. See Editorial, "Peking's Adventurist Course," *Pravda*, Aug. 28. 1969, pp. 2–3; *CDSP* (Sept. 24, 1969), 3–5; *New York Times*, Sept. 28, 1969, p. 5; and Henry Kissinger, *The White House Years* (Boston: Little, Brown, 1979), p. 183.

3. Henry Kissinger reports that Mao Tse-tung told him Lin was removed because of his opposition to the rapprochement. For Kissinger's report on Chinese views, see *White House Years*, pp. 768, 690, 693, 711, 1062–63, 1073. Also see Henry Kissinger, *Years of Upheaval* (Boston: Little, Brown, 1982), pp. 689–95.

4. See Harold Hinton, *The Sino-Soviet Confrontation: Implications for the Future* (New York: Crane, Russak, 1976), pp. 31–32.

5. See Kissinger, *The White House Years*, pp. 171–72, 177.

6. Henry Kissinger, for example, in his famous book *Nuclear Weapons and Foreign Policy*, abr. ed. (New York: Norton, 1969), developed a picture of the Soviet Union that fits well with the "enemy" stereotype.

7. The Nixon administration perceived the Syrian intervention in Jordan, which followed King Hussein's attack on the Palestinians, as a Soviet challenge and responded by pressing Israel to prepare an attack backed by American might. Whether the "Soviet threat" in this case was phantom or real, the Nixon team acted as could be expected in a containment pattern. See Jon Glassman, *Arms for the Arabs: The Soviet Union and War in the Middle East* (Baltimore: Johns Hopkins University Press, 1975), pp. 87–89; and Kissinger, *The White House Years*, pp. 626–29. Also see Seymour M. Hersh, *The Price of Power: Kissinger in the Nixon White House* (New York: Summit, 1983), pp. 234–49.

8. Henry Kissinger depicted the Bengali crisis as "incontestably" Pakistan's doing but attributed the outbreak of war to Indian and Soviet hegemonic ambitions. Operating with this interpretation, he ordered a U.S. air carrier task force into the Bay of Bengal apparently to deter further Soviet actions (*The White House Years*, pp. 885–906, 889, 906).

9. Ibid., pp. 524, 688, 690, 693, 698, 711, 963–65.

10. See L. I. Brezhnev, "Report at a Gala Joint Meeting of the C.P.S.U. Central Committee, the U.S.S.R. Supreme Soviet and the R.S.F.S.R. Supreme Soviet, December 21, 1972," in *Our Course: Peace and Socialism* (Moscow: Novosti, 1975), pp. 302–04; Academician P. Fedoseyev, "On the Ideological and Political Essence of Maoism," *Pravda,* Dec. 5, 1971, pp. 3–5; *CDSP* 23 (Jan. 4, 1972), 9.

11. Staff, "The Maoist Leadership Unmasks Itself," *Pravda,* Dec. 17, 1971, p. 5, and *Izvestia,* Dec. 17, 1971, p. 2, *CDSP* 23 Jan. 11, 1972, 6; Editors, "The Situation in China and the Peking Leadership's Maneuvers," *Pravda,* Feb. 8, 1972, p. 5, *CDSP* 24 (Mar. 8, 1972), 11. Also see V. Kudryavtsev, "Policy With a False Bottom," *Izvestia,* Jan. 18, 1972, p. 4, *CDSP* 24 (Feb. 16, 1972), 24.

12. See, for example, G. Yakubov, "Conflict in Hindustan and the Mao Group's Provocative Role," *Pravda,* Dec. 28, 1971, p. 4, *CDSP* 23 (Jan. 25, 1972), 1–3. Also see Viktor Mayevsky, "Peace and Security in Asia Is All Nations' Concern," *Pravda,* Mar. 28, 1972, p. 4, *CDSP* 24 (Apr. 26, 1972), 22; "The Peking Leaders Are Traitors to the National Liberation Movement," *Pravda,* Dec. 22, 1971, p. 5, *CDSP* 23 (Jan. 18, 1972), 5.

13. Brezhnev, "Report at a Gala Joint Meeting," pp. 302–03.

14. Staff, "The Indian-Pakistani Conflict and Peking's Anti-Sovietism," *Pravda,* Dec. 8, 1971, p. 5, and *Izvestia,* Dec. 9, 1971, p. 3, *CDSP* 23 (Jan. 4, 1972), 2; Viktor Mayevsky, "Clash in Hindustan," *Pravda,* Dec. 9, 1971, p. 5, *CDSP* 23 (Jan. 4, 1972), 2–4; V. Kudryavtsev, "Flames Over South Asia," *Izvestia,* Dec. 12, 1971, p. 2, *CDSP* 23 (Jan. 11, 1972), 8; and T. Kolesnichenko, "Hand in Hand with the Imperialists," *Pravda,* Dec. 17, 1971, p. 5, *CDSP* 23 (Jan. 11, 1972), 6–7.

15. The Soviet Union stationed forty-four divisions on the border, including two in Mongolia (*The Military Balance: 1972–73* [London: IISS, 1972], p. 7). This was an increase of twenty-nine divisions since 1967. On Korean issues, see Chong-Sik Lee, "The Detente and Korea," in *The World and the Great-Power Triangles* ed. William E. Griffith (Cambridge, Mass.: MIT Press, 1975), pp. 344–45, 349. Also see Chin O. Chung, *P'yongyang Between Peking and Moscow: North Korea's Involvement in the Sino-Soviet Dispute, 1958–1975* (University: University of Alabama Press, 1978), p. 141. In late January, just prior to President Nixon's trip to Peking, the Soviet foreign minister visited Tokyo. A joint communique emphasized Soviet-Japanese cooperation and the positive benefits of a Soviet-Japanese peace treaty. The Soviet Union reportedly revised its traditional position and said it was willing to consider the territorial dispute. See Rodger Swearingen, *The Soviet Union and Post War Japan: Challenge and Response* (Stanford, Calif.: Hoover Institution Press, 1978); Staff, "Talks in Tokyo," *Pravda,* Jan. 25, 1972, p. 4, *CDSP* 24 (Feb. 23, 1972), 18–19; "Joint Soviet-Japanese Communique," *Pravda,* Jan. 28, 1972, p. 4, and *Izvestia,* Jan. 29, 1972, p. 3, *CDSP* 24 (Feb. 23, 1972), 18–19; and Paul Langer, "Japan and the Great-Power Triangles," in *Great Power Triangles,* ed. Griffith, p. 315. The USSR never did agree to discuss the northern territories. Following the normalization of Chinese-Japanese relations in September, the Soviet Union's rhetoric hardened. It dismissed Japan's territorial claims as "pointless," "absurd," and as instigated by the PRC, and rejected any discussion of the frontier issue. See V. Kudryavstev, "Wandering in Search of New Paths," *Izvestia,* Nov. 2, 1972, p. 4, *CDSP* 24 (Nov. 29, 1972), 1–3; Viktor Mayevsky, "Searching for a New Course," *Pravda,* Dec. 17, 1972, p. 5, *CDSP* 24 (Jan. 10, 1973), 3–5; M. Yurchenko, "Instigators From Peking," *Izvestia,* Dec. 14, 1972, p. 3, *CDSP* 24 (Jan. 10, 1973), 4–5.

16. L. I. Brezhnev, "Speech at the 15th Congress of the Trade Unions of the U.S.S.R., March 20, 1972," in *Our Course: Peace and Socialism,* p. 249.

17. L. I. Brezhnev, "Address to a Meeting of Soviet-Hungarian Friendship, November 30, 1972," in *Our Course: Peace and Socialism*, p. 278.

18. Brezhnev, "Speech at the 15th Congress of the Trade Unions," p. 246.

19. Brezhnev, "Address to a Meeting of Soviet-Hungarian Friendship," p. 277.

20. Editorial, "Fighters' Solidarity in Struggle," *Pravda*, Jan. 19, 1972, p. 1, *CDSP* 24 (Feb. 16, 1972), 21; Brezhnev, "Speech at the 15th Congress of the Trade Unions," p. 246. Also see Brezhnev, "Report at a Gala Joint Meeting," pp. 301–02.

21. "Soviet Government Statement," *Pravda* and *Izvetsia*, May 12, 1972, p. 1, *CDSP* 24 (May 24, 1972), 5; "Soviet Government Statement," *Pravda*, Dec. 31, 1971, p. 1, *CDSP* 23 (Jan. 25, 1972), 15; Editorial, "The Aggressor's Provocations and Maneuvers in Indochina," *Pravda*, Jan. 27, 1972, p. 5, *CDSP* 24 (Feb. 23, 1972), 7; Brezhnev, "Speech at the 15th Congress of the Trade Unions," pp. 246–47. Also see Brezhnev, "Speech at the Sixth Congress of the Polish United Workers' Party," in *Our Course: Peace and Socialism*, p. 226. For journalistic images following the prevailing line, see Yury Zhukov, "The Pentagon's Designs Are Failing," *Pravda*, May 13, 1972, p. 4, *FBIS-95;* A. Kislov, "Zionists in the Services of American Imperialism," *Izvestia*, Jan. 20, 1972, p. 4, *CDSP* 24 (Feb. 16, 1972), 21.

22. Brezhnev, "Speech at the 15th Congress of the Trade Unions," p. 246. For one of the sharpest journalistic developments, see V. Kudryavtsev, "Flames Over South Asia," and "Hypocrisy of the 'Peacemakers,' " *Izvestia*, Dec. 18, 1971, *CDSP* 23 (Jan. 11, 1972), 17.

23. Brezhnev, "Report at a Gala Joint Meeting," p. 306.

24. G. Arbatov, "The Strength of a Policy of Realism," *Izvestia*, June 22, 1972, pp. 3–4, *CDSP* 24 (July 17, 1972), 4–6.

25. Brezhnev, "Speech at the 15th Congress of the Trade Unions," p. 246. Also see Brezhnev, "Report at a Gala Joint Meeting."

26. Academician N. Inozemtsev, "Integrity and Effectiveness of Soviet Foreign Policy," *Pravda*, June 9, 1972, pp. 4–5, *CDSP* 24 (July 5, 1972), 1–4.

27. Arbatov, "The Strength of a Policy of Realism," p. 5.

28. Ibid.

29. Brezhnev, "Report at a Gala Joint Meeting," p. 302.

30. L. I. Brezhnev, "Speech at Dinner In Honour of Party and Government Delegation of the People's Republic of Bulgaria, November 13, 1972," in *Our Course: Peace and Socialism*, p. 267. Also see G. Trofimenko, "Sober Voices," *Pravda*, May 18, 1972, p. 4, *CDSP* 24 (June 14, 1972), 4–5; S. Vishnevsky, "From Positions of Realism," *Pravda*, May 19, 1972, p. 4, *CDSP* 24 (June 14, 1972), 5.

31. Brezhnev, "Speech at Dinner in Honour of Party and Government Delegation of the People's Republic of Bulgaria," p. 267.

32. Trofimenko, "Sober Voices," p. 4. Also see V. Osipov, "Life Demands Realism in Policy," *Izvestia*, May 19, 1972, p. 2, *CDSP* 24 (June 14, 1972), 6; and T. Kolesnichenko, "Desire of the Majority of Americans," *Pravda*, May 20, 1972, p. 5, *CDSP* 24 (June 14, 1972), 6.

33. Brezhnev, "Report at a Gala Joint Meeting" p. 310.

34. Arbatov, "The Strength of a Policy of Realism," p. 6.

35. Roger Labrie, ed., *SALT Handbook: Key Documents and Issues 1972–1979* (Washington, D.C.: American Enterprise Institute, 1979), p. 50.

36. Ibid., pp. 50–51.

37. "Basic Principles of Relations Between the Union of Soviet Socialist Republics and the United States of America," *Pravda* and *Izvestia*, May 30, 1972, p. 1, *CDSP* 24 (June 28, 1972), 22–23. "Joint Soviet-American Communique," *Pravda* and *Izvestia*, May 31, 1972, pp. 1–2, *CDSP* 24 (June 28, 1972),

23–25. Also see Alexander George, "The Basic Principles Agreement of 1972: Origins and Expectations," in *Managing U.S.-Soviet Rivalry: Crisis Prevention*, ed. George (Boulder, Colo.: Westview, 1983), pp. 107–18.

38. U.S. agricultural exports to the USSR remained at low levels from 1945 to 1970. Except for a high of $137 million in 1964, yearly exports in this period never exceeded $35 million. Beginning in late 1971, Soviet purchases rose dramatically, peaking at $1 billion in 1973 (David S. Schoonover, "Soviet Agricultural Trade and the Feed-Line Stock Economy," in Joint Economic Committee, *Soviet Economy in Perspective* [Washington, D.C.: GPO, 1976], pp. 814, 821).

39. David Carey and Joseph Havelka, "Soviet Agriculture: Progress and Problems," in Joint Economic Committee, *Soviet Economy in a Time of Change* 2 (Washington, D.C.: GPO, Oct. 10, 1979), pp. 55–86.

40. See John Newhouse, *Cold Dawn: The Story of SALT* (New York: Holt, Rinehart and Winston, 1973).

41. International Institute for Strategic Studies, *The Military Balance, 1972–1973* (London: IISS, 1972), p. 83.

42. Ibid., pp. 83–86.

43. International Institute for Strategic Studies, *Strategic Survey 1974* (London: IISS, 1975), pp. 60–65.

44. See Hearings of Senate Foreign Relations and Senate Armed Services Committee in Labrie, *SALT Handbook*, pp. 67–94, 95–140.

45. See William E. Griffith, *The Ostpolitik of the Federal Republic of Germany* (Cambridge, Mass.: MIT Press, 1978), pp. 181–82; and Keesing's Research Report, *Germany and Eastern Europe Since 1945: From the Potsdam Agreement to Chancellor Brandt's Ostpolitik* (New York: Scribner's, 1973), pp. 239–70.

46. Foreign Affairs Committees, Supreme Soviet Council of the Union and Council of Nationalities, "In the Interests of the Peoples of Europe," *Pravda*, Apr. 13, 1972, p. 2, and *Izvestia*, Apr. 13, 1972, pp. 1, 3, *CDSP* 24 (May 10, 1972), 1–5; Editorial, "Great Strength of the Party's Leninist Policy," *Pravda*, May 21, 1972, p. 1, *CDSP* 24 (June 14, 1972), 9.

47. Y. Goloshubov and V. Nakaryakov, "Session of the Presidium of the U.S.S.R. Supreme Soviet," *Izvestia*, June 1, 1972, p. 1, *CDSP* 24 (June 28, 1972), 12–13. Also see Brezhnev, "Speech at the 15th Congress of the Trade Unions," p. 245.

48. Brezhnev, "Speech at Dinner in Honour of Party and Government Delegation of the People's Republic of Bulgaria," pp. 266–67; and "Speech at the Fifteenth Congress of the Trade Unions," p. 244. Also see Inozemtsev, "Integrity and Effectiveness," p. 3., and Spectator, "What Debates in the F.R.G. Bundestag Showed," *Pravda*, Mar. 4, 1972, p. 4, *CDSP* 24 (Mar. 29, 1972), 18–19, Foreign Affairs Committees, "In the Interests of the Peoples of Europe."

49. Suslov also expressed concern about the persisting danger by the "reactionary elite" in Bonn (Foreign Affairs Committees, of the U.S.S.R. Supreme Soviet's Council of the Union and Council of Nationalities, "In the Name of Peace and Cooperation").

50. Academician Inozemtsev, "Integrity and Effectiveness," p. 4; Spectator, "What Debates in the F.R.G. Bundestag Showed"; Foreign Affairs Committees, "In the Interest of the Peoples of Europe."

51. Willy Brandt, *People and Politics: The Years 1960–1975*, trans. J. Maxwell Brownjohn (Boston: Little, Brown, 1976), p. 318. Also see Helmut Schmidt, *The Balance of Power: Germany's Peace Policy and the Superpowers*, trans. Edward Thomas (London: Kimber, 1971), pp. 16–18, 38–39, 211–13, 225, 231–32.

52. Brandt, *People and Politics*, pp. 335–36. Also see Kissinger, *The White House Years*, p. 966.

53. Brandt, *People and Politics,* p. 367.

54. Ibid., pp. 296, 356. Also see Schmidt, *Balance of Power,* pp. 31, 36, 226.

55. Brandt, *People and Politics,* pp. 355, 421. Also see Frans Joseph Strauss, *Challenge and Response: A Programme for Europe* (New York: Atheneum, 1970).

56. See Foreign Affairs Committees, "In the Interests of the Peoples of Europe," pp. 4–5.

57. See Gerhard Wettig, *Community and Conflict in the Socialist Camp: The Soviet Union, East Germany and the German Problem 1965–1972,* trans. E. Moreton and H. Adomeit (New York: St. Martin's, 1973), p. 89.

58. Brezhnev, "Speech at the 15th Congress of Trade Unions," p. 245.

59. Henry Wilcox Schaefer, *Comecon and the Politics of Integration* (New York: Praeger, 1972), pp. 127–32, 152–73.

60. Kissinger, *White House Years,* pp. 392–94, 401–03, 966.

61. Ibid., pp. 402, 409–10, 529–30.

62. See Wolfgang Berner et al., *The Soviet Union, 1973: Domestic Policy, Economics, Foreign Policy* (New York: Holmes and Meier, 1975), pp. 110–11.

63. In 1972 the USSR had concluded treaties with Egypt and Iraq and offered a treaty to Syria (which Syria declined). It had poor relations with Libya as Libyan leaders criticized the USSR for selling out the "anti-imperialist" struggle. Soviet-Libyan relations began to improve in 1974. Even a cursory look at the comparative military might makes the importance of Egypt, Syria, and Iraq clear:

	Egypt	Syria	Iraq	South Yemen	Libya
Army personnel	285,000	100,000	90,000	15,200	20,000
Tanks	2,000	1,170	905	50	221
Aircraft	618	210	189	27	22

Source: The Military Balance 1972–1973 (London: IISS, 1972), pp. 30–35; *The Military Balance 1975–1976,* p. 39.

64. Glassman, *Arms for the Arabs,* pp. 71–80.

65. See Alvin Rubinstein, *Red Star on the Nile: The Soviet-Egyptian Influence Relationships Since the June War* (Princeton, N.J.: Princeton University Press, 1977), pp. 105, 111; and George Breslauer, "Soviet Policy in the Middle East, 1967–1972: Unalterable Antagonism or Collaborative Competition," in *Managing U.S.-Soviet Rivlary,* ed. George, pp. 77–81.

66. By the end of 1970 the USSR deployed over 220 pilots, 150 aircraft, and 22,000 troops in Egypt, manning 75 to 85 SAM sites and 6 airfields (*Strategic Survey 1970* [London: IISS, 1971], p. 47).

67. The USSR continued to deny offensive weapons and counselled caution on the Arabs, encouraging Egypt to accept a political settlement. See Mohamed Heikal, *The Sphinx and the Commissar: The Rise and Fall of Soviet Influence in the Middle East* (New York: Harper and Row, 1978), p. 217.

68. See Anwar Sadat, *In Search of Identity: An Autobiography* (New York: Harper and Row, 1977), pp. 227–28. Also see Glassman, *Arms for the Arabs,* pp. 93–94. Also see Galia Golin, *Yom Kippur and After: The Soviet Union and the Middle East Crisis* (Cambridge: Cambridge University Press, 1977), pp. 21–34, 42–43, 45–46. Soviet President Podgorny visited Cairo in late April 1972. Soviet Defense Minister Grechko, just prior to the Nixon-Brezhnev Summit in May 1972, flew to Cairo and apparently urged Sadat to

publicize the USSR's willingness to supply offensive air power. This rhetorical willingness did not translate into actual material supply (Kissinger, *The White House Years*, pp. 368–69, 378, 559, 1288–90.

69. Sadat, *In Search of Identity*, pp. 317–24. Apparently, the weapons the Soviet Union refused to provide Egypt were TU-22 medium bombers, SCUD missiles of 150–450-km. range and MiG-25 aircraft.

70. The Soviet Union reduced its personnel in Egypt from nearly 20,000 in early 1972 to less than 800 by the end of the year. It withdrew MiG-25 and SU-11 aircraft, as well as mobile SA-6 and jamming equipment. See Rubinstein, *Red Star on the Nile*, pp. 188–92; and Glassman, *Arms for the Arabs*, pp. 95–96. Also see *Strategic Survey: 1972* (London: IISS, 1973), pp. 26–27.

71. In October 1972 Egyptian Minister Sidqi visited Moscow. Reportedly, he was treated so badly the Egyptians considered breaking relations despite the Soviet Union's willingness to reinitiate the supply of spare parts and SAMs (Glassman, *Arms for the Arabs*, p. 96; Sadat, *In Search of Identity*, p. 234). Using unidentified Israeli sources, Jon Glassman reports that in 1973 the USSR began to supply Egypt with SCUD missiles. The Stockholm International Peace Research Institute (SIPRI) reports that in 1973 40 to 60 SS-TC SCUD missiles with a range of 150 km. were manned by Soviet personnel (SIPRI, *Arms Trade Registers: The Arms Trade with the Third World* [Stockholm: Almquist and Wiksell International, 1975], p. 45). *The Military Balance: 1973–1974* (London: IISS, 1973), pp. 31, 6–7, does not list any SCUD missiles for Egypt nor specify that the USSR had any SCUDs deployed in Egypt during 1973–1974.

72. Sadat charged that Soviet Ambassador Vinogradov attempted on October 6 to "trick" him into accepting a cease-fire by telling him Syria desired a cease-fire (*In Search of Identity*, pp. 247, 252–53). Also see Rubinstein, *Red Star on the Nile*, pp. 259–62; and Robert O. Freedman, *Soviet Policy Toward the Middle East Since 1970* (New York: Praeger, 1978), p. 141; Karen Dawisha, *Soviet Foreign Policy Toward Egypt* (New York: St. Martin's, 1979), pp. 67–70.

73. Kissinger, *Years of Upheaval*, pp. 471–73, 486–87, 498–500, 525. The Soviet Union vetoed UN cease-fire proposals which called for a return to the October 5 positions. It was not willing to deny their allies the occupied territory they had regained. On October 10, the United States accepted a cease-fire in place and the USSR quickly agreed.

74. At the outset, the Soviet Union backed the Egyptians and Syrians with propaganda, and called on other Arabs to provide material aid. On October 9, Israel began bombing deep into Syria. The next day the USSR began to airlift SAMs and antitank ammunition to Syria and Egypt. See Glassman, *Arms for the Arabs*, pp. 144–47; Rubinstein, *Red Star on the Nile*, pp. 265–71; and Heikal, *Sphinx and Commissar*, p. 257.

75. Sadat, *In Search of Identity*, pp. 258–60. Sadat said that after the Kosygin visit he felt that the UAR was fighting the United States and Israel without Soviet help. Rubinstein concludes that the emerging Israeli battlefield advantage at this time could have been reversed with serious Soviet aid, but the USSR refused and forced Sadat to accept the cease-fire (*Red Star on the Nile*, p. 272).

76. Reportedly the U.S. communicated to the Israelis that if they failed to honor the cease-fire the United States would not block Soviet intervention (Rubinstein, *Red Star on the Nile*, pp. 275–76; Glassman, *Arms for the Arabs*, p. 165; and Freedman, *Soviet Policy*, p. 145).

77. Kissinger, *Years of Upheaval*, pp. 211, 493–94.

78. In the fall of 1970 King Hussein sent his army against the Palestinians in Jordan. Syria intervened to defend the Palestinians. In Washington the Syrian move was seen as a Soviet challenge. It brought forth an immediate response

which hinted at an Israeli attack backed by direct American force. This response stood in marked contrast to the Soviet toleration of Israeli intervention, bombing, and persistent occupation of Egyptian and Syrian territory. It is unclear whether or not the Soviet Union was involved in the Syrian decision to intervene. Intra-Arab politics were probably far more important than Soviet advice. In any case, the USSR acted quickly to restrain the Syrians even though this meant the Syrian troops in Jordan would be mauled and the Palestinians annihilated. See William B. Quandt, *Decade of Decisions: American Policy Toward the Arab-Israeli Conflict, 1967–1976* (Berkeley and Los Angeles: University of California Press, 1977), pp. 105–27; and Malcolm Kerr, *The Arab Cold War: Gamal 'Abd al-Nasir and His Rivals, 1958–1970* (London: Oxford University Press, 1971), pp. 14–53.

79. See Breslauer, "Soviet Policy in the Middle East," pp. 65–98.

80. Kissinger, *Years of Upheaval*, pp. 196–200, 220–21, 298–99.

81. Kissinger, *The White House Years*, pp. 368–69, 378, 559, 1288–90; and *Years of Upheaval*, pp. 298–99.

82. Kissinger, *Years of Upheaval* pp. 209–12, 295–300, 469–72.

83. Ibid., pp. 196–200, 298–300, 543–52.

84. Richard Cottam, "The Case of the Kurds: Minorities in the Middle East," presented at the annual meeting of the American Political Science Association, 1977.

85. Ibid., pp. 23–26.

86. "The Pike Papers," *Village Voice*, Feb. 16, 1976, pp. 85, 87–88.

87. Cottam, "The Case of the Kurds."

88. Robert O. Freedman, "Soviet Policy Toward Ba'athist Iraq, 1968–1979," in *The Soviet Union in the Third World: Successes and Failures*, ed. Robert Donaldson (Boulder, Colo.: Westview, 1981), pp. 161–91, 170–72.

89. Cottam, "The Case of the Kurds," p. 31.

90. Howard Hensel, "Soviet Policy Toward the Kurdish Question, 1970–75," *Soviet Union/Union Sovietique* 6 (1979), 65–67.

91. Between 1965 and 1974 the United States transferred $2,703 milliion in arms to Iran. At the same time, the USSR delivered $1,343 million to Iraq (U.S. Arms Control and Disarmament Agency, *World Military Expenditures and Arms Transfers: 1966–1975* [Washington, D.C.: Arms Control and Disarmament Agency, 1976], p. 78).

92. Freedman, "Soviet Policy Toward Ba'athist Iraq," p. 175.

93. Hensel, "Soviet Policy Toward the Kurdish Question," pp. 75–76.

94. See, for example, A. Ignatov, "Iraq Today," *New Times* 21 (May 1974), 22–24. According to the Pike papers, U.S. officials agreed with the shah that the Kurds would be used but not allowed to prevail. The Pike Commission described the U.S. role as a "cynical enterprise" (see "The Pike Papers").

95. Alvin Rubinstein, "Air Support in the Arab East," in *Diplomacy of Power: Soviet Armed Forces as a Political Instrument*, ed. Stephen Kaplan (Washington, D.C.: Brookings, 1981), pp. 499–510. Rubinstein cites Kurdish reports of Soviet pilots and MiG-23s that he concludes Iraqis were not trained to fly.

96. Freedman, "Soviet Policy Toward Ba'athist Iraq," p. 173.

97. Congress moved to prohibit further U.S. arms deliveries to Pakistan because of the violence. The U.S. consulate in Dacca compared the violence to genocide. Moral outrage was reported to be widespread in the foreign policy bureaucracy. Formal dissents were lodged in the face of perceived insensitivity in the White House. See Cristopher Van Hollen (deputy assistant secretary of state for Near Eastern and South Asian Affairs, 1969–1972), "The Tilt Policy Revisited: Nixon-Kissinger Geopolitics and South Asia," *Asian Survey* 20 (April 1980), 342–43. Also see Roger Morris, *Uncertain*

Greatness: Henry Kissinger and American Foreign Policy (New York: Harper and Row, 1977), pp. 213–18.

98. Robert H. Donaldson, *Soviet Policy Toward India: Ideology and Strategy* (Cambridge, Mass.: Harvard University Press, 1974), pp. 218–19, 227–31; and Bhabani Sen Gupta, "South Asia and the Great Powers," in *The World and the Great-Power Triangles,* ed. William E. Griffith (Cambridge, Mass.: MIT Press, 1975), pp. 229–30, 438. Also see J. P. Jain, *Soviet Policy Towards Pakistan and Bangladesh* (New Delhi: Radiant, 1974), pp. 125–26.

99. The CIA reported that "the Soviets may have regarded the treaty as an instrument through which they could exercise restraint over the Indians; "C.I.A. analysts reasoned that Soviet aid might relax Indian anxieties and enhance their willingness to remain patient in the face of the mounting refuge burden and U.S.-Chinese-Pakistani cooperation" (Van Hollen, "The Tilt Policy," pp. 347–48).

100. See Bhabani Sen Gupta, "South Asia," p. 230. Also see *Strategic Survey: 1971* (London: IISS, 1972), p. 48.

101. Morris, *Uncertain Greatness,* pp. 216–18, 227. Also see Jack Anderson, with George Clifford, *The Anderson Papers* (New York: Random House, 1973), pp. 37–39. Anderson obtained internal CIA reports and published some of their content.

102. See Van Hollen, "The Tilt Policy," p. 349. The leaders of the Awami League remained in jail and Pakistani leaders were unwilling to deal with them. The United States refused to support a UN call for Rahman's release. Given the Awami League's role, it does not seem reasonable to assume a settlement was imminent when its major leaders were still being declared unimportant (Anderson and Clifford, *The Anderson Papers,* p. 258).

103. *Strategic Survey: 1971,* p. 48. Despite congressional efforts to stop U.S. deliveries to Pakistan, they continued until November. Congress then acted to stop the administration's policy (Morris, *Uncertain Greatness,* p. 222; and Anderson and Clifford, *The Anderson Papers,* p. 258).

104. Kissinger, *The White House Years,* pp. 901–02. Jack Anderson reports that the CIA detected Chinese activity in the Himalayas, December 8–11, 1971. According to the CIA, the USSR moved ground and air forces into position along the Sinkiang frontier. Anderson, still quoting U.S. intelligence, reports that the Soviet ambassador in New Delhi, Nikolay Pegov, told Indian officials that if China moved in the Himalayas, Russia would mount a "diversionary action in Sinkiang" (Anderson and Clifford, *The Anderson Papers,* pp. 260–66). The Chinese gave no signal that they intended to take any actions other than expressing loud verbal and diplomatic condemnation. Attacking across the Himalayas in winter seems an option unlikely to appeal to leaders in Peking.

105. Anderson and Clifford, *The Anderson Papers,* pp. 258; Van Hollen, "The Tilt Policy," pp. 352–56.

106. Van Hollen, "The Tilt Policy," pp. 351–52.

107. Anderson and Clifford, *The Anderson Papers,* pp. 232–34.

108. Ibid.

109. Ibid.

110. See David K. Hall, "The Indo-Pakistani War of 1971," in *Force Without War: U.S. Armed Forces as a Political Instrument,* ed. Barry M. Blechman and Stephen S. Kaplan (Washington, D.C.: Brookings, 1978), p. 200.

111. Kissinger, *The White House Years,* pp. 885–89.

112. Ibid., pp. 1117–20.

113. Ibid., pp. 1144–45.

114. Ibid., pp. 1151–56.

115. Ibid., p. 1196. In response to the bombings, the USSR sent submarines and six surface warships to the McClesfield Bank area some 300 miles from the principal operations area of U.S. carriers. The ships remained 300 miles away until June. See Bradford Dismukes, "Soviet Employment of Naval Power for Political Purposes, 1965–1975," in *Soviet Naval Influence: Domestic and Foreign Dimensions,* ed. Michael McGwire and John McDonnell (New York: Praeger, 1977), pp. 484–509, 501–02.

116. Kissinger, *The White House Years,* p. 1201.

117. Ibid., pp. 1126–29.

118. See Gareth Porter, *A Peace Denied: The United States, Vietnam and the Paris Agreement* (Bloomington: Indiana University Press, 1975), pp. 186, 206–09, 216–18. Also see Frank Snepp, *Decent Interval: An Insider's Account of Saigon's Indecent End Told by the CIA's Chief Strategy Analyst in Vietnam* (New York: Vintage Books, 1978), p. 58; and Ambassador Martin in U.S. Congress, House Committee on Foreign Affairs, *Hearing Before the Subcommittee on Asia and Pacific Affairs,* 93rd Cong., 2d sess., July 31, 1974 (Washington, D.C.: GPO, 1974), p. 27.

119. Porter, *A Peace Denied,* pp. 188–94, 206–09, 216–18, 240–47; and Snepp, *Decent Interval,* pp. 61, 91.

120. The agency estimated that combined Chinese-Soviet military aid to the DRV in 1973 was $290 million, less than half the estimated $600 million delivered in 1972 (Porter, *A Peace Denied,* p. 188; Snepp, *Decent Interval,* p. 65).

121. *Facts on File* (1974), pp. 797, 862, 881, 904, 931, 1011. Also see Porter, *A Peace Denied,* pp. 269–73; Snepp, *Decent Interval,* pp. 117–20.

122. According to the CIA, the DRV was not increasing its forces in the south. In 1973–1974 it replaced around 70,000, keeping the total number around 160,000–170,000. The CIA also reported that the DRV did not engage in offensive military activities during 1973 (Porter, *A Peace Denied,* pp. 188–94, 202, 266, 268; Snepp, *Decent Interval,* pp. 52–56, 91, 104).

123. Thieu withdrew troops from Tong Le Chan and then claimed that the PRG had forcefully overrun the village. Frank Snepp reports that officials in the U.S. Embassy knew the Tong Le Chan episode was a fraud (*Decent Interval,* p. 105).

124. CIA analysts felt the PRG had cautious battlefield objectives, and kept negotiations as the interim objective (Snepp, *Decent Interval,* pp. 106, 122). Also see Porter, *A Peace Denied,* pp. 267–70.

125. In 1974, according to U.S. government sources, the Soviet Union and China delivered to North Vietnam $400 million in military assistance and from $1.0 to $1.4 billion in economic aid. U.S. aid to South Vietnam in 1974 totaled $700 million in military assistance and from $2.2 to 3.0 billion in economic aid (U.S. Intelligence Community report cited in the *New York Times,* Mar. 28, 1975, p. 1; Martin, "Hearings," pp. 26–27; Snepp, *Decent Interval,* p. 111). The *New York Times,* May 1, 1975, p. 20, reported that Pentagon officials estimated that from 1961 to 1975 the United States had provided South Vietnam $141 billion in total aid, while the USSR and China together had provided North Vietnam with $7.5 billion in total aid.

126. See *The Military Balance: 1974–1975* (London: IISS, 1974), pp. 60–61.

127. For a text of Secretary Brezhnev's congratulations, see *FBIS-SOV-75-86,* May 2, 1975, pp. L1–2. For an example of the Soviet Union's media, see B. Vasilyev, "Vietnam's Feat," *Izvestia,* May 5, 1975, p. 3, *FBIS-SOV-75-90,* pp. L1–3.

Chapter 5
Soviet Perceptions and Foreign Policy, 1979

1. See Wang Bingnan, "Growth of the Friendship Between the Chinese and American People," *Beijing Review* 4 (Jan. 26, 1979), 9–13; and "Powerful Factor for Maintaining Asian and World Peace," *Beijing Review* 7 (Feb. 16, 1979), 20.

2. See Senator Henry Jackson, 90th Cong. 1st sess., in *Congressional Record* 113, pt. 4 (Feb. 24, 1967), 4,443–44; and ibid., pt. 22 (Oct. 19, 1967), 529,496–98.

3. See Jimmy Carter, *Keeping Faith: Memoirs of a President* (New York: Bantam, 1982), p. 206. Also see Zbigniew Brzezinski, *Power and Principle: Memoirs of the National Security Adviser, 1977–1981* (New York: Farrar, Straus, Giroux, 1983), pp. 408–11.

4. See the *New York Times*, Jan. 31, 1976, p. 11, July 28, 1976, p. 3, and Aug. 14, 1976, p. 18.

5. See Kenneth Lieberthal, "The Foreign Policy Debate in Peking as Seen Through Allegorical Articles, 1973–1976," *China Quarterly* 71 (Sept. 1977), 528–54.

6. Ole Holsti and James Rosenau, *American Leadership in World Affairs: Vietnam and the Breakdown of Consensus* (Boston: Allen and Unwin, 1984).

7. See, for example, W. Scott Thompson, ed., *National Security in the 1980s: From Weakness to Strength* (San Francisco: Institute for Contemporary Studies, 1980).

8. For two examples, see Rodger Morris, *Uncertain Greatness: Henry Kissinger and American Foreign Policy* (New York: Harper and Row, 1977); and Seymour Hersh, *The Price of Power: Kissinger in the Nixon White House* (New York: Summit, 1983).

9. Brzezinski, *Power and Principle*, pp. 6, 146–56, 178–90.

10. Cyrus Vance, *Hard Choices: Critical Years in American Foreign Policy* (New York: Simon and Schuster, 1983), pp. 45–47, 84–92.

11. For an analysis of the March 1977 SALT proposal, see Strobe Talbott, *Endgame: The Inside Story of SALT II* (New York: Harper and Row, 1979), pp. 38–78.

12. Jimmy Carter, "A Foreign Policy Based on America's Essential Character," *Department of State Bulletin* 77 (June 13, 1977), 621–25. Also see Jimmy Carter, "U.S.-Soviet Relationship," *Department of State Bulletin* 77 (Aug. 15, 1977), 193–97.

13. See Vance, *Hard Choices*, pp. 79–83. Also see Steven I. Levine, "China Policy During Carter's Year One," *Asian Survey* 18 (May 1978), 437–47.

14. Brzezinski, *Power and Principle*, pp. 146–55, 164–90, 316–25. Also see *Facts on File* (1978), pp. 9, 137, 140, 178.

15. Brzezinski, *Power and Principle*, pp. 196–97, 203–11. Also see Michael Oksenberg (an expert on China serving on the NSC), "The United States and China," in *China and Japan: A New Balance of Power*, ed. Donald Hellmann (Lexington, Mass.: Lexington Books, 1976), pp. 269–72, 277; and "Statement of Michael Oksenberg," in House Subcommittee on Future Foreign Policy Research and Development, Committee on International Relations, 94th Cong., *United States—Soviet Union—China: The Great Power Triangle* (Washington, D.C.: GPO, 1976), pp. 120–24.

16. Brzezinski, *Power and Principle*, pp. 202–09, 419–25, 551–55; Vance, *Hard Choices*, pp. 75–83, 113–19, 390–91.

17. Brzezinski, *Power and Principle*, pp. 404–10. Also see Richard Burt,

"Zbig Makes It Big," *New York Times Magazine*, July 30, 1978, pp. 8–20, 28–30.

18. See Jimmy Carter, "The President: The United States and the Soviet Union," *Department of State Bulletin* 78 (July 1978), 14–16; and President Carter, "Text of Speech at Georgia Institute of Technology," *New York Times*, Feb. 21, 1979, p. A4.

19. Carter, *Keeping Faith*, p. 256.

20. See Willaim R. Heaton, Jr., *A United Front Against Hegemonism: Chinese Foreign Policy into the 1980s*, National Security Affairs Monograph ser. 80-3, National Defense University (Washington, D.C.: GPO, March 1978).

21. See, for example, "Social-Imperialist Strategy in Asia," *Beijing Review* 3 (Jan. 19, 1979), 13–16; Huang Hua, "The International Situation and China's Foreign Policies," *Peking Review* 40 (Oct. 6, 1978), 12–17, 35; "Moscow's Outcries Can Never Harm China," *Peking Review* 42 (Oct. 20, 1978), 22–25; and "Communique of the Third Plenary Session of the 11th Central Committee of the Communist Party of China," *Peking Review* 52 (Dec. 29, 1978), 6–16.

22. Jonathan Pollak, "China's Agonizing Reappraisal," in *The Sino-Soviet Conflict: A Global Perspective*, ed. Herbert Ellison (Seattle: University of Washington Press, 1982), pp. 71–72. Also see Jonathan Pollack, "The Implications of Sino-American Normalization," *International Security* 3 (Spring 1979), 37–57.

23. David Lampton, "Misreading China," *Foreign Policy* (Winter 1981–82), 104–05.

24. *Facts on File* (1978), p. 974. Also see Deng Xiaoping, "Text of Interview of Vice-Premier Deng Xiaoping by U.S. T.V. Commentators," *Beijing Review* 7 (Feb. 16, 1979), 17–18.

25. I. Aleksandrov, "Contrary to Historical Truth," *Pravda*, Dec. 8, 1979, p. 4, *FBIS-SOV-79-238*, pp. B1–4.

26. I. Aleksandrov, "A Road Without a Future," *Pravda*, Apr. 7, 1979, pp. 4–5, *FBIS-SOV-80-069*, pp. B1–5; I. Aleksandrov, "Contrary to Historical Truth," p. B2. Also see Editorial, "On the U.S. President's State of the Union Message," *Pravda*, Jan. 29, 1980, p. 1, *FBIS-SOV-80-020*, p. A4; Nikolay Fedorov, "Good Neighborliness Is in the Interests of the Peoples," *Izvestia*, Feb. 13, 1980, p. 4, *FBIS-SOV-80-032*, pp. B1–2; N. Kapchenko, "Beijing Policy: Calculation and Miscalculation," *International Affairs (Moscow)*, July 1979, p. 39; and N. Kapchenko, "The Threat to Peace from Peking's Hegemonistic Policy," *International Affairs (Moscow)*, Feb. 1980, p. 68.

27. Editorial, "Peoples Against Imperialism," *Pravda*, Nov. 23, 1979, p. 1, *FBIS-SOV-79-231*, pp. CC3–4. A. Bovin, "Beijing's European Flirtation," *Izvestia*, Nov. 11, 1979, p. 4, *FBIS-SOV-79-222*, p. B1; and A. Petrov, "Beijing's Intrigues Against the Nonalignment Movement," *Pravda*, Aug. 11, 1979, p. 4, *FBIS-SOV-79-158*, pp. B1–4.

28. *The Military Balance: 1980–81* (London: IISS, 1980), p. 11. For example, Soviet and Chinese forces clashed on the Kazakhstan-Sinkiang border in July 1979; see *Facts on File* (1979), p. 554. Also see ibid., pp. 258, 803, 917–18; and Harry Gelman, "The Outlook for Sino-Soviet Relations," *Problems of Communism* 28 (Sept./Dec. 1979), 50, 58–59. The Soviet Union's relations with Mongolia remained very close. See William R. Heaton, Jr., "Mongolia 1979: Learning from 'Leading Experiences,' " *Asian Survey* 20 (Jan. 1980), 77–83.

29. Before Prime Minister Desai received President Carter in January 1978, he visited Moscow in October 1977. The USSR remained India's number one arms supplier, giving $0.6 billion in military assistance in 1977. In 1977 the USSR delivered to India $340 million of the $392 million economic aid it gave to Third World countries. See Robert Donaldson, "Soviet Policy in South Asia," in *Soviet Policy in the Third World*, ed. W. Raymond Duncan (New York:

Pergamon, 1980), pp. 229–31; *Facts on File* (1977), p. 348; Central Intelligence Agency, *National Basic Intelligence Factbook* (Washington, D.C.: GPO, Jan. 1979), p. 214.

30. *New York Times,* Feb. 1, 1979, p. 5, Feb. 14, 1979, p. 6, Feb. 16, 1979, p. 6, and Feb. 19, 1979, p. 10.

31. Sheldon Simon, "Southeast Asia in Soviet Perspective," in *Soviet Policy,* ed. Duncan, p. 243. Also see *Strategic Survey: 1977* (London: IISS, 1978), pp. 83–84.

32. *Facts on File* (1979), p. 122. For text of Soviet declaration see the *New York Times,* Feb. 19, 1979, p. 11. On March 2 the Soviet government warned China of "severe retribution" if it did not halt its attack and withdraw from Vietnam (*New York Times,* Mar. 3, 1979, p. 1).

33. See Harlan Jencks, "China's 'Punitive war on Vietnam: A Military Assessment," *Asian Survey* 19 (Aug. 1979), 801–15. Daniel Tretiak also summarizes the Soviet support as in line with the limited nature of China's attack and the unimpressive performance by China's army ("China's Vietnam War and Its Consequences," *China Quarterly* 80 [Dec. 1979], 740–67). Also see C. G. Jacobsen, *Sino-Soviet Relations Since Mao: The Chairman's Legacy* (New York: Praeger, 1981), pp. 97–105.

34. See Joseph. M. Ha, "Moscow's Policy Toward Japan," *Problems of Communism* 26 (Sept.–Oct. 1977), 61–72. Also see P. Falkenheim, "The Impact of the Peace and Friendship Treaty on Soviet-Japanese Relations," *Asian Survey* 19 (Dec. 1979), 1220–21.

35. *Facts on File* (1978), pp. 637, 801. For examples of Soviet press reactons, see Yu. Bandura, "A Dubious Deal," *Izvestia,* Aug. 15, 1978, p. 4, *FBIS-SOV-78-163,* p. M1; B. Orekhov, "A Risky Step," *Pravda,* Aug. 25, 1978, p. 4, *FBIS-SOV-78-169,* pp. M1–2; and Yu. Vasilyev, "Concerning the Japanese-Chinese Treaty," *Izvestia,* Aug. 25, 1978, p. 3, *FBIS-SOV-78-169,* pp. M3–5. The Soviet Union officially protested to Japan over the treaty August 23, 1978.

36. L. I. Brezhnev, "In the Name of the Happiness of Soviet People," TASS, Mar. 2, 1979, *FBIS-SOV-79-044,* p. R5. Also see V. Borisov, "Beijing's Expansionist Plans in Southeast Asia," *International Affairs (Moscow),* June 1979, pp. 15–24.

37. Yuriy Zhukov, "International Review," *Pravda,* Sept. 2, 1979, p. 4; and P. Zhilin (corresponding member of the USSR Academy of Sciences), "The Lessons of History Must Not Be Forgotten: On the 40th Anniversary of the Start of World War II," *Pravda,* Aug. 31, 1979, pp. 3–4, both in *FBIS-SOV-79-175,* pp. CC9–18. Also see O. Vasilyev and V. Petrusenko, "Lessons of WWII: History Does Not Forgive the Accomplices of Aggression," *Izvestia,* Aug. 31, 1979, p. 5; and Army General A. Yepishev, chief of the Soviet Army and Navy Main Political Directorate, "Lessons of History Which Call for Vigilance," *Izvestia,* Sept. 1, 1979, p. 3, both in *FBIS-SOV-79-177,* pp. CC12–18.

38. I. Aleksandrov, "Road Without A Future," p. B4. Also see A. Bovin, "Short-sighted Calculations," *Izvestia,* Jan. 8, 1980, p. 5, *FBIS-SOV-80-007,* pp. B1–2.

39. L. I. Brezhnev, "Pravda Interviews Leonid Brezhnev," *Pravda,* Jan. 13, 1980, p. 1; *FBIS-SOV-80-009,* pp. A1–6; Editorial, "On the U.S. President's State of the Union Message"; and B. N. Ponamarev (candidate member of the Politburo), "In the Interests of Detente: In the Interest of the Peoples of the World," *Pravda,* Nov. 18, 1979, p. 4; *FBIS-SOV-79-225,* pp. G1–5.

40. L. I. Brezhnev, "Speech at Meeting of Electors of the Baumansky Electoral Okrug," *Moscow Domestic Service,* Feb. 22, 1980, *FBIS-SOV-80-038,* pp. R4–6. Also see Marshal D. Ustinov, "Military Detente is the Imperative of the Time," *Pravda,* Oct. 25, 1979, pp. 4–5, *FBIS-SOV-79-210,* pp.

AA1–8; and Vsevolod Ovchinnikov, "The Gendarme's Fist," *Pravda*, Jan. 12, 1980, p. 4, *FBIS-SOV-80-010*, pp. A14–16.

41. Editorial, "On the U.S. President's State of the Union Message," pp. A1–5; and Editorial, "Following the Leninist Course of Peace," *Pravda*, Feb. 4, 1980, p. 1, *FBIS-SOV-80-027*, pp. CC1–2. Also see S. Vishnevsky, "Following a Dangerous and Slippery Path: In Connection with Carter's 5-Year Military Program," *Pravda*, Dec. 15, 1979, p. 4, *FBIS-SOV-79-244*, pp. A3–5. Also see A. Bovin, "A Political Observer's Opinion: Those Who Sow the Wind," *Izvestia*, Jan. 16, 1980, p. 5, *FBIS-SOV-80-012*, pp. A1–4.

42. Brezhnev, "Speech at Meeting of Electors of the Baumansky Electoral Okrug," pp. R4–7; and Brezhnev, "Pravda Interviews Leonid Brezhnev," pp. A1–6.

43. Brezhnev, "Speech at Meeting of Electors of the Baumansky Electoral Okrug," p. R6.

44. Editorial, "On the U.S. President's State of the Union Message," p. A5. Also see Editorial, "With the Mighty Weapon of Truth," *Pravda*, Oct. 30, 1979, p. 1, *FBIS-SOV-79-214*, pp. BB1–3.

45. A. Petrov, "Captive to Cold War Dogmas," *Pravda*, Jan. 19, 1980, p. 4, *FBIS-SOV-80-014*, pp. A1–5. Also see Editorial, "Peoples Against Imperialism," pp. CC3–4.

46. Editorial, "On the President's State of the Union Message," pp. A1–5.

47. Brezhnev, "Pravda Interviews Leonid Brezhnev," p. A5; and A. Kirilenko (Politburo member), "The Banner of October Is the Banner of Peace and Creativity," *Moscow Domestic Service*, Nov. 6, 1979, *FBIS-SOV-79-217*, pp. P2–13.

48. Brezhnev, "Speech at Meeting of Electors of the Baumansky Electoral Okrug," p. R5; Brezhnev, "Pravda Interviews Leonid Brezhnev," pp. A1, A5; and Editorial, "With the Mighty Weapon of Truth."

49. L. I. Brezhnev, "Speech October 6, 1979," TASS, Oct. 6, 1979, *FBIS-SOV-79-196*, p. 3. Also see Ponomarev, "In the Interests of Detente: In the Interests of the Peoples of the World," pp. G1–5; and Editorial, "For Talks Instead of New Armaments," *Pravda*, Nov. 17, 1979, p. 1, *FBIS-SOV-79-224*, pp. AA1–6.

50. S. Vishnevsky, "Following a Dangerous and Slippery Path," p. A4.

51. Editorial, "On the U.S. President's State of the Union Message," p. A5.

52. Bovin, "A Political Observer's Opinion," p. A2.

53. For a journalist's elaboration on the common theme, see G. Vasilyev, "Spectators on the Bank of the Potomac," *Pravda*, Jan. 22, 1980, p. 4, *FBIS-SOV-80-018*, p. A9; V. Korionov, "The World of the Eighties: Challenge of the Century," *Pravda*, Jan. 14, 1980, p. 6, *FBIS-SOV-80-012*, pp. A5–7; and M. Stura, "Position of Strength Policy—That Is Washington's Militarist Course," *Izvestia*, Jan. 31, 1980, p. 5, *FBIS-SOV-80-025*, pp. A15–19.

54. B. Pyadyshev, "The Military-Industrial Complex," *International Affairs (Moscow)*, Feb. 1980, pp. 47–54. Also see Editorial, "Lasting Peace for Peoples," *Izvestia*, Aug. 9, 1979, p. 1, *FBIS-SOV-79-157*, pp. AA3–4; and Editorial, "For Peace and Cooperation in Europe," *Pravda*, July 31, 1979, p. 1, *FBIS-SOV-79-149*, pp. G1–2.

55. Editorial, "On the U.S. President's State of the Union Message"; M. Mikhaylov, "Rebuffing the Intrigues of Imperialism: The Afghan Revolution Has Entered a New State," *Izvestia*, Jan. 1, 1980, p. 4, *FBIS-SOV-80-003*, pp. D7–10; Y. Glukhov, "Rebuffing Imperialist Aggression," *Pravda*, Jan. 8, 1980, p. 4, *FBIS-SOV-80-007*, pp. D7–8.

56. Arthur Macy Cox, "The C.I.A.'s Tragic Error," *New York Review of Books* 27 (Nov. 6, 1980), 21–24, and *Russian Roulette: The Superpower Game* (New York: Times Books, 1982), pp. 103–08.

57. Daniel O. Graham, *Shall America Be Defended? SALT II and Beyond* (New Rochelle, N.Y.: Arlington House, 1979), pp. 173–74, 180.

58. Henry Rowen (chairman, National Intelligence Council), CIA Briefing on the Soviet Economy to Subcommittee on International Trade, Finance, and Security Economics, Joint Economic Committee, December 1, 1982, photocopy, p. 11.

59. Franklyn D. Holzman, "Are the Soviets Really Outspending the U.S. on Defense?" *International Security* 4 (Spring 1980), 91, 98–99, 101.

60. For a discussion of the limitation of static comparison, see Fritz Ermarth, "Contrasts in American and Soviet Strategic Thought," *International Security* 3 (Fall 1978), 138–55; and Richard Burt, "Reassessing the Strategic Balance," *International Security* 5 (Summer 1980), 37–52.

61. See Richard Pipes, "Why the Soviet Union Thinks It Could Fight and Win a Nuclear War," *Commentary* 64 (July 1977), 21–34; Colin Gray, "Nuclear Strategy: The Case for a Theory of Victory," *International Security* 4 (Summer 1979), 54–87, and "Strategic Stability Reconsidered," *Daedalus* 109 (Fall 1980), 135–54. Also see Ermarth, "Contrasts in American and Soviet Strategic Thought."

62. See Harriet Fast Scott and William F. Scott, *The Armed Forces of the U.S.S.R.* (Boulder, Colo.: Westview Press, 1979), p. 381. Also see David Holloway, "Military Power and Political Purpose in Soviet Policy," *Daedalus* 109 (Fall 1980), 18–24.

63. See Robert Lee Arnett, "Soviet Attitudes Toward Nuclear War Survival (1962–1977): Has There Been a Change?" Ph.D. diss., Ohio State University, 1979.

64. See Sidney Drell, "Arms Control: Is There Still Hope?" *Daedalus* 109 (Fall 1980), 177–88. Also see Michael Howard, "The Forgotten Dimension of Strategy," *Foreign Affairs* 57 (Summer 1979), 975–86; and Jan Lodal, "Deterrence and Nuclear Strategy," *Daedalus* 109 (Fall 1980), 155–75.

65. See Raymond L. Garthoff, "Mutual Deterrence and Strategic Arms Limitation in Soviet Policy," *International Security* 3 (Summer 1978), 122.

66. See David Holloway, *The Soviet Union and the Arms Race* (New Haven, Conn.: Yale University Press, 1983), pp. 33, 54–58.

67. Arnett, "Soviet Attitudes," pp. 90–102.

68. See Garthoff, "Mutual Deterrence"; and John Erickson, "The Soviet View of Deterrence: A General Survey," in *The Nuclear Arms Race—Control or Catastrophe?* ed. Frank Barnaby and Geoffrey Thomas (London: Frances Pinter, 1982), pp. 73–93. For a Soviet view, see Henry Trofimenko, "Changing Attitudes Toward Deterrence," Paper #25 (Los Angeles: UCLA Center for International and Strategic Affairs, 1980).

69. For a discussion of the problem and possible U.S. options, see Congressional Budget Office, *Counterforce Issues for the U.S. Strategic Nuclear Forces* (Washington, D.C.: GPO, 1978).

70. See Stansfield Turner, "The Folly of the MX Missile," *New York Times Magazine*, Mar. 13, 1983, p. 95.

71. See Office of Technology Assessment, *The Effects of Nuclear War* (Washington, D.C.: GPO, 1979), p. 57; and Congressional Budget Office, *Retaliatory Issues for the U.S. Strategic Nuclear Forces* (Washington, D.C.: GPO, 1978), pp. 21–28, 37–48.

72. See Congressional Budget Office, *Counterforce Issues*, pp. xi–xii, 14–20.

73. Arthur M. Katz, *Life After Nuclear War: The Economic and Social Impacts of Nuclear Attacks on the United States* (Cambridge, Mass.: Ballinger, 1982), p. 333.

74. Randall Forsberg, "A Bilateral Nuclear-Weapon Freeze," *Scientific American* 247 (Nov. 1982), 52–61.

75. See Herbert Scoville, Jr., *MX: Prescription for Disaster* (Cambridge, Mass.: MIT Press, 1981); and Joel S. Wit, "American S.L.B.M.: Counterforce Options and Strategic Implications," *Survival* (Summer 1982), 163–74.

76. Pipes, "Why the Soviet Union Thinks It Could Win"; and Gray, "Strategic Stability," pp. 140–42; and Gray, "Nuclear Strategy," pp. 76–77.

77. The SALT II Treaty set a limit of 2,250 on all strategic launchers, including land- and sea-based missiles as well as bomber aircraft. It set sublimits of 1,320 on all launchers with MIRVs (including ICBMs, SLBMs and some bombers), 1,200 on missile launchers with MIRVs (including ICBMs and SLBMs), and 820 on all ICBMs with MIRVs. For a review of the negotiations and tradeoffs in SALT, see Talbott, *Endgame;* and Thomas W. Wolfe, *The SALT Experience* (Cambridge, Mass.: Ballinger, 1979).

78. See Paul Nitze, "Is SALT II a Fair Deal for the United States?" and "Statement of the Board of Directors of the Arms Control Association on the SALT II Agreements," in *SALT Handbook: Key Documents and Issues 1972–1979*, ed. R. Labrie (Washington, D.C.: AEI, 1979), pp. 667–85, 685–704.

79. The United States in March made two proposals. The limited version would simply exclude cruise missiles from consideration. Because this major new technology could radically alter the number of warheads the United States and the Western European countries could deliver, the USSR not unexpectedly rejected the offer. The more comprehensive proposal would cover cruise missiles and reduce overall ceilings on strategic launchers to between 1,800 and 2,000. Additionally, the proposal suggested a sublimit on ICBMs with MIRVs at 550 and on SS-18s at 150. This was completely unacceptable to the Soviets. At this time the USSR had not completed ICBM modernization but, more important, it had just begun putting MIRVs on SLBMs. This proposal would force equal limits on ICBMs with MIRVs at a time when the United States deployed 496 SLBMs with MIRVs (4,960 warheads) and the Soviets none (*Strategic Survey 1977* [London: IISS, 1978], p. 93; *The Military Balance 1977–1978* [London, IISS, 1978], p. 77).

80. Nitze, "Is SALT II a Fair Deal?" pp. 684–85; and Paul Nitze, "Salt II and American Strategic Considerations," *Comparative Strategy* 2 (1980), 9–34.

81. The sixteenth meeting of the WTO's Political Consultative Committee took place November 28, 1978 in Moscow. For a flavor of the themes the USSR stressed, see L. I. Brezhnev, "In Friendly Atmosphere," TASS, Nov. 23, 1978, *FBIS-SOV-78-277;* and Editorial, "For Lasting Peace and Broad Cooperation," *Izvestia,* Nov. 25, 1978, p. 1, *FBIS-SOV-78-234,* pp. CC1–2; and Editorial, "In the Interests of All People," *Pravda,* Nov. 25, 1978, p. 1, *FBIS-SOV-78-228,* pp. CC7–8. Also see "Declaration of Warsaw Treaty Member Countries," TASS, May 15, 1980, *FBIS-SOV-80-097,* pp. BB3–17.

82. See Melvin Croan, *East Germany: The Soviet Connection,* Washington Papers 4, no. 36 (Beverly Hills, Calif.: Sage Publications, 1976), pp. 16–19.

83. Brzezinski, *Power and Principle,* pp. 296–301. For an enunciation of the policy toward Romania, see Kissinger, *The White House Years,* pp. 154–58.

84. Tad Szulc, "Lisbon and Washington: Behind the Portuguese Revolution," *Foreign Policy* 21 (Winter 1975–1976), 3–62.

85. Reports vary on the financial assistance the USSR gave to Portuguese parties. Western intelligence sources estimated Soviet aid to the PCP at $2–$10 million per month (*Facts on File* [1975], p. 620). The *Washington Post,* Aug. 25, 1975, estimated Soviet aid for 1975 at $45 million, while UK Prime Minister Wilson claimed it was $100 million a year (*Facts on File* [1975], p. 854). The *New York Times,* Sept. 25, 1975, p. 1, reported that the CIA sent $2–$10 million per month to Portuguese Socialists through West European Socialists,

although the latter denied this (*Facts on File* [1975], p. 853). The *New York Times*, Sept. 27, 1975, p. 2, reported a U.S. State Department official as saying that the United States sent $2–$10 million per month to the Socialists and reported that Henry Kissinger explained that he had received approval for aid from congressional oversight committees.

86. See Szulc, "Lisbon and Washington," pp. 33–34.

87. Eusebio M. Mujal-Leon, "The P.C.P. and the Portuguese Revolution," *Problems of Communism* 26 (Jan.–Feb. 1977), 21–32; *Facts on File* (1975), pp. 546, 619. Evidence of Soviet encouragement for the coup is difficult to find, with Western newspapers like the *New York Times*, Sept. 10, 1975, p. 19, reporting that their sources said USSR representatives in Lisbon were cool to the idea of a communist takeover. An act often cited as encouragement, albeit only propaganda, is Konstantin Zarodov (editor of *Problems of Peace and Socialism*) writing in *Pravda*, Aug. 6, 1975, criticizing West European communist parties for cooperating with socialist parties (*Facts on File* [1975], p. 776; *New York Times*, Oct. 4, 1975, p. 8, and Oct. 8, 1975, p. 3).

88. The United States and the EEC, after the ouster of Gonçalves, granted Portugal $272 million in emergency aid (*Facts on File*, [1975], p. 853). For Soviet press coverage, see B. Kotov, "The Situation is Becoming Complicated," *Pravda*, Nov. 24, 1975, p. 3, *FBIS-SOV-75-231*, pp. E7–8; and L. Agapov, "The Situation is Deteriorating," *Izvestia* Nov. 25, 1975, *FBIS-SOV-75-232*, p. E2.

89. For the details of Soviet efforts to court Turkey, see Alvin Z. Rubinstein, *Soviet Policy Toward Turkey, Iran, and Afghanistan: The Dynamics of Influence* (New York: Praeger, 1982), pp. 25–55.

90. See Sarah M. Terry, "The Implications of Interdependence for Soviet-East European Relations: A Preliminary Analysis of the Polish Case," in *The Foreign Policies of East Europe: New Approaches*, ed. R. H. Linden (New York: Praeger, 1980), pp. 186–266; and Zbigniew Fallenbuchl, "Poland's Economic Crisis," *Problems of Communism* 31 (Mar.–Apr. 1982), 1–21.

91. See Adam Bromke, "The Opposition in Poland," *Problems of Communism* (Sept.–Oct. 1978), pp. 37–51; "Experience and the Future" Discussion Group, *Poland Today: The State of the Republic*, intro. Jack Bielasiak, trans. A. Swidlick et al. (Armonk, N.Y.: M.E. Sharpe, 1981); and Richard Herrmann, "Comparing World Views in East Europe: Contemporary Polish Perceptions," in *Foreign Policies of East Europe*, ed. Linden, pp. 46–95.

92. See the reports of J. B. de Weydenthal, in "Solidarity's First National Congress: Stage One," and "Stage Two" *Radio Free Europe Research Reports*, BR/270 (Sept. 21, 1981), BR/291 (Oct. 19, 1981), "Polish Authorities Call for End to Strikes," BR/312 (Nov. 11, 1981), and "Situation Report" 17 (Oct. 5, 1981).

93. Philip Windsor, *Germany and the Western Alliance: Lessons from the 1980 Crisis*, Adelphi Paper 170 (London: IISS, 1981); Brzezinski, *Power and Principle*, pp. 291–96, 301–11; and Carter, *Keeping Faith*, pp. 536–38.

94. For a report on differences in NATO and within the Carter administration over the decision to introduce new medium-range missiles, see Fred Kaplan, "Warring Over New Missiles for N.A.T.O.," *New York Times Magazine*, Dec. 9, 1979, and *New York Times*, Feb. 25, 1979, p. 8. Also see Gregory F. Treverton, *Nuclear Weapons in Europe*, Adelphi Paper 168 (London: IISS, 1981), pp. 22–24; and Raymond L. Garthoff, "The NATO Decision on Theater Nuclear Forces," *Political Science Quarterly* 98 (Summer 1983), 197–214.

95. Helmut Schmidt, "Government Statement on Bonn Visit of Soviet Party and State Head Brezhnev," May 11, 1978, *FBIS-WEU-78-92*, pp. J1–5. Alfons Pawelyzyk (SPD deputy and chairman of the Bundestag Disarmament Committee), "Speech to Bundestag," Mar. 6, 1979, *FBIS-WEU-79-047*, p. J6.

96. Helmut Schmidt, "Speech at S.P.D. Security Congress in Cologne,"

Bonn Tagesdienst Bulletin of the S.P.D., Bundestag Faction, Apr. 20, 1980, pp. 1–19, *FBIS-WEU-80-080,* p. J10.

97. "Government Statement by Chancellor Helmut Schmidt to Bundestag," *Cologne Westdeutscher Rundfunk Network,* Jan. 17, 1980, *FBIS-WEU-80-013,* p. J3. Giscard d'Estaing and Schmidt, meeting in early February, called for a Soviet withdrawal from Afghanistan, but did not endorse President Carter's calls for sanctions (Helmut Schmidt and Valery Giscard d'Estaing, "Joint Communique," *AFP,* Feb. 5, 1980, *FBIS-WEU-80-025,* p. K2).

98. "Government Statement by Chancellor Helmut Schmidt," pp. J4–6. Also see "Interview with Helmut Schmidt," *Der Spiegel,* Feb. 4, 1980, pp. 24–33, *FBIS-WEU-80-026,* pp. J3–15.

99. *New York Times,* Jan. 7, 1979, p. 13; Helmut Schmidt, "Speech to the Bundestag," Mar. 9, 1979, *FBIS-WEU-70-049,* pp. J1–20. For the view of Willy Weisskirch, Chairman of the Working Circle for Defense of C.D.U./C.S.U. Bundestag Faction," *Mainz Domestic Service,* Jan. 9, 1979, *FBIS-WEU-79-9,* pp. J1–2; and "Interview with C.S.U. Chairman F. J. Strauss," *Cologne Domestic Service,* Jan. 14, 1979, *FBIS-WEU-79-11,* pp. J1–9.

100. "Speech by Defense Minister Hans Apel," *Federal German Information Service Bulletin,* Feb. 20, 1979, *FBIS-WEU-79-038,* pp. J7–8.

101. L. I. Brezhnev, "Speech October 6, 1979 in Berlin." Also see Andrei Gromyko, "Speech in Bonn," TASS, Nov. 22, 1979, *FBIS-SOV-79-227,* pp. G3–5, and "Statement and Press Conference," *Moscow Domestic Service,* Nov. 24, 1979, *FBIS-SOV-79-228,* pp. G1–7.

102. *Facts on File* (1979), p. 938; *New York Times,* Dec. 6, 1979, p. 3. The CIA reported in June 1980 that while the Soviet Union carried out its pledge to withdraw forces from East Germany, it strengthened its forces in Eastern Europe by 30,000 troops, 1,000 artillery pieces, and 2,000 tanks and APCs (*New York Times,* June 8, 1980, p. 4).

103. "Communique from the Meeting of the Committee of Ministers of Foreign Affairs of the Warsaw Treaty Member States," TASS, Dec. 6, 1979, *FBIS-SOV-79-236,* pp. BB1–7.

104. Stephen Szabo concludes: "Anywhere from 63% to 81% of Germans questioned between 1976 and 1981 believe N.A.T.O. is essential for German security" ("West Germany: Generations and Changing Security Perspectives," in *The Successor Generation: International Perspectives of Postwar Europeans* ed. Stephen Szabo [London: Butterworth, 1983], p. 66). Also see Elizabeth Noelle-Neumann, *The Germans: Public Opinon Polls, 1967–1980* (Westport, Conn.: Greenwood, 1981), pp. 435–37. Erich Weede, Dietmar Schossler, and Mattias Jung found that 90 percent of the West German elite favored close and continuous ties to the U.S. 82 percent of the S.P.D. and 96 percent of the CDU respondents were so inclined. However, 79 percent of the SPD respondents said they would resist further reinforcements of the FRG's military commitment ("West German Elite Views on National Security Issues: Evidence from a 1980/1981 Survey of Experts," *Journal of Strategic Studies* 6 [Mar. 1983], 86, 91).

105. J. A. Stockfish, *Models, Data, and War: A Critique of the Study of Conventional Forces* R-1526-PR (Santa Monica, Calif.: Rand, 1975); and Robert Shishko, "The European Conventional Balance: A Primer" (Santa Monica, Calif.: Rand, 1981), p. 6707.

106. The Defense Department calculates an Armored Division Equivalent (ADE) to summarize mobility, survivability, and firepower. See John J. Mearsheimer, "Why the Soviets Can't Win Quickly in Central Europe," *International Security* 7 (Summer 1982), 8. Also see *The Military Balance 1979–1980* (London: IISS, 1979), pp. 108–13.

107. IISS, *Military Balance 1979–1980,* pp. 113, 117. Also see Mearsheimer, "Why the Soviet's Can't Win," pp. 3, 9, 36; and Robert Metzger and

Paul Doty, "Arms Control Enters the Gray Area," *International Security* 3 (Winter 1978), 43.

108. Metzger and Doty, "Arms Control," pp. 22–23.

109. Christopher D. Jones, "Equality and Equal Security in Europe," *Orbis* 26 (Fall 1982), 637–64.

110. Metzger and Doty, "Arms Control," pp. 22–23.

111. See Holloway, *The Soviet Union and the Arms Race,* pp. 65–70.

112. See Treverton, *Nuclear Weapons in Europe,* p. 10.

113. Raymond Garthoff, "Moscow's Less Than Ominous Reasons for Deploying SS-20s," *New York Times,* May 13, 1983, p. 26, emphasis in original.

114. Szabo reports, "A host of surveys have clearly indicated that a Soviet invasion of Western Europe is not viewed as either a realistic possibility or a cause for concern by a majority of Europeans." In March 1981 32 percent of West Germans said they were either very or fairly concerned about a Soviet attack, and 54 percent were not concerned at all. Szabo concludes that the data suggests "that the danger of neutralism among the young stems not from a perception of growing Soviet superiority but rather from a sanguine perception of the military balance" ("West Germany" pp. 55–56, 58).

115. Helmut Schmidt, "Interview," May 8, 1978, *FBIS-WEU-78-91,* pp. J1–3.

116. Juergen Kellermeir, "Interview with S.P.D. H. Wehner," *Cologne Domestic Service,* Feb. 3, 1979, *FBIS-WEU-79-26,* pp. J3–5.

117. Franz Schmidt, "Interview with Chancellor Helmut Schmidt," *Neue Osnabruecker Zeitung,* June 1, 1978, *FBIS-WEU-78-107,* p. J11.

118. Elisabeth Noelle-Neuman, "Are the Germans 'Collapsing' or 'Standing Firm'?" *Encounter* 58 (Feb. 1982), p. 77.

119. Weede et al. "West German Elite Views," p. 91; and Szabo, "West Germany," pp. 66–67.

120. Bruce Russett and Donald R. Deluca find similar results. See "Theater Nuclear Forces: Public Opinion in Western Europe," *Political Science Quarterly* 98 (Summer 1983), 185–86.

121. Schmidt, "Interview," May 8, 1978, p. J2.

122. "Speech by Chancellor Helmut Schmidt During Debate in the Bundestag on Disarmament," *Cologne Domestic Service,* Feb. 15, 1979, *FBIS-WEU-79-034,* p. J3. In one survey only 13 percent of the experts asked identified deterrence and detente as alternatives, whereas 67 percent felt detente complements military deterrence or that military deterrence ensures strategic stability as a prerequisite of detente. An additional 20 percent felt detente should promote the political prerequisites for overcoming deterrence (Weede et al., "West German Elite Views," p. 86).

123. Helmut Schmidt, "Speech at S.P.D. Security Congress in Cologne," *Bonn Tagesdienst Bulletin of the S.P.D. Bundestag Faction,* Apr. 20, 1980, pp. 1–19, *FBIS-WEU-80-080,* p. J10.

124. Karen Dawisha, *Soviet Foreign Policy Towards Egypt* (New York: St. Martin's Press, 1979); Mohamed Heikal, *The Sphinx and the Commissar: The Rise and Fall of Soviet Influence in the Middle East* (New York: Harper and Row, 1978); and Robert Freedman, *Soviet Policy Toward the Middle East Since 1970* (New York: Praeger, 1978).

125. *Facts on File* (1979), p. 762; ibid. (1980), p. 11.

126. K. Dawisha, *Soviet Foreign Policy,* pp. 76–77; Alvin Rubinstein, *Red Star on the Nile: The Soviet-Egyptian Influence Relationship Since the June War* (Princeton, N.J.: Princeton University Press, 1977), pp. 324–25.

127. The Egyptian Communist party was reestablished. The USSR did not supply it with enough support to challenge Sadat's rule (Heikal, *Sphinx and Commissar,* p. 272).

128. American participants at Camp David have reported that Sadat was more conciliatory than his advisers and that he tended to ignore or override them (Carter, *Keeping Faith*, p. 342; and Brzezinski, *Power and Principle*, pp. 237–38).

129. Libya deployed an army of 45,000 troops with 2,400 tanks and an air force of 287 combat aircraft, compared to Egypt's army of 320,000 with 1,600 tanks and an air force with 363 combat aircraft. See *The Military Balance 1980–1981* (London: IISS, 1980), pp. 41, 45.

130. See V. Pereosada, "Left Party Congress," *Pravda*, Apr. 11, 1980, p. 5, *FBIS-SOV-80-076*, pp. H6–7, and "For Egypt's National Interests," *Pravda*, Apr. 13, 1980, p. 5, *FBIS-SOV-80-082*, pp. H1–2.

131. On March 31, 1979, eighteen Arab League members imposed an economic boycott of Egypt and severed diplomatic relations. Moreover, they expressed their hope that Sadat would be overthrown (*Facts on File* [1979], p. 248). For an example of the Soviet Union's propaganda surrounding this decision, see P. Demchenko, "New Realities, Old Problems," *Pravda*, Mar. 30, 1979, p. 5, *FBIS-SOV-79-065*, pp. H1–3; and Yevgeniy Primakov (member of the USSR Academy of Sciences and director of the Institute of Oriental Studies), "Interview," *Novosti Press, Beirut, FBIS-SOV-79-131*, pp. H1–10.

132. After 1975 the USSR endorsed the inclusion of the PLO at Geneva and the creation of a Palestinian state. Arms sales to Libya escalated significantly in 1976–1979. The USSR, however, continued to endorse the Geneva format and Israel's right to exist within the 1967 frontiers. See Freedman, *Soviet Policy Toward the Middle East*, pp. 279–80; and K. Dawisha, *Soviet Foreign Policy*, p. 80. Also see L. I. Brezhnev, "Message to Yasir Arafat," *Pravda*, Nov. 29, 1979, p. 1, *FBIS-SOV-79-237*, p. H6; and P. Demchenko, "The Palestinians Continue the Struggle," *Pravda*, Dec. 7, 1979, p. 4, *FBIS-SOV-79-240*, pp. H3–6.

133. Ilana Kass, "Moscow and the Lebanese Triangle," *Middle East Journal* 33 (Spring 1979), 164–87; and Freedman, *Soviet Policy Toward the Middle East*, pp. 255–62, 273–74.

134. Walid Khalidi, *Conflict and Violence in Lebanon: Confrontation in the Middle East* (Cambridge, Mass.: Harvard University Center for International Affairs, 1979), pp. 82–84. Also see Itamar Rabinovich, "The Limits of Military Power: Syria's Role," in *Lebanon in Crisis: Participants and Issues*, ed. P. Edward Haley and Lewis Snider (Syracuse, N.Y.: Syracuse University Press, 1979), pp. 56–57.

135. Kass, "Moscow and the Lebanese Triangle," pp. 164–87; 170–72. Also see Galia Golin, "Syria and the Soviet Union Since the Yom Kippur War," *Orbis* 21 (Winter 1978), 795–96.

136. See James Collins, "The Soviet Union," in *Lebanon in Crisis*, ed. Haley and Snider, pp. 209–23.

137. PLO spokesmen publicly complained about the lack of Soviet support. They asked the USSR to at least "show the flag" if it would not provide material aid (Golin, "Syria and the Soviet Union," p. 797; and Freedman, *Soviet Policy Toward the Middle East*, pp. 255–56).

138. See A. A. Gromyko, "Address to the U.N. General Assembly," *Izvestia*, Sept. 27, 1978, p. 3, *FBIS-SOV-78-189*, pp. A1–12; "On the Leninist Foreign Policy Course," *Pravda*, Sept. 25, 1978, p. 1, *FIBS-SOV-78-190*, pp. A1–2; and Editorial, "On Lasting Peace and the Peoples' Security," *Izvestia*, Sept. 30, 1978, p. 1, *FBIS-SOV-78-193*, pp. A4–6. Also see P. Demchenko, "The Near East: A Just Peace, Not Separate Deals," *Pravda*, Dec. 29, 1977, p. 4, *FBIS-SOV-78-1*, pp. F5–8.

139. See Yuriy Glukhov, "Results of Baghdad," *Pravda*, Nov. 11, 1978, p. 5, *FBIS-SOV-78-221*, pp. F1–2; and V. Kudryavtsev, "Near East: After Baghdad," *Izvestia*, Nov. 18, 1978, p. 4, *FBIS-SOV-78-225*, pp. F2–5.

140. *Facts of File* (1978), pp. 10–11, 78–79, 762–63. It was only two weeks later that the Syrian-Iraqi Summit met and worked out plans for cooperation (ibid., p. 802).

141. See Alan Taylor, *The Arab Balance of Power* (Syracuse, N.Y.: Syracuse University Press, 1982), pp. 73–96.

142. Israel invaded southern Lebanon in 1978. Under U.S. pressure, it withdrew but continued to strike Palestinian and Lebanese sites. In 1979 Israel repeatedly delivered air, sea, and ground assaults on Lebanon. Two days of air attacks on Lebanon in June evoked "concern" from Washington and when Israel launched air attacks, July 6–24, the U.S. State Department "condemned" the raids and suggested they possibly breached U.S. restrictions prohibiting the use of American weapons in "offensive" operations. The Israelis struck Lebanon with air attacks again, August 6–21 (*Facts on File* [1979], pp. 278, 296, 340, 378, 436, 462, 496, 551, 592, 625).

143. *New York Times*, Apr. 10, 1980, p. 16. Reportedly Brzezinski was a proponent of exploring contacts with Iraq (*New York Times*, May 5, 1980, p. 18). Also see Adeed Dawisha, "Iraq: The West's Opportunity," *Foreign Policy* 41 (Winter 1980–1981), 134–53; and Steven B. Kashkett, "Iraq and the Pursuit of Nonalignment," *Orbis* 26 (Summer 1982), 477–94.

144. *New York Times*, Oct. 9, 1980, p. 17. See "Soviet-Syrian Joint Communique," *Pravda*, Oct. 11, 1980, pp. 1, 4, *FBIS-SOV-80-201*, pp. H4–8; and Editorial, "Dictated by Aims of Peace," *Izvestia*, Oct. 15, 1980, p. 1, *FBIS-SOV-80-202*, pp. H1–3.

145. Israel's success in Lebanon and confidence in striking the nuclear facilities in Baghdad seem to give weight to these judgments. See *The Military Balance 1980–1981*, pp. 43, 45, 48.

146. See Dennis Ross, "The Soviet Union and the Persian Gulf," Working Paper #4 (Providence, R.I.: Brown University Center for Foreign Policy Development, June 1983), pp. 25–26.

147. Colin Legum reports NATO planners' surprise at the USSR's airlift capacity and ability to project force ("Angola and the Horn of Africa," in *Diplomacy of Power: Soviet Armed Forces as a Political Instrument*, ed. Stephen Kaplan (Washington D.C.: Brookings, 1981), p. 623. In August the CIA reported that between 11,000 and 14,000 Cuban troops remained in Ethiopia along with 2,000 Soviet advisers (*Facts on File* [1979], pp. 271, 406, 673, 791, 825). According to the CIA, the USSR committed $2 billion in military aid to Ethiopia in 1977–1978 (National Assessment Center, *Communist Aid Activities in Non-Communist Less Developed Countries, 1979* [Washington D.C.: CIA, Sept. 1979], p. 3; and Orah Cooper and Carol Fogarty, "Soviet Economic and Military Aid to the Less Developed Countires, 1954–1978," in Joint Economic Committee, *Soviet Economy in a Time of Change*, 96th Cong., 1st sess. (Washington, D.C.: GPO, 1979), p. 652.

148. Major revolts began in February 1974 and escalated into a general strike in March (*New York Times*, Feb. 27, 1974, p. 1, Mar. 8, 1974, p. 3). After several months in which Emperor Haile Selassie talked of holding a constitutional convention the army assumed control in July. It began to arrest former government officers and eventually deposed the emperor, ending his fifty-eight-year tenure. Lt. Gen. Aman Michael Andom, as chief of staff, assumed control (*Facts on File* [1974], p. 180; and the *New York Times*, July 5, 1974, p. 38, July 10, 1974, p. 6, and Sept. 13, 1974, p. 1).

149. The United States continued aid, delivering $22.5 million in 1975 and authorized the sale of $53 million more over the next two years. See *Strategic Survey 1977* (London: IISS, 1977), pp. 18–19. Also see the *New York Times*, Oct. 22, 1975, p. 11, which reports U.S. aid as $23.5 million in economic and $12.5 in military supply. Two weeks after Mengistu made public

overtures to the Soviets, the United States announced it was stopping its aid. The decision was said to be a response to human rights violations. The USSR had already signed a $385 million arms deal with Ethiopia in December 1976 (*Strategic Survey 1977*, p. 19).

150. In March 1977 Fidel Castro mediated at a summit meeting in Aden between South Yemen, Somalia, and Ethiopia urging an anti-imperialist alliance (Maria Ottaway and David Ottaway, *Ethiopia: Empire in Revolution* [New York: Africana Publishing, 1978], p. 170; *Strategic Survey 1977*, pp. 17–18; and *Facts on File* [1977], p. 249).

151. *Facts on File* (1977), pp. 587–88; and the *New York Times*, Sept. 1, 1977, p. 1. Secretary Vance and Security Adviser Brzezinski disagreed over U.S. policy. Vance advised against an American military action and for strict adherence to Somali withdrawal; Brzezinski favored a show of force as a method of demonstrating U.S. resolve. See Vance, *Hard Choices*, pp. 73–74, 85–88; and Brzezinski, *Power and Principle*, pp. 182–83.

152. *Facts on File* (1977), pp. 684, 715.

153. Legum, "Angola and the Horn," p. 617; *Facts on File* (1977), p. 829.

154. The Sudanese, Somali, Yemeni summit meeting occurred on May 11–12 (*Strategic Survey 1977*, p. 18). For Carter's statement, see the *New York Times*, June 12, 1977, p. 1.

155. Larry Napper, "The Ogaden War: Some Implications for Crisis Prevention," in *Managing U.S.-Soviet Rivalry: Problems of Crisis Prevention*, ed. Alexander George (Boulder, Colo.: Westview Press, 1983), pp. 236, 248.

156. *New York Times*, Mar. 30, 1978, p. 10. Eritrean Liberation Fronts (ELF-EPLF), at the time united, were backed by the Sudan, Saudia Arabia, Egypt, and Syria. Iraq also backed the Eritreans and reportedly threatened to break diplomatic relations with the USSR (*Facts on File* [1978], pp. 415–16).

157. *Facts on File* (1978), p. 100.

158. Secretary of State Cyrus Vance disclosed that the United States was given assurances from the USSR that Ethiopia would not invade Somalia. Apparently National Security Council delegate David Aaron received similar pledges when he visited Ethiopia in February 1979, and in March Foreign Minister Gromyko assured President Carter directly. Carter announced that if the USSR did help Ethiopia invade Somalia the United States would help Somalia (*New York Times*, Feb. 19, 1978, p. 10, Feb. 22, 1978, p. 1, and Feb. 11, 1978, p. 1). Also see Napper, "The Ogaden War," pp. 236–37; and Vance, *Hard Choices*, pp. 86–87.

159. *Strategic Survey 1978* (London: IISS, 1978), p. 99.

160. The South Yemeni ambassador was reported to have left Ethiopia June 7, 1978, in protest over the Eritrean policy (*Facts on File* [1978], p. 584).

161. Ibid., pp. 498–99; and Fred Halliday, *Soviet Policy in the Arc of Crisis* (Washington, D.C.: Institute for Policy Studies, 1981), pp. 90–92. Also see *Facts on File* (1979), p. 791; and ibid. (1980), pp. 10, 67.

162. For those who see the Soviet relationship as the primary issue in South Yemeni politics, Ismail's ascendancy is seen as circumstantial evidence indicating a Soviet role. Others who emphasize a range of issues in Yemeni affairs perceive the effects of the Ismail coup as more varied and as circumstantially indicating many other candidates for involvement. Alvin Rubinstein argues that the USSR was involved, Fred Halliday that it was not. See Alvin Z. Rubinstein, "The Soviet Union and the Arabian Peninsula, *The World Today* 35 (Nov. 1979), 442–52; and Halliday, *Soviet Policy in the Arc*, pp. 92–93.

163. *Facts on File* (1979), p. 89; and the *New York Times*, Feb. 12, 1979, p. 4.

164. In early March the United States decided to dispatch a naval task force to the Arabian Sea and sent eighteen F-15 fighter planes and two AWACs

to Saudia Arabia. Representative Les Aspin noted, in criticizing the administration's actions, that U.S. deliveries to the YAR in 1979 would total $540 million, making it the third largest recipient of American arms, following only Israel and Saudi Arabia (*Facts on File* [1979], p. 199; *New York Times,* Feb. 25, 1979, p. 11, Mar. 3, 1979, p. 3, Mar. 8, 1979, p. 3, Mar. 10, 1979, p. 1).

165. See, for example, Nimrod Novik, *Between Two Yemen's Regional Dynamics and Superpower Conduct in Riyadh's 'Backyard'* (Tel Aviv: University of Tel Aviv Center for Strategic Studies, Dec. 1980), pp. 9–14.

166. William B. Quandt, *Saudi Arabia in the 1980s: Foreign Policy, Security, and Oil* (Washington, D.C.: Brookings, 1981), pp. 22, 26–28.

167. *New York Times,* Mar. 13, 1979, p. 11.

168. Deputy Assistant Secretary for Near Eastern and South Asian Affairs William R. Crawford confirmed that Soviet aid to the PDRY over the "last several years: exceeded $400 million" (U.S. Congress, House, Committee on Foreign Affairs, *Proposed Arms Transfers to the Yemen Arab Republic: Hearings Before the Subcommittee on Europe and the Middle East,* 96th Cong., 1st sess., p. 31). Two CIA analysts report that in 1977–1978 Afghanistan, South Yemen, and Iraq together bought $600 million worth of Soviet arms (Cooper and Fogarty, "Soviet Economic and Military Aid," p. 655).

169. See Alvin Rubinstein, "The Soviet Union in the Middle East," *Current History* 77 (Oct. 1979), 106–09, 132–33; and John Campbell, "Soviet Policy in the Middle East," *Current History* 80 (Jan. 1981), 1–4, 42–43. For Soviet propaganda said to "court" Saudia Arabia, see C. K. Dudarev, "Washington's Policy Harms Saudi Arabia's Interests," *ZA Rubezhom* 17 (Apr. 19, 1979), 4–5, *FBIS-SOV-79-082,* pp. H7–8. Also see Igor Belyayev, "Saudi Arabia: What Next?" *Literaturnaya Gazeta,* Jan. 31, 1979, p. 14, *FBIS-SOV-79-024,* pp. F7–11.

170. The PDRY and YAR announced a decision to unify on March 29, 1979 (*Facts on File* [1979], pp. 199, 250). *Pravda* called the decision to unify North and South Yemen "an important factor promoting stability and peace in the region" ("Report on Communique issued by P.D.R.Y. and Y.A.R.," *Pravda,* Apr. 1, 1979, p. 1, *FBIS-SOV-79-067,* p. H9).

171. *Washington Post,* June 5, 1980, p. 1.

172. *Facts on File* (1980), p. 468; *New York Times,* June 15, 1980, p. 4, June 27, 1980, p. 18, June 30, 1980, p. 3.

173. See, "Joint Communique," *Pravda,* Oct. 27, 1979, pp. 1, 4, *FBIS-SOV-79-211,* pp. H1–5; and V. Peresada, "12 Years Independence for Democratic Yemen," *Pravda,* Nov. 30, 1979, p. 4, *FBIS-SOV-79-237,* pp. H4–5.

174. In February 1979 U.S. Secretary of Defense Brown visited Cairo to discuss Egypt's requests for arms (*Facts on File* [1979], p. 143). In 1979 the United States provided $1.2 billion in financial aid and $3.5 billion in longer-term arms commitments to Egypt, and by October 1979 Egypt had received twelve of thirty-five ordered F-4 Phantoms, and forty of 800 M-113 APCs (*Facts on File* [1979], p. 762; *Strategic Survey 1979* [London: IISS, 1980], p. 79). Somalia first raised the issue of access to military facilities in 1977 in an apparent effort to attract U.S. support in its contest with Ethiopia. In 1978 the issue was again discussed by a U.S. congressional delegation visiting Somalia, and in February 1979 Secretary Harold Brown, while visiting Saudi Arabia, explained that in light of the Iranian revolution the United States was considering the issue of a military presence in the area (*Facts on File* [1979], pp. 143–44). In December 1979, before the USSR's invasion of Afghanistan, a team from the U.S. State and Defense Departments visited Saudi Arabia, Oman, Somalia, and Kenya to examine the possibility of "port calls and the use of airfields" (*Facts on File* [1979], p. 958; *New York Times,* Dec. 23, 1979, p. 1). In April 1980 the United States agreed to arrangements with Oman and Kenya that

would allow it to maintain military facilities in those countries in exchange for military aid (*Facts on File* [1980], pp. 303, 436).

175. See Rosenau and Holsti, *American Leadership in World Affairs*, pp. 213–14.

176. See Alfred Monks, *The Soviet Invasion of Afghanistan* (Washington, D.C.: AEI, 1981); and Anthony Arnold, *Afghanistan: The Soviet Invasion in Perspective* (Stanford, Calif.: Hoover Institution Press, 1981).

177. See, for example, Alexander Dallin, "The Road to Kabul: Soviet Perceptions of World Affairs and the Afghan Crisis," in Vernon Aspaturian, Alexander Dallin, Jiri Valenta, *The Soviet Invasion of Afghanistan: Three Perspectives* (Los Angeles: UCLA Center for International and Strategic Affairs, 1980), pp. 56–71. Also see George Kennan in U.S. Congress, Senate, Hearings, Subcommittee on Near Eastern and South Asian Affairs, Committee on Foreign Relations, *U.S. Security Interests and Policies in Southwest Asia*, Feb.–Mar. 1980 (Washington, D.C.: GPO, 1980), pp. 90–95; 105–12.

178. Daoud came to power in 1973, reportedly with Parchami help. While Parcham had had ties to Moscow, there is little evidence that Soviet involvement had much to do with Daoud's rise. Since the 1950s the USSR had supplied 95 percent of Kabul's economic and military aid. See Shabeen F. Dil, "The Cabal in Kabul: Great Power Interaction in Afghanistan," *American Political Science Review* 71 (June 1977), 468–76. Also see Nancy P. Newell and Richard S. Newell, *The Struggle for Afghanistan* (Ithaca, N.Y.: Cornell University Press, 1981), pp. 45–50.

179. See Louis Dupree, "Afghanistan Under the Khalq," *Problems of Communism* 28 (July 1979), 34–50; and Robert Donaldson, "Soviet Policy in South Asia," in *Soviet Policy in the Third World*, ed. W. Raymond Duncan (New York: Pergamon Press, 1980), p. 226; Newell and Newell, *The Struggle for Afghanistan*, pp. 67–72, 112–13.

180. Newell and Newell, *The Struggle for Afghanistan*, pp. 52–65. Also see Dupree, "Afghanistan," pp. 39–45.

181. *New York Times*, Feb. 16, 1979, p. 1, and Feb. 18, 1979, p. 13.

182. Newell and Newell, *The Struggle for Afghanistan*, pp. 79–85. While reports on the size and character of the resistance in Afghanistan varied, reports of escalating fighting persisted throughout 1979 (*New York Times*, Jan. 8, 1979, p. 3, Jan. 11, 1979, p. 5, Mar. 23, 1979, p. 1, June 24, 1979, p. 1; *Facts on File* [1979], p. 368). On August 18, 1979, an Islamic regime was reportedly established within the opposition (*Facts on File* [1979], p. 666).

183. See Donaldson, "Soviet Policy in South Asia," p. 227; *Facts on File* (1979), p. 589; and the *New York Times*, Aug. 2, 1979, p. 10. Also see Newell and Newell, *The Struggle for Afghanistan*, pp. 87–88, 114.

184. The struggle between Taraki and Amin occurred just five days after Taraki returned from discussions in Moscow. The CIA reported increased activity among Soviet military units near the Afghan border following Taraki's death and reported later that the USSR had tried to oust Amin in September but failed (*New York Times*, Sept. 20, 1979, p. 10, and Jan. 2, 1980, p. 14). Also see Jiri Valenta, "Soviet Invasion of Afghanistan: The Difficulty of Knowing Where to Stop," *Orbis* 24 (Summer 1980), 205.

185. The Soviet Union dispatched Lt. General Viktor S. Paputin, first deputy minister of internal affairs, to Kabul in the middle of December 1979, evidently to "persuade" Amin to step aside. Paputin was reportedly wounded in Afghanistan and in any case returned to Moscow and was confirmed by Soviet authorities as dead (*Facts on File* [1980], pp. 26, 44; *New York Times*, Jan. 4, 1980, p. 8, Feb. 3, 1980, p. 10).

186. See Thomas G. Hart, "Perceiving 'Afghanistan': Some Questions about the Applicability of Theoretical Insights in Analyzing Perceptions in a

Current Crisis," in *Cognitive Dynamics and International Politics,* ed. Christer Jonsson (London: Frances Pinter, 1982), pp. 178–98.

187. For a concise example of the prevailing Soviet image, see *The Truth About Afghanistan: Documents, Facts, Eyewitness Report* (Moscow: Novosti Press, 1980).

188. Brzezinski, *Power and Principle,* p. 430.

189. On the Iranian revolution, see Richard Cottam, *Nationalism in Iran,* 2d ed. (Pittsburgh: University of Pittsburgh Press, 1978); Homa Katouzian, *The Political Economy of Modern Iran: 1926–1979* (New York: New York University Press, 1981); and Nikki Keddie, *Roots of Revolution: An Interpretive History of Modern Iran* (New Haven, Conn.: Yale University Press, 1981).

190. The revolt in Iran escalated throughout 1978 with protests in Qom in January, riots in Tabriz in February, demonstrations in Teheran in May–July, massacres in September, such as at Jaleh Square on "Black Friday," and major strikes among oil workers. Soviet propaganda continued to attribute the disturbances to problems associated with industrialization, errors in planning, excess bureaucracy, excess military expenditures, and rising expectations. Not until late October and November did Soviet propaganda emphasize "repression" and "corruption" as causes of the "social antagonisms" and even then refrained from criticizing the shah. See A. Bovin, "Iran: Consequences and Reasons," *Literaturnaya Gazeta,* Oct. 25, 1978, p. 14, *FBIS-SOV-78-212,* pp. F10–13. Also see Barry Rubin, *Paved with Good Intentions: The American Experience in Iran* (New York: Oxford University Press, 1980), p. 206.

191. See Shahram Chubin, *Soviet Policy Toward Iran and the Gulf,* Adelphi Paper 157 (London: IISS, 1980), pp. 21–22. According to the CIA, the USSR in 1978 had 5,100 economic technicians stationed in Iran. See National Foreign Assessment Center, *Communist Aid Activities in Non-Communist Less Developed Countries: 1978* (Washington D.C.: CIA, 1978), pp. 4, 15.

192. In early December the USSR's propaganda began to describe the shah's "SAVAK butchers," his "personal corruption," and his "vassal" relationship vis-à-vis the United States and began to encourage the opposition. See, for example. S. Kondrashov, "Around the Events in Iran," *Izvestia,* Dec. 6, 1978, p. 3, *FBLS-SOV-78-237,* pp. F1–3; and A. Akhmedzyanov, "Iran's Hot Winter," *Izvestia,* Dec. 14, 1978, p. 5, *FBIS-SOV-78-244,* pp. F4–7. .

193. See the *Washington Post,* Nov. 7, 1978, p. 1, 16; and the *New York Times,* Nov. 15, 1978, p. A3.

194. "Leonid Brezhnev's Reply to a Question by *Pravda* Correspondent," *Pravda,* Nov. 19, 1978, p. 1, *FBIS-SOV-78-224,* p. F1.

195. Brzezinski records that he did advocate a military coup, urging the president to attempt this option in early 1979. The groundwork was reportedly laid and, as the former NSC adviser regrets, he failed to persuade President Carter to order the action. See Brzezinski, *Power and Principle,* pp. 378–96; also see William Sullivan, "Dateline Iran: The Road Not Taken," *Foreign Policy* 40 (Fall 1980), 175–186; *New York Times,* Jan. 9, 1979, p. A12, Jan. 11, 1979, p. A3; and the *Washington Post,* Jan. 13, 1979, pp. 1, 13, Jan. 19, 1979, pp. 1, 16. For examples of the Soviet propaganda broadcast to Iran, see *FBIS-SOV-79-005,* Jan. 8, 1979, pp. F3–4; and *FBIS-SOV-79-002,* Jan. 3, 1979, pp. F2–3. For Soviet domestic propaganda, see A. Filippov, "U.S. Military Pressure on Iran," *Pravda,* Jan. 11, 1979, p. 5, *FBIS-SOV-79-010,* p. F3; A. Maksimov, "Iran: On the Threshold of a Military Putsch?" *Izvestia,* Jan. 13, 1979, p. 4, *FBIS-SOV-79-012,* p. F1; and V. Ovchinnikov, "What, Then, Is Interference?" *Pravda,* Jan. 13, 1979, p. 5, *FBIS-SOV-79-012,* pp. F2–3.

196. The U.S. government warned the USSR against providing military assistance to the Afghan government in its struggle against domestic opposition

in March 1979 (*Facts on File* [1979], p. 232; *New York Times*, Mar. 24, 1979, p. 4, and Aug. 3, 1979, p. 1).

197. See, for example, Mansour Farhang, *U.S. Imperialism: The Spanish-American War to the Iranian Revolution* (Boston: South End Press, 1981). Farhang served as President Banisadr's ambassador to the UN. Also see Abolhassan Banisadr, *The Fundamental Precepts of Islamic Government*, trans. M. Ghanoonparvar (Lexington, Ky.: Mazda, 1981), pp. 59–70.

198. *Facts on File* (1980), p. 644; *New York Times*, June 13, 1979, p. 11.

199. Aleksander Bovin, for example, explained that the "hope" concerning the revolution "had been replaced by anxiety and alarm, uncertainty and disappointment" ("With Koran and Saber!!!" *Nedelya* 36 [Sept. 4, 1979], 6, *FBIS-SOV-79-176*, pp. H1–2).

200. For an illustration of the shift in propaganda after the hostage crisis began and U.S.-Iranian relations collapsed, contrast Bovin, ibid., with Aleksander Bovin, "International Panorama," *Moscow Domestic Television*, Nov. 18, 1979, *FBIS-SOV-79-239*, pp. H2–3.

201. For coverage of fighting in Turkmenistan and Kurdistan, see the *New York Times*, Mar. 28, 1979, p. 3, Mar. 29, 1979, p. 3, Mar. 30, 1979, p. 6, Apr. 2, 1979, p. 6; and *Facts on File* (1979), pp. 145, 198, 321.

202. For an example of Soviet propaganda broadcast to Iran, see *FBIS-SOV-79-059*, Mar. 26, 1979, pp. H13–18, and *FBIS-SOV-79-067*, Apr. 5, 1979, p. H8. Also see A. Grachev, "The Policy Line is Goodneighborliness," *Pravda*, Mar. 24, 1979, p. 5, *FBIS-SOV-79-060*, pp. H8–9; and A. Akmuradov, "Slander—The Tool of Reaction," *Pravda*, Apr. 4, 1979, p. 5, *FBIS-SOV-79-068*, pp. H6–7.

203. See A. Filippov, "Situation in Iran," *Pravda*, Sept. 14, 1979, p. 5; and A. Filippov, "Problem Remains Unresolved: Situation in Kordestan," *Pravda*, Sept. 16, 1979, p. 5, both in *FBIS-SOV-79-184*, pp. H9–10.

204. Soviet propaganda, for example, blamed the December 1979–January 1980 clashes in Tabriz as a result of "CIA," "SAVAK" efforts to "unleash fratricidal disagreements" (*Moscow Domestic Service*, Jan. 7, 1980, *FBIS-SOV-80-005* p. H1, Jan. 10, 1980, *FBIS-SOV-80-008*, p. H1.

205. See Selig Harrison, *In Afghanistan's Shadow: Baluch Nationalism and Soviet Temptations* (Washington, D.C.: Carnegie Endowment for International Peace, 1981), pp. 71–92, 112–20.

206. Ibid., pp. 136–40.

207. Ibid., pp. 108–09, 126–32.

208. Ibid., pp. 146–49.

209. See the U.S. Defense Department report entitled, "Capabilities in the Persian Gulf," reported by Richard Burt in the *New York Times*, Feb. 2, 1980, pp. 1, 4.

210. Ibid. The Defense Department report cited above, for example, suggested that the Soviet Union could easily destroy key facilities as Ras Tanura, and Ju Ay Mah, Saudi Arabia, and Kharg Island, off the coast of Iran, with SU-19 fencers and Backfire bombers launched from air bases inside the USSR. Fighter aircraft escorting the Soviet bombers would need to be refueled. See Dennis Ross, "Considering Soviet Threats to the Persian Gulf," Woodrow Wilson Center, working paper no. 29, September 1981.

211. For a discussion of the difficulties the USSR might encounter in trying to occupy Iran, see Joshua Epstein, "Soviet Vulnerabilities in Iran and the R.D.F. Deterrent," *International Security* 6 (Fall 1981), 126–58.

212. For one evaluation of the military balance, see Staff of the Carnegie Panel on U.S. Security and the Future of Arms Control, *Challenges for U.S. National Security: Assessing the Balance Defense Spending and Conventional Forces* (Washington, D.C.: Carnegie Endowment for International Peace, 1981),

pp. 149–94. The Defense Department estimated that the USSR could mobilize to full readiness twenty-three divisions north of Iran within a month. See Richard Burt, "Capabilities in the Persian Gulf." The U.S. RDF might land a brigade in a week and perhaps 20,000 troops in a month, assuming there were friendly harbors in Iran.

213. For a discussion of many of the obstacles confronting U.S. conventional activity in the Persian Gulf, see Jeffery Record, *The Rapid Deployment Force and U.S. Military Invention in the Persian Gulf* (Cambridge, Mass.: Fletcher School of Law and Diplomacy Institute for Foreign Policy Analysis, 1981), pp. 19–42.

214. See Richard K. Betts, *Surprise Attack: Lessons for Defense Planning* (Washington D.C.: Brookings, 1982), pp. 266–73.

215. Robert Tucker has argued that the magnitude of U.S. interests in the Gulf makes the nuclear deterrent credible. See *The Purposes of American Power: An Essay on National Security* (New York: Praeger, 1981), pp. 69–114.

216. Brzezinski compares the Carter Doctrine to the Truman Doctrine, arguing that deterrence can be extended by verbal commitment. The changed strategic balance is not mentioned in the analogy (*Power and Principle*, pp. 443–48).

217. The Soviet Union pledged its neutrality in the war on September 23, 1980, and reportedly rebuffed Iraqi requests for arms, calling instead for a cease-fire and negotiations (*Facts on File* [1980], pp. 718, 719, 733, 758, 879). See Aleksey Leonidov, "Who Benefits from the Iranian-Iraqi Conflict," *Izvestia,* Sept. 23, 1980, *FBIS-SOV-80-187*, pp. H1–3; and Yu. Glukov, "Who Benefits by This? Surrounding the Iranian-Iraqi Conflict," *Pravda,* Sept. 24, 1980, p. 5, *FBIS-SOV-80-188*, pp. H3–4.

Chapter 6
Theories of Motivation and Soviet Foreign Policy: Lessons from the Analysis

1. This data base was created under the direction of Philip Stewart at Ohio State University. It includes every speech and article by a Politburo member from 1970 to 1979. The speeches are coded into 2,000 themes and the data base includes over 250,000 items. See Philip Stewart, "Foreign Policy Perceptions of the Soviet Politburo in the 1970s: Analysis and Data for Final Report," unpublished, Department of Political Science, Ohio State University, 1981; and Philip Stewart, James Warhola, and Roger Blough, "Issue Salience and Foreign Policy Role Specialization in the Soviet Politburo of the 1970s," *American Journal of Political Science* 28 (1984), 1–22.

2. For reasons of political interest, Yuri Andropov was also included even though he said relatively little in the 1970s.

3. See, for example, William Jackson, "Soviet Images of the U.S. as Nuclear Adversary, 1969–1979," *World Politics* 33 (1981), 614–38. Robert Cutler, "The Soviet Union in the 1974 Cyprus Affair," paper presented at the 15th National Convention of the American Association for the Advancement of Slavic Studies, Kansas City, 1983). Also see Thomas N. Bjorkman and Thomas J. Zamostny, "Soviet Politics and Strategy toward the West: Three Cases," *World Politics* 36 (1984), 189–214.

4. This finding parallels that of William Zimmerman and Glen Palmer,

"Words and Deeds in Soviet Foreign Policy: The Case of Soviet Military Expenditures," *American Political Science Review* 77 (1983), 358–67.

5. The increasing complexity represented by the rise in the relative mix of "degenerate" with "enemy" items reflects the recognition by these members of economic problems, social problems, and racial conflicts in the United States. These three items account for 83 percent of all of the "degenerate" items coded. In the eight years coded there were no references by any member to Soviet moral superiority, the disintegration of spiritual values in the West, U.S. weakness, or Soviet military superiority.

6. The small range of differences on the national liberation dimension and the lack of clear patterns across years warn against placing too much confidence in conclusions about specific members. Images of Grechko and the military as favoring intervention in regions like the Middle East partially contradict these findings and give reason for caution. On military attitudes toward involvement in the Middle East, see Ilana Kass, *Soviet Involvement in the Middle East: Policy Formulation, 1966–1973* (Boulder, Colo.: Westview Press, 1978), pp. 205–12.

7. Hans Morgenthau, *Politics Among Nations: The Struggle for Power and Peace*, 5th ed. (New York: Knopf, 1973), pp. 154–55.

8. See Thomas Etzold and John Gaddis, eds., *Containment: Documents on American Policy and Strategy, 1945–1950* (New York: Oxford University Press, 1982), p. 89.

9. This is a common perceptual impairment. See Alexander George, *Presidential Decision-Making in Foreign Policy: The Effective Use of Information and Advice* (Boulder, Colo.: Westview Press, 1980), pp. 48–49.

10. See Alexander George and Richard Smoke, *Deterrence in American Foreign Policy: Theory and Practice* (New York: Columbia University Press, 1974); Alexander George, David Hall, and William Simons, *The Limits of Coercive Diplomacy: Laos, Cuba, Vietnam* (Boston: Little, Brown, 1971). Also see Leslie Gelb and Richard Betts, *The Irony of Vietnam: The System Worked* (Washington, D.C.: Brookings, 1979), pp. 363–69.

11. This argument is also made by Dennis Ross (deputy director of the Office of Net Assessment, Department of Defense). See "Considering Soviet Threats to the Persian Gulf," Woodrow Wilson Center for International Security Studies, paper no. 29, September 1981, pp. 7–8.

12. George Breslauer, "The Dynamics of Soviet Policy Toward the Arab-Israeli Conflict: Lessons of the Brezhnev Era," working paper #8 (Providence, R.I.: Brown University Center for Foreign Policy Development, Oct. 1983) p. 19, emphasis in original.

13. Seth Tillman, *The United States in the Middle East: Interests and Obstacles* (Bloomington: Indiana University Press, 1982), pp. 230–89.

14. Robert Jervis, *Perception and Misperception in International Politics* (Princeton, N.J.: Princeton University Press, 1976), pp. 319–80; and John Steinbruner, *The Cybernetic Theory of Decision: New Dimensions of Political Analysis* (Princeton, N.J.: Princeton University Press, 1974), pp. 88–139.

15. Davis Bobrow's study of Soviet perceptions, 1966–1980, found this to be the case ("Uncoordinated Giants," in *Foreign Policy USA/USSR*, ed. Charles Kegley Jr. and Pat McGowan [Beverley Hills, Calif.: Sage, 1982], p. 42).

16. See Ole Holsti and James Rosenau, *American Leadership in World Affairs: Vietnam and the Breakdown of Consensus* (Boston: Allen & Unwin, 1984), pp. 188, 229, 231, 233, 271, 282.

17. Franklyn Griffiths has completed one very interesting study of Soviet academic journals that finds four views of the sources of American foreign policy. The images he finds all share something in common with the "enemy" pattern but range from the very simple indicating intense threat to the quite

complex indicating a more relaxed posture. He concludes as I do that in the late 1970s the simpler and more stereotypical views have prevailed over the more complex images and have led to more aggressive and competitive Soviet international behavior ("The Sources of American Conduct: Soviet Perspectives and Their Policy Implications," *International Security* 9 (Fall 1984), 3–50).

18. Edward Jones and Richard Nisbett find that subjects tend to attribute their own actions to situational requirements and the actions of others to predispositional factors. Balance theory would predict that praiseworthy acts of an "enemy" would be attributed to situational requirements, and blameworthy acts to predisposition. It would predict the opposite interpretation of similar acts taken by the observer's country. See "The Actor and Observer: Divergent Perceptions of the Causes of Behavior," in *Attribution: Perceiving the Causes of Behavior,* ed. Edward Jones et al. (Morristown, N.J.: General Learning Press, 1971), pp. 79–94. Also see E. J. Phares, *Locus of Control in Personality* (Morristown, N.J.: General Learning Press, 1976).

19. See Hans Morgenthau, *Politics Among Nations: The Struggle for Power and Peace,* 5th ed. (New York: Knopf, 1973), pp. 4–7, and J. D. Singer, "The Levels of Analysis Problem in International Relations," in *The International System: Theoretical Essays,* ed. Klaus Knorr and Sidney Verba (Princeton, N.J.: Princeton University Press, 1961), pp. 77–92.

Bibliography

Abelson, Robert. "Script Processing in Attitude Formation and Decision Making." In *Cognition and Social Behavior,* ed. J. Carroll and J. Payne, 33–45. Hillsdale, N.J.: Lawrence Erlbaum Associates, 1976.

Adomeit, Hannes. *Soviet Risk-Taking and Crisis Behavior: A Theoretical and Empirical Analysis.* London: George Allen and Unwin, 1982.

Anderson, Jack, and George Clifford. *The Anderson Papers.* New York: Random House, 1973.

Armstrong, John. "The Domestic Roots of Soviet Foreign Policy." In *The Conduct of Soviet Foreign Policy,* ed. E. Hoffman and F. Fleron, 50–60. Chicago: Aldine Atherton, 1972.

Arnold, Anthony. *Afghanistan: The Soviet Invasion in Perspective.* Stanford, Calif.: Hoover Institution Press, 1981.

Arrow, Kenneth. *Social Choice and Individual Values.* New Haven, Conn.: Yale University Press, 1963.

Asch, Solomon. *Social Psychology.* Englewood Cliffs, N.J.: Prentice-Hall, 1952.

Aspaturian, Vernon. *Process and Power in Soviet Foreign Policy.* Boston: Little, Brown, 1971.

Aspaturin, Vernon, Alexander Dallin, and Jiri Valenta. *The Soviet Invasion of Afghanistan: Three Perspectives.* Los Angeles: Center for International and Strategic Affairs, University of California at Los Angeles, 1980.

Axelrod, Robert, ed. *The Structure of Decision: The Cognitive Maps of Political Elites.* Princeton, N.J.: Princeton University Press, 1976.

Banisadr, Abolhassan. *The Fundamental Precepts of Islamic Government.* Trans. M. Ghanoonparvar. Lexington, Ky.: Mazda, 1981.

Barnet, Richard. *The Giants: Russia and America.* New York: Simon and Schuster, 1977.

———. "U.S.-Soviet Relations: The Need for a Comprehensive Approach." *Foreign Affairs* 75 (Spring 1979):779–95.

Barnett, A. Doak. *China and the Major Powers in East Asia.* Washington, D.C.: Brookings, 1977.

Bem, D. J., and A. Allen. "On Predicting Some of the People Some of the Time: The Search for Cross-Situational Consistencies in Behavior." *Psychological Review* 81(1974): 506–20.

Betts, Richard. *Surprise Attack: Lessons for Defense Planning.* Washington, D.C.: Brookings, 1982.

Berner, Wolfgang, et al. *The Soviet Union, 1973: Domestic Policy, Economics, Foreign Policy.* New York: Holmes and Meier, 1975.

Bialer, Seweryn. "Poland and the Soviet Imperium." *Foreign Affairs* 59 (1980): 522–39.

———. *Stalin's Successors: Leadership, Stability, and Change in the Soviet Union.* Cambridge: Cambridge University Press, 1980.

Bialer, Seweryn, and J. Afferica. "Reagan and Russia." *Foreign Affairs* 61 (Winter 1982/1983): 249–71.

Bialer, Seweryn, and T. Gustafson. *Russia at the Crossroads: The 26th Congress of the C.P.S.U., 7–38.* London: George Allen and Unwin, 1982.

Bieri, James. "Cognitive Structures in Personality." In *Personality Theory and Information Processing,* ed. H. Schroder and P. Suedfeld, 178–208. New York: Ronald Press, 1971.

Bjorkman, T., and T. Zamostny. "Soviet Politics and Strategy Toward the West: Three Cases." *World Politics* 36 (January 1984): 189–214.

Blechman, B., and S. Kaplan. *Force Without War: U.S. Armed Forces as a Political Instrument.* Washington, D.C.: Brookings, 1978.

Bobrow, Davis. "Uncoordinated Giants." In *Foreign Policy USA/USSR,* ed. C. Kegley, Jr., and P. McGowan, 23–49. Beverly Hills, Calif.: Sage, 1982.

Booth, Ken. *Strategy and Ethnocentrism.* New York: Holmes and Meier, 1979.

Boulding, Kenneth. *The Image.* Ann Arbor: University of Michigan Press, 1956.

———. "National Images and International Systems." *Journal of Conflict Resolution* 3 (1959): 120–31.

Bowers, K. S. "Situationism in Psychology: An Analysis and a Critique." *Psychological Review* 80 (1973): 307–36.

Brandt, Willy. *People and Politics: The Years 1960–1975.* Trans. J. Maxwell Brownjohn. Boston: Little, Brown, 1976.

Breslauer, George. "The Dynamics of Soviet Policy Toward the Arab-Israeli Conflict: Lessons of the Brezhnev Era." Working Paper 8. Providence, R.I.: Center for Foreign Policy Development, Brown University.

———. *Khrushchev and Brezhnev as Leaders: Building Authority in Soviet Politics.* London: George Allen and Unwin, 1982.

———. "Soviet Policy in the Middle East, 1967–1972: Unalterable Antagonism or Collaborative Competition." In *Managing U.S.-Soviet Rivalry: Problems of Crises Prevention,* ed. Alexander George, 65–106. Boulder, Colo.: Westview, 1983.

Bromke, Adam. "The Opposition in Poland." *Problems of Communism* (September/October 1978): 37–51.

Brzezinski, Zbigniew. *Power and Principle: Memoirs of the National Security Adviser, 1977–1981.* New York: Farrar, Straus, Giroux, 1983.

Burt, Richard. "Reassessing the Strategic Balance." *International Security* 5 (Summer 1980): 37–52.

Campbell, John. "Soviet Policy in the Middle East." *Current History* 80 (January 1981): 1–4, 42–43.

Carter, James. *Keeping Faith: Memoirs of a President.* New York: Bantam Books, 1982.

Chubin, Shahram. *Soviet Policy Toward Iran and the Gulf.* Adelphi Papers 157. London: IISS, 1980.

Chung, Chin O. *P'yongyang, Between Peking and Moscow: North Korea's Involvement in the Sino-Soviet Dispute 1958–1975.* University, Ala.: University of Alabama Press, 1978.

Congressional Budget Office. *Counterforce Issues for the U.S. Strategic Nuclear Forces.* Washington, D.C.: GPO, 1978.

———. *Retaliatory Issues for the U.S. Strategic Nuclear Forces.* Washington, D.C.: GPO, 1978.

Conquest, Robert. *Present Danger: Towards a Foreign Policy.* Stanford, Calif.: Hoover Institution Press, 1979.

Cottam, Richard. *Foreign Policy Motivation: A General Theory and a Case Study.* Pittsburgh: University of Pittsburgh Press, 1977.

————. *Nationalism in Iran.* 2d ed. Pittsburgh, Pa.: University of Pittsburgh Press, 1978.

Cottam, Richard, and Gerard Galluci. *The Rehabilitation of Power in International Relations.* Pittsburgh, Pa.: University Center for International Studies, 1978.

Cox, Arthur M. *Russian Roulette: The Superpower Game.* New York: Times Books, 1982.

Croan, Melvin, *East Germany: The Soviet Connection.* The Washington Papers, vol. 4, no. 36. Beverly Hills, Calif.: Sage, 1976.

Cronbach, L. J. "The Two Disciplines of Scientific Psychology." *American Psychologist* 12 (1957): 671–84.

————. "Beyond the Two Disciplines of Scientific Psychology." *American Psychologist* 30 (1975): 116–27.

Dagan, Avigdor. *Moscow and Jerusalem.* New York: Abdlard-Schuman, 1970.

Dallin, Alexander. "Soviet Foreign Policy and Domestic Politics: A Framework for Analysis." In *The Conduct of Soviet Foreign Policy,* ed. E. P. Hoffman and F. J. Fleron, 36–49. Chicago: Aldine Atherton, 1971.

Dawisha, Adeed. "Iraq: The West's Opportunity." *Foreign Policy* 41 (Winter 1980–1981): 134–53.

Dawisha, Karen. *Soviet Foreign Policy Toward Egypt.* New York: St. Martin's, 1979.

Deutsch, Morton. "Field Theory in Soviet Psychology." In *The Handbook of Social Psychology,* 2d ed., ed. G. Lindzey and E. Aronson, 412–87. Reading, Mass.: Addison-Wesley, 1968.

Dil, Shabeen. "The Cabal in Kabul: Great Power Interaction in Afghanistan." *American Political Science Review* 71 (June 1977): 468–76.

Dismukes, Bradford. "Soviet Employment of Naval Power for Political Purposes, 1965–1975." In *Soviet Naval Influence: Domestic and Foreign Dimensions,* ed. M. McGwire and J. McDonnell, 484–509. New York: Praeger, 1977.

Donaldson, Robert H. *Soviet Policy toward India: Ideology and Strategy.* Cambridge, Mass.: Harvard Univesity Press, 1974.

————. *The Soviet Union in the Third World: Successes and Failures.* Boulder, Colo.: Westview, 1981.

Donley, Richard, and David Winter. "Measuring the Motives of Public Officials at a Distance: An Exploratory Study of American Presidents." *Behavioral Science* 15 (1970): 227–36.

Drell, Sidney. "Arms Control: Is There Still Hope?" *Daedalus* 109 (Fall 1980): 177–88.

Duncan, Raymond, ed. *Soviet Policy in the Third World,* 239–61. New York: Pergamon, 1980.

Dupree, Louis. "Afghanistan Under the Khalq." *Problems of Communism* 28 (July 1979): 34–50.

Epstein, Joshua. "Soviet Vulnerabilities in Iran and the R.D.F. Deterrent." *International Security* 6 (Fall 1981): 126–58.

Erickson, John. "The Soviet View of Deterrence: A General Survey." In *The Nuclear Arms Race—Control or Catastrophe?* ed. F. Barnaby and G. Thomas, 73–93. London: Frances Pinter, 1982.

Ermarth, Fritz. "Contrasts in American and Soviet Strategic Thought." *International Security* 3 (Fall 1978): 138–55.

Etzioni, Amitai. "Social-Psychological Aspects of International Relations." In vol. 5 of *The Handbook of Social Psychology.* 2d ed., ed. G. Lindzey and E. Aronson. Reading, Mass.: Addison-Wesley, 1968.

Etzold, Thomas, and John Gaddis, eds. *Containment: Documents on American Policy and Strategy, 1945–1950.* New York: Oxford University Press, 1982.

Experience and the Future Discussion Group. *Poland Today: The State of the Republic.* Intro. J. Bielasiak. Trans. A. Swidlick, T. Mollin, M. Vale, et al. Armonk, N.Y.: M. E. Sharpe, 1981.

Falkenheim, P. "The Impact of the Peace and Friendship Treaty on Soviet/Japanese Relations." *Asian Survey* 19 (December 1979): 1220–21.

Fallenbuchl, Zbigniew. "Poland's Economic Crisis." *Problems of Communism* 31 (March–April 1982): 1–21.

Farhang, Mansour. *U.S. Imperialism: The Spanish-American War to the Iranian Revolution.* Boston: South End Press, 1981.

Ferris, Wayne. *The Power Capabilities of Nation-States.* Lexington, Mass.: D. C. Heath, 1973.

Finlay, D. J., Ole Holsti, and Richard Fagan. *Enemies in Politics.* Chicago: Rand McNally, 1967.

Fiske, Susan, and Shelley Taylor. *Social Coginition.* Menlo Park, Calif.: Addison-Wesley, 1984.

Forsberg, Randall. "A Bilateral Nuclear-Weapon Freeze." *Scientific American* 247 (November 1982): 52–61.

Freedman, Lawrence. *U.S. Intelligence and the Soviet Strategic Threat.* Boulder, Colo.: Westview, 1977.

Freedman, Robert O. *Soviet Policy Toward the Middle East Since 1970.* New York: Praeger, 1978.

———. "Soviet Policy Toward the Ba'athist Iraq." In *The Soviet Union in the Third World: Successes and Failures,* ed. R. Donaldson, 161–91. Boulder, Colo.: Westview, 1981.

Gaddis, John L. *Strategies of Containment: A Critical Appraisal of Postwar American National Security Policy.* Oxford: Oxford University Press, 1982.

Gamson, William, and Andre Modigliani. *Untangling the Cold War: A Strategy for Testing Rival Theories.* Boston: Little, Brown, 1971.

Garthoff, Raymond L. "Mutual Deterrence and Strategic Arms Limitation in Soviet Policy." *International Security* 3 (Summer 1978): 112–47.

———. "The NATO Decision on Theater Nuclear Forces." *Political Science Quarterly* 98 (Summer 1983): 197–214.

Gelb, Leslie, and Richard Betts. *The Irony of Vietnam: The System Worked.* Washington, D.C.: Brookings, 1979.

Gelman, Harry. "The Outlook for Sino-Soviet Relations." *Problems of Communism* 28 (September/December 1979): 50–66.

George, Alexander. "Case Studies and Theory Development: The Method of Structured, Focused Comparisons." In *Diplomacy: New Approaches in History, Theory, and Policy,* ed. P. G. Lauren, 43–68. New York: Free Press, 1979.

———. "The Causal Nexus Between Cognitive Beliefs and Decision-Making Behavior: The 'Operational Code' Belief System." In *Psychological Models in International Politics,* ed. L. Falkowski, 95–124. Boulder, Colo.: Westview, 1979.

———. *Presidential Decisionmaking in Foreign Policy: The Effective Use of Information and Advice.* Boulder, Colo.: Westview, 1980.

———, ed. *Managing U.S.-Soviet Rivalry: Problems of Crisis Prevention.* Boulder: Westview, 1983.

George, Alexander, and Richard Smoke. *Deterrence in American Foreign Policy: Theory and Practice.* New York: Columbia University Press, 1974.

George, Alexander, D. Hall, and W. Simons. *The Limits of Coercive Diplomacy: Laos, Cuba, Vietnam.* Boston: Little, Brown, 1971.

Gibert, Stephen. *Soviet Images of America.* New York: Crane, Russak, 1977.

Glassman, Jon D. *Arms for the Arabs*. Baltimore: Johns Hopkins University Press, 1975.

Golin, Galia. *Yom Kippur and After: The Soviet Union and the Middle East Crisis*. Cambridge: Cambridge University Press, 1977.

———. "Syria and the Soviet Union Since the Yom Kippur War." *Orbis* 21 (Winter 1978): 777–801.

Graham, Daniel O. *Shall America Be Defended?: SALT II and Beyond*. New Rochelle, N.Y.: Arlington House, 1979.

Gray, Colin. "Nuclear Strategy: The Case for a Theory of Victory." *International Security* 4 (Summer 1979): 54–87.

———. "Strategic Stability Reconsidered." *Daedalus* 109 (Fall 1980): 135–54.

Griffith, William E. *The Sino-Soviet Rift*. Cambridge, Mass.: MIT Press, 1964.

———. *Sino-Soviet Relations, 1964–1965*. Cambridge, Mass.: MIT Press, 1967.

———. *The World and the Great-Power Triangles*. Cambridge, Mass.: MIT Press, 1975.

———. *The Ostpolitik of the Federal Republic of Germany*. Cambridge, Mass.: MIT Press, 1978.

Griffiths, Franklyn. *Genoa Plus 51: Changing Soviet Objectives in Europe*. Wellesley paper 4. Toronto: Canadian Institute of International Affairs, 1974.

Guroff, Gregory, and Steven Grant. "Soviet Elite: World View and Perceptions of the U.S." U.S. International Communication Agency, June 1980 and September 1981.

Ha, Joseph M. "Moscow's Policy Toward Japan." *Problems of Communism* 26 (September/October 1977): 61–72.

Haas, Ernst. "Why Collaborate? Issue Linkage and International Regimes." *World Politics* 32 (1980): 357–405.

Hall, David. "The Indo-Pakistani War of 1971." In *Force Without War: U.S. Armed Forces as a Political Instrument*, ed. B. Blechman and S. Kaplan, 175–218. Washington, D.C.: Brookings, 1978.

Halliday, Fred. *Soviet Policy in the Arc of Crisis*. Washington, D.C.: Institute for Policy Studies, 1981.

———. *The Making of the Second Cold War*. London: Verso and NLB, 1983.

Halperin, Morton. *Bureaucratic Politics and Foreign Policy*. Washington D.C.: Brookings, 1974.

Harrison, Selig. *In Afghanistan's Shadow: Baluch Nationalism and Soviet Temptations*. Washington, D.C.: Carnegie Endowment for International Peace, 1981.

Hart, Thomas. *The Cognitive World of Swedish Security Elites*. Stockholm: Esselte Stadium, 1976.

———. "Perceiving 'Afghanistan': Some Questions about the Applicability of Theoretical Insights in Analyzing Perceptions in a Current Crises. In *Cognitive Dynamics and International Politics*, ed. C. Jonsson, 178–98. London: Frances Pinter, 1982.

Harvard Nuclear Study Group. *Living With Nuclear Weapons*. New York: Bantam, 1983.

Hastorf, Albert, David Schneider, Jr., and Judith Polefka. *Person Perception*. Reading, Mass.: Addison-Wesley, 1970.

Heaton, William R. *A United Front Against Hegemonism: Chinese Foreign Policy into the 1980's*. Washington, D.C.: GPO, 1978.

Heider, Fritz. *The Psychology of Interpersonal Relations*. New York: John Wiley, 1958.

Heikal, Mohamed. *The Cairo Documents*. Garden City, N.Y.: Doubleday, 1973.

————. *The Sphinx and the Commissar: The Rise and Fall of Soviet Influence in the Middle East.* New York: Harper and Row, 1978.

Hensel, Howard. "Soviet Policy Toward the Kurdish Question, 1970–1975." *Soviet Union/Union Sovietique* 6 (1979): 61–80.

Heradstveit, Daniel. *The Arab-Israeli Conflict: Psychological Obstacles to Peace.* Oslo: Universitetsforlaget, 1981.

Herrmann, Richard. "Comparing World View in East Europe: Contemporary Polish Perceptions." In *Foreign Policies of East Europe,* ed. R. H. Linden. New York: Praeger, 1980.

————. "Perceptions and Foreign Policy Analysis." In *Foreign Policy Decision Making: Perception, Cognition and Artificial Intelligence,* ed. D. Sylvan and S. Chan, 25–52. New York: Praeger, 1984.

Hersh, Seymour M. *The Price of Power: Kissinger in the Nixon White House.* New York: Summit, 1983.

Hinton, Harold. *The Sino-Soviet Confrontation: Implications for the Future.* New York: Crane, Russak, 1976.

Holloway, David. "Military Power and Political Purpose in Soviet Policy." *Daedalus* 109 (Fall 1980): 13–30.

————. *The Soviet Union and the Arms Race.* New Haven, Conn.: Yale University Press, 1983.

Holsti, Ole R. "Cognitive Dynamics and Images of the Enemy." In *Enemies in Politics,* ed. D. J. Finlay, O. R. Holsti and R. R. Fagen, 25–96. Chicago: Rand McNally, 1967.

————. "Foreign Policy Viewed Cognitively." *The Structure of Decision: The Cognitive Maps of Political Elites,* 18–54. Princeton, N.J.: Princeton University Press, 1976.

Holsti, Ole R., and James Rosenau. *American Leadership in World Affairs: Vietnam and the Breakdown of Consensus.* Boston: Allen and Unwin, 1984.

Holzman, Franklyn D. "Are the Soviets Really Outspending the U.S. on Defense?" *International Security* 4 (Spring 1980): 86–104.

Horelick, Arnold, Ross Johnson, and John Steinbruner. *The Study of Soviet Foreign Policy: Decision Theory Related Approaches.* Sage Professional Papers in International Studies, vol. 4. Beverly Hills, Calif.: Sage, 1975.

Hough, Jerry. *Soviet Leadership in Transition.* Washington, D.C.: Brookings, 1980.

Howard, Michael. "The Forgotten Dimension of Strategy." *Foreign Affairs* 57 (Summer 1979): 975–86.

Hugo, Grant. *Appearance and Reality in International Relations.* New York: Columbia University Press, 1970.

Hybel, A., and D. B. Robertson. "Assessing the Dynamic Reaction of the U.S.S.R. to American and Chinese Actions and to its Nuclear Gap with the U.S.A." *International Interactions* 4 (1978): 125–54.

Hyland, William. "U.S.-Soviet Relations: The Long Road Back." *Foreign Affairs* 60 (1981): 525–50.

Jackson, William. "Soviet Images of the U.S. as Nuclear Adversary, 1969–1979." *World Politics* 33 (1981): 614–38.

Jacobsen, C. G. *Sino-Soviet Relations Since Mao: the Chairman's Legacy.* New York: Praeger, 1981.

Jain, J. P. *Soviet Policy Towards Pakistan and Bangladesh.* New Delhi: Radiant Publishers, 1974.

Jencks, Harlan. "China's Punitive War on Vietnam: A Military Assessment." *Asian Survey* 19 (August 1979): 801–15.

Jervis, Robert. *Perception and Misperception in International Politics.* Princeton, N.J.: Princeton University Press, 1976.

————. "Beliefs About Soviet Behavior." In *Containment, Soviet Behavior, and*

Grand Strategy, ed. R. Osgood, 56–59. Berkeley: Institute of International Studies, University of California, 1981.

Johnson, Lyndon B. *The Vantage Point: Perspectives of the Presidency, 1963–1969.* New York: Holt, Rinehart and Winston, 1971.

Jones, Christopher. "Equality and Equal Security in Europe." *Orbis* 26 (Fall 1982): 637–64.

Jones, Edward E., et al. *Attribution: Perceiving the Causes of Behavior.* Morristown, N.J.: General Learning Press, 1971.

Kaplan, Morton. *System and Process in International Politics.* New York: Krieger, 1975.

Kashkett, Steven B. "Iraq and the Pursuit of Nonalignment." *Orbis* 26 (Summer 1982): 477–94.

Kass, Ilana. *Soviet Involvement in the Middle East: Policy Formulation, 1966–1973.* Boulder, Colo.: Westview, 1978.

———. "Moscow and the Lebanese Triangle." *The Middle East Journal* 33 (Spring 1979): 164–87.

Katouzian, Homa. *The Political Economy of Modern Iran: 1926–1979.* New York: New York University Press, 1981.

Katz, Arthur M. *Life After Nuclear War: The Economic and Social Impacts of Nuclear Attacks on the U.S..* Cambridge, Mass.: Ballinger, 1982.

Katz, Mark. *The Third World in Soviet Military Thought.* London: Croom Helm, 1982.

Keddie, Nikki. *Roots of Revolution: An Interpretive History of Modern Iran.* New Haven, Conn.: Yale University Press, 1981.

Keesing's Research Report. *Germany and Eastern Europe Since 1945: From the Potsdam Agreement to Chancellor Brandt's Ostpolitik.* New York: Charles Scribner's Sons, 1973.

Kelly, Harold. "Causal Schemata and the Attribution Process." In *Attribution: Perceiving the Causes of Behavior,* ed. E. Jones et al., 151–74. Morristown, N.J.: General Learning Press, 1971.

Kennan, George. *The Cloud of Danger: Current Realities of American Foreign Policy.* Boston: Atlantic Monthly Press and Litte, Brown, 1977.

———. *The Nuclear Delusion: Soviet-American Relations in the Atomic Age.* New York: Pantheon, 1982.

Kerr, Malcolm. *The Arab Cold War: Gamal Abd al-Nasir and His Rivals, 1958–1970.* London: Oxford University Press, 1971.

Khalid, Walid. *Conflict and Violence in Lebanon: Confrontation in the Middle East.* Cambridge, Mass.: Center for International Affairs, Harvard University, 1979.

Kiesler, C. A., B. E. Collins, and N. Miller. *Attitude Change: A Critical Analysis of Theoretical Approaches.* New York: Wiley, 1969.

Kirsh, Marian. "Soviet Security Objectives in Asia." *International Organization* 24 (Summer 1970): 451–78.

Kissinger, Henry. *Nuclear Weapons and Foreign Policy.* Abr. ed. New York: Norton, 1969.

———. *The White House Years.* Boston: Little, Brown, 1979.

———. *Years of Upheaval.* Boston: Little, Brown, 1982.

Klinghoffer, Arthur J. *The Angolan War: A Study in Soviet Foreign Policy in the Third World.* Boulder, Colo.: Westview, 1980.

Krasner, Stephen. "Are Bureaucracies Important? (or Allison Wonderland)?" *Foreign Policy* 7 (Summer 1972): 157–79.

Krasnow, Wladislaw. "Richard Pipes' Foreign Strategy: Anti-Soviet or Anti-Russian?" *Russian Review* 38 (April 1979): 180–97.

Kuhn, Thomas. *The Structure of Scientific Revolutions.* 2d ed. Chicago: University of Chicago Press, 1970.

Labrie, Roger, ed. *SALT Handbook: Key Documents and Issues 1972–1979*. Washington, D.C.: AEI, 1979.

Lampton, David. "Misreading China." *Foreign Policy* (Winter 1981–82): 103–14.

Langer, Paul. "Japan and the Great-Power Triangles." In *The World and the Great Power Triangles,* ed. W. E. Griffith, 271–320. Cambridge, Mass.: MIT Press, 1975.

Laqueur, Walter. "Containment for the 80's." *Commentary* 70 (October 1980): 33–42.

———. "Pity the Poor Russians?" *Commentary* 71 (February 1981): 32–41.

Laudan, Larry. *Progress and Its Problems: Toward a Theory of Scientific Growth*. Berkeley and Los Angeles: University of California Press, 1977.

Lebow, Richard N. *Between Peace and War: The Nature of International Crises*. Baltimore: Johns Hopkins University Press, 1981.

Lee, Chong-Sik. "The Detente and Korea." In *The World and the Great Power Triangles,* ed. W. E. Griffith, 321–96. Cambridge. Mass.: MIT Press, 1975.

Legum, Colin. "Angola and the Horn of Africa." In *Diplomacy of Power: Soviet Armed Forces as a Political Instrument,* ed. S. Kaplan, 570–637. Washington D.C.: Brookings, 1981.

Legvold, Robert. "Containment Without Confrontation." *Foreign Policy* 40 (Fall 1980): 74–98.

———. "The 26th Party Congress and Soviet Foreign Policy." In *Russia at the Crossroads: The 26th Congress of the C.P.S.U.,* ed. S. Bialer and T. Gustafson, 156–77. London: George Allen and Unwin, 1982.

Leites, Nathan. *The Operational Code of the Politburo*. New York: McGraw-Hill, 1951.

Lenczowski, John. *Soviet Perceptions of U.S. Foreign Policy: A Study of Ideology, Power and Consensus*. Ithaca, N.Y.: Cornell University Press, 1982.

Levine, Steven I. "China Policy During Carter's Year One." *Asian Survey* 18 (May 1978): 437–47.

Levy, Jack. "Misperception and the Cause of War: Theoretical Linkages and Analytical Problems." *World Politics* 36 (October 1983): 76–99.

Lieberthal, Kenneth. "The Foreign Policy Debate in Peking as Seen Through Allegorical Articles, 1973–1976." *China Quarterly* 71 (September 1977): 528–54.

Linden, Carl. *Khrushchev and the Soviet Leadership: 1957–1964*. Baltimore: Johns Hopkins Press, 1966.

Lisann, Maury. "Moscow and the Chinese Power Struggle." *Problems of Communism* 18 (November–December 1969): 32–41.

Lodal, Jan. "Deterrence and Nuclear Strategy." *Daedalus* 109 (Fall 1980): 155–75.

London, Kurt L. "Vietnam: A Sino-Soviet Dilemma." *Russian Review* 26 (January 1967): 26–37.

Low, Alfred. *The Sino-Soviet Dispute: An Analysis of the Polemics*. Rutherford: Fairleigh Dickinson University Press, 1976.

McClelland, Charles A. "Let the User Beware." *International Studies Quarterly* 27 (June 1983): 169–77.

MacFarquhar, Roderick. *Sino-American Relations, 1949–1971*. New York: Praeger, 1972.

McGovern, Raymond L. "Moscow and Hanoi," *Problems of Communism* 16 (May–June 1967): 64–71.

Mearsheimer, John J. "Why the Soviets Can't Win Quickly in Central Europe." *International Security* 7 (Summer 1982): 3–44.

Medvedev, Roy. *On Socialist Democracy*. New York: Norton, 1975.

Menon, Rajan. "Military Power, Intervention, and Soviet Policy in the Third World." In *Soviet Foreign Policy in the 1980's*. ed. R. Kanet, 263–84. New York: Praeger, 1982.

Metzger, Robert, and Paul Doty. "Arms Control Enters the Gray Area." *International Security* 3 (Winter 1978): 17–52.

Michael, Franz. "Moscow and the Current Chinese Crises." *Current History* 53 (September 1967): 141–47.

Mischel, W. "Toward a Cognitive Social Learning Reconceptualization of Personality." *Psychological Review* 80 (1973): 252–83.

Mitchell, R. J. "A New Brezhnev Doctrine: The Restructuring of International Relations." *World Politics* 30 (April 1978): 366–90.

Monks, Alfred. *The Soviet Invasion of Afghanistan*. Washington, D.C.: AEI, 1981.

Morgenthau, Hans. *Politics Among Nations: The Struggle for Power and Peace*. 5th ed. New York: Knopf, 1973.

Morris, Roger. *Uncertain Greatness: Henry Kissinger and American Foreign Policy*. New York: Harper and Row, 1977.

Mujal-Leon, Eusebio M. "The P.C.P. and the Portuguese Revolution." *Problems of Communism* 26 (January/February 1977): 21–41.

Napper, Larry. "The Ogaden War: Some Implications for Crisis Prevention." In *Managing U.S.-Soviet Rivalry: Problems of Crisis Prevention*, ed. A. George, 225–53. Boulder: Westview Press, 1983.

Neal, Fred W., ed. *Detente or Debacle: Common Sense in U.S.-Soviet Relations*. New York: Norton, 1979.

Newell, Nancy P., and Richard S. Newell. *The Struggle for Afghanistan*. Ithaca, N.Y.: Cornell University Press, 1981.

Newhouse, John. *Cold Dawn: The Story of SALT*. New York: Holt, Rinehart and Winston, 1973.

Nisbett, Richard, and Lee Ross. *Human Inferences: Strategies and Shortcomings of Social Judgment*. Englewood Cliffs, N.J.: Prentice-Hall 1980.

Nitze, Paul. "Salt II and American Strategic Considerations." *Comparative Strategy* 2 (1980): 9–34.

Nixon, Richard M. *The Memoirs of Richard Nixon*. New York: Grosset and Dunlap, 1978.

Noelle-Neumann, Elizabeth. *The Germans: Public Opinion Polls, 1967–1980*. Westport, Conn.: Greenwood Press, 1981.

———. "Are the Germans 'Collapsing' or 'Standing Firm'?" *Encounter* 58 (February 1982): 76–81.

Northrop, F.S.C. *The Logic of the Sciences and Humanities*. New York: World Publishing 1959.

Novik, Nimrod. *Between Two Yemens: Regional Dynamics and Superpower Conduct in Riyadh's Backyard*. Tel Aviv: Center For Strategic Studies, University of Tel Aviv, December 1980.

Office of Technology Assessment. *The Effects of Nuclear War*. Washington, D.C.: GPO, 1979.

Oksenberg, Michael. "The United States and China." In *China and Japan: A New Balance of Power*, ed. D. Hellman, 269–96. Lexington, Mass.: Lexington Books, 1976.

Oskamp, Stuart. "Attitudes Toward U.S. and Russian Actions: A Double Standard." *Psychological Reports* 16 (1965): 43–46.

Oskamp, Stuart, and A. Harty. "A Factor-Analytic Study of the Double Standard in Attitudes Toward U.S. and Russian Actions." *Behavioral Science* 13 (1968): 178–88.

Ottaway, Maria, and David Ottaway. *Ethiopia: Empire in Revolution*. New York: Africana Publishing, 1978.

Phares, E. J. *Locus of Control in Personality*. Morristown, N.J.: General Learning Press, 1976.

Pipes, Richard. "Why the Soviet Union Thinks It Could Fight and Win a Nuclear War." *Commentary* 64 (July 1977): 26–29.

———. "Militarism and the Soviet State." *Daedalus* 109 (Fall 1980): 1–12.

———. U.S.-Soviet Relations in the Era of Detente: A Tragedy of Errors. Boulder, Colo.: Westview Press, 1981.

———, ed. *Soviet Strategy in Europe*. New York: Crane, Russak, 1976.

Pollack, Jonathan. "The Implications of Sino-American Normalization." *International Security* 3 (Spring 1979): 37–57.

———. "China's Agonizing Reappraisal." In *The Sino-Soviet Conflict: A Global Perspective*, ed. H. Ellison, 50–72. Seattle: University of Washington Press, 1982.

Porter, Gareth. *A Peace Denied: The United States, Vietnam and the Paris Agreement*. Bloomington: Indiana University Press, 1975.

Prados, John. *The Soviet Estimate: U.S. Intelligence Analysis and Russian Military Strength*. New York: Dial Press, 1982.

Quandt, William B. *Decade of Decisions: American Policy Toward the Arab-Israeli Conflict, 1967–1976*. Berkeley and Los Angeles: University of California Press, 1977.

———. *Saudi Arabia in the 1980's: Foreign Policy, Security and Oil*. Washington, D.C.: Brookings, 1981.

Rabinovich, Itamar. "The Limits of Military Power: Syria's Role." In *Lebanon in Crisis: Participants and Issues*, ed. P. E. Haley and L. Snider, 55–74. Syracuse, N.Y.: Syracuse University Press, 1979.

Record, Jeffery. *The Rapid Deployment Force and U.S. Military Intervention in the Persian Gulf*. Cambridge, Mass.: Institute for Foreign Policy Analysis, 1981.

Remington, Robin A. *The Warsaw Pact: Case Studies in Communist Conflict Resolution*. Cambridge, Mass.: MIT Press, 1971.

Ross, Dennis. "Considering Threats to the Persian Gulf." Paper 29. Washington, D.C.: Woodrow Wilson Center for International Security Studies, 1981.

Rostow, W. W. *The Diffusion of Power: An Essay in Recent History*. New York: Macmillan, 1972.

Rubin, Barry. *Paved with Good Intentions: The American Experience in Iran*. New York: Oxford University Press, 1980.

Rubinstein, Alvin. *Red Star on the Nile: The Soviet-Egyptian Influence Relationship Since the June War*. Princeton, N.J.: Princeton University Press, 1970.

———. "The Soviet Union in the Middle East." *Current History* 77 (October 1979): 106–09, 132–33.

———. "The Soviet Union and the Arabian Peninsula." *World Today* 35 (November 1979): 442–52.

———. "Air Support in the Arab East." In *Diplomacy of Power: Soviet Armed Forces as a Political Instrument*, ed. S. Kaplan, 468–518. Washington, D.C.: Brookings, 1981.

———. *Soviet Policy Toward Turkey, Iran, and Afghanistan: The Dynamics of Influence*. New York: Praeger, 1982.

Rummel, R. J. *Peace Endangered: The Reality of Detente*. Beverly Hills, Calif.: Sage, 1976.

Rusk, Dean. *The Winds of Freedom*. Boston: Beacon Press, 1963.

Russett, Bruce, and Donald Deluca. "Theater Nuclear Forces: Public Opinion in Western Europe." *Political Science Quarterly* 98 (Summer 1983): 179–96.

Sadat, Anwar. *In Search of Identity: An Autobiography*. New York: Harper and Row, 1977.

Safran, Nadav. *From War to War: The Arab-Israeli Confrontation 1948–1967*. Indianapolis: Pegasus, Bobbs-Merrill, 1969.

Schaefer, Henry W. *Comecon and the Politics of Integration*. New York: Praeger, 1972.

Schmidt, Helmut. *The Balance of Power: Germany's Peace Policy and the Superpowers*. Trans. E. Thomas. London: Kimber, 1971.

Schwartz, Morton. *Soviet Perceptions of the United States*. Berkeley and Los Angeles: University of California Press, 1978.

Scott, Harriet S., and William F. Scott. *The Armed Forces of the U.S.S.R.* Boulder, Colo.: Westview, 1979.

Scoville, Herbert, Jr. *MX: Prescription for Disaster*. Cambridge, Mass.: MIT Press, 1981.

Shaver, Kelly G. *An Introduction to Attribution Processes*. Cambridge, Mass.: Winthrop, 1975.

Shulman, Marshall D. "Recent Soviet Foreign Policy: Some Patterns in Retrospect." *Journal of International Affairs* 22 (1968): 26–47.

Simes, Dimitri. "The Death of Detente." *International Security* 5 (Summer 1980): 3–25.

———. "Deterrence and Coercion in Soviet Policy." *International Security* 5 (Winter 1980–1981): 80–103.

———. "Disciplining Soviet Power." *Foreign Policy* 43 (Summer 1981): 33–52.

———. "The Clash Over Poland." *Foreign Policy* 46 (Spring 1982): 49–66.

Singer, J. David. "The Levels of Analysis Problem in International Relations." In *The International System: Theoretical Essays*, ed. K. Knorr and S. Verba, 77–92. (Princeton, N.J.: Princeton University Press, 1961):

Skillings, Gordon, and Franklyn Griffiths. *Interest Groups in Soviet Politics*. Princeton, N.J.: Princeton University Press, 1971.

Slusser, Robert. *The Berlin Crisis of 1961: Soviet American Relations and the Struggle for Power in the Kremlin, June–November 1961*. Baltimore: Johns Hopkins University Press, 1973.

Snepp, Frank. *Decent Interval: An Insider's Account of Saigon's Indecent End Told By the CIA's Chief Strategy Analyst in Vietnam*. New York: Vintage, 1978.

Snyder, Glen, and Paul Diesing. *Conflict Among Nations: Bargaining, Decision Making, and System Structure in International Crises*. Princeton, N.J.: Princeton University Press, 1977.

Solzhenitsyn, Alexander. "Misconceptions About Russia Are a Threat to America." *Foreign Affairs* 58 (Spring 1980): 797–834.

Stein, Arthur. "When Misperceptions Matter." *World Politics* 34 (1982): 505–26.

Steinbruner, John. *The Cybernetic Theory of Decision: New Dimensions of Political Analysis*. Princeton, N.J.: Princeton University Press, 1974.

Strauss, Frans J. *Challenge and Response: A Programme for Europe*. New York: Atheneum, 1970.

Stuart, Douglas, and Harvey Starr. "Inherent Bad Faith Reconsidered: Dulles, Kennedy and Kissinger." *Political Psychology* 3 (1982): 1–33.

Sullivan, Michael. "Foreign Policy Articulations and U.S. Conflict Behavior." In *To Augur Well: Early Warning Indicators in World Politics*, ed. J. D. Singer and M. D. Wallace, 215–35. Beverly Hills, Calif.: Sage, 1979.

Sullivan, William. "Dateline Iran: The Road Not Taken." *Foreign Policy* 40 (Fall 1980): 175–86.

Swearingen, Rodger. *The Soviet Union and Post War Japan: Challenge and Response*. Stanford, Calif.: Hoover Institution Press, 1978.

Szabo, Stephen. *The Successor Generation: International Perspectives of Postwar Europeans*, 43–75. London: Butterworths, 1983.

Szulc, Tad. "Lisbon and Washington: Behind the Portuguese Revolution." *Foreign Policy* 21 (Winter 1975–1976): 3–62.

Talbott, Strobe. *Endgame: The Inside Story of SALT II.* New York: Harper and Row, 1979.

Taylor, Alan. *The Arab Balance of Power.* Syracuse, N.Y.: Syracuse University Press, 1982.

Terry, Sarah M. "The Implications of Interdependence for Soviet-East European Relations: A Preliminary Analysis of the Polish Case." In *The Foreign Policies of East Europe: New Approaches,* ed. R. H. Linden, 186–266. New York: Praeger, 1980.

Thompson, Scott W., ed. *National Security in the 1980's: From Weakness to Strength.* San Francisco: Institute for Contemporary Studies, 1980.

Tillman, Seth. *The United States in the Middle East: Interests and Obstacles.* Bloomington: Indiana University Press, 1982.

Tretiak, D. "China's Vietnam War and Its Consequences." *China Quarterly* 80 (December 1979), 740–67.

Treverton, Gregory F. *Nuclear Weapons in Europe.* Adelphi Paper 168. London: IISS 1981.

Triska, J., and D. Finley. *Soviet Foreign Policy.* New York: Macmillan, 1968.

Trofimenko, Henry. "Changing Attitudes Toward Deterrence." Paper 25. Center for International and Strategic Affairs, University of California, Los Angeles, 1980.

Tucker, Robert. *The Purposes of American Power: An Essay on National Security.* New York: Praeger, 1981.

U.S. Arms Control And Disarmament Agency. *World Military Expenditures and Arms Transfers: 1966–1975.* Washington, D.C.: Arms Control and Disarmament Agency, 1976.

U.S. Congress, House. Subcommittee on the Far East and the Pacific of the Committee on Foreign Affairs. *Sino-Soviet Conflict.* Hearings, 89th Cong., 1st sess. Washington, D.C.: GPO, 1965.

———. Subcommittee on the Far East and the Pacific of the Committee on Foreign Affairs. *United States Policy Toward Asia.* Hearings, 89th Cong., 2d sess. Washington, D.C.: GPO, 1966.

———. Subcommittee on Future Foreign Policy Research and Development of the Committee on International Relations. *United States—Soviet Union—China: The Great Power Triangle.* Hearings, 94th Cong., Washington, D.C.: GPO, 1976.

———. Committee on International Relations. *The Soviet Union Internal Dynamics of Foreign Policy: Present and Future.* Hearings, 95th Cong., 2d sess. Washington, D.C.: GPO, 1978.

U.S. Congress, Senate. Committee on Foreign Relations. *U.S. Policy With Respect to Mainland China.* Hearings, 89th Cong., 2d sess. Washington D.C.: GPO, 1966.

———. Committee on Foreign Relations. *U.S. Security Interests and Policies in Southwest Asia.* Hearings, 96th Cong., 2d sess. Washington D.C.: GPO, 1980.

Valenta, Jiri. "The Bureaucratic Politics Paradigm and the Soviet Invasion of Czechoslovakia." *Political Science Quarterly* 94 (Spring 1979): 55–76.

———. *Soviet Intervention in Czechoslovakia, 1968: Anatomy of a Decision.* Baltimore: Johns Hopkins University Press, 1979.

———. "Soviet Invasion of Afghanistan: The Difficulty of Knowing Where to Stop." *Orbis* 24 (Summer 1980): 201–18.

Van der Kroef, Justus M. "The Soviet Union and South East Asia." In *The Soviet Union and the Developing Nations,* ed. R. Kanet, 79–118. Baltimore: Johns Hopkins University Press, 1974.

Van Hollen, Christoper. "The Tilt Policy Revisited: Nixon-Kissinger Geopolitics and South Asia." *Asian Survey* 20 (April 1980): 339–61.

Vance, Cyrus. *Hard Choices: Critical Years in American Foreign Policy*. New York: Simon and Schuster, 1983.

Vasquez, John A. *The Power of Power Politics: A Critique*. New Brunswick, N.J.: Rutgers University Press, 1983.

Waltz, Kenneth. *Man, The State and War*. New York: Columbia University Press, 1954.

———. *Theory of International Politics*. Reading, Mass.: Addison-Wesley, 1979.

Warburg, James P. *Germany: Key to Peace*. Cambridge, Mass.: Harvard University Press, 1953.

Weber, Max. *The Theory of Social and Economic Organization*. Trans A. M. Henderson and T. Parsons. New York: Free Press, 1964.

Weede, Erich, Schossler Dietmar, and Mattias Jung. "West German Elite Views on National Security Issues: Evidence from a 1980/1981 Survey of Experts." *Journal of Strategic Studies* 6 (March 1983): 82–95.

Weiner, Bernard. *Theories of Motivation: From Mechanism to Cognition*. Chicago: Rand McNally, 1972.

Welch, William. *American Images of Soviet Foreign Policy: An Inquiry into Recent Appraisals from the Academic Community*. New Haven, Conn.: Yale University Press, 1970.

Wettig, Gerhard. *Community and Conflict in the Socialist Camp: The Soviet Union, East Germany and the German Problem 1965–1972*. Trans. E. Moreton and H. Adomeit. New York: St. Martin's, 1975.

White, Ralph K. *Nobody Wanted War: Misperceptions in Vietnam and Other Wars*. New York: Anchor, 1970.

Windsor, Philip. *Germany and the Western Alliance: Lessons from the 1980 Crisis*. Adelphi Paper 170. London: IISS, 1981.

Wit, Joel S. "American S.L.B.M.: Counterforce Options and Strategic Implications." *Survival* (Summer 1982): 163–74.

Wolfe, Thomas A. *Soviet Power and Europe 1945–1970*. Baltimore: Johns Hopkins Press, 1970.

———. *The SALT Experience*. Cambridge, Mass.: Ballinger, 1979.

Yanov, Alexander. *Detente After Brezhnev: The Domestic Roots of Soviet Foreign Policy*. Berkeley: Institute of International Studies, University of California at Berkeley, 1977.

Yim Kwan H., ed., *China and the U.S., 1964–1972*. New York: Facts on File, 1975.

Yodfat, Aryeh. *The Soviet Union and the Arabian Peninsula: Soviet Policy Toward the Persian Gulf and Arabia*. London: Croom Helm, 1983.

Zagoria, Donald. *The Sino-Soviet Conflict, 1956–1961*. Princeton, N.J.: Princeton University Press, 1962.

———. *Vietnam Triangle: Moscow, Peking, Hanoi*. New York: Pegasus, 1967.

Zimmerman, William, and Robert Axelrod. "The 'Lessons' of Vietnam and Soviet Foreign Policy." *World Politics* 34 (October 1981): 1–24.

Zimmerman, William, and Robert Axelrod. "The Soviet Press on Soviet Foreign Policy: A Usually Reliable Source." *British Journal of Political Science* 11 (1981): 183–200.

Zimmerman, William, and Glen Palmer. "Words and Deeds in Soviet Foreign Policy: The Case of Soviet Military Expenditures." *American Political Science Review* 77 (1983): 358–67.

Index